A Planters' Republic

A PLANTERS' REPUBLIC

*The Search for
Economic Independence in
Revolutionary Virginia*

BRUCE A. RAGSDALE

MADISON HOUSE

Madison 1996

Ragsdale, Bruce A.
A Planters' Republic
The Search for Economic Independence in Revolutionary Virginia

LIBRARY OF CONGRESS CATALOGING-IN-PUBLICATION DATA

Ragsdale, Bruce A.
    A planters' republic : the search for economic independence in
  Revolutionary Virginia / Bruce A. Ragsdale.
      p.   cm.
    Includes bibliographical references and index.
    ISBN 0-945612-40-0
      1. Virginia—Economic conditions.   2. Virginia—Commerce—
  History—18th century.   3. Virginia—Politics and government—To
  1775.   I. Title.
  HC107.V8R33   1995
  330.9755'01—dc20   95-18435
                                                                 CIP

Printed in the United States of America on acid free paper.

Published by Madison House Publishers, Inc.
P.O. Box 3100, Madison, Wisconsin 53704

FIRST EDITION

CONTENTS

For Richard Scobey

ACKNOWLEDGMENTS

I WAS FORTUNATE TO EMBARK ON THIS STUDY of political economy in Revolutionary Virginia at a time when numerous scholars were greatly expanding our understanding of economy and society in the early Chesapeake. Their work has helped me to establish the context for this examination of political strategy and the Virginia planters' response to the commercial challenges of revolution and independence. In writing this book, I have incurred many personal debts as well.

More than twenty years ago, when I was an undergraduate student, William W. Abbot first introduced me to the study of the American Revolution. He kindled an interest in that era and, perhaps more important, conveyed a sense of the community of scholars who had transformed the study of early America in the previous twenty-five years. He made a career in history seem a worthy aspiration. Since that time Bill Abbot served as my dissertation adviser and as the director of the Papers of George Washington project while I worked there. I owe him a great deal.

At the University of Virginia, fellow graduate students helped me to define this study and offered support. Mark Barr, Colleen Berge, Daniel Borus, Jean Lee, William Link, Lynda Morgan, Libby O'Connell, and John Oldfield all contributed in important ways. The staff of the Papers of George Washington provided an ideal place to work while I was completing the dissertation and when I returned for additional research. In particular, Dorothy Twohig was a valued source of information and enthusiasm, and Beverly Runge always was eager to share her extensive knowledge of Virginia. At several points in the work on this study, John M. Hemphill offered his expert advice on colonial Virginia and eighteenth-century commerce. Merrill D. Peterson, Thad W. Tate, and James Sterling Young read the dissertation on which this study is based and added helpful comments.

At repositories throughout Virginia and in Washington, D.C., numerous archivists assisted my research. Among the most helpful were Edmund Berkeley, Jr., Janet Linde, and Michael Plunkett at the Alderman Library, University of Virginia; Howson Cole and Frances S. Pollard of the Virginia Historical Society; and Gail Terry, then of Colonial Williamsburg Foundation library. Barbara McMillan of the Mount Vernon Ladies Association and Catherine H. Grosfils of Colonial Williamsburg Foundation helped to locate illustrations. Sara B. Bearss of the Virginia Historical Society was especially generous in sharing her knowledge of prints related to early Virginia.

The Society of the Cincinnati for the State of Virginia awarded a grant that contributed to the completion of the dissertation. The Virginia Foundation for the Humanities offered a fellowship that allowed me to take leave from the Office of the Historian at the U. S. House of Representatives and conduct further research for the manuscript. Robert Vaughan of the Virginian Center for the Humanities provided the ideal atmosphere for both research and collegiality. Raymond W. Smock helped to arrange for leave from the U. S. House of Representatives.

Kenneth R. Bowling of the First Federal Congress Project read the manuscript and encouraged me to publish it. Sylvia R. Frey reviewed the manuscript for Madison House and presented a thoughtful critique. As an editor, Gregory M. Britton has maintained his excitement about the project and offered solid advice.

Rick Scobey read the manuscript, offered the perspective of an economist, and provided critical support for the completion of the book. His greatest contribution to this work, as well as to our life together, has been his unfailing confidence and trust in the author.

Bruce A. Ragsdale
Washington, D.C.

INTRODUCTION

During the autumn of 1765, in the midst of the American protest of the Stamp Act, George Washington made preparations to discontinue the cultivation of tobacco at Mount Vernon and his other Potomac lands. In the seven years since he returned from service in the Virginia Regiment, attentive supervision of his tobacco fields had led only to repeated disappointments in the sale of the estate's crop on British markets. Washington finally decided to abandon the commodity that had been the foundation of Virginia's prosperity for nearly a century and a half. He inquired of merchants in England and Virginia what markets he might expect to find for flour, grain, hemp, and flax as replacements for his annual shipments of Potomac tobacco. At the same time he ordered from London the tools and equipment that would allow him to initiate more ambitious domestic manufactures at Mount Vernon. Soon thereafter he enlarged the estate's commercial fishery and experimented with a variety of commodities that would not be dependent solely on British markets or London creditors.[1]

The political crisis surrounding the Stamp Act provided the final impetus for Washington's reorganization of his estate. Great Britain's

[1]George Washington to Capel and Osgood Hanbury, 20 Sep. 1765, idem to James Gildart, 20 Sep. 1765, and idem to Robert Cary & Co., 20 Sep. 1765, in *The Papers of George Washington, Colonial Series*, eds., W. W. Abbot and Dorothy Twohig (Charlottesville: University Press of Virginia, 1983–), 7:393–94, 397, 398–402.

imposition of a direct tax violated both the rights of the Virginia assembly and colonial assumptions about the commercial benefits of Empire. Washington reminded British correspondents that "the whole produce of our labour hitherto has centred in Great Britain." Additional economic demands from Parliament, he warned, would drive commerce away from the course that for so many years had tied Virginia to the center of Empire. Confronted by an increasingly restrictive imperial policy and discouraging returns from British trade, Washington envisioned the development of an independent economy safe from the constraints of parliamentary regulation and the influence of British merchants. The Stamp Act politicized Washington's long-standing dissatisfaction with the British tobacco trade and made the improvement of plantation management an enticing means of protecting American liberties as well as advancing the material interests of individual planters. Washington emerged from the Stamp Act crisis convinced of the logic of a strategy of commercial resistance that utilized Virginia's great wealth to force concessions from Parliament and secure fair terms of trade from British merchants.

In April 1769, in the face of yet another assertion of Parliament's authority to tax the colonies, George Washington urged his fellow Virginians to seek redress from the British "by starving their Trade & manufactures." He proposed that the Virginians join in an association to refuse British imports and thereby deprive merchants and manufacturers of their most valuable market in the North American colonies. The economic coercion, if effective, would mobilize British traders to seek repeal of the Townshend duties and all other parliamentary acts that infringed on the rights of colonial governments. The first goal of Washington was to "maintain the liberty which we have derived from our Ancestors." Yet the prospect of a commercial association held further advantages that excited Washington even more than the political design. If it accomplished nothing else, a nonimportation association, by freeing the colony's gentry from the pursuit of English fashion and luxury, would reduce the Virginians' "considerable" debt to Great Britain and release "the Country from the distress it at present labours under."[2]

Again in 1774, during the American protest of the Coercive Acts, Washington was instrumental in drafting the county resolves that served as the model of commercial resistance for the provincial convention

[2]George Washington to George Mason, 3 Apr. 1769, *Papers of George Washington, Colonial Series*, eds., Abbot and Twohig, 8:177–80.

and the First Continental Congress. An association that prohibited all British imports and threatened a suspension of Virginia's valuable tobacco exports to Great Britain promised to bring repeal of the Parliamentary acts at the same time that it laid the foundation for a diversified economy flourishing outside the confines of the Empire. After the Revolutionary War, in the years immediately following his resignation from the Continental Army, Washington resumed his efforts to diversify his own estate and encourage commercial development in Virginia. He introduced agricultural reforms at Mount Vernon, sought private support and governmental sponsorship for internal improvements, and encouraged mercantile investment in trading centers of the state. At the same time he worked to establish interstate commercial agreements and advocated revisions in the national government such as would facilitate independent commerce. Throughout the revolutionary era, from the earliest resistance to imperial policy in the 1760s to the debate on ratification of the Federal Constitution in 1788, Washington pursued a vision of economic independence that he considered a prerequisite for the liberty, security, and prosperity of Virginia. That vision reflected a determination to free planters from the demands of British merchants and the restrictions of the tobacco trade while maintaining the viability of Virginia's plantation system of agriculture.

That Virginia's most prominent leader of the Revolution should devote so much energy and attention to the search for economic independence was evidence of the centrality of commercial relations in the conflict with Great Britain. Washington, as clearly as any individual of his generation, exemplified the confluence of political and economic objectives that characterized the Revolution in Virginia. Yet he was hardly alone. The process by which Washington moved from private grievances regarding British trade to an endorsement of commercial resistance and, ultimately, a commitment to economic independence was repeated innumerable times among the gentry planters of his native Northern Neck and the Tidewater, and, on the eve of Revolution, among yeoman planters throughout the colony. Three times in the decade preceding Independence, Virginians organized commercial associations as a means of protest against specific legislation of the British Parliament. In each of these nonimportation associations, as in the informal commercial resistance to the Stamp Act, the great planters who historically were at the center of the tobacco trade with Great Britain endeavored to diversify agricultural production, increase domestic manufactures, and strengthen the native merchant community in Virginia. Beyond the immediate political goal, their intent was to enable Virginia's agricultural economy to develop its full potential free from imperial regulation and the limitations of merchants' capital.

◼   ◼   ◼

The gentry's challenge to the commercial bonds of Empire signified a sharp break with the colonial past. Virginia, through ties of trade and culture, had been as closely attached to Great Britain as any of the thirteen colonies that joined in revolution. Since the days of the Virginia Company, Chesapeake tobacco was the basis of the most valuable trade from British North America. A return trade in British manufactures made Virginia the ideal mercantilist colony, eagerly purchasing finished goods in return for the sale of a raw commodity demanded by buyers in Great Britain and throughout Europe. The tobacco trade, with its organization reliant on resident factors and personal exchanges with colonial planters, established direct links between British merchants and a majority of landholding colonists. In no other colony were so many people in such frequent contact with citizens of Great Britain.

The great planters in Virginia owed their ascendancy in large part to the operation of the British tobacco trade. Access to the personal services of English merchants had offered an emergent planter gentry the most advantageous sales of tobacco and the credit extensions necessary for the purchase of new lands and slaves to work in the tobacco fields. Established relationships with London consignment merchants made the great planters the colony's principal intermediaries with London and further enhanced their influence within Virginia. The plantation system of agriculture that arose in a tobacco economy employing slave labor served as the foundation of the gentry's political and social authority in a colony where most landholders shared the bonds of race and the interests of the staple trade.

The thriving commercial connection between Virginia and Great Britain sustained a cultural identification of colonist with the metropolitan center of Empire. Through most of the colonial era, Virginians, particularly the great planters who aspired to the English ideal of an independent gentry, looked across the Atlantic for models of political and social order. From the innumerable Virginia place names that commemorated English royalty to the ubiquitous British consumer goods that defined genteel taste in the colony, a provincial gentry proclaimed its attachment to the Mother Country.

The very ties of commerce that supported the rise of the great planters eventually proved confining for the expansive society of the crown's
Old Dominion. The transatlantic trade that offered Virginia's gentry
material prosperity and cultural identity also placed the planters at the
forefront of the development of commercial capitalism in the mid-eighteenth century. Great Britain's increasingly sophisticated financial structure, which contributed to a concentration of mercantile firms and the
mobilization of credit, supported the expansion of the tobacco economy
at the same time that it imposed on the colony requirements for commercial regularity that often were at odds with the rhythms and resources of plantation agriculture. By the third quarter of the eighteenth
century, in a variety of ways ranging from experiments with new export
crops that might be attractive on alternative markets to denunciations
of the luxuries that filled the great planters' mansions, Virginia planters
evinced a widespread concern that the colony's great estates could not
protect their interests against the demands of a highly-organized and
capital-intensive trading establishment in Great Britain.

By the 1760s, the more restrictive demands of British commerce
coinciding with the associated reorganization of imperial administration prompted Virginia's leading planters to reevaluate the benefits of
the British connection. The strategy of commercial resistance that was
a centerpiece of the revolutionary movement in Virginia was a response
to the twin threats to the authority and well-being of the great planters
and marked the formal beginning of a struggle for economic independence that would continue long after the withdrawal of royal officials
and the surrender of British armies. The earliest leaders of commercial
resistance were concentrated in the Northern Neck region where a decline in the fortunes of the premium tobacco trade had prompted widespread interest in agricultural diversification. Washington and allies like
George Mason and Richard Henry Lee found support for their ideas of
commercial resistance from a broad group of wealthy Tidewater and
Piedmont planters who constituted much of the political leadership of
Virginia in the second half of the eighteenth century. Their design of
commercial association shaped the nature of the resistance to Great Britain before the Revolution and defined notions of economic independence in the decade following the war.

The scheme of commercial resistance propounded in Virginia aimed
to check the risks of debt and dependency at the same time that it maintained the basic structure of a plantation society that had been the foundation for the most stable and secure elite in British North America.
The architects of the commercial associations anticipated, and indeed

preferred, that Virginia's economy would remain primarily agricultural. So too did they insist on continuing their participation in the trade of the Atlantic economy. The natural riches of Virginia and the advanced state of manufactures in Europe, once free of the restrictions of imperial policy and the British merchants' monopoly on shipping and marketing, would no doubt result in a balanced trade based on reciprocal advantages.

In the meantime, Virginia planters resolved to reorganize plantations so as to make them more responsive to the demands of transatlantic trade. Nonimportation, with its requirements for thrift, self-reliance, and austerity, sought to cultivate the personal characteristics thought necessary for successful participation in foreign trade. The temporary suspension of imports would encourage the development of local manufactures and free plantations from the need to import basic goods. The strict regulation of British merchant activity in Virginia would enable native traders to expand their business and thereby carry Virginia produce to new markets. Finally, a cessation of slave imports would attract free laborers skilled in the supporting crafts required by plantations.

This model of economic independence recalled a supposed golden age of the great planters' self-reliant estates at the same time that it anticipated an era of free trade in which Virginia's diverse production might find new markets throughout Europe and the Americas. The paradox of attempting to preserve the structures of a colonial society and simultaneously pursuing the opportunities of liberal commerce would haunt the Virginia planters long after the Revolution, but not before the colony's political leaders embraced commercial resistance as a means of expanding economic opportunities and extending the development of British North America's wealthiest colony. These leaders pursued their revolutionary course confident in their faith that the great riches of Virginia would insure the prosperity and preeminence of an independent state.

■   ■   ■

The Political Economy of
a Tobacco Colony

VISITORS TO THE GREAT ESTATES OF PRE-REVOLUTIONARY VIRGINIA were invariably impressed with the variety and quality of English goods that filled the houses of the colony's wealthiest planters. Furniture, porcelain, paintings, and silver, even the clothing of the planter's family were predominantly of English manufacture and of the latest fashion. Those aspects of the estate that the planters could not import—the architecture of the house, the design of the interior, or the layout of the gardens—they drew from English pattern books and more sophisticated treatises that were imported along with the volumes that lined the shelves of the planters' libraries.

That the elite of British North America's wealthiest colony should gather these possessions in their midst is perhaps not surprising. Fine English goods were the most tangible evidence of the planters' economic prosperity and of an assumed social superiority. Display of English fashion signified not only wealth but access to the metropolitan center of London where personal agents selected the custom-ordered goods. The imitation of styles associated with England's country gentry reassured the provincial gentlemen and their families of their own sophistication and offered an illusion of approximating the ideal of the independent landed class in the Mother Country.

A traveler who visited the nearby farms of yeoman planters might be more surprised to find them filled with English goods as well. These small planters, masters of at most two or three slaves and themselves workers of the soil producing just a few hogsheads of tobacco a year,

I

relied on imported items to supply the household and clothe the family. Here were not the elegant items that graced the gentry houses, but instead common sorts of cloth, tools, cooking utensils, and table ware.

Most surprising of all to a visitor would have been to return to the estates of the great planters and inspect the quarters of the slaves who constituted the very bottom rank of Virginia society. Here the blankets under which slaves slept, the clothes worn for field work, and the grubbing and hilling hoes used to cultivate tobacco were all likely to be of British manufacture or European goods shipped by British merchants.

In all but the poorest and most remote regions of pre-revolutionary Virginia one found pervasive evidence of a material link with Great Britain. Although Virginians by the eighteenth century were capable of manufacturing most of these goods, British merchants offered them at well below the production costs for colonial artisans and craftsmen. The economy of scale in British manufactures and the credit structure of the British trade provided inexpensive goods in return for colonial produce and freed Virginia's capital and labor for the cultivation of export crops and the development of estates. By the eve of the Revolution, the imports that were both a source of identity and a practical necessity for Virginians were also an indication of the degree to which the colony's prosperity rested on its commercial ties to Great Britain.[1]

The consumption of British manufactures throughout Virginia society and the display of English manners among the gentry was made possible by a combination of tobacco and slaves that made the Chesapeake the most valuable center of trade in British North America. Virginia, the wealthiest and most populous colony, together with Maryland accounted for fifty to sixty percent of the value of American exports to Great Britain and absorbed thirty to forty percent of British imports in the mainland colonies. A steady flow of merchant ships seeking cargoes of tobacco distributed goods to the wharves of the great estates and to

[1]For overview of consumption patterns in eighteenth-century Anglo-American world, see *Consumption and the World of Goods*, eds., John Brewer and Roy Porter (London and New York: Routledge, 1993); *Of Consuming Interests: The Style of Life in the Eighteenth Century*, eds., Cary Carson, Ronald Hoffman, and Peter J. Albert (Charlottesville and London: The University Press of Virginia, 1994); and Neil McKendrick, John Brewer, and J. H. Plumb, *The Birth of a Consumer Society: The Commercialization of Eighteenth-Century England* (Bloomington: Indiana University Press, 1982); Lorena Walsh, "Urban Amenities and Rural Sufficiency: Living Standards and Consumer Behavior in the Colonial Chesapeake, 1643–1777," *Journal of Economic History* 43 (March 1983): 109–117.

an extensive network of British-run stores that traded with smaller planters.[2]

The reliance on British goods was only the most visible manifestation of the pervasive influence of the tobacco trade that remained the foundation of Virginia's economy until after the Revolution. Tobacco had so thoroughly dominated Virginia's economic development since the early seventeenth century that nearly every aspect of colonial society reflected the crop's influence. The appearance of the landscape was as much a result of the tobacco trade as were the furnishings of the dwellings. The marketing and cultivation requirements of the staple crop contributed to a distinctive settlement pattern where settlers, rather than gather in fortified communities, trading towns, or governmental centers, preferred to patent individual estates along the Tidewater rivers where they found rich soil and direct access to the ships of tobacco traders from England. In the following century, as the availability of Tidewater land disappeared, the marketing structure of the tobacco trade encouraged landless Virginians and immigrants to move into the Piedmont region and repeat the pattern of settling on isolated farms with access to the four great river systems or roads to the tobacco wharves. Since tobacco required relatively little processing in the colony and the mercantile organization of the trade was concentrated in Great Britain, no port cities developed in Virginia as entrepôts of the tobacco trade.

Throughout the colonial era, the social and political structure of Virginia owed much to the tobacco economy and the trade in that commodity. During the first seventy-five years of tobacco cultivation in Virginia, as productivity gains maintained the profits of the staple export, planters invested available capital in agricultural production and farm-building. Consequently, few material distinctions marked gradations of wealth and status. While some accumulated great wealth, small planters predominated among tobacco producers. Political offices, particularly on the county level, were also open to smaller planters, and while wealthier planters held the highest offices of the county and seats in the House of Burgesses, the lack of continuity in leadership and the uncertainties of life in the seventeenth-century Chesapeake precluded the development of a stable political establishment.[3]

[2]Jacob M. Price, "New Time Series for Scotland's and Britain's Trade with the Thirteen Colonies and States, 1740–1791," *William and Mary Quarterly* 3rd ser., 32 (April 1975): 322–25.

[3]Allan Kulikoff, *Tobacco and Slaves: The Development of Southern Cultures in the Chesapeake, 1680–1800* (Chapel Hill: University of North Carolina Press,

Beginning in the 1680s, a more structured and settled social order emerged in response to developments in the tobacco trade and demographic changes in the colony. During a prolonged depression in the late seventeenth century, planters faced stagnant demand for tobacco in Europe and low prices for all but the highest grade of leaf in Virginia. At the same time, the immigration of indentured servants from England dwindled, thereby depriving planters of their most important source of labor. Planters with sufficient capital made the costlier but ultimately more profitable investment in newly-available slaves. Employing these slave laborers in the production of high-quality leaf on fertile lands, the planters were able to gain the best prices available on the English market. The transition to slave labor provided planters with a more valuable and flexible labor force. Slave women were employed along with men in field work, and their children became part of the planter's work force. Young slaves joined the elderly in home manufactures and other domestic tasks. During the uncertain tobacco markets of the late-seventeenth and early-eighteenth centuries, slave-holding planters held the additional advantage of diversified estates and a measure of self-sufficiency possible only on the largest plantations in the colony.[4]

The resources of land and labor were valuable to Virginia planters only if they could gain access to the most favorable tobacco markets in England. In the absence of a rigid trading structure, planters through much of the seventeenth century participated in a variety of marketing arrangements in the hopes of finding the highest sales in any given season. By the 1690s, the largest growers of tobacco relied primarily on the consignment system. Originally conceived as a trade between merchants, the consignment system consisted of the shipment of tobacco to an

---

1986), 23–44; James Horn, "Servant Emigration to the Chesapeake in the Seventeenth Century," in *The Chesapeake in the Seventeenth Century: Essays on Anglo-American Society and Politics*, eds., Thad W. Tate and David Ammerman (New York: W. W. Norton and Company, 1979), 51–95; Edmund S. Morgan, *American Slavery, American Freedom: The Ordeal of Colonial Virginia* (New York: W. W. Norton and Co., 1975), 133–57.

[4]John J. McKusker and Russell R. Menard, *The Economy of British America, 1607–1789* (Chapel Hill: University of North Carolina Press, 1985), 122–26; Kulikoff, *Tobacco and Slaves*, 37–44, 77–92; Lorena Walsh, "Plantation Management in the Chesapeake, 1620–1820," *Journal of Economic History* 49 (June 1989): 393–97.

English merchant, most commonly in London, who then sold the crop on the best terms available. The shipper, whether planter or merchant, retained ownership of the tobacco until the final sale and thus was responsible for all charges accrued in the shipping, payment of duties, and unloading and storage of the cargo. Although these costs were high (as much as 75 percent of the final sales price), the merchants' personal attention to the individual cargoes increased the likelihood of a profitable sale. A commission of 2 ½ to 3 percent of the sales price encouraged merchants to search for the most favorable purchaser. This personal service was particularly valuable in the years between 1690 and 1720 when Chesapeake prices were low and demand stagnant, but London prices were frequently high due to the expenses of shipping during wartime. The volume required for personal service and the delay in receipt of sales limited the viability of the consignment system to large producers of tobacco.

As the consignment trade evolved in the early eighteenth century, merchants provided additional services that enhanced the benefits of the trade for large planters. Virginians with an established correspondence relied on their merchant as a banker, drawing bills of exchange in return for tobacco sales or on credit in expectation of future shipments. These bills became an important medium of exchange in Virginia and were a principal source of credit for planters intent on expanding their estates. Planters also drew on their accounts for the purchase of British goods personally selected by the merchant according to the colonist's orders. Merchants usually chose to limit their business to a size that permitted the personal attendance prized by Virginia planters. In the many long-standing relationships between planters and merchants, the English trader became an agent for the Virginian in legal business or family concerns such as the education of a planter's children in English schools. The tobacco trader furnished everything from political intelligence to advice on the current London fashions. What originated as a business relationship often evolved into the Virginians' most important connection with the metropolitan center of the Empire.[5]

The reorganization of tobacco markets and the introduction of slave labor coincided with demographic shifts that contributed to the new

[5]Samuel M. Rosenblatt, "The Significance of Credit in the Tobacco Consignment Trade: A Study of John Norton & Sons, 1768–1775," *William and Mary Quarterly* 3rd ser., 19 (July 1962): 383–99; Robert Polk Thomson, "The Merchant in Virginia, 1700–1775" (Ph.D. diss., University of Wisconsin, 1955), ch. 2.

social order in Virginia. Declining mortality rates, a balanced gender ratio, and the emergence of a native-born majority made possible a more stable society than that of the middle decades of the seventeenth century. Planters who spent a lifetime accumulating land and chattel slaves were able to bequeath their wealth to the next generation, providing estates for daughters as well as sons and laying the foundation for the great family dynasties that would dominate so much of provincial society in the eighteenth century.

By the time tobacco prices began to recover during the second decade of the eighteenth century, Virginia was characterized by a hierarchical society in which an individual's rank in large part reflected access to the profits of the tobacco market and the credit resources of British tobacco merchants. At the highest level of provincial society were the great planters who owned the most fertile Tidewater lands, controlled a disproportionate share of Virginia's slave labor, and traded directly with the consignment merchants of London and the British outports. The wealth of Virginia's gentry families was never as concentrated as in the plantation colonies of South Carolina and the British West Indies, but a recognized elite based on wealth and political influence gained ascendancy by the early eighteenth century and continued to strengthen its dominion over provincial society. Comprising no more than five percent of the colony's population, the gentry families were distinguished by their freedom from physical labor in their own fields and by estates large enough to provide a livable inheritance for their children. Most were descendants of seventeenth-century immigrants who were sufficiently wealthy to take advantage of opportunities during depressions in the tobacco trade. Many also had used their political influence to speculate in land.[6]

The expanded scale of production on Virginia's largest tobacco plantations and the concomitant costs of land and labor made it increasingly difficult for smaller growers to enter the highest ranks of colonial society. Yet while the rise of the great planters limited social mobility, the expansion of tobacco cultivation in the eighteenth century created a

[6]Bernard Bailyn, "Politics and Social Structure in Virginia," in *Seventeenth-Century America*, ed., James Morton Smith (Chapel Hill: University of North Carolina Press, 1959), 90–115; Kulikoff, *Tobacco and Slaves*, 9–10, 263–80; Jack P. Greene, *Pursuits of Happiness: The Social Development of Early Modern British Colonies and the Formation of American Culture* (Chapel Hill: University of North Carolina Press, 1986), 92–94.

Tobacco Paper, Seventeenth-century woodcut. An early label on a tobacco package offered an image of the type of ship that provided the most important link between Virginia and the center of Empire. (Colonial Williamsburg Foundation)

shared economic interest between the gentry and the yeoman planter families who made up the majority of the population in the eastern half of Virginia. Drawing on their own estates and their access to English credit, the great planters extended credit to small planters who hoped to purchase a slave or improve their lands. The larger planters also provided access to export markets and the services of an English merchant. The yeoman planter families came to accept the dominance of the great planters in return for a share of expanding economic opportunities.[7]

The wide-scale introduction of black slaves laid the foundation for Virginia's hierarchical society and made possible the increased production of tobacco. In the last decade of the seventeenth century, more slaves arrived in Virginia than in all the previous years since English settlement. From just under 17,000, or thirteen percent of the colony's population, in 1700, the number of slaves grew through continued importations and in later years through a rate of reproduction unknown in other plantation colonies. By the eve of the Revolution, the approximately 200,000 slaves in Virginia made up forty percent of the population. While slaves were concentrated on the estates of the wealthiest planters, by 1770 more than half of the white families in Virginia owned slaves. In Tidewater counties closer to two-thirds of the households owned slaves. Their common investment in the labor of black slaves and the racial distinctions embodied in law and culture sustained additional interdependencies between large and small planters.[8]

Gentry planters translated their success in the tobacco economy into a more secure control of political authority. By the eighteenth century the wealthy planters who long had dominated the county courts were able to nominate their own successors, and the colonial governor invariably complied with a commission for the new justice. At election gatherings the great planters competed for the support of small tobacco producers whose participation in the political process lent greater legitimacy to the authority of the gentry. From this secure political base in the counties, the great planters in the House of Burgesses advanced their privileges until by the second quarter of the eighteenth century they had made the assembly the most powerful legislative body in the British colonies.

[7]Kulikoff, *Tobacco and Slaves*, 261–63, 280–82, 288–90; Darrett B. Rutman and Anita H. Rutman, *A Place in Time: Middlesex County, Virginia, 1650–1750* (New York: W. W. Norton & Co., 1984), 204–33; Morgan, *American Slavery, American Freedom*, esp. ch. 17, 18; Charles S. Sydnor, *Gentlemen Freeholders: Political Practices in Washington's Virginia* (Chapel Hill: University of North Carolina Press, 1952).

[8]Kulikoff, *Tobacco and Slaves*, 37–44; McKusker and Menard, *The Economy of British America*, 136–38.

The children of the gentry frequently intermarried and reinforced the sense of identity within this self-conscious elite. Brick mansion houses, filled with luxury goods imported through tobacco merchants, further marked the eighteenth-century gentry families and set them apart from other Virginians. The awareness of social distinctions, denoted in residence, dress, and manners, permitted an easy and secure commerce among all ranks of Virginians, especially at public gatherings or sporting events which served as important sources of community in this society with few urban centers. To be sure, there were economic losers among white Virginians, but many moved on to the west or to areas peripheral to the tobacco trade. Others accepted a dependency on the great planters as tenants. Many certainly were disaffected by a gentry culture in which they had no hope of participation, but throughout the pre-Revolutionary period no one within Virginia seriously threatened the hegemony of the great planters and their political establishment. The gentry leaders of Virginia society enjoyed a social and political stability unparalleled in the colonies of British America. Significantly, that stability endured as tobacco production expanded and continued to guide the economic growth of the colony.[9]

By mid-century, the steady demand for tobacco and the commercial structure of the British trade had supported the extension of tobacco cultivation into the Piedmont, the Southside, and even parts of the lower Shenandoah Valley and with it the culture of the Tidewater planters. Despite a diversification of agricultural production and occasional, short-lived increases in grain exports, tobacco continued to account for 85 percent of the value of the colony's exports to Great Britain and 60 to 70 percent of total exports. The staple crop remained the only significant means of attracting British credit and determined the areas of greatest population and economic growth. The rate of new settlement paralleled the expansion of the tobacco trade, and migration into the Piedmont was centered in those areas favored by British tobacco traders. Demand for slave imports also was concentrated in counties where tobacco production was on the rise. This revival of the tobacco trade that began in the 1720s and continued with only short interrup-

[9]Jack P. Greene, "Foundations of Political Power in the Virginia House of Burgesses, 1720–1776," *William and Mary Quarterly* 3rd ser., 16 (October 1959): 485–506; Rhys Isaac, *The Transformation of Virginia, 1740–1790* (Chapel Hill: University of North Carolina Press, 1982), 18–42; Kulikoff, *Tobacco and Slaves*, 261–300.

tions until the early 1770s increased the wealth of most Virginia house-holds at the same time that it further attached the colonists to the staple trade.[10]

■   ■   ■

The tobacco trade that made possible Virginia's economic prosper-ity and social stability never instilled in the planters a sense of security and confidence; certainly not the sort of confidence the great planters exhibited in their roles as domestic patriarchs or political leaders. In part the planters' anxiety about tobacco resulted from the short-term risks endemic in the staple trade. Cycles of overproduction followed by lower prices, dependence on foreign markets, shortages of capital and credit, and reliance on British shipping and financial services all contin-ued to restrict Virginia tobacco growers in the eighteenth century. The vicissitudes of eighteenth-century shipping when combined with vola-tile, seemingly capricious markets could erase the profits of an entire years' crop.

The planters' persistent apprehension was more significantly a re-sponse to a fundamental reorganization of the tobacco trade, the full implications of which Virginians only gradually came to comprehend. In the forty years preceding the American Revolution the commerce that was such an important part of most Virginians' lives underwent a profound transformation. Chesapeake tobacco growers soon found themselves more deeply enmeshed than ever in an Atlantic economy over which they had little influence. Distant markets, the fiscal require-ments of foreign states, and the credit resources of British wholesalers more often than not determined the success or failure of a given year's tobacco crop. Demand for tobacco, marketing arrangements, and the financial structure of British commerce all changed in ways that affected opportunities in the colony and restricted the flexibility of Virginia plant-ers. At the same time, these developments in the tobacco trade initiated nearly a half century of economic prosperity in the colony.

Responding to the particular demands of expanding Continental markets and taking advantage of newly-available credit, British mer-chants encouraged Virginia planters to increase production and extend

[10]McKusker and Menard, *The Economy of British America*, 119–27; Kulikoff, *Tobacco and Slaves*, 118–31.

tobacco cultivation into new areas. While large planters continued to rely on the consignment trade, British merchants increasingly purchased tobacco through the direct trade. This arrangement by which factors of British trading firms purchased tobacco outright in the colony and shipped it for sale as bulk cargoes in England or Scotland originated in the seventeenth century and came to dominate the trade after 1730. This trading structure was particularly well-suited for European markets where quantity was more important than quality. Demand from these Continental markets increased throughout the eighteenth century until the 1770s when Great Britain reexported 85 percent of the tobacco imported from the American colonies.[11]

Of the several European markets, France was the most influential in reviving the Chesapeake trade and determining the marketing structure in Virginia. The fiscal requirements of the French government and the operation of the tobacco trade through a state monopoly guided the growing French demand toward the direct traders in Great Britain and a particular group of producers in Virginia. The Chesapeake crop, especially the Oronoco grown in Virginia and along Maryland's Potomac shore, suited French tastes and was cheap enough to carry the burden of heavy French duties. The availability of Chesapeake tobacco contributed to a seven-fold increase in French consumption between 1715 and 1775. Unlike the Dutch markets where numerous buyers competed for reexported tobacco from Great Britain, the French monopoly presented a single purchaser for the nation's market. The several agents of the monopoly who operated in Great Britain each needed to procure as many as several thousand hogsheads a year. Rejecting the small and often more expensive cargoes from consignment merchants, the agents of

[11]Charles Wetherell, "'Boom and Bust' in the Colonial Chesapeake Economy," *Journal of Interdisciplinary History* 15 (Autumn 1984): 185–210; McKusker and Menard, *The Economy of British America*, 120–25; for rise of the direst trade see the work of Jacob M. Price: "The Economic Growth of the Chesapeake and the European Market, 1677–1775," *Journal of Economic History* 24 (December 1964): 496–511; *France and the Chesapeake: A History of the French Tobacco Monopoly, 1674–1791, and Its Relationship to the British and American Tobacco Trades*, 2 vols. (Ann Arbor: University of Michigan Press, 1973); *Capital and Credit in British Overseas Trade: The View from the Chesapeake, 1700–1776* (Cambridge: Harvard University Press, 1980); and Jacob M. Price and Paul G. E. Clemens, "A Revolution of Scale in Overseas Trade: British Firms in the Chesapeake Trade, 1675–1775," *Journal of Economic History* 47 (March 1987): 1–43.

the French monopoly instead purchased their tobacco from the largest direct trade merchants who offered entire shiploads at a bulk rate.[12]

At the same time that British merchants won the business of the French monopoly, Virginia's assembly enacted a statute that made that colony's tobacco most attractive for the direct trade and the French market. The Inspection Act of 1730 provided for the destruction of all trash tobacco and the establishment of warehouses for the storage of tobacco approved for exportation. A system of inspection notes guaranteed the quality of approved tobacco and permitted planters to negotiate the sale of their crop without the actual transport of hogsheads. Although Governor Gooch in his report to the Board of Trade emphasized the utility of the act in the enforcement of customs collection, he and the originators of the act intended the inspection system to limit the kind of overproduction that repeatedly depressed tobacco prices. In fact, the operation of the act restricted the amount of tobacco acceptable for export. The guarantee of a minimum quality for all Virginia tobacco exports and the construction of centrally located warehouses also gave the Inspection Act an importance never anticipated by its sponsors. Direct trade merchants henceforth were able to purchase tobacco sight unseen and trust that it would sell on the reexport market. The collection of purchases from a few or even a single warehouse reduced the time a ship captain spent in Virginia and the merchants' overall costs. The failure of Maryland's assembly to enact a similar inspection system before 1747 gave Virginia tobacco producers an edge in the critical years when the direct trade merchants expanded their operations in the Chesapeake.[13]

On the eve of the Revolution at least two-thirds to three-fourths of Virginia's tobacco traveled to Great Britain through the direct trade. The shift in marketing arrangements had profound implications for economic development in Virginia. Whereas the consignment trade represented a coalescence of planters' and merchants' interests, the direct trade of the eighteenth century imposed on Virginians the requirements of a new commercial organization. Planters could benefit from

[12]Price, "The Economic Growth of the Chesapeake and the European Market," 496–511; idem., *France and the Chesapeake*, 649–77.

[13]John M. Hemphill II, *Virginia and the English Commercial System, 1689–1733: Studies in the Development and Fluctuations of a Colonial Economy under Imperial Control* (New York and London: Garland Publishing, Inc., 1985), 156–71; Aubrey C. Land, *Colonial Maryland, A History* (Millwood, N.Y.: KTO Press, 1981), 180–81.

the advance of tobacco markets only if they organized their production to fit the demands of direct trade merchants. Within these limits, however, the effect of the various services of the factors was to raise small farmers above the level of subsistence and to increase the production of tobacco for reexport markets. At the same time, the direct trade tied an ever wider segment of Virginia society to the opportunities and risks of European markets.

In Virginia the clearest evidence of the restructuring of the tobacco trade was the influx of Scottish merchants during the forty years before the Revolution. Even before Virginians understood the demands of new European markets, they recognized that the business practices of the Glasgow firms forever changed commercial life in the colony. The operation of the direct trade by concentrated Glasgow partnerships came to affect every aspect of tobacco production in Virginia. By 1770, Glasgow merchants purchased half the tobacco exported from the Chesapeake. Their share of the trade during the third quarter of the eighteenth century enabled the Scots to influence the areas of expansion, the type of tobacco grown, and the price levels for the crop in London and the British outports. On the eve of the Revolution, many Virginia planters understandably believed the Scots were responsible for most of the commercial changes of the previous four decades.

The rise of the Scots signified the far-flung developments that transformed economic life in Virginia. Although Scottish merchants had traded with Virginia since before the Act of Union, as late as 1738 they purchased only ten percent of the tobacco exports from the Chesapeake. Their activity in Virginia increased only after the French began to make large tobacco purchases in Scotland around 1740. During the first twelve years of significant French purchases in Scotland (1739–1751), Chesapeake tobacco exports to the Glasgow area increased 350 percent. Scottish merchants reexported almost all of this tobacco, over half of it to France. The importance of the French market in the 1740s, when Scottish merchants enlarged their business in Virginia, accentuated the distinctive nature of Glasgow firms and determined many of the characteristics of Scotland's trade with the colony. The steady French purchases in cash supported a general expansion of credit in Scotland. This credit and the Scottish practice of reinvesting a high portion of profits made the Glasgow firms bigger than ever. By 1770, the three largest trading syndicates in Glasgow controlled 50 percent of Scotland's trade with the Chesapeake. With this greater concentration of capital, Scots were able to organize their Virginia trade to meet the special demands of the reexport market. The assets of the Glasgow trading houses enabled the Scots to overwhelm their competition in the other outports and to set the terms of trade in many parts of Virginia.[14]

Drawing on the capital from French purchases in the 1740s, the Scottish merchants developed a system of stores that became the base of their operation in Virginia and a model for all tobacco merchants. Glasgow firms established chains of stores at key locations, usually near tobacco inspection warehouses or in Virginia's few towns. At the individual stores, a young Scotsman served as factor, buying tobacco from local growers and selling imported goods in return. The larger firms employed a central agent who managed the loading of company ships and maintained uniform policy among the various stores. Planters might use cash or bills of exchange to purchase goods from the Scottish stores, or more commonly accepted goods on credit in expectation of future sales of tobacco. At a typical store operated by John Glassford and Company, 80 percent of the accounts were on credit, most of it repaid with tobacco in less than a year. Cloth and haberdashery articles were the most commonly-purchased goods, though nearly a third of the debts at the store were for cash loans.[15]

The store trade was particularly well designed for newly settled areas where generous offers of credit for goods and loans promoted tobacco cultivation and drew a dependable clientele. Scottish factors preferred to deal with smaller growers who could devote all of their resources to the demands of markets served by the Glasgow firms. The factors designed the services of their stores to meet the need of these small or middling planters. The location of stores in newly settled areas and throughout the Piedmont provided outlets for planters who lived away from Virginia's great rivers. The credit resources of the direct trade freed the small planters' limited capital for the purchase of land and slaves or investment in property improvements. Scottish stores stocked

[14]Jacob M. Price, "The Rise of Glasgow in the Chesapeake Tobacco Trade, 1707–1775," *William and Mary Quarterly* 3rd ser., 11 (April 1954): 179–99; idem., *France and the Chesapeake*, 604–17, 662–63; idem., *Capital and Credit in the British Overseas Trade*, 23–29; T. M. Devine, *The Tobacco Lords: A Study of the Tobacco Merchants of Glasgow and their Trading Activities c. 1740–90* (Edinburgh: Edinburgh University Press, 1990).

[15]J. H. Soltow, "Scottish Traders in Virginia, 1750–1775," *Economic History Review*, 2nd ser., 12 (August 1959): 83–98; Thomson, "The Merchant in Virginia"; Price, "The Rise of Glasgow"; Devine, *The Tobacco Lords*; Carole Shammas, *The Pre-Industrial Consumer in England and America* (Oxford: Clarendon Press, 1990), 269–70.

large quantities of inexpensive household goods which raised the planters' standard of living and eliminated the need for domestic manufactures.

In settled areas such as the Potomac shore, the Scots attracted business by offering the highest prices for tobacco. In order to load quickly the company's ships, cash purchases were almost always necessary as a supplement to the tobacco received on accounts at the stores. By meeting the highest price demands for tobacco, the Scottish factors reduced the time spent in the Chesapeake, lowered freight rates, and met the best British markets, especially those for cash sales to the French. Virginia traders and independent British merchants were helpless against the generous offers from the large Scottish firms. In 1769, Harry Piper, a merchant of Alexandria, complained "the Scotch don't much mind prices." The arrival of the Scottish ships in the Potomac initiated a process of bidding up the price of tobacco as the Glasgow men "carry all before them."[16]

The large capital investment required for the services and organization of the Scottish trade overwhelmed any potential competition. The £3,000 needed to open a single store in the 1740s and 1750s was beyond the means of all but the wealthiest Virginians. Glasgow firms commonly had a capitalization of between £10,000 and £20,000. The few firms that carried over half of Scotland's tobacco trade were much larger. In 1773 William Cunninghame & Company was capitalized at close to £80,000, and the largest single importer, Speirs, Bowman & Company, was capitalized at a spectacular £150,000.

These investments in the Chesapeake trade proved to be exceptionally profitable. The most important source of profit for Glasgow firms was the sale of goods at the factors' stores rather than tobacco sales. The mark-up, or advance, for goods sold on credit was frequently 80 percent above the sterling price in Great Britain, plus another advance based on the prevailing rate of exchange between sterling and Virginia currency. Factors usually applied an advance of 50 percent plus the prevailing exchange rate to goods sold for cash. In many instances the actual advances may have been higher. As the sales of these goods increased, the Scottish merchants organized their tobacco trade to in-

[16]Price, *France and the Chesapeake*, 664–66; Soltow, "Scottish Traders in Virginia"; Thompson, "The Merchant in Virginia"; Harry Piper to Dixon & Littledale, 7 January and 12 May 1769, Piper Letterbook, Alderman Library, University of Virginia.

sure a high turnover in capital and a reinvestment in the lucrative store business. Offering top prices for tobacco in Virginia and occasionally selling at below cost in Great Britain, the Scottish firms quickly reapplied their tobacco receipts to the purchase of more goods for the factors' stores. The sale of these goods on lenient terms in turn became one of the principal sources of credit in Virginia.[17]

The distribution of credit through the store trade and the competitive prices offered for tobacco enabled the Scottish merchants and other British direct traders to guide regional development in Virginia. The Scottish firms focused their attention on areas that would most likely serve the needs of their particular organization of the direct trade. They ignored established areas along the York River and the lower Rappahannock where large planters concentrated on quality tobacco for sale on the British domestic market. In 1769 Roger Atkinson of Petersburg reported only "one concern f[ro]m Glasgow in all York River . . . & the principal . . . tells me that the Tobo does not answer in Glasgow as well as the James River."[18] The Scottish factors were more likely to establish stores along the Potomac where the local Oronoco leaf sold well on the French market or increasingly in the Upper James district and throughout the Piedmont. Typical was William Cunninghame & Company which started with stores at Dumfries on the Potomac and at fall line towns like Falmouth and Fredericksburg. By the 1770s, the company added stores along the James and in the Southside area of Halifax and Mecklenburg. As each of the company's fourteen stores opened, the local factor repeated the process of extending credit to attract small landholders who would organize their lands to satisfy the demands of Glasgow and the reexport market.

The greatest expansion of tobacco cultivation after 1750 was concentrated in those regions where the Scottish traders were most active. The strongest rate of growth was in the Upper James River naval district, especially in the region west and south of Petersburg. Exports from this district increased in the same years that the Scottish merchants extended their operations. From 6,000 hogsheads in 1739, the region's

[17]Price, *Capital and Credit*, 24–29, 149–55; Price, *France and the Chesapeake*, 665–66; Price and Clemens, "A Revolution of Scale in Overseas Trade," 30–31.

[18]Roger Atkinson to Messrs Lionel and Samuel Lyde, 25 August 1769, Roger Atkinson Letterbook, 1769–1776, Alderman Library, University of Virginia.

exports reached a level of 16,000 in 1752 and maintained that level through the colonial period. By 1773, the district produced over 38 percent of the colony's tobacco grown for export, as opposed to 19 percent in 1739. Glasgow firms bought over half of the tobacco shipped from the Upper James in the 1770s, and the largest Scottish tobacco merchant, Speirs, Bowman & Company, operated exclusively in this region.

The districts shunned by Scottish traders suffered a relative and occasionally absolute decline in the tobacco trade. In the Rappahannock naval district, where Scots were present but not dominant, the share of Virginia's tobacco exports dropped from 30 percent in 1739 to around 20 percent in the 1760s and 1770s. In the York River district, the central source of the sweet-scented tobacco produced for the consignment trade, the share of Virginia's tobacco trade dropped from 36 percent in 1727 to 14 percent in 1768. This represented an absolute decline from 14,620 hogsheads to 6,272 as tobacco production in the area became almost exclusively the activity of large planters.[19]

Despite appearances that the Scottish controlled all, the Glaswegians' organization of the direct trade was only one of several instruments in the centralization of British commerce and the consequent restructuring of Virginia's tobacco trade. Enticed by the successful example of the Scottish traders and growing European demand, London tobacco merchants frequently entered the direct trade after 1740. Their direct purchases in Virginia accelerated the reorientation of tobacco production toward Continental markets and brought to London the kind of concentrated companies first found in Glasgow. In 1775, six London firms controlled over 50 percent of the metropolis' tobacco trade, each firm importing over 2,000 hogsheads in the year.[20]

These concentrated merchant firms in the Virginia trade augmented their working capital by borrowing from individuals or banks, by reinvesting their profits, and, most important, through credit extended by

[19]Price, *France and the Chesapeake*, 666–71; for list and description of Virginia stores of William Cunninghame & Company, see Virginia Claims of Wm. Cunninghame & Co., Public Record Office, AO13/29 (Virginia Colonial Records Project microfilm); Robert Polk Thomson, "The Tobacco Export of the Upper James River Naval District, 1773–75," *William and Mary Quarterly* 3rd ser., 18 (July 1961): 392–407; Peter V. Bergstrom, *Markets and Merchants: Economic Diversification in Colonial Virginia, 1700–1775* (New York and London: Garland Publishing, Inc., 1985), 141, 144–46.

[20]Price, *France and the Chesapeake*, 657–58; Price and Clemens, "A Revolution of Scale in Overseas Trade."

commercial businesses. Warehousemen, shopkeepers, and tradesmen sold goods on credit, with no interest charged for the first twelve months. As long as expanding markets made tobacco a secure form of remittance on Virginia debts, British merchants were eager to offer Virginians these goods at an advanced price and under similar credit arrangements. Firms with sufficient capital on hand paid for the goods in under twelve months, thereby qualifying for a discount from the wholesaler. The merchants frequently allowed planters' debts to run three or four years, with five percent annual interest charges after the first year.[21]

The expansion of mercantile credit and its particular origin in commercial businesses precipitated an influx of British imports into the Chesapeake during the middle decades of the eighteenth century. In 1740, the two Chesapeake colonies imported £356,680 worth of goods from Great Britain; by 1771, the value of British imports into the region reached a colonial-era high of £1,223,726. Virginia's Scottish imports alone grew from £74,724 in 1740 to £250,401 in 1771. England's exports to the Chesapeake grew by more than 200 percent as London warehousemen provided goods on credit to tobacco merchants throughout the British Isles.[22]

With access to affordable imports, Virginians of almost every economic rank became beneficiaries of the consumer revolution of eighteenth-century Great Britain. Innovations in production and marketing reduced the price of manufactured goods and increased consumption on all levels of British society. Notions of style and fashion, and the manipulation of those notions by merchandisers, created new markets for every type of commodity from luxury goods to common household wares. These consumption patterns quickly spread to the Chesapeake through the efficient organization of the tobacco trade which in turn came to rely on British goods to attract the crops of planters. The dramatic increase in the volume of imports after 1750, as the system of factors' stores spread throughout the colony, resulted in decreased prices for most British manufactures. Whether gentry or yeoman, Virginia

[21]Price, *Capital and Credit*, 44–123.

[22]Price, "New Time Series for Scotland's and Britain's Trade with the Thirteen Colonies and States," 322–25. Colonial import and export statistics combine the colonies of Virginia and Maryland. A separate accounting was recorded only during the years 1768–1772, in Ledger of Imports and Exports (America), 5 January 1768–5 January 1773, Public Record Office, Customs, 16/1 (Virginia Colonial Records Project microfilm).

Tobacco Paper, Eighteenth-century woodcut. This common image featured on English tobacco labels identified the renowned York River tobacco with the African and African American slaves who worked the fields, not the planters who owned the land. (Colonial Williamsburg Foundation)

planter families during the middle decades of the eighteenth century were able to increase their consumption of imported goods and raise their standard of living without spending more of their income on durable goods.

As early as the second decade of the eighteenth century, gentry families regularly purchased fashionable items with which to decorate their increasingly elaborate houses and to clothe their families. Within another 20 years, the establishment of factors' stores brought similar, if less expensive, concepts of fashion to the families of yeoman planters. Such basic indicators of gentility as table ware were common among wealthy families by 1730 and among middling families by mid-century. In the third quarter of the century, fashionable items appeared in Virginia almost as quickly as they did in Great Britain. Josiah Wedgewood's popular Queensware pottery, one of the very symbols of the consumer revolution, appeared on Virginia tables, including that of George Washington, within a few years of its introduction in Great Britain. By 1771, another Northern Neck planter reported it "much in use here." Robert Beverley might refer to fashion as a "Foolish Passion," but he urged his merchant to consider current tastes in London as he selected goods for Beverley's new house. Beverley also provided a description of Governor Botetourt's interior design as a guide to what was considered "a pretty Effect" in Virginia. These fashionable goods as well as the common imported articles that were ubiquitous in Virginia households further cemented cultural ties with Great Britain and created new levels of dependence on the center of Empire.[23]

For all the prosperity exemplified by new consumer goods, the Virginia economy remained distinctly colonial. Even in flush times as the Virginia economy grew, it was marked by a lack of development as was typical of staple economies, especially those dependent on slave labor. The predominance of tobacco culture and a plantation system of agriculture impeded the creation of domestic markets, local manufactures, an indigenous commercial class, and a more skilled and flexible labor force. Wealth remained concentrated among a gentry class that found that its investment options were sharply restricted by the distribution of credit through the tobacco trade. Acceptance of the merchants' exten-

---

[23]Richard L. Bushman, *The Refinement of America: Persons, Houses, Cities* (New York: Alfred A. Knopf, 1992); Shammas, *The Pre-Industrial Consumer in England and America*, 86–95, 181–85; Susan Gray Detweiler, *George Washington's Chinaware* (New York: Harry N. Abrams, 1982), 53–62; Enclosure to Robert Cary & Co., 25 July 1769, *Papers of George Washington, Colonial Series*, eds., Abbot and Twohig, 8:232; Raleigh Downman to Clay and Midgley, 2 July 1771, Joseph Ball Letterbook, Library of Congress; Robert Beverley to Samuel Athawes, 15 Apr. 1771, Robert Beverley Letterbook, Library of Congress.

sions almost invariably entailed a further commitment to tobacco cultivation as the principal means of making remittances. The merchants'
enhanced ability to demand repayment made it difficult for planters to
divert capital to the long-term development of alternative staple crops
or local manufactures. Once growers were indebted to the factors' stores,
Archibald Cary found that the Scottish merchants "take every step in
their power to keep the Planters imploy'd in that Commodity [tobacco],
and often refuse to purchase Hemp by which means many People are
deterred from Cultivating it, for want of a certain market."[24]

The expansion of British credit during the middle decades of the
eighteenth century perpetuated the colony's dependence on the tobacco
trade at precisely the time when population growth, westward settlement, and diversification of agricultural production made possible and
at times necessitated the development of new export trades. The rapid
settlement of lands east of the Blue Ridge and rising land prices made
the exhaustive soil demands of tobacco culture more costly than ever.
The declining ratio of land to labor, the large acreage required for the
successful rotation of tobacco, and declining fertility forced young men
to delay the formation of separate households and persuaded many to
move beyond the Blue Ridge. Faced with reduced yields in tobacco fields,
many established planters increased their cultivation of grains and other
crops less demanding of soil and labor than tobacco. The regimen of
plantation agriculture easily accommodated the cultivation of wheat and
corn, both of which provided work for those slaves who could not meet
the more arduous demands of tobacco. The commercial production of
these grains for both domestic and export markets helped compensate
for losses during poor tobacco markets and made a significant contribution to most planters' incomes after mid-century.[25]

Unfortunately, the West Indies and southern Europe, the principal
export markets for Virginia grains, never provided the steady demand
that might have enabled planters in the colony to abandon tobacco. Nor

[24]For distinction between growth and development, see McKusker and
Menard, *The Economy of British America*, 24–26; Archibald Cary to Governor
Fauquier, 17 Apr. 1766, Public Record Office, CO5/1345, pp. 134–35 (Virginia
Colonial Record Project microfilm).

[25]Peter V. Bergstrom, *Markets and Merchants;* Harold B. Gill, Jr., "Wheat
Culture in Colonial Virginia," *Agricultural History* 52 (July 1978): 380–93;
Kulikoff, *Tobacco and Slaves*, 131–34; Walsh, "Plantation Management in the
Chesapeake."

did these trade routes provide the financial services and distribution of consumer goods available through the British tobacco trade. In the years before the Revolution, only areas unsuited for tobacco cultivation concentrated exclusively on grain production, and trade from these peripheral regions never approached the value of trade from tobacco-producing regions. The grain trade, however, was responsible for the growth of the most substantial port towns in Virginia, such as Norfolk and Alexandria.[26]

The rise of these few port towns in the years before the Revolution only accentuated the general lack of commercial services in a tobacco-dominated export economy. Despite the value of its trade with other colonies and Great Britain, Virginia had no commercial centers comparable to Charleston, South Carolina or the port cities of the northern colonies. Tobacco required little processing in the colony beyond the prizing of leaf in massive hogsheads that were difficult to transport across land. Consequently, no town ever served as the central point for the collection of tobacco and distribution of British imports. The administrative center of the tobacco trade remained in Great Britain where the Navigation Acts required all tobacco first be landed and where tobacco buyers and wholesalers provided indispensable financial services. Small trading centers developed around the tobacco inspection warehouses where tobacco was loaded in Virginia, but these crossroads developed no significant artisan communities or commercial services. In a colony where slaves provided much of the labor, aspiring merchants found few independent seamen for hire.[27]

Just as the structure of the colonial tobacco trade inhibited the development of commercial ports and alternative export trades in Virginia, so too did it retard the growth of manufactures in the Chesapeake. The efficient distribution of inexpensive British goods made it impossible for provincial manufactures to compete with imports. Virginia offered prosperity to coopers, blacksmiths, and shipbuilders, all of whom

[26]Jacob M. Price, "Economic Function and the Growth of American Port Towns in the Eighteenth Century," *Perspectives in American History* 8 (1974): 123–86; Walsh, "Plantation Management in the Chesapeake"; Thomas M. Preisser, "Alexandria and the Evolution of the Northern Virginia Economy, 1749–1776," *Virginia Magazine of History and Biography* 89 (July 1981): 282–93.

[27]Carville Earle and Ronald Hoffman, "Urban Development in the Eighteenth-Century South," *Perspectives in American History* 10 (1976): 7–80; Price, "Economic Function and the Growth of American Port Towns," 123–86.

assisted the tobacco trade, but not to artisans and manufacturers producing household goods, particularly cloth. Larger estates initiated cloth manufacturing, but few if any were self-sufficient. When the tobacco trade fell into the recessions that recurred even during generally prosperous years, planters large and small had no alternative but to continue to import goods for the provisioning of their families and slaves.

▪   ▪   ▪

In the quarter century before the Revolution, more and more Virginians, particularly great planters faced with the fixed costs of maintaining estates, recognized the liabilities of dependence on British capital as it was distributed through the tobacco trade. Most alarming was the sharp rise in the personal indebtedness that always had characterized the colonial economy. Precise levels of indebtedness before 1775 are difficult to determine, but all indications suggest a significant increase in colonial debts after 1740. By 1775, when levels of debt were recorded, and after a year of nonimportation during which debts were sharply reduced, Virginia and the other tobacco colony of Maryland held a per capita debt triple the average for all other colonies in British North America. The debt that was so much larger was also more pervasive. As more and more landholders traded directly with British merchants, every level of tobacco producer owed debts to British merchants or their factors in the colony. The larger debt owed by Virginians was in many ways a reflection of the greater wealth of the colony and the confidence among planters and merchants that the tobacco trade would support a sustained growth of the colonial economy. Yet for those who wished to promote a more diversified and independent economy, the debt was both a symbol of the colony's persistent reliance on Great Britain and a practical obstacle to all planters who wished to protect their estates from the hazards of the tobacco trade.[28]

For planters familiar with an older, personal style of business and apprehensive about the risks of a more highly commercialized Atlantic

[28]Price, *Capital and Credit*, 10–16; Emory G. Evans, "Planter Indebtedness and the Coming of the Revolution in Virginia," *William and Mary Quarterly* 3rd ser., 19 (October 1962): 511–33; Lawrence Henry Gipson, "Virginia Planter Debts Before the American Revolution," *Virginia Magazine of History and Biography* 69 (July 1961): 259–77.

economy, the enlarged debt represented a threat to the traditional sources of social stability. A seemingly permanent debt, owed to merchants in Great Britain, undermined personal independence and moral character. As luxury imports came to fill the houses of the colony's gentry, the debt itself appeared to be a consequence of excessive and indulgent purchases. Others attributed the debt to a reckless disregard for the productive capacity of the planters' estates. The debt was simply a trap into which the planters "have brought themselves by their own luxury and extravagance." Richard Corbin considered personal indebtedness one of the principal "Errors of his countrymen" and warned that only "the strongest Efforts of Industry and its attendant Virtue Frugality" could restore Virginia's good credit. Such concerns with the moral effects of indebtedness were also common in eighteenth-century England, where the expanded scale of business and finance rendered debts both more common and more impersonal. The particular Chesapeake variation on this widespread anxiety denoted the special dilemma of a planter economy engaged in distant commercial activity. Repeated criticism of immoderate purchases and inattention to the management of estates betrayed a fear that Virginia's great planters did not possess the character traits required for successful transactions with the concentrated mercantile establishments of Great Britain. If Virginians were to regain economic security and protect their estates from the demands of British creditors, they needed to adopt a simpler standard of living and a more disciplined management of their estates.[29]

John Wayles, perhaps because he was colonial agent for an English merchant as well as a native planter, understood that the mobilization of credit was more responsible for indebtedness than was the extravagance of planters. "Luxury & expensive living have gone hand in hand with the increase of wealth," he wrote to a Bristol merchant in 1766. "In 1740 I don't remember to have seen such a thing as a turkey carpet in the Country . . . now nothing are so common as Turkey or Wilton Carpets, the whole furniture of the Rooms Elegant & every appearance of

---

[29]*Virginia Gazette* (Rind), 1 June 1769; Richard Corbin to Dinwiddie, 10 July 1761, Richard Corbin to Philip Ludwell, 13 Aug. 1764, Richard Corbin Papers, Colonial Williamsburg Foundation (University of Virginia microfilm); discussion of eighteenth-century debate on moral effects of a commercial economy in Drew R. McCoy, *The Elusive Republic: Political Economy in Jeffersonian America* (Chapel Hill: University of North Carolina Press, 1980); for different analysis of the significance of debt among Virginia's gentry planters, see T. H. Breen, *Tobacco Culture: The Mentality of the Great Tidewater Planters on the Eve of Revolution* (Princeton: Princeton University Press, 1985).

Opulence. All this is in great Measure owing to the credit which the Planters have had from England & which has enabled them to Improve their Estates to the pitch they are arrived at, tho' many are ignorant of the true cause."[30]

Richard Henry Lee acknowledged instances of "extravagance & want of Industry" but was more inclined to attribute chronic indebtedness to the structure of the tobacco trade. Lee was especially critical of the store trade, which he claimed exploited the restrictions on colonial trade by imposing "most oppressively both in the price and quality of goods." The high advances on inferior goods sold at the factors' stores produced the "enormous debt due at the stores." Robert Beverley blamed merchants in Great Britain as well. He was "of opinion that our being so much incumbered arises wholly from their [the merchants'] own Conduct, for they dispose of our Comodities upon such wretched Terms that I am conscious upon the strictest Frugality & Œconomy tis impossible for us to keep the Balance of Trade in our Favour."[31]

After the Revolution, Thomas Jefferson was even more insistent that British merchants were responsible for the chronic and pervasive indebtedness of colonial Virginia. The organization of the tobacco trade, he charged, had been calculated to increase the colonists' debts and perpetuate their dependence on the British-controlled tobacco trade.

> The advantages made by the British merchants on the tobaccoes consigned to them were so enormous that they spared no means of increasing those consignments. A powerful engine for this purpose was the giving good prices and credit to the planter, till they got him more immersed in debt than he could pay without selling his land or slaves. They then reduced the prices given for his tobacco so that let his shipments be ever so great, and his demand of necessaries ever so œconomical, they never permitted him to clear off his debt. These debts had become hereditary from father to son for many generations, so that the planters were a species of property annexed to certain mercantile houses in London.[32]

[30]John Wayles to Farrell & Jones, 30 August 1766, American Loyalist Claims, Public Record Office, T.79/30.

[31]"Rusticus" [Richard Henry Lee] to Rind, [176–], *Lee Family Papers* (University of Virginia microfilm publication); Robert Beverley to [. . .], 18 Aug. 1765, Robert Beverley Letterbook, Library of Congress.

[32]Additional Queries of Démeunier with Jefferson's Answers, [ca. Jan.– Feb. 1786], *The Papers of Thomas Jefferson*, ed. Julian P. Boyd (Princeton: Princeton University Press, 1954), 10:27.

Jefferson certainly exaggerated the conspiratorial design of the merchants and failed to appreciate the forces of the market, but like Lee and the many others who suspected the motives of the merchants, he understood well the value of easy credit in attracting customers and encouraging increased tobacco production.

The two most common explanations of Virginia's indebtedness, one emphasizing extravagance, indolence, and reckless management, the other centering on the connivance of British merchants and imperial officials, appear unrelated if not contradictory. The former represented a suspicion of the commercial activity associated with expanded tobacco markets while the latter indicated an impatience with the mercantilist policies that inhibited economic growth in the colony. From either perspective or from a mixture of the two, however, planters concluded that a reduction of debt depended on the curtailment of British imports and the development of commerce less reliant than tobacco on British merchants.

The debt that grew ever larger and more dispersed threatened to become additionally burdensome for Virginians in the quarter century preceding Independence. British merchants exercised their influence with Parliament, the Board of Trade, and Virginia's provincial government to win new protection for creditors' interests in the colonial courts. Virginia statute and local court actions traditionally had offered a more lenient treatment of debtors than was the practice in Great Britain. Reflecting an economy where almost everyone accumulated some kind of debt, the colonial legal code and its application during the first half of the eighteenth century presented debtors with the most liberal terms acceptable while maintaining the colony's legitimacy for British investment. A series of statute revisions increased protection of debtors' property, reduced the likelihood of incarceration, and limited the ability of creditors to collect the full value of debts. After Parliament in 1732 enacted a statute subjecting a debtor's land and slaves to creditors' claims, the local courts prevented a successful enforcement of the law. The assembly further enhanced debtors' flexibility in an act of 1749 that permitted the discharge of sterling debts in local currency at a fixed exchange rate of £1 sterling to £1.25 Virginia currency; a rate considered par but frequently below the true value of sterling debts.[33]

---

[33]Peter J. Coleman, *Debtors and Creditors in America: Insolvency, Imprisonment for Debt, and Bankruptcy, 1607–1900* (Madison: The State Historical Society of Wisconsin, 1974), 191–206; Gipson, "Virginia Planter Debts Before the American Revolution," 260–61.

The centralized merchant firms that came to dominate the tobacco trade after mid-century demanded greater security and regularity of payments for their credit extensions in Virginia. The Assembly's act of 1749 particularly incensed the British merchants. The extent of British-held debt in Virginia was so widespread by 1750, and the credit obligations in the complex organization of the direct trade so pressing, that British merchants no longer could accept the casual treatment of recovery suits or the unpredictability of exchange rates. Merchant agitation and pressure from the Board of Trade convinced the burgesses in 1755 to revise the act of 1749 and permit local courts to determine judgments at current exchange rates. Any potential goodwill emanating from the revision vanished when the burgesses followed with approval of the colony's first issue of paper money. Convinced that the provincial assembly would do nothing to protect creditor interests, English merchants campaigned for a prohibition on all colonial currency as legal tender. Glasgow merchants, whose accounts were generally in local currency, were less concerned about legal tender but also wanted to reduce the exchange rates that could eliminate all profits in the time between the sale of goods on credit and collection of the debt. One result of the merchants' efforts was the Currency Act of 1764, by which Parliament permitted the issuance of paper money in Virginia but prohibited it as legal tender in private transactions.[34]

Merchants resident in the colony also attempted to secure more regular and favorable payment of debts. A merchants' petition to the assembly in 1764 requested some sort of regulation of the county courts in their treatment of suits for recovery. According to the traders, the action of these courts and their sheriffs delayed any decision on debt cases and flagrantly protected the debtors' interests. Among the suggested remedies was adoption of the practice of taking bonds, with warrant of attorney, to confess judgment, "which is the common Security of *England, Ireland,* and the *English* Dominions in *America* (this colony only excepted)." Some such security, the merchants contended, was necessary for any further extensions of credit.[35]

[34]Gipson, "Virginia Planter Debts Before the American Revolution," 275; *Journals of the House of Burgesses of Virginia, 1761–1765,* eds., John Pendleton Kennedy and H. R. McIlwaine (Richmond: The Colonial Press, 1905–1915), 233–35; Joseph A. Ernst, "Genesis of the Currency Act of 1764: Virginia Paper Money and the Protection of British Investments," *William and Mary Quarterly* 3rd ser., 22 (January 1965): 33–74.

[35]*Journals of the House of Burgesses, 1761–1765,* eds., Kennedy and McIlwaine, 233–35.

Members of the House of Burgesses recognized that certain concessions to merchant creditors were necessary in order to maintain the flow of credit from Great Britain to the colony. After passing a bankruptcy act that would have granted insolvent debtors greater protection than under English law, the assembly quickly accepted Governor Fauquier's recommendation for a repeal, even before the Privy Council disallowed the act. A writer to the *Virginia Gazette* in 1766 pleaded for reform of the county courts in the treatment of debt cases. The repeated delays in action on recovery suits had become "a very great Discouragement of Trade." Although the burgesses were loath to interfere with the structure of local courts, in the 1760s they approved several revisions of statutes that had made it difficult to imprison insolvent debtors. In 1769, the assembly acceded to merchant appeals and provided for the security of bonds, with warrant of attorneys, to confess judgment.[36]

Individual burgesses found little success in their attempts to curtail what they considered the unfair privileges of merchant-creditors. In 1766, Richard Henry Lee sponsored a bill to revise an earlier act allowing merchants to prove book debts solely by their own oath. According to Lee, the factors and store merchants, who already "received by much the greatest part of the annual produce of our lands and labor," did not deserve a legislative favor denied all others in Virginia. Lee's bill, however, failed to gain the assembly's approval. In 1769, a majority of burgesses agreed to limit the action of the Williamsburg Court of Hustings to cases arising within the city limits. Since 1736, the Williamsburg court had accepted suits from all parts of Virginia as a convenience for people attending the General Court and the assembly. Merchants came to rely on this court because of its expeditious action on suits for recovery and its reputation as one of the most favorable courts for merchants. Although Richard Jackson, legal counsel to the Board of Trade, found no technical objections to the act restoring the court's original jurisdiction, he recognized that the broader authority was "of Singular Utility in the recovery of Mercantile Debts" and "highly useful to the Trade of this Kingdom." The Board of Trade recommended disallowance on the

---

[36]Coleman, *Debtors and Creditors in America*, 196–97; "Benvolus" to Rind, *Virginia Gazette* (Rind), 11 Dec. 1766; *The Statutes at Large: Being a Collection of all the Laws of Virginia, From the First Session of the Legislature, in the Year 1619*. Edited by William Waller Hening, 13 vols. (New York, Philadelphia, Richmond, 1819–23), 8:326–32.

same grounds. In February 1772, the Privy Council declared the act void.[37]

The cumulative effect of statute revisions and imperial regulations after 1750 was to make it easier for British merchants and their factors to collect debts in Virginia. With less flexibility and owing greater amounts, colonial debtors found the periodic fluctuations in tobacco and credit markets more problematic than ever. Infusions of British capital and the long-term expansion of tobacco markets on the Continent never eliminated the periodic depressions that plagued Virginia's staple economy since the seventeenth century. Twice after 1760, the imperial economy suffered sharp restrictions of available credit, and on both occasions tobacco prices fell. Following the close of the Seven Years War, a brief expansion of credit collapsed into a depression that persisted through the mid-1760s. A credit crisis in 1772, the worst in the imperial economy since the South Sea Bubble of 1720, followed the largest expansion of credit in the colonial period. These sharp fluctuations in the Atlantic economy and the lesser shifts affecting every plantation underscored the constraints imposed on the colonial economy by the British-held debt.

■   ■   ■

The transformation of the tobacco trade in the mid-eighteenth century presented Virginia's gentry planters with a special predicament. While large producers of tobacco reaped many of the advantages of a general expansion of British credit and increased availability of British imports, they gained few benefits from the direct trade that came to dominate the commerce in tobacco. Direct traders deliberately avoided any personal transactions with the great planters. William Cunninghame & Company instructed its Virginia agents to solicit the trade of mid-

[37]*Journals of the House of Burgesses, 1766–1769*, eds., Kennedy and McIlwaine, 56,61, 62, 67–68; "Rusticus" [Richard Henry Lee] to Rind, [176-], *Lee Family Papers* (University of Virginia microfilm publication); James H. Soltow, *The Economic Role of Williamsburg* (Williamsburg, Va.: Colonial Williamsburg, 1965), 143; *Hening's Statutes*, 8:401–02; Richard Jackson report, Public Record Office, CO5/1333, ff. 64–65; Journal of the Board of Trade, Public Record Office, CO391/78, pp.155, 161–62, 166; Privy Council Register, Public Record Office, PC2/115, pp. 288–89, PC2/116, pp. 92–93 (Virginia Colonial Records Project microfilm).

dling planters who were seldom in debt rather than that of the "first crop Masters who are continually so." Large planters demanded too much of their merchants and regularly allowed debts to accumulate for several years before shifting their business and begging credit from another merchant. After several years in the colony, the company's manager concluded "nothing can justify Large debts owing by a few and lying over from year to year." If the Cunninghame factors wanted to buy tobacco from the "Great Men," let the transaction be in cash.[38]

Great planters, in fact, regularly offered all or a portion of their crop to direct traders in the colony. The planter might agree to sell lower quality tobacco to country purchasers who offered a set price and cash payment. Large planters also often sold small amounts of tobacco to pay for incidental goods at a factor's store. In years of low prices on the London market, the cash prices offered by Scottish buyers were tempting. In 1765, Richard Corbin warned his London merchants, Capel and Osgood Hanbury, that "the Sales of Tob. from the Out Ports are almost double those from London, and if there is not a very great Alteration in the London market I shall not do Justice to my Family, if I do not send the greatest part of my Tobo to the best Market."[39]

Yet few planters with the responsibilities of managing a large estate could disengage from the consignment system that was increasingly on the periphery of the tobacco trade. The consignment merchants still offered the kind of credit extensions that Cunninghame & Company and other Scottish firms refused to grant large planters. By limiting the size of their clientele, the consignment merchants were able to offer the regular and long-term loans required for the development and maintenance of a large plantation. The merchant's role as a banker, paying out bills of exchange drawn on credit or account, provided an additional service not available from the factors in the colony. And only the consignment merchants had the time and means to sell the sweet-scented tobacco produced on the richest lands in Virginia. English markets for this higher quality leaf remained steady through the eighteenth cen-

[38]William Cunninghame & Company to James Robinson, 16 May 1772, Cunninghame of Lainshaw Muniments, 1761–1778, Scottish Record Office (Virginia Colonial Records Project microfilm).

[39]George Washington to Richard Washington, 10 Aug. 1760, *Papers of George Washington, Colonial Series*, ed., Abbot, 6:452–53; Richard Corbin to Messrs. Hanbury, 31 May 1765, Richard Corbin Letterbook, Colonial Williamsburg Foundation (University of Virginia microfilm).

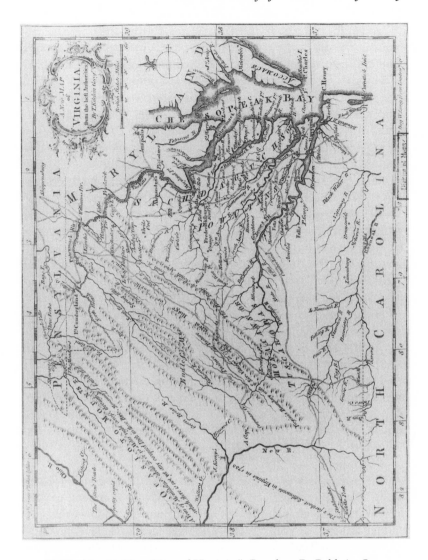

T. Kitchin. "A New Map of Virginia." (London, R. Baldwin, Jun., 1761). Printed in *The London Magazine*, vol. 33, November 1761, 512–13. The establishment of tobacco warehouses fostered the development of small towns and the network of internal roads that facilitated the extension of tobacco culture into the Piedmont region. (Library of Congress)

tury, and as long as consignment merchants devoted their personal attention to the marketing of sweet-scented leaf, Virginia's larger planters found it to be a worthwhile means of obtaining London credit.

The consignment merchants' credit and personal service enabled large planters to purchase a quality and quantity of goods not to be found in the factors' stores or elsewhere in Virginia. Through their contacts with shopkeepers and artisans in London, the consignment merchants gathered the furniture, clothing, and other fashionable items that came to characterize the houses of the colony's wealthiest planters. A more practical and absolutely essential service was the merchants' selection of large quantities of provisions for an estate's slaves. Such goods were commonly available in Virginia, but not in the amounts required by a large estate nor on the terms offered by consignment merchants. One wealthy planter, responsible for the maintenance of an extensive estate, grew "quite tired with Dealing in the Stores at their exorbitant Rates" and vowed to send for England "for every thing I shall ever want."[40]

The personal selection of goods was among the many services that made the consignment trade a distinct privilege of the colony's wealthiest planters. Furthermore, the direct communication with influential traders at the center of the Empire enhanced the great planters' own authority in the colony. Even when the material advantages of the trade declined, the intimate connection with a merchant in London or other English ports remained a significant definition of the status of gentry families in Virginia. A planter could sincerely describe a "Commercial Friendship . . . glowing in my own breast, which takes its rise from a long Correspondence."[41]

The advantages of consignment, however, became increasingly costly as the trade slipped into the margins of Virginia's commerce with Great Britain. Landon Carter thought "it must be madness that can continue attached to such a trade and the favour or whatever it is that inclines a man to trade to London is very dearly purchased." And, indeed, the charges for freight, duties, insurance premiums, loading and unloading, storage, brokerage, and the merchants' commission inflated the costs of marketing the crop, all at the expense of the planter. The

[40]Robert Beverley to John Bland, 11 Oct. 1763, Robert Beverley Letterbook, Library of Congress.

[41]Richard Corbin to [John Hanbury], 13 June 1758, Richard Corbin Letterbook, Colonial Williamsburg Foundation (University of Virginia microfilm).

sources of the merchants' profit was the commission of 2 1/2 or 3 percent on the final sales price and the manipulation of customs duties. The total duties on imported tobacco by 1759 amounted to 8 1/3 pence per pound. Merchants received various discounts for cash payment, though they charged the planters for bonded payment. The difference, though less than a penny per pound, produced as much revenue as the commission charge. The costs of maintaining sufficient cash reserves justified the merchants' charge on the planter's account, but the structure of the trade proved to be an expensive way for planters to market their tobacco.[42]

During good markets, when sweet-scented tobacco sold for more than five times the price of other leaf, the consignment of individual cargoes was profitable, even lucrative. In other years the carefully shipped tobacco sold on the export market for no more than the cheaper grades shipped to Great Britain in bulk. Those reliant on the consignment trade faced the further risks of a very personal form of commerce dependent on the cooperation and skills of a few individuals. Captains who delayed loading a cargo in Virginia might miss the most advantageous markets in England. The successful sale of a cargo and timely collection of outbound merchandise in England hinged on a fragile network of brokers and wholesalers.

In the face of such unpredictable returns from the tobacco trade, the private correspondence between planters and merchants, even among those with long-standing family connections, almost always betrayed an element of contest. Planters presented a protest of disappointment in the sale of nearly every shipment which they assured the trader was the best in many years, well-cured and carefully packed. They challenged the various charges involved in the shipping and sale of the cargoes and frequently reproached the merchants for offering Virginians inferior goods and services. Although Virginians understood the advantages of cash payment of duties, few had the capital to lodge with a merchant for this purpose. Planters were left with few alternatives other than to distribute their crop among merchants in an attempt to bargain or to purchase cheaper goods in the outports.

[42]Landon Carter, *The Diary of Landon Carter of Sabine Hall, 1752–1775*, ed., Jack P. Greene, 2 vols. (Charlottesville: University Press of Virginia, 1965), 1:413; Rosenblatt, "The Significance of Credit in the Tobacco Consignment Trade," 387–88; for example of merchants' charges see various receipts of Robert Cary & Co. in Custis Papers, Virginia Historical Society.

During the 1760s and 1770s, John Tayloe, a wealthy planter in Richmond County, simultaneously shipped tobacco to merchants in Liverpool, Bristol, Dublin, and Edinburgh as well as to several London firms. John Turbeville informed merchants William Lee, James Russell, and William Molleson that he would distribute his crop among them and annually rotate the size of their shares. George Washington confronted Robert Cary & Company and James Gildart with the returns from other correspondents and with reports of what his neighbors received for similar tobacco. In a nearly formulaic response to consignment merchants, Washington and other planters threatened to suspend shipments if profits did not increase. Yet Washington continued to consign tobacco even when he realized that the sales of sweet-scented tobacco in London were often below what he could obtain for Oronoco in the country.[43]

Washington's involvement in the consignment trade was indicative of the frustrations confronting an ambitious planter in a restricted market. Washington had shipped his earliest tobacco crops to consignment merchants in London and Bristol in order to establish a source of credit and supply of British goods. Following his marriage to Martha Custis, he transferred his business to Robert Cary & Company and Capel and Osgood Hanbury, two prominent consignment firms that had long associations with the Custis family. Even these well-connected merchants could not provide satisfactory sales for Washington in depressed markets. How could it be, Washington asked his principal London correspondent, Robert Cary & Company, that the growers of high quality tobacco, "who by a close and fixed correspondence with you, contribute so largely to the dispatch of your Ships in this Country should meet with such unprofitable returns."[44]

Twice during the 1760s, Washington chose to sell his Potomac crop to a merchant in Alexandria rather than risk the London market. But

[43]Rosenblatt, "The Significance of Credit," 392–94; John Tayloe (1721–1779) Account Books, Virginia Historical Society; Robert Carter Accounts, Virginia Historical Society; George Washington to Robert Cary & Co., 20 Sep. 1765, *Papers of George Washington, Colonial Series*, eds., Abbot and Twohig, 7:398–402; George Washington to James Gildart, 3 Apr. 1761, in ibid, 7:32.

[44]Bruce A. Ragsdale, "George Washington, the British Tobacco Trade, and Economic Opportunity in Prerevolutionary Virginia," *Virginia Magazine of History and Biography* 97 (April 1989): 133–62; George Washington to Robert Cary & Co., 20 Sep. 1765, *Papers of George Washington, Colonial Series*, eds., Abbot and Twohig, 7:398–402.

new investments and the requirements of operating several plantations forced Washington to continue consignments to London firms. His uncharacteristic debt of £1,800 to Cary & Company in 1764, after a series of bad crops, defaulted payments from his own debtors, and purchases of land and slaves, was distressing evidence of the need to ship tobacco to London as long as he relied on the credit from consignment merchants. After 1765, Washington experimented with hemp, flax, and grain in the hope of finding a more dependable commodity for the London market. His success with new crops, however, was limited to the West Indies trade which provided none of the credit services or manufactured goods offered by tobacco traders in London. Washington's diversification of production at Mount Vernon, moreover, was possible only while tobacco shipments from the valuable Custis estates on York River maintained his credit with London merchants.[45]

Washington's extensive purchases of British imports proved no more satisfactory than the marketing of his tobacco. The dubious quality and the inflated price of the goods were, to him, aggravating reminders of Virginia's commercial dependence on Great Britain. Washington complained of receiving articles "that could only have been used by our Forefathers in the days of yore." "'Tis a custom," Washington had reason to believe, "with many Shop keepers and Tradesmen in London when they know Goods are bespoke for Exportation to palm sometimes old, and sometimes very slight and indifferent Goods upon us taking care at the sametime to advance 10, 15 or perhaps 20 prCt upon them." When ordering a chariot for Fielding Lewis, Washington instructed his merchant not to inform the tradesmen that the vehicle was intended for the colonies. The omission of goods and mistakes in quantity or size were particularly annoying after the wait of nine or more months between ordering and receiving the goods. Cary & Company suggested that Washington return unsatisfactory goods, but this could require as long as two years for any response. At the same time that Washington discontinued tobacco production at Mount Vernon, he initiated cloth manufactures in an effort to reduce the plantation's reliance on imported clothing. Although the operation was soon furnishing more than 1,200 yards of homespun a year, it was incapable of replacing the supplies from Great Britain.[46]

[45]Ragsdale, "George Washington, the British Tobacco Trade, and Economic Opportunity in Prerevolutionary Virginia."

[46]Ibid.; George Washington to Robert Cary & Co., 28 Sep. 1760, *Papers of George Washington, Colonial Series*, ed., Abbot, 6:459–61.

Other wealthy planters diversified export crops, established domestic manufactures, and invested in commercial ventures in the hopes of lessening the influence of British merchants and broadening opportunities in the colony. In the Northern Neck, men like Robert Carter of Nomini Hall and John Tayloe of Mount Airy established iron forges and grain mills and operated ships for the marketing of new commodities. A broader group of Virginians looked to the West for both speculation and the expansion of plantation agriculture. The Ohio Company and similar land schemes attracted the investments of those who hoped the West might support commercial development within Virginia. These ambitious endeavors, however, like those of Washington, did little to relieve the individual planter's dependence on the tobacco trade for credit and essential imports.[47]

If the transactions between Washington and his consignment merchants illustrate the great planters' dissatisfaction with the trade, they also reveal the commitment to a system of agriculture and a standard of living that perpetuated the dependence on British merchants. As long as Washington and other gentry planters organized their estates around slave labor and the cultivation of export crops, they needed to maintain a correspondence with British merchants in order to secure a flow of credit and the necessary provisions for a household and laborers. The personal selection of goods expected by Washington and his immediate family also required the services of a London merchant. For other gentry families in Virginia, far more deeply entangled in debt to British merchants, the consignment trade was a nearly inescapable means of reducing their obligations at the same time that they preserved a source of supplies for their plantations.

■   ■   ■

From the perspective of planters long accustomed to the consignment trade, the rise of the Scottish merchants became the most disturbing indication of the gentry's perceived loss of autonomy and influence over the colony's commercial life. The rapid success of the factors and their trading firms convinced planters and native merchants alike that the Scots dominated the economic life of the colony. Petersburg mer-

---

[47]Louis Morton, *Robert Carter of Nomini Hall* (Williamsburg: Colonial Williamsburg, Inc., 1941), chs.5–8; Account Book of John Tayloe, Virginia Historical Society.

chant Roger Atkinson asserted that "in a little time they will engross the whole," while William Lee claimed "Glasgow has allmost monopolized Virginia and its inhabitants." In the early 1770s, a newcomer to the colony understandably, if mistakenly, concluded that "all the Merchants & Shopkeepers . . . through the Province are young Scotch-Men."[48]

The Scottish organization of the tobacco trade so quickly overwhelmed earlier trading arrangements that both Virginian and English observers suspected various types of fraud. London merchants accused the Scots of exploiting their country's irregular coastline and sparse population to smuggle tobacco past customs inspectors. William Nelson, as president of the governor's council in Virginia, received similar reports of Scottish ships concealing inspection manifests for hogsheads when they cleared from the colony and illegally landing the surplus cargo in Scotland without paying proper duties. Although Nelson, a prosperous merchant himself, understood the importance of the store trade in explaining Scottish profits, the alleged customs violations were the more common explanation of the Scots' baffling practice of paying more for tobacco in Virginia than it would fetch on British markets. "There is something very Mysterious in the Glasgow trade," wrote William Lee from London, "their factors raise the price nominally in Virginia & the principals always begin to lower it here in Britain."[49]

What Virginians could not explain with rumors of illegal and unethical business, they attributed to a cultural degeneracy of the Scots. Despite the achievements of the Scottish renaissance, many in Virginia as well as England viewed Scotland as a backward, uncivilized nation, "cursed . . . with Barrenness and Vice."[50] Yet however widespread anti-Scottish sentiment appeared, and it was prevalent, Virginians fully ac-

---

[48]Roger Atkinson to Samuel Gist, 25 Aug. 1769, Roger Atkinson Letterbook, University of Virginia; William Lee to Landon Carter, 26 Aug. 1771, William Lee Letterbook, 1770–1771, Lee Family Papers at Stratford Hall; Philip Vickers Fithian, quoted in Alan L. Karras, *Sojourners in the Sun: Scottish Migrants in Jamaica and the Chesapeake, 1740–1800* (Ithaca and London: Cornell University Press, 1992), 89.

[49]Price, "The Rise of Glasgow"; William Nelson to Samuel Athawes, 5 July, 1769, Nelson Letterbook, 1765–1775, Virginia State Library; William Lee to James Mills, 24 September 1770, William Lee Letterbook, 1769–1771, Stratford Hall (University of Virginia microfilm).

[50]William Lee to Francis Lightfoot Lee, 5 Sep. 1774, *Lee Family Papers* (University of Virginia microfilm publication); for broader discussion of English attitudes toward Scotland, see Linda Colley, *Britons: Forging the Nation, 1707–1837* (New Haven and London: Yale University Press, 1992), 117–32.

cepted many individual Scots as respected members of provincial society. Scottish-born Virginians frequently served in political offices on a
local and provincial level. Native-born Virginians reserved their hostility almost exclusively for those Scots associated with the concentrated
tobacco firms of Glasgow.

That the Glasgow tobacco merchants alone provoked the great
planters' worst suspicions about national character suggests that the anti-
Scottish attacks reflected apprehensions about business rather than cultural prejudices. The colonists' stereotypical notion of a humorless, dour
Scot, single-mindedly attached to business was a sharp contrast to the
image of an expansive, self-confident Virginia planter moving easily
among all ranks of society; and each stereotype contained a certain truth.
But what appeared to Virginians to be innate differences of character
were the manifestation of very dissimilar approaches to business and
commerce. Arthur Lee confronted this disparity of manners while studying in Scotland. On a trip to Glasgow, Lee attempted to establish personal contacts that might assist his family in commerce, but the Virginian
was repelled by the merchants' brusque demeanor. "Their strict attention to business, had rendered them an uncivil, unsociable People, and
utterly strangers to Politeness," he lamented to his brother Richard
Henry Lee in Virginia.[51]

Virginia's great planters, from a long involvement in the consignment trade, thought of tobacco commerce as a slow-moving business in
which merchants steadily expanded a network of personal contacts until
they secured a profitable level of annual crop shipments. As Arthur Lee's
efforts in Glasgow indicated, the gentry planters' own business dealings
were naturally connected to various types of social interaction. The Lees
of Stratford, like innumerable other estate owners in Virginia, regularly
transacted business in the midst of social gatherings or community meetings. Ship captains in the consignment trade combined their collection
of tobacco with social visits to the familiar planters along Virginia's rivers. The gentry's business affairs in the colony and in Great Britain also
were intertwined with family connections. For the great planter, social
position, political connection, and family ties all insured access to economic opportunity.

The Scottish commercial structure, which was neither slow nor
personal, more neatly segregated economic transactions from the broader

---

[51]Arthur Lee to Richard Henry Lee, 21 October 1761, in *Lee Family Papers*
(University of Virginia microfilm publication).

life of the community. The factor in Virginia served no other function than to provide the services associated with the marketing of tobacco and sale of British imports. The efficiency and superiority of these services, rather than social position or family connection in the colony, determined the success of a Scottish agent. Each factor established himself by drawing on his company's resources to attract a steady supply of tobacco and new customers for the store. Particularly in newly-settled areas, the factor's business was unrelated to community contacts, political influence, or social status.

This modern notion of the exclusivity of economic life was a local reflection of the rational, centralized organization of the Glasgow merchants houses. The directors of the tobacco firms structured their operations so that the loyalties and interests of the factors remained in Scotland throughout their service in the Chesapeake. The factors' job was temporary by design. Companies selected as agents young, single men who could devote their undivided attention to business affairs before returning to advanced positions with the firm in Scotland. While resident in the colony, factors socialized almost exclusively with a close network of their fellow Scots. Hiring contracts barred the factors from engaging in any kind of business of their own while in Virginia and forbade factors from owning any land except that immediately connected to the store. Resident for only two to three years at most, the young factors had little opportunity or need to establish community ties in Virginia. William Cunninghame & Company went so far as to instruct its factors not to develop "too great an Intimacy" with the Virginians in order not to compromise their advantages in negotiation. In a directive that Arthur Lee and his family surely would not have comprehended, the resident manager for the company "strongly advised" against "much visiting at the planters houses." When one Cunninghame factor married a Virginia woman, the company discharged him.[52]

Virginians were particularly apprehensive about the factors' transient position in colonial society. "They neither value us or our country . . . no sooner are they feathered (like birds of migration) they fly away," complained a "Planter" in 1771. Landon Carter thought the Scots' lack of attachment explained their failure to support American resistance to imperial policy. Only "a very few who seem to intend this Colony as their chief residence" supported the patriot cause, while the rest ac-

---

[52]Soltow, "Scottish Traders in Virginia," 85–89; Karras, *Sojourners in the Sun*, 81–117, 131–66.

tively encouraged compliance with the offensive British acts. Long before the imperial crisis the factors' allegiance to Scotland and their companies posed problems for Virginians, particularly the gentry planters. The Scots not only threatened to displace the great planters as an economic elite, they introduced a trading structure that redefined the relationship between economic activity and the local community. Since the early decades of the eighteenth century, the great planters had adhered to a paternalistic ideal of public service that tempered the exploitative character of Virginia society in the preceding century. A flexible system of local administration, a commitment to political leadership, and a sense of public obligation balanced the great planters' disproportionate control of land and labor. This code of public virtue secured for the gentry the most stable social structure in British North America and eliminated all but the most inconsequential challenges to their authority. The Scottish factors' economic influence, which rivaled and in areas excelled that of the wealthiest planters, was unchecked by any similar obligation or connection to the public life of Virginia.[53]

The Scottish merchants in Virginia became the special object of the great planters' fears and resentments because they so clearly, even exaggeratedly, represented the risks of the direct trade and of continued dependence on Great Britain. The immediate and obvious threat was Glasgow's potential domination of the tobacco trade. The Scots had been the most visible agents in the transition away from the consignment system favored by great planters. Their system of stores further displaced the great planters as intermediaries between smaller planters and British markets. Within the tobacco trade, the efficient, rationally organized, and capital intensive companies in Glasgow were at the forefront of the kind of commercial development that threatened to engulf the plantation-based gentry in Virginia.

As the Scots' particular commercial system infiltrated Virginia and set a model for other traders, it appeared to have implications far beyond the issue of relative economic advantages or questions of who controlled the tobacco trade. Scottish trading activity threatened to undermine an important basis of political stability by dividing the common interest that once had united tobacco growers. For the great planters to protect their economic interests and social position would require more than the diversification of their estates or compensation for de-

<hr />

[53]A "Planter" to Rind, *Virginia Gazette* (Rind), 31 Oct. 1771; *Diary of Landon Carter*, ed., Greene, 2:821.

clining opportunities in the consignment trade. The broad threat presented to the gentry by the Scots and other concentrated commercial enterprises in Great Britain would not be checked until the entire colonial economy was weaned from its reliance on tobacco exports and the merchants residing in the colony were incorporated in the planter-dominated political culture of Virginia.

◼   ◼   ◼

    Virginia planters in the third quarter of the eighteenth century found themselves ever more deeply enmeshed in a web of commerce that spanned the Atlantic world. The gentry along the James River, the yeoman planters of the Piedmont, and every other producer of tobacco for export traded directly with British merchants who personified the advance of commercial capitalism in the eighteenth century. As the center of the richest trade of British North America, Virginia reaped many of the benefits of the mobilization of capital and rise of consumerism that had transformed the economy of Great Britain in the eighteenth century. Yet the expansion of the British tobacco trade that increased the wealth of most Virginia households and advanced territorial settlement exacted a heavy cost from many Virginians. The efficient organization of the British trade, supported by the power of a mercantilist state, overwhelmed commercial competition, diminished the personal influence of even the wealthiest landowners in Virginia, and confined economic development to a narrow path. Ultimately, the growth of the tobacco trade in the middle decades of the eighteenth century reinforced the colonial character of the Chesapeake economy.

    For the great planters, the reorganization and centralization of the tobacco trade ironically threatened to undermine the very authority that they had attained through their special connection with Great Britain. A larger and more strictly regulated debt, the commercial influence of British factors resident in Virginia, and the fading advantages of the consignment trade all restricted the great planters' ability to utilize the land and labor resources that constituted the material foundation for their ascendancy. The owners of Virginia's great estates sought in the management of their plantations and in their transactions with merchants to establish the kind of regularity and certainty that would allow them to meet the demands of a highly organized and increasingly concentrated commercial establishment in Great Britain. These efforts, however, inevitably confronted the limitations inherent in a staple economy with few commercial institutions and reliant on slave labor. Frustrated in their efforts to protect the independence of their individual estates, the gentry planters looked beyond their own plantations to question the structure of Virginia's economy and eventually the value of the British connection itself.

An Imperial Crisis and the Origins of Commercial Resistance

Until the end of the French and Indian War, the tobacco trade remained the most significant bond between Virginia and Great Britain. For the great majority of the colony's residents, the Empire was one of commerce and goods rather than administrative bureaucracies or military force. Virginians were far more likely to deal regularly with a resident British factor or a merchant in England than with an imperial official. News of politics and imperial policy traveled through an unofficial network connecting merchants in London with the planters who dominated the political life of the colony. When Virginians appealed to imperial administrators or Parliament, it was frequently through the mediation of influential merchants in the tobacco trade.

For decades the effective operation of the Empire had depended largely on the informal ties linking colonists with powerful groups in London, and no colony in British North America enjoyed as many attachments to London as did the tobacco-rich Virginia. The Virginians' regular communication with British merchants helped to maintain the allegiance of the Old Dominion and averted many a direct confrontation with imperial authority. The personal services of British merchants and the accessibility of British fashions for wealthy Virginians further encouraged the colonists' cultural identification with the center of Empire. As long as they enjoyed a degree of political autonomy and their economic interests coincided with those of the British commercial establishment, Virginia's great planters were content, indeed often gratified, to consider themselves members of the British Empire.[1]

While the colony's proud and assertive gentry often clashed with royal governors over questions of political prerogatives, before the 1760s Virginians only occasionally challenged imperial authority over the provincial economy. The relative lack of opposition to mercantilist regulation in part reflected the mixed effects of British policy. Although they restricted the marketing of colonial produce, the Navigation Acts and customs duties also protected Virginia's tobacco growers from competition with Spanish colonies and the Continent. Parliament also encouraged the cultivation of desired staples such as hemp through offers of bounties for colonial planters, albeit with little success.

Virginia's colonists were most likely to criticize imperial restrictions on the colonial economy during periods of depressed tobacco prices when growers absorbed a higher proportion of the customs duties and planters struggled to expand domestic manufactures. During a recession in the 1720s, a number of Virginians recognized that regulation of the tobacco trade favored the interests of British merchants and retarded agricultural diversification. As tobacco prices continued to fall, the burgesses attempted to lessen dependence on that crop by curbing slave importations and establishing a quota on the number of plants tended by each worker, but these efforts fell to the combined opposition of the Crown and new planters eager to compete with the established gentry of Tidewater.[2]

The Virginia assembly periodically challenged the excessive tobacco duties which steadily increased between 1660 and 1759 when they reached 8 ⅓ pence per pound, a sum 200–300 percent above the price of tobacco before importation. In 1732, the burgesses campaigned for an excise tax on the sale of tobacco in England to replace all customs duties on the crop. Despite the ministry's support for the excise, British merchants defeated the scheme. When Parliament added an extra penny per pound to tobacco duties in 1747, the burgesses unsuccessfully petitioned for its removal. Despite the burden customs duties placed on the producers, particularly at a time of poor tobacco prices, the political

---

[1]Alison Gilbert Olson, *Making the Empire Work: London and American Interest Groups, 1690–1790,* (Cambridge and London: Harvard University Press, 1992); John M. Hemphill II, *Virginia and the English Commercial System, 1689–1733: Studies in the Development and Fluctuations of a Colonial Economy under Imperial Control* (New York and London: Garland Publishing, Inc., 1985).

[2]Hemphill, *Virginia and the English Commercial System,* 52–97.

effort to reduce import duties subsided during prosperous markets and was not a persistent objective of the colonists.[3]

Nor did Virginians before the 1760s express any serious opposition to British restrictions on colonial manufactures. A parliamentary act of 1750 prohibited the erection of new slitting mills or steel furnaces, which might have been beneficial to Virginia, but Parliament simultaneously encouraged the production of pig iron for export to Great Britain. Iron foundries provided a viable opportunity for wealthy planters intent on diversification, and pig iron became Virginia's most important manufacture. British prohibitions on colonial exports of wool and the act of 1732 prohibiting shipment of hats from one colony to another had no effect in a colony where clothing items were usually cheaper to import than manufacture. In fact, the inexpensive production of consumer goods in Great Britain and the efficient marketing arrangements of the tobacco trade proved to be the most effective restriction on Virginia manufactures.[4]

The entire operation of the trade between Great Britain and Virginia mitigated against criticism of imperial regulations of the economy. The British government prevented the development of an independent economy less by means of strict regulation of the colonists than through its support of the British merchants' monopoly on the Virginia trade. Credit legislation increasingly favored the interests of the merchants at the expense of the colonists; the customs system placed the financial burden on the producers and consumers rather than the traders; the operation of the customs service required capital-intensive merchant firms to establish headquarters in Great Britain; and the Board of Trade discouraged any attempts to limit the size of Virginia's tobacco crop, thereby aiding merchants whose profits depended more on quantity than quality. The merchants rather than royal officials or customs collectors thus became the principal agents of a governmental strategy that per-

[3]Complete account of the excise scheme in Ibid., 190–286; see also Lawrence H. Gipson, *The British Empire Before the Revolution, The Southern Plantations*, 2:130–32; and Peter Linebaugh, *The London Hanged: Crime and Civil Society in the Eighteenth Century* (Cambridge and New York: Cambridge University Press, 1992), 153–83; customs duties detailed in Samuel M. Rosenblatt, "The Significance of Credit in the Tobacco Consignment Trade: A Study of John Norton & Sons, 1768–1775," *William and Mary Quarterly* 3rd ser., 19 (July 1962): 383–99.

[4]Oliver M. Dickerson, *The Navigation Acts and the American Revolution* (Philadelphia: University of Pennsylvania Press, 1951), 18–21.

Tobacco Paper, Line Engraving, 1733. This ribald English tobacco label declared colonial leaf "the Best in Christendom" following the defeat of the excise scheme that would have shifted the burden of revenue from Chesapeake producers to British consumers. (Colonial Williamsburg Foundation)

petuated the colonists' reliance on staple crop production and discouraged commercial development outside of Great Britain. When Virginians criticized commercial relations with Great Britain, as they often did before the 1760s, they were more likely to attack the merchants' monopoly on credit and marketing than the imperial regulations that supported the merchants' advantages.

The reorganization of imperial administration and stricter enforcement that began in the 1740s only gradually came to affect Virginia's internal politics or its commerce with Great Britain. The Board of Trade's close examination and partial disallowance of a general revision of colonial statutes at mid-century signaled Whitehall's intention to monitor the provincial legislatures just as the controversy over Dinwiddie's pistole fee marked a determination to exact greater revenue from the American colonies. As alarming as these incidents were for some Virginia political leaders, neither seriously disrupted imperial relations or the necessary, though fragile, cooperation that developed between Virginia and Great Britain during the French and Indian War. Only in the wake of the peace of 1763 did the British government impose regulations that challenged traditional assumptions regarding both imperial administration and the operation of a transatlantic trade that was for Virginians the most important link with the center of Empire.[5]

■   ■   ■

Within a matter of months in 1764, Virginians received notice of Parliament's approval of two acts and the proposal for a third that together would undermine the political prerogatives of provincial assemblies and restrict a local economy already in the throes of a post-war depression. For a colony so intimately tied to Great Britain through networks of trade and material goods, any shift in imperial administration necessarily entailed a further straining of commercial bonds. Announcement of these British statutes and recognition of the larger policy goals they portended induced Virginia's political leadership for the first

[5]Warren M. Billings, John E. Selby, and Thad W. Tate, *Colonial Virginia: A History* (White Plains, N.Y.: KTO Press, 1986), 253–66; Jack P. Greene, "An Uneasy Connection: An Analysis of the Preconditions of the American Revolution," in *Essays on the American Revolution*, eds., Stephen G. Kurtz and James H. Hutson (New York: W. W. Norton, 1973), 32–80.

time to examine the commercial limitations of the colony fully within the context of imperial authority. The new acts, with their demands for revenue and restrictions on trade, immediately politicized the planters' chronic economic grievances. What had been personal dilemmas of trade and plantation management suddenly became matters of public affairs. Virginia's commercial disadvantages no longer appeared to be the result solely of merchant collusion and exploitation, but also the consequence of imperial policy. The cumulative effect of the new acts convinced one prominent planter "that the Ministry are as ignorant of our Situation, with Respect to Trade, as they have long appeared to be of Government."[6]

The Currency Act of 1764 forbade in the colonies south of New England all future emissions of paper money as legal tender, as well as the reissue of any paper money already in circulation. Although the act went into effect in all colonies not subject to the Currency Act of 1751, Parliament's principal object was to prevent Virginians from discharging their British debts in inflated paper currency. The House of Burgesses had approved the colony's first paper issue in 1755 in order to finance Braddock's expedition. Braddock's defeat and renewed military expenses made necessary twelve further emissions before 1763. At least £230,000 in Virginia notes remained outstanding in 1764.

English merchants, as part of a broader effort to protect creditors' interests in Virginia, persuaded the Board of Trade that the colony's emissions of paper money were a threat to the security of sterling debts. In May 1763, Governor Francis Fauquier presented the House of Burgesses with the Board's recent resolution, threatening to prohibit all local currency. The assembly rejected the governor's plea for a modicum of protection for sterling debts and refused to eliminate the treasury notes as legal tender. According to the burgesses' reply, all sterling debts were protected by the Virginia assembly's law of 1755 providing for court determination of prevailing exchange rates between local currency and sterling. If the merchants had the right to decide exchange rates, they could "extort such Differences as might be very oppressive." Robert Beverley considered the threat of a parliamentary statute restricting currency "too Tyrannical for a free born People."[7]

[6]Robert Beverley to Landon Carter, 9 Oct. 1765, Landon Carter Papers, 1763–1775, Virginia Historical Society.

[7]Joseph A. Ernst, *Money and Politics in America, 1755–1775: A Study in the Currency Act of 1764 and the Political Economy of Revolution* (Chapel Hill: University of North Carolina Press, 1973), Ch. 3; Fauquier's address to the Burgesses in *Journals of the House of Burgesses, 1761–1765*, eds. Kennedy and McIlwaine,

Parliament's approval of the Currency Act provoked no immediate protest from the burgesses who had feared their recalcitrance would provoke a ban on all circulating legal tender issues. Since the act permitted outstanding currency to remain in circulation, the most important practical effect of the legislation was to eliminate currency emissions as a means of relieving the periodic distress of credit restriction, rising exchange, and cash shortages. The Currency Act thus strengthened the position of Richard Henry Lee and others in Virginia who maintained that the solution to short-term credit restrictions was a long-term improvement in Virginia's balance of trade. But even for Lee and the many burgesses who opposed paper money in principle, the Currency Act was the clearest evidence yet of Parliament's willingness to regulate the colonial economy in the interest of protecting merchants' debts and crown revenues, even when that regulation overturned the consensus of the colonial assembly.[8]

Parliament's regulation of colonial currency came shortly on the heels of a reorganization and strengthening of colonial customs in the Revenue Act of 1764, also known as the Sugar Act. The act reduced molasses duties to one-half of the six pence a gallon levied (though seldom if ever collected) under the terms of an act of 1733. Parliament's new Revenue Act imposed taxes on a variety of additional commodities and provided for the effective collection of all duties as well as the stricter enforcement of standing trade regulations. This measure differed from earlier acts respecting trade in its stated intention to raise a revenue; proceeds were to help defray the costs of stationing British troops in North America.[9]

Although Virginia was much less affected than the northern colonies which depended on the importation of French West Indian sugar, the burgesses were "very uneasy" about this "Attempt made in Parliament to lay a Duty on the several Commodities mentioned" and regret-

---

171–72; Burgesses' reply of 20 May, ibid., 173–74; Burgesses offered more extensive defense on 27 May, ibid., 188–92; Robert Beverley to John Bland, 5 May 1763, Robert Beverley Letterbook, Library of Congress.

[8]Ernst, *Money and Politics*, 63; idem., "The Robinson Scandal Redivivus: Money, Debts, and Politics in Revolutionary Virginia," *Virginia Magazine of History and Biography* 77 (April 1969): 146–73.

[9]Edmund S. Morgan and Helen M. Morgan, *The Stamp Act Crisis: Prologue to Revolution* (Chapel Hill: University of North Carolina Press, 1953), Ch. 3; Bernhard Knollenberg, *Origins of the American Revolution, 1759–1766*, Rev. Ed. (New York: The Macmillan Company, 1961), Ch. 12.

ted they had not received word in time to register a protest through their London agent, Edward Montague. Of greatest concern to the Virginians was the new duty of £7 per ton on Madeira wine. Wine was important to the colony, not only as a favored drink of the gentry but also as a valuable return cargo in Virginia's emerging grain trade with Southern Europe.[10]

Opposition to the Revenue Act in Virginia was secondary to the colonists' reaction to a proposed stamp tax. When Edward Montague sent the assembly's committee of correspondence a report on the approval of the Revenue Act, he included a description of George Grenville's proposal for raising additional revenue through a stamp tax on the colonies. The committee instructed Montague to exert every effort to prevent passage of the Stamp Act. At the assembly's fall session in 1764, the full House of Burgesses with the concurrence of the council issued more protests in an address to the King and memorials to Parliament. If Montague should be unable to submit the memorial to the Commons, the burgesses requested that he print copies and distribute them throughout England.[11]

The appeals of Virginia and other colonies failed to restrain the House of Commons which approved the Stamp Act without any formal consideration of the various American petitions. The Act, which was to go into effect on November 1, 1765, levied a duty on almost every type of paper in use in the colonies. The schedule of fees covered documents used in court actions, customs papers, newspapers and pamphlets, even playing cards. Rates were generally lower than for similar levies in England, but all were to be paid in specie. When word of the act's passage reached the colonies, Virginia's House of Burgesses took the lead in protesting the measure with the approval of Patrick Henry's resolves in May. These statements of principal reasserted the colonists' right to representative government and offered a model imitated by other colo-

---

[10]Virginia Committee of Correspondence to Edward Montague, 15 June 1764, *Virginia Magazine of History and Biography* 12 (July 1904): 6–14.

[11]Virginia Committee of Correspondence meeting, 15 June 1764; Committee of Correspondence to Edward Montague, 28 July 1764, *Virginia Magazine of History and Biography* 12 (July 1904): 6–14; Address and Memorials in *Journals of the House of Burgesses, 1761–1765*, eds., Kennedy and McIlwaine, 302-04; Committee of Correspondence to Edward Montague, 19 Dec. 1764, *Virginia Magazine of History and Biography* 12 (April 1905): 353–55.

nies, but the Virginia assembly did not define a particular strategy of resistance to the Stamp Act.[12]

■   ■   ■

Virginians, like other American colonists, considered the Stamp Act indicative of a fundamental redefinition of the relationship between Great Britain and its North American colonies. The collection of revenue through a parliamentary-imposed tax violated the established political privileges of the provincial assemblies and betrayed colonial assumptions about the mutual obligations of the Empire. In their earliest protests against the Stamp Act, Virginians grasped the parallels between the political infringements and commercial restrictions imposed by the new tax. Parliament's assumption of the authority to tax the colonies threatened the assemblies' right to approve all taxes for each colony just as it simultaneously demonstrated a clear example of the monetary costs resulting from a loss of that legislative sovereignty.

The immediate economic effects of the Stamp Act were obvious to Virginians in the mid-1760s. Passage of the Stamp Act came at a time when the colony was under an unusually heavy tax burden owing to the expenses of the French and Indian War and the cost of retiring paper currency. "For God's Sake," asked Charles Carter of Corotoman upon word of the Stamp Act's passage, "what will become of our poor colony of Virginia which is already so heavy laden with Debts & Taxes." The burgesses' committee of correspondence found the new tax particularly objectionable because the existing taxes had been "contracted chiefly in Defence of the Common Cause" during the late war.[13]

---

[12]Morgan and Morgan, *The Stamp Act Crisis*, Ch.5; Merrill Jensen, *The Founding of a Nation: A History of the American Revolution, 1763–1776* (New York: Oxford University Press, 1968), Ch. 2, esp. 59–66.

[13]Charles Carter to Messrs Stewart & Campbell, 15 May 1765, Carter Letterbook, Alderman Library, University Virginia; Virginia Committee of Correspondence to Edward Montague, 28 July 1764, *Virginia Magazine of History and Biography* 12 (July 1904): 9; see also *Journals of the House of Burgesses, 1761–1765*, eds., Kennedy and McIlwaine, (Remonstrance to the House of Commons) 304; and Petition of Edward Montague, 7 Mar. 1766, Main Papers, House of Lords Record Office (Virginia Colonial Records Project microfilm).

Parliament's demand for payment in specie created additional problems in a colony suffering from a shortage of all types of circulating currency and of specie in particular. The burgesses' memorials to the Lords and Commons in 1764 warned of the colonists' "total want of specie." In the spring of 1765, Governor Fauquier alerted the ministry that a general scarcity of specie was already causing distress. Merchants in the Virginia trade estimated that in the entire colony there was not one-tenth the specie needed to pay the levy for a single year. Even if more specie became available, merchants worried that the payments on the stamp tax would reduce the colonists' ability to repay British debts in sterling.[14]

The scarcity of specie was one consequence of the current depression in the tobacco trade. Following the peace of 1763, tobacco prices had fallen, resulting in a withdrawal of British credit from Virginia. The poor returns on tobacco and the shortage of coin and bills of exchange made it difficult for planters to make remittances on the debts that they accumulated before 1765. Fauquier was convinced "this private Distress which every man feels encreases the general Dissatisfaction at the Duties laid by the late Stamp Act." The Stamp Act added to the problems of the depression by taxing every court action involved in the recovery and processing of debts. Edward Montague told the House of Lords that credit was so short in Virginia that securities were demanded for the smallest debts. The entry of these bonds also required a revenue stamp. Virginia merchants feared that if the Stamp Act were enforced the greatest burden would fall on the yeoman planters, those with debts under £5, who "can neither Buy or sell but affected by it nor proceed in law proceedings." The act was adding insult to injury by taxing the very type of litigation that hard times necessitated.[15]

But court cases for debt recovery and the entry of bonds were not simply a product of an economic depression, they were integral to the

[14]*Journals of the House of Burgesses, 1761–1765*, eds., Kennedy and McIlwaine, 302–04; Francis Fauquier to Halifax, 14 June 1765, Public Record Office, CO5/1345, 80–81 (Virginia Colonial Records Project microfilm); Hearings of the Committee on the American Papers, Etc., British Museum, Add. Mss. 33030, testimony of George Mercer 124, and Capel Hanbury 107.

[15]Fauquier to Halifax, 14 June 1765, Public Record Office, CO5/1345, 80–81 (Virginia Colonial Records Project microfilm); Petition of Edward Montague, 7 Mar 1766, House of Lords Record Office; Hearings of the Committee on the American Papers, Etc., testimony of James Balfour 114, and George Mercer, 124.

operation of Virginia's economy in the best of times. Early opponents of the Stamp Act recognized that a tax on court proceedings constituted a permanent hardship in an economy like Virginia's. According to Landon Carter, the duty was indeed a tax upon necessities of life because people could not survive without buying and selling, and this was "a tax upon every branch of Trade." Merchants in London feared that the costs of court proceedings would further limit the colonists' ability and readiness to make remittances on British debts.[16]

■   ■   ■

Challenged by the immediate costs of the Stamp Act and fearful of its long-term effects on the colony's trade, Virginia's leading planters and political leaders responded to the imperial reorganization with an articulation of their own ideal of the proper commercial balance between Mother Country and colony. This public discussion was part of a broader examination of every aspect of imperial relations from the distribution of political power to the mutual benefits of Navigation Acts. Just as the resulting defense of constitutional rights strengthened the attachment to political liberties and advanced colonial notions of sovereignty, so the analysis of Virginia's commercial position within the Empire heightened awareness of the colony's great wealth at the same time that it emphasized the various hazards of dependence on British trade.

In its earliest remonstrance to the House of Commons in December 1764, the Virginia assembly declared the proposed stamp tax unreasonable because the colony already contributed so much to the benefit of the Empire. Virginia willingly had met British requests for defense appropriations during the French and Indian War, and the provincial government continued to expend money for the protection of the colony's frontier. More important than any specific appropriation of revenue was the wealth that the colony's trade provided for Great Britain. The Navigation Acts already exacted the just price for commercial protection and imperial defense. According to the assembly, "the Plantation Trade, confined as it is to the Mother Country, hath been a prin-

[16]Landon Carter, essay of 30 November 1765, in Jack P. Greene, "'Not to be Governed or Taxed But by . . . Our Representative': Four Essays in Opposition to the Stamp Act by Landon Carter," *Virginia Magazine of History and Biography* 76 (July 1968): 284.

cipal Means of multiplying and enriching her Inhabitants." The members of the Stafford County court maintained the American colonies were "the most invaluable part of [the King's] Dominions for increasing the trade, Navigation, and manufactures of Great Britain." This wealth from the American trade arose through no costs to the British government, but rather "at the Expence of the private Adventurers our Ancestors; the Fruit of whose Toil and Danger we now enjoy."[17]

Most commentators in Virginia still adhered to the ideal of an Empire that might offer endless bounty for both the colonies and the Crown. Again and again, opponents of the Stamp Act insisted that Great Britain would magnify its revenue from the American trade by freeing the colonial economies from governmental regulation rather than by levying taxes or imposing new trade restrictions. The assembly assured members of the House of Commons that the colonial trade, "if not too much discouraged, may prove an inexhaustible Source of Treasure to the Nation." "If by opening the Channels of Trade," George Mason proposed to the merchants of London, "you afford Us a ready Market for the Produce of our Lands, and an Opportunity of purchasing cheap the Conveniencys of Life, all our superfluous Gain will sink into your Pockets, in Return for British Manufactures." The justices of Stafford County promised Governor Fauquier that with "indulgencies and proper encouragement" from the British government, instead of threats to their property and liberty, the Virginians would be able to supply Great Britain with the most valuable sorts of commodities. And the relief from taxation would better enable the colonists "to pay their unreasonable British creditors."[18]

Various opponents of the Stamp Act warned that the enforcement of the new revenue acts would undermine economic growth and dimin-

[17]Remonstrance to House of Commons, 18 Dec. 1764, *Journals of the House of Burgesses, 1761–1765*, eds., Kennedy and McIlwaine, 304; George Washington to Robert Cary & Co., 20 Sep. 1765, in *Papers of George Washington, Colonial Series*, eds., Abbot and Twohig, 7:398–402; Stafford County Court to Governor Francis Fauquier, 5 Oct. 1765, in *Revolutionary Virginia: The Road to Independence*, comp., William J. Van Schreeven, eds., Robert L. Scribner and Brent Tarter, 7 vols., (Charlottesville: University Press of Virginia, 1973–83), 7:722–23; George Mason to the Committee of Merchants in London, 6 June 1766, in George Mason, *The Papers of George Mason*, ed., Robert A. Rutland, 3 vols. (Chapel Hill: University of North Carolina Press, 1970), 1:69.

[18]Remonstrance to the House of Commons, 18 Dec. 1764, *Journals of the House of Burgesses, 1761–1775*, eds., Kennedy and McIlwaine, 304; George Ma-

ish the commercial opportunities that Virginia heretofore had provided for British merchants and manufacturers. Landon Carter feared that the British had forgotten "that every duty has its additional expence, clear of the money paid into the revenue." Carter pointed out that American demand for British goods "depends solely on the luxury of the consumer" and required "an indulgence given in price; especially where the consumption principally depends upon the poorer sort of people." Revenue duties would necessarily limit that consumption and consequently injure British traders, manufacturers, and the laborers they employed. In further ramifications of the stamp tax, the new excise also would impede the Americans' ability to pay their British creditors, thereby disrupting the flow of payments to shopkeepers, manufacturers, and seamen to whom the merchants owed money. As George Mason reminded the London merchants, the colonies and Great Britain formed a single "Commercial Chain; break but one Link of it, and the whole is destroyed." Another Chesapeake planter cautioned a British merchant that "all fetters upon our trade & impositions on our property will ultimately affect you more than us." Many merchants both in Great Britain and in the colony also feared that enforcement of the act would make it impossible to resume normal commerce. Virginia merchant James Balfour while in London swore he would not return to the colony with a farthing, neither would he give fifty shillings for his extensive business in Virginia if the act were continued.[19]

■   ■   ■

At the same time that the burgesses defended the established political rights of the colony, they and many other Virginians embraced a strategy of commercial resistance designed to apply pressure directly

---

son to the Committee of Merchants in London, 6 June 1766, *Papers of George Mason*, ed., Rutland, 1:69–70; Stafford County Court to Fauquier, 5 October 1765, in *Revolutionary Virginia*, eds., Scribner and Tarter, 7:722–23.

[19]Remonstrance to the House of Commons, *Journals of the House of Burgesses, 1761–1765*, eds., Kennedy and McIlwaine, 304; Landon Carter, essay of 30 Nov. 1765, in Greene, "'Not to Be Governed or Taxed . . .'" 289, 294–95; George Mason to the Committee of Merchants in London, 6 June 1766, *Papers of George Mason*, ed., Rutland, 1:69–70; *Virginia Gazette* (Purdie), 11 July 1766; Hearings of the Committee on the American Papers, Etc., testimony of Capel Hanbury, 107, 112; James Balfour, 115.

on those who might bring about a repeal of the Stamp Act. By with-holding from British merchants and manufacturers the business of the colony, the Virginians also hoped to protect what they considered the mutual benefits of Empire and to reduce the vulnerability of a colonial staple economy. With few alternative avenues to influence in London, Virginians appealed to the tobacco merchants whom they frequently accused of intrigue and conspiracy. Planters who recently blamed bur-densome imperial policy on "the very Merchts who draw their Suste-nance as it were from our very Vitals" and who despaired of the possibility of resistance from an indebted population, now hoped to utilize the colony's wealth in order to engage the material interests and enlist the political support of traders who had long been the Virginians' principal intermediaries in Great Britain.[20]

In their initial remonstrance against the proposed Stamp Act, the burgesses recognized that the cost of the new duties might compel colo-nists to initiate domestic manufactures as an alternative to British im-ports. But what the assembly formally described as a necessity of "extreme poverty" was for many individuals an opportunity to shield the colony from imperial demands for revenue and, more important, a means to lessen permanently their fellow Virginians' dependence on imported manufactures. Arthur Lee first suggested domestic manufactures in Vir-ginia as a proper defense against the Revenue Act of 1764. Writing from Scotland where he was studying medicine, Lee urged his brother Rich-ard Henry Lee to cultivate support in the House of Burgesses for the public encouragement of colonial manufactures. Virginians might fol-low the Scottish example of local improvement societies in which arti-sans instructed the community in basic crafts. Lee also suggested that the assembly dispatch several young Virginians on a tour of manufac-turing regions of Europe in order to learn new technologies and recruit skilled workers for emigration to the colony. The ever-suspicious Lee warned his brother and other burgesses to be secretive so as to avoid "the vigilance of that jealous eye, with which Britain will ever view the rise & progress of Arts & Manufactures in America."[21]

---

[20]Robert Beverley to John Bland, 5 May 1763, Robert Beverley Letterbook, 1761–1793, Library of Congress.

[21]*Journals of the House of Burgesses, 1761–1765*, eds., Kennedy and McIlwaine, 302–04; Arthur Lee to Richard Henry Lee, 13 Jan. 1765, *Lee Family Papers*, (University of Virginia microfilm).

Several northern colonies more adversely affected by the Revenue Act had responded to the new duties with the sort of commercial resistance recommended by Lee. In 1764 Bostonians entered nonconsumption agreements, and in New York the Society for the Promotion of Arts, Agriculture and Economy offered bounties for improvements in local manufactures. Throughout New England and the Middle Atlantic colonies, experiments in domestic manufactures testified to a determination to suspend imports from Great Britain until Parliament approved a satisfactory revision of the Revenue Act. Interest in manufacturing schemes and commercial resistance in these colonies escalated after passage of the Stamp Act. By the fall of 1765, merchants in New York, Philadelphia, and Boston approved formal nonimportation associations which were to remain in effect until repeal of the Stamp Act.[22]

A comprehensive and formal plan of commercial resistance faced far greater obstacles in the Chesapeake than in northern colonies where the principal importers were native merchants gathered together in a handful of port cities. The much higher volume of goods imported into Virginia entered through innumerable planters' wharves and dozens of factors' stores dispersed throughout the colony. Compared to the northern colonies, Virginia had far fewer domestic manufactures to supply replacements for the ordinary and necessary goods normally imported through the tobacco trade. In the absence of a principal commercial center tied through trading networks to local communities, the only institution uniting the entire colony was the assembly which took the lead in the early protests against the Stamp Act. But Fauquier dissolved the House of Burgesses in May of 1765 and had no intention of reconvening it until the crisis passed. The governor also suspended publication of the *Virginia Gazette*, thereby silencing the most important means of communication in this colony with few urban centers.

Deprived of the means of organizing a formal, colony-wide association, many Virginians privately responded to the Stamp Act by initiating domestic manufactures and reducing their consumption of British goods. The emphasis on cloth production reflected Virginia's overwhelming dependence on Great Britain for all varieties of that article. Governor Fauquier reported that the Stamp Act prompted a "strong attempt" in the colony to convert hemp into osnaburg, a coarse European fabric essential for clothing slaves. Capel Hanbury, a London mer-

---

[22]Arthur M. Schlesinger, *The Colonial Merchants and the American Revolution, 1763–1776* (New York: Columbia University, 1918), 63–65, 76–81.

chant, heard of schemes for weaving linen and woolens, as well as the construction of fulling mills for the preparation of wool for weaving. The reports he received from Virginia mentioned a "spirit of emulation for wearing their own manufactures," which had replaced the proud display of British clothing. Hanbury's reference to "premiums for making linen and woolen" indicates that some planters, at least, organized public support for domestic manufactures. Certain communities also entered agreements not to kill lambs in order to increase the supply of wool.[23]

During the Stamp Act crisis, planters established schools, "which were never thought of before," in order to teach children the skills needed for home manufactures. George Mercer knew of two planters who each had transferred forty workers from agriculture "into the manufacturing way." One of these men had established a rope walk for the full processing of his plantation's hemp. The type of manufactures initiated in response to the Stamp Act crisis yielded various benefits for Virginia planters. The curtailment of purchases that pressured British merchants and rallied political support for repeal also reduced the debts planters owed Great Britain. The promotion of weaving provided valuable employment for slaves. Domestic manufactures brought plantations a step closer to full seasonal labor and created profitable work for the otherwise idle among the children and the elderly. In its widest implications, the new interest in manufacturing and agricultural diversification earned colonial plantations a new measure of independence and security from the demands of merchants or imperial authorities.[24]

No one held higher expectations for the far-reaching benefits of commercial resistance than George Washington. He was convinced that nonimportation and the attention to manufactures would relieve the problems of commercial dependence and perpetual indebtedness as well

[23]Fauquier to the Board of Trade, 5 June 1765, in Francis Fauquier, *The Official Papers of Francis Fauquier, Lieutenant Governor of Virginia, 1758–1768*, ed. George Reese, 3 vols. (Charlottesville: University Press of Virginia, 1980–83) 3:1250–51; Fauquier to the Board of Trade, 6 Dec. 1766, Public Record Office, CO5/1345, 76–77 (Virginia Colonial Records Project microfilm); Hearings of the Committee on the American Papers, Etc., British Museum, Add. Mss. 33030, testimony of Capel Hanbury, 108–112; George Mercer, 130 (Virginia Colonial Records Project microfilm).

[24]Hearings of the Committee on the American Papers, Etc., British Museum, Add. Mss. 33030, testimony of Capel Hanbury, 109; James Balfour, 115, 120; George Mercer, 129.

as provide a defense against the immediate threat of the revenue acts. In a letter to his principal London merchant in September 1765, Washington predicted that once Virginia initiated wide scale domestic manufactures "The Eyes of our People (already beginning to open) will perceive, that many of the Luxuries which we have heretofore lavished our Substance to Great Britain for can well be dispensed with whilst the Necessaries of Life are to be procurd (for the most part) within ourselves. This consequently will introduce frugality; and be a necessary stimulation to Industry. Great Britain may then load her Exports with as Heavy Taxes as She pleases but where will the consumption be? I am apt to think no Law or usage can compel us to barter our money or Staple Commodities for their Manufactures, if we can be supplied within ourselve upon the better Terms—nor will her Traders dispose of them without a valuable consideration and surety of Pay—where then lyes the utility of these Measures?" For his own part, Washington asked his merchant to ship from London various tools needed to convert wool, flax, and hemp into cloth.[25]

Robert Beverley, who found "nothing less profitable or more troublesome than tob[acco]," also concluded that the costs of the Stamp Act made some shift in agriculture imperative. For Beverley the defense against the Stamp Act was intertwined with a new interest in agricultural diversification that might permanently relieve Virginians of the encumbering debt associated with their traditional staple. Beverley knew "of nothing that can extricate this Colony at this Time if making Hemp does not contribute largely, for since we are to be taxed on all Quarters, & Expences of every kind increase daily it will be almost impossible for us to discharge our Debts to Britain."[26]

◾   ◾   ◾

The scope of support for commercial resistance in Virginia became more evident and decidedly more public after November 1, 1765, when the colonists' determination not to use stamps forced them to choose between breaking the law or suspending all business requiring stamps.

[25]George Washington to Robert Cary & Co., 20 Sep. 1765, with enclosure, *Papers of George Washington, Colonial Series*, eds., Abbot and Twohig, 7:398–404.

[26]Robert Beverley to [. . .], 8 May 1765, Robert Beverley Letterbook, Library of Congress.

In each colony, the decision of whether or not to continue court proceedings or to allow the free flow of foreign commerce varied according to the commercial character of the region and the preferred strategy of resistance. Although several northern colonies opened local courts in defiance of the required use of stamps, Richard Henry Lee explained that "the very different situation of our affairs from theirs with respect to Great Britain" required Virginia to close the courts in order to prevent the enforcement of the Stamp Act.[27] Virginians hoped that by closing the colony's courts, on which British merchants relied for the collection of debts, and by opening its ports, through which Virginians might improve their balance of trade and promote independent commerce, they would mobilize British merchants to campaign for repeal and offer the colony's planters an opportunity to pursue their schemes for diversification.

As early as the summer of 1765, some Virginians announced their intention to shut the county courts on the first of November. Landon Carter promised not to serve in any public office including that of court commissioner after November when the law would "fix the justice and equity, only in the sterling ability of the Person to authenticate his proofs." Robert Beverley agreed that Parliament's refusal to consider Virginia's remonstrance left no recourse for redress save the closing of the courts "for some time." "This of course would effect some change, for the better it maybe, but for worse it cannot." In September and October, the courts of Westmoreland, Stafford, and Culpeper Counties apprised Governor Fauquier of their refusal to sit once the Stamp Act went into effect. Fauquier was reluctant to appoint new commissioners for fear of the type of men who might take over the courts, so after November 1 these three courts and all but one other in Virginia closed.[28]

Court members anticipated that the suspension of justice and consequent delay in the recovery of British debts, like the nonimportation of British cloth, would persuade merchants to bring pressure on Parliament for the repeal of the Stamp Act. Six weeks before the act went into

[27]Richard Henry Lee to Landon Carter, 24 Feb. 1766, Richard Henry Lee Correspondence, Virginia Historical Society.

[28]Landon Carter, "To the Freeholders of the County of Richmond," in Greene, "'Not to be Governed or Taxed but by . . .'" 266–68; Robert Beverley to Landon Carter, 9 Oct. 1765, Landon Carter Papers, Virginia Historical Society; Francis Fauquier to the Board of Trade, 3 Nov. 1765, Public Record Office, CO5/1345, 101–10 (Virginia Colonial Records Project microfilm).

effect, George Washington warned his principal London merchant that if the courts closed "it may be left to yourselve, who have such large demands upon the Colonies, to determine, who is to suffer most in this event—the Merchant, or the Planter." To another English correspondent, he predicted that "if a stop be put to our Judicial proceedings I fancy the Merchants of G. Britain will not be among the last to wish for a Repeal of it." Even the cautious Edmund Pendleton approved of closing the courts as a means of "engaging the interest of the British merchants toward a repeal." Several county commissioners, including Pendleton in Caroline County, eventually opened the courts to business not requiring stamps and in their defiance offered further evidence of their determination to mobilize the political support of merchant creditors in Great Britain. Only in the Eastern Shore's Northampton County, where British trade was inconsequential, did the courts declare the Stamp Act unconstitutional and proceed with business as usual.[29]

Although the refusal to use stamps where required was the ostensible justification for closing the courts, Virginians had no compunction about continuing to clear out trading vessels without the stamps. In the fall of 1765, Virginia suffered from an unfavorable balance of payments with Great Britain, a high exchange rate, and a shortage of currency. Any interruptions in the colony's valuable export trade would magnify these problems and further subject Virginia planters to the mercy of their British creditors. Tobacco shipments to Great Britain were the principal means of reducing the planters' debts, and the commodities trade to the West Indies and Southern Europe was a badly needed source of credit and coin. In an effort to maintain these advantages, Virginians proceeded to clear outward bound vessels within two days of the Stamp Act's going into effect. Peter Randolph, surveyor general for the southern colonies, advised the Virginia collectors on November 2 that they should clear ships as usual since no stamps were available. Governor Fauquier gave a veneer of official sanction to this move on November 7 when he provided naval district officers with printed certificates that

---

[29]George Washington to Robert Cary & Co., 20 Sep. 1765, George Washington to Francis Dandridge, 20 Sep. 1765, *Papers of George Washington, Colonial Series*, eds., Abbot and Twohig, 7:398–402, 395–96; Edmund Pendleton to James Madison, Sr., 17 Feb. 1766, in Edmund Pendleton, *The Letters and Papers of Edmund Pendleton, 1734–1803*, ed., David Mays, 2 vols. (Charlottesville: University Press of Virginia, 1967), 1:21–24, 168–70; *Revolutionary Virginia*, eds., Scribner and Tarter, 1:20–21.

were intended to protect vessels from seizure by the King's men. The certificates stated that George Mercer swore he brought no stamps with him and that the ship was otherwise cleared as required.[30]

Between November 1, 1765, and May 1, 1766, the officers in five of Virginia's six naval districts cleared a total of 155 vessels, most of them bound for the West Indies, Southern Europe, or the port cities of the northern colonies. In other colonies some captains were reluctant to sail to London for fear of reprisals, and this may have been true for Virginia, as only three ships, according to the Naval Office records, aimed for London before May 1. But this was the slowest season for the London tobacco trade, particularly among consignment merchants. A total of 36 ships did set off for Great Britain, and in the Upper James River district alone, nineteen heavily-laden tobacco ships returned to the outports where merchants were attempting to establish a steady, year-round trade with Virginia. English and Scottish ports admitted numerous ships, some with papers "unstamped but signed by proper officers," and others with Governor Fauquier's certificate attesting that the stamps were unavailable.[31]

Virginia merchants and British merchants resident in the colony were generally supportive of the opposition to the Stamp Act and the strategy of commercial resistance. Certainly, Fauquier found few royal allies among the merchant community when George Mercer, the appointed stamp officer for Virginia, arrived at Williamsburg in late October 1765. Mercer reached the capital at the most inopportune moment,

[30]*Revolutionary Virginia*, eds., Scribner and Tarter, 1:20–21; Morgan and Morgan, *The Stamp Act Crisis*, 159–60.

[31]Francis Fauquier to Naval Officers of Virginia, 7 Nov. 1765, Public Record Office, CO5/1331 (Virginia Colonial Records Project microfilm); naval district records for this period survive for all but the York River district, Public Record Office, CO5/1449, 1450 (Virginia Colonial Records Project microfilm); Morgan and Morgan, *The Stamp Act Crisis*, 167; John Carter Matthews, "Two Men on a Tax: Richard Henry Lee, Archibald Ritchie, and the Stamp Act," in *The Old Dominion*, ed., Darrett B. Rutman (Charlottesville: University Press of Virginia, 1964), 96–108; Account of all Ships arrived in the ports of this Kingdom since 1 November last, 1 Feb. 1766, and Register of the General Office of Shipping, 5 Mar. 1766, in Wentworth Woodhouse Muniments, Letters and Papers of the Second Marquis of Rockingham, Sheffield City Libraries (Virginia Colonial Records Project microfilm); on efforts to establish year-round trade, see Price and Clemens, "A Revolution of Scale in Overseas Trade: British Firms in the Chesapeake Trade, 1675–1775."

as the town was filled with the planters and merchants gathered from all over the colony for the meeting of the General Court. A large contingent of planters and merchants publicly confronted Mercer and demanded his oath that he would not distribute the stamps. Fauquier labeled the crowd a mob but admitted that it consisted of the "Gentlemen of property in the Colony, some of them at the head of their respective Counties, and the Merchants of the Country whether English, Scotch or Virginians, for few absented themselves." Fauquier later conferred with many of the merchants in an effort to convince them that observance of the Stamp Act was in their material interest, but his appeal fell on deaf ears.[32]

On the rare occasions when merchants attempted to abide by the Stamp Act, they faced convincing demonstrations of the popular determination to prevent enforcement of the tax. Archibald Ritchie, a merchant from Hobb's Hole in Essex County, publicly stated his intention to use stamped paper in clearing out a grain shipment in February 1766. After a crowd of seventy residents of Essex County failed to gain a public apology from Ritchie, Richard Henry Lee organized a regional association aimed at forcing Ritchie's recantation, even though the merchant privately had admitted his decision not to use the stamped paper. At a meeting in Leedstown on February 27, Lee gained approval for the so-called Westmoreland Association, which pledged its subscribers to resist any attempt to make use of the revenue stamps. On the following day, in their only public action, the Westmoreland associators, along with crowds from counties south of the Rappahannock, converged on Hobb's Hole and presented Ritchie with a prepared declaration. "After some little Hesitation," Ritchie read the statement of apology before the four hundred people assembled.[33]

In Norfolk, Virginia's only sizable port, opponents of the Stamp Act formed a Sons of Liberty group that circulated resolves similar to those of the Westmoreland Association. Soon afterward, a Norfolk mob

---

[32]Francis Fauquier to the Board of Trade, 3 Nov. 1765, Public Record Office, CO5/1345, 101–10 (Virginia Colonial Records Project microfilm).

[33]*Maryland Gazette*, 27 Mar. 1766; *Virginia Gazette* (Rind), 16 May 1766; Richard Parker to Richard Henry Lee, 23 Feb. 1766; Samuel Washington to Richard Henry Lee, 22 Feb. 1766, *Lee Family Papers* (University of Virginia microfilm publication); Richard Henry Lee to Landon Carter, 24 Feb. 1766, in Richard Henry Lee, *The Letters of Richard Henry Lee*, ed., James C. Ballagh, 2 vols. (New York: The Macmillan Company, 1911), 1:14–15.

terrorized a ship captain who allegedly informed on traders who had smuggled goods without proper and stamped clearance papers. The crowd tarred and feathered Captain William Smith before pelting him with rotten eggs, parading him through the streets while tied to a cart, and finally throwing him into the harbor where he was saved only by a passing ship. Smith testified that the crowd included all the "principal men," who were encouraged by Norfolk's mayor, Maximillian Calvert. Like the Westmoreland associators in their confrontation with Ritchie, the Norfolk Sons of Liberty demonstrated that an extra-legal association and organized popular demonstrations might effectively coerce the few merchants who failed to join in the resistance to the parliamentary statute.[34]

When the *Virginia Gazette* of May 2, 1766, reported Parliament's repeal of the Stamp Act, Virginians were satisfied that their strategy of commercial resistance had been effective. Faced with the suspension of court actions on debt cases and the threat of reduced British imports, merchants on both sides of the Atlantic heartily supported and often led the campaign for a repeal of the Stamp Act. In Virginia, all types of merchants, British factors as well as native traders, joined with the planters in a united opposition to the parliamentary tax, despite the best efforts of Fauquier to separate commercial and agricultural interests in the colony. In London, merchants from the Virginia trade petitioned and cajoled members of Parliament to rescind the Stamp Act. Traders in London, Bristol, Liverpool, and Glasgow petitioned the Lords and Commons, reporting the threat of bankruptcies due to the interruption of trade with the colonies. The Glasgow merchants specifically referred to the closing of Virginia's courts as a grave threat to the security of their outstanding debts. Virginia merchants testifying before a parliamentary committee were unanimous in their conviction that only repeal would restore British–Virginia trade to its previous status.[35]

[34]The 3 Apr. 1766 account of Captain William Smith enclosed in Capt. J. Morgan to Fauquier, 5 Apr. 1766, sent in Fauquier to Commissioners for Trade & Plantations, 7 Apr. 1766, Public Record Office, CO5/1331 (Virginia Colonial Records Project microfilm).

[35]Francis Fauquier to the Board of Trade, 3 Nov. 1765, Public Record Office, CO5/1345 (Virginia Colonial Records Project microfilm); Petition of London merchants, 5 Mar. 1766, petition of Bristol merchants, 5 Mar. 1766, and petition of Glasgow merchants, 7 Mar. 1766, in House of Lords Record Office; Charles Goore to Richard Henry Lee, 17 Aug. 1766, *Lee Family Papers* (Uni-

"The Repeal, or the Funeral Procession." London, March 18, 1766. While a handful of government ministers mourn the repeal of the Stamp Act, British commerce comes alive in the background. Warehouses representing the manufacturing cities of England load their good on ships destined for reopened markets in the American colonies. (Colonial Williamsburg Foundation)

The Stamp Act crisis briefly forged a commonalty of interests between the Virginia planters and British merchants who in recent years had grown increasingly suspicious of one another. In 1766, Virginia planters had every reason to believe that their brief experiment in commercial resistance had mobilized British traders to a defense of American political rights and a recognition of the colony's contributions to the wealth of the Empire. As numerous merchants acknowledged in petitions to Parliament and during testimony before parliamentary committees, the huge debt owed them by Virginia planters had created their own kind of dependence on the smooth flow of commerce and a regular administration of justice. Nonimportation was particularly alarming because, as John Glassford testified, the sale of goods through the factors' stores was "the only way to recover Debts." Glasgow merchants were keenly aware that "the greatest part of our fortune lyes in America, chiefly in Debts." Any curtailment of tobacco production or replace-

versity of Virginia microfilm publication); Hearings of the Committee on the American Papers, Etc., testimony of Capel Hanbury, James Balfour, and John Glassford.

ment of imports with domestic manufactures would ruin the British merchants who invested so much in the Chesapeake trade. British tobacco merchants also recognized that the transfer of labor from tobacco to manufactures prompted by the Stamp Act carried the double threat of fewer remittances on debts and lower demand for the goods in the factors' stores.[36]

Individual merchants in Great Britain hastened to assure their Virginia correspondents that they had done everything possible to satisfy American demands and that the advantages of the Chesapeake trade would soon be restored for colonials and Britons alike. Capel and Osgood Hanbury told George Washington that they attempted "to prevent the Act passing when first it was in agitation & have ever since it passed spar'd no endeavours to demonstrate the necessity of Repealing it." After recounting the efforts of Liverpool merchants to secure support for repeal among members of Parliament, Charles Goore promised Richard Henry Lee that the American colonies were now safe from Parliamentary interference since "A Spirit prevails, especially in the trading Ports, and manufacturing Countys, to oppose the Members that argued & voted against the repeal of the Stamp Act." In its letter of congratulations upon the repeal of the Stamp Act, the London merchant firm of Bosworth and Griffith assured Edmund Berkeley that they anticipated a "return to tranquility"[37]

As the British merchants hoped and expected, trade with Virginia returned to its familiar course in the months immediately following the repeal of the Stamp Act. Only gradually during the next several years did the lasting commercial effects of the Stamp Act crisis become apparent. For many Virginians, the debate over the proper commercial structure of the Empire had contributed to a more profound awareness of the colony's dependence on British trade and the significance of im-

---

[36]Petition of Glasgow Merchants, 7 Mar. 1766, in House of Lords Records Office (Virginia Colonial Records Project microfilm); testimony of John Glassford, testimony of James Balfour, Hearings of Committee on the American Papers, Etc., British Museum, London, Add. Ms. 33030, 115–22, 161–68 (Virginia Colonial Records Project microfilm).

[37]Capel and Osgood Hanbury to George Washington, 27 Mar. 1766, *Papers of George Washington, Colonial Series*, eds., Abbot and Twohig, 7:431; Charles Goore to Richard Henry Lee, 17 August 1766, *Lee Family Papers* (University of Virginia microfilm publication); Bosworth & Griffith to Edmund Berkeley, 31 Mar. 1766, Berkeley Family Papers, Alderman Library, University of Virginia.

perial regulations in perpetuating that dependence. The experience of organizing various forms of commercial resistance offered these same Virginians a glimpse of the possibilities for reducing the colony's reliance on British merchants and the tobacco trade. In the aftermath of the Stamp Act resistance, these Virginians attempted to fulfill some measure of the colony's potential for economic independence.

"A Virginian" writing in the *Virginia Gazette* of December 11, 1766, was confident that the recent experiments in nonimportation and domestic manufactures would continue to protect the colonists from the worst disadvantages of the imperial economy. Although Virginians had no control over the Navigation Acts that contributed to the colony's "declining state," they were able to limit the influence of British merchants who exploited Virginia's restricted trade. Through excessive mark-ups on imported goods, the merchants had forced chronic debts upon the Virginians and maintained their dependence on foreign goods. A continuation of "the Frugal and industrious schemes they have lately adopted" would eliminate the Virginians' debts to British merchants and permit the colonists to patronize the colony's native merchants. The subsequent growth in Virginia's native commercial establishment "shall bring the tobacco market home to us as the Brit[ish] merchts will always find it worthwhile to employ their vessels for our Commodity which they must buy with Cash or Bills of Exchange." This would be the only effective means of halting the drain of payments that currently resulted in the "impoverishment of this Colony." According to this writer, delivering Virginia from the "Brink of Destruction" required a permanent restructuring of the trade, not "Quack medicines" like the proposed loan office or bank.[38]

For certain planters not too tightly caught in the web of debt and tobacco production, the commercial resistance to the Stamp Act inaugurated a permanent reorganization of their economic activity. Such wealthy planters as Landon Carter and Robert Beverley emphasized the cultivation of hemp and flax in the wake of the Stamp Act crisis. Most striking, perhaps, was the example of George Washington, whose order for weaving equipment was one part of a broad reorganization of Mount Vernon that was precipitated by the Stamp Act crisis. Following the fall harvest of 1765, Washington completely abandoned tobacco cultivation at his Potomac estate in favor of a variety of crops and produce that would not depend on one market or creditor. Experiments

---

[38]"A Virginian" in *Virginia Gazette* (Rind), 11 Dec. 1766.

with hemp and flax were part of Washington's search for new exports suitable for British markets, where he also hoped to market flour in place of tobacco. The increased production of grain and the establishment of a fishery at Mount Vernon allowed Washington opportunities to trade with West Indian markets as well. The weaving operation established in response to the Stamp Act was by 1768 producing more than 1,200 yards of homespun a year. Within a few years of the Stamp Act, Washington began converting his tenants' leases from tobacco to cash payments, thus encouraging further diversification and forcing those who continued to produce tobacco to bear the risks of fluctuating prices.[39]

The impediments to a successful diversification of a large plantation remained obvious to Washington, whose accomplishments at Mount Vernon were made possible in large part by the continued production of tobacco on the Custis estates along the York River. Tobacco from those lands maintained Washington's credit with his London merchants and guaranteed a source of goods with which to provision the estates while he introduced domestic manufactures and established new trading outlets. However marginal their impact on the Virginia economy at large, the private efforts to reorient plantation management were among the most important legacies of the Stamp Act crisis. The success of commercial resistance and the new confidence in Virginia's potential for economic development inspired individual planters like Washington to explore options outside of the cultivation of tobacco and British commerce. At the same time, the assembly's attempt to restrict the slave trade in 1767 exemplified the collective efforts to promote the goals of economic diversification that had attracted such widespread interest during the Stamp Act crisis. When, after 1767, Parliament enacted further restrictions on trade and demanded new revenue from the colonies, the individual interests of the great planters and the public support for an independent economy would coalesce in a more formal and ambitious plan of commercial resistance.

[39]See invoice for goods ordered from Robert Cary & Co., 20 September 1765, inclosed in letter of same date, *Papers of George Washington, Colonial Series*, ed., Abbot and Twohig, 7:398–404; Washington's interests in grain crops and other new trades discussed in his correspondence throughout the late 1760s and early 1770s; Bruce A. Ragsdale, "George Washington, the British Tobacco Trade, and Economic Opportunity in Prerevolutionary Virginia," 133–62; *The Diary of Landon Carter*, ed., Greene, for 1766 discusses experiments with hemp and flax.

NONIMPORTATION AND
THE CHESAPEAKE ECONOMY

T RADE BETWEEN VIRGINIA AND GREAT BRITAIN barely returned to normal before the determined enforcement of new revenue legislation from
Parliament compelled Virginia's burgesses, emboldened by their success against the Stamp Act, to organize a more formal though still extra-legal strategy of commercial resistance. The repeal of the Stamp
Act, accompanied as it was by a Declaratory Act asserting Parliament's
right to legislate for the colonies, never completely eased the tensions
between Great Britain and America. During the following year colonial
political leaders remained suspicious of the British government's intentions; while in England, all too many officials readily accepted exaggerated reports of continued American resistance. A confused ministry with
no clear leadership soon exacerbated imperial relations with its disregard of American expectations about the proper commercial and constitutional order of the Empire. With William Pitt, now earl of Chatham,
increasingly disabled by illness and Lord Shelburne, the secretary of
state for the southern department, unable to organize a majority in Parliament, the ambitious chancellor of the exchequer, Charles Townshend,
seized the initiative in formulating colonial policy in the spring of 1767.[1]

Townshend insisted that his proposed legislation for the colonies
would raise sufficient revenue to offset a tax reduction in Great Britain
and fund a portion of the salaries of royal officials in North America.
The new revenues would arise from an import duty which colonists
would pay on British-manufactured glass, painters' colors, and paper as
well as on all tea imported into British North America. To insure the

---

[1]Jensen, *The Founding of a Nation*, 215–23.

collection of these and existing duties, Townshend proposed another bill that would strengthen the enforcement of all trade regulations through the creation of an American board of customs. Finally, in a move threatening coercion of any colonists who did not comply with British revenue demands, Townshend recommended the suspension of the New York assembly until it complied with all the provisions of the Quartering Act of 1765.[2]

Parliament's approval of the three acts in June 1767 temporarily satisfied Townshend's domestic political goals, but the legislation was inadequate for raising the promised revenue and dangerously escalated American opposition. Each of the acts challenged rights that Americans during the Stamp Act crisis had affirmed as their own. The import duty was obviously a revenue tax, made no more palatable by its deference to the distinction between external and internal levies. The use of the revenue for salaries and royal administration further challenged the prerogatives of colonial legislatures, and the suspension of the New York assembly demonstrated Parliament's willingness to alter the constitutional structure of colonial governments. The board of customs represented an additional incursion of British authority into provincial politics, and placement of the board in Boston appeared to be a deliberate provocation of American merchants. Townshend's duties, by arbitrarily raising the prices for goods which the Navigation Acts prevented the colonists from buying elsewhere, confirmed the Virginians' accusation that Parliament intended to exploit the restricted American trade for revenue.[3]

The colonists quickly responded to the several challenges of the Townshend Acts. John Dickinson, in his *Letters From a Farmer in Pennsylvania*, offered the most articulate expression of American constitutional rights and recommended a petition campaign aimed at a parliamentary repeal. The Massachusetts House of Representatives led the official response with a petition to the King, followed by the more extraordinary step of distributing to the other colonial assemblies a circular letter urging a concerted resistance to the Townshend Acts. Virginia had been without an assembly since before passage of the acts, but when the burgesses convened at the end of March 1768, they unanimously approved Massachusetts' appeal, issued their own circular letter, and petitioned to the King, Lords, and Commons for repeal of the three acts.[4]

[2]Ibid., 225–26.
[3]Ibid., 226–28.
[4]Ibid., 241–43, 250; Pauline Maier, *From Resistance to Revolution* (New York: Alfred A. Knopf, 1972), 169–70; *Journals of the House of Burgesses, 1766–1769*, eds., Kennedy and McIlwaine, 174, 165–71.

Dickinson's influential *Letters From a Farmer* identified the commercial threat posed by the new acts. The import duties, even more than the stamp tax, imposed further disadvantages on Americans in a trading relationship that already favored the British. The establishment of a permanent board of customs portended more onerous trade restrictions and additional duties. According to Dickinson, a duty on British manufactures betrayed the established commercial relationship between America and the Mother Country. Great Britain had a right to prohibit foreign imports in the colonies and therefore could not tax items for which Americans were dependent on the British. Ancient history provided Dickinson with the example of nations starved into submission by their acquiescence to the trading restrictions imposed by powerful empires. If his proposed petition campaign failed to secure repeal, Dickinson favored some form of commercial resistance, although he feared that any ambitious manufacturing schemes in the colonies would provoke new restrictions from Parliament.[5]

From the perspective of Virginia, Arthur Lee concluded that commercial resistance should be the first response to the Townshend Acts. Lee's *Monitor* letters, published in Virginia between February and April of 1768, reiterated the constitutional arguments of Dickinson's *Farmer* and stressed the colonies' potential for economic independence. Echoing the arguments Virginians had marshaled against the Stamp Act, Lee asserted that the colonies were already the principal support of Great Britain's economy, providing resources and offering an eager market for British manufactures. With dedication and industry, Americans might establish an economy independent of Great Britain and retain their natural wealth. Lee favored a commercial association, not simply as a form of political pressure on the English commercial classes, but also as a means of initiating the long-term growth that would make American trade less vulnerable to British regulation. In addition to the petitions recommended by Dickinson, Lee advocated the formation of associations for the encouragement and purchase of domestic manufactures. Lee was confident that such schemes would succeed in Virginia where, he trusted, the example of the gentry would persuade smaller planters to initiate household manufactures.[6]

---

[5]John Dickinson, "Letters from a Farmer," No. 2, 3, in *The Farmer's and Monitor's Letters*, with an introduction by William J. Van Schreeven (Richmond: Whittet and Shepperson, 1969), 4–14.

[6]Arthur Lee's "The Monitor" was published in the *Virginia Gazette* (Rind) between February and late April 1768. *The Farmer's and Monitor's Letters*, "Monitor," No. 6, 7, 8, pp. 80–92.

The earliest organized protests of the Townshend Acts included consideration of the kind of commercial resistance that had been effective during the Stamp Act crisis. Boston, which was so directly affected by the import duties and the board of customs, was the source of the first attempts to organize a boycott of British goods. As early as August 1767, the *Boston Gazette* published a plan for nonimportation, and in October, one month before the Townshend Acts went into effect, the Boston town meeting approved a voluntary nonconsumption agreement. In March 1768, the popular party in Boston gained approval of a formal boycott of British commodities, though the resistance of merchants forced the inclusion of a proviso making the association contingent upon the adoption of similar agreements in New York and Philadelphia. New York followed with an association conditional on the participation of Philadelphia, but the plan unraveled when Philadelphia's merchants defeated these initial proposals for commercial resistance.[7]

When the Virginia assembly met in April 1768, there was no public discussion of proposals for commercial resistance in the northern colonies nor consideration of the kind of association suggested by Lee, but the Burgesses' petition to the King and Parliament shared Lee's view that the Townshend duties violated accepted notions of the trading relationship between Britain and America. The petition to the assembly from Westmoreland County freeholders went so far as to declare that America's complete dependence on Great Britain for supplies of manufactures rendered the duties "both cruel and unconstitutional."[8]

Support for nonimportation and manufacturing associations grew throughout 1768 as the British government revealed its determination to counter American resistance. In August 1768, Massachusetts proponents of nonimportation, capitalizing on the reaction to the arrival of the board of custom and Britain's order to rescind the colony's circular letter, won approval of another boycott agreement. The Boston association, which was to be in effect only for the calendar year of 1769, prohibited the importation of all but a few British goods necessary to carry on Massachusetts' own manufactures. Later that month, New York followed with a stricter agreement to remain in effect until Parliament repealed the Townshend duties. Philadelphia merchants delayed the decision on nonimportation in hopes that repeal would make a boycott unnecessary, but receiving no encouragement from London, they suc-

[7]Arthur M. Schlesinger, *The Colonial Merchants*, 104–20; Jensen, *The Founding of a Nation*, 266–73.

[8]*Journals of the House of Burgesses*, 1766–1769, eds., Kennedy and McIlwaine, 165–71, 146.

cumbed to popular pressure in March 1769 and approved an association similar to those adopted in New York and Boston.[9]

In February 1769, Lord Botetourt, the new governor of Virginia, assured the secretary of state for America, Lord Hillsborough, that the Virginians opposed Parliament's revenue legislation but obeyed the laws and paid the duties "without a shadow of resistance from any Mortal." By the time Philadelphia approved an association in March, however, a number of Virginia's political leaders had concluded that petitions alone were incapable of forcing repeal of the Townshend legislation. British response to the circular letter of Massachusetts, the activity of the American board of customs, and the stationing of British troops in Boston in September of 1768, all indicated an imperial resolve to enforce the Townshend Acts. Private correspondence from London and dispiriting reports of the organizational weakness of America's friends in Parliament offered Virginians little prospect for repeal. By early March, Francis Lightfoot Lee found Virginians "grow more determined every day to defend their rights." Lingering hopes for a response to American claims evaporated in late March when the *Virginia Gazette* reported Parliament's intention to resurrect a statute of Henry VIII that would allow the transportation of Americans to England for trial on treason charges. When the Virginia assembly convened on May 8, the majority of burgesses agreed on the need for a more vigorous opposition to the Townshend legislation, and for many of them this meant some form of commercial resistance.[10]

However much Virginians might wish for the colonies to present a unified opposition to British policy, the broad commercial associations of the northern colonies were not viable in the Chesapeake economy. The collaboration of two Fairfax County neighbors, George Mason and George Washington, produced the first formal plan of nonimportation designed for the particular character of Virginia's trade and its plantation system of agricultural production. In early April of 1769, David

[9]Jensen, *The Founding of a Nation*, 283–87; Schlesinger, *Colonial Merchants*, 120–31.

[10]Governor Botetourt to Secretary of State, 17 Feb. 1769, Public Record Office, CO5/1347, ff. 66–67 (Virginia Colonial Records Project microfilm); Arthur Lee to Richard Henry Lee, 27 Dec. 1769, *Lee Family Papers* (University of Virginia microfilm publication); Arthur Lee to [Francis Lightfoot Lee], 23 Mar. 1769, in ibid. (recipient is incorrectly identified as Richard Henry Lee); [Francis Lightfoot Lee] to William Lee, 9 Mar. 1769, Brock Collection, Huntington Library (Colonial Williamsburg microfilm); *Virginia Gazette* (Purdie & Dixon), 23 Mar. 1769.

Ross of Bladensburg, Maryland, forwarded to George Washington a copy of the Philadelphia association along with a proposed scheme of nonimportation devised by a group of Annapolis merchants. The Maryland merchants wished to observe the Philadelphia boycott but recognized the practical difficulties facing that kind of agreement in a colony where only a few importing merchants lived in port towns and where merchants accounted for only a fraction of British imports. To be effective, a Maryland nonimportation agreement must encompass the entire colony and embrace planters as well as merchants. The scarcity of manufactures in the Chesapeake also compelled Maryland associators to exempt from the boycott a greater variety of goods.[11]

Colonial petitions clearly had failed to sway the King or Parliament, and economic coercion would be preferable to the armed defense that Washington privately conceded he was prepared to endorse. Yet Washington realized nonimportation would face even greater obstacles in Virginia where the resident merchants were both fewer in number and more dispersed than in Maryland and where factors of British merchants were responsible for a larger share of the colony's imports. Washington concluded that a practical association in Virginia must emphasize nonconsumption if it were to offset the importations by British factors. Like Arthur Lee's *Monitor*, Washington was confident that "the Gentlemen in their several counties" would be able "to explain matters to the people, & stimulate them to a cordial agreement to purchase none but certain innumerated articles out of any of the Stores after such a period." Public censure of those who violated the association would further discourage purchases at the factors' stores.[12]

Washington's enthusiasm for a nonimportation association grew as he contemplated the "private, as well as public advantages to result from it." The certainty of the private benefits made him eager to initiate a formal commercial association regardless of the practical difficulties of organizing nonimportation in Virginia or reservations about its potential political impact. Washington was convinced, as he had been during the Stamp Act crisis, that a scheme of commercial resistance would alleviate the worst burdens of economic dependence on Great Britain and the tobacco trade. He was particularly worried about the recent rise in

---

[11]Philadelphia Merchants to Annapolis merchants, with reply, 15 Mar. 1769; Annapolis merchants to Virginia Merchants, 25 Mar. 1769, Washington Papers, Library of Congress; note in *Papers of George Washington, Colonial Series*, eds., Abbot and Twohig, 8:180–81.

[12]George Washington to George Mason, 5 Apr. 1769, *Papers of George Washington, Colonial Series*, eds., Abbot and Twohig, 8:177–80.

personal indebtedness by which "many families are reduced, almost, if not quite, to penury & want." Restricting imports and promoting local manufactures would be the best means of extricating these estates from their debt. "A scheme of this sort will contribute more effectually than any other I can devise to immerge the Country from the distress it at present labours under . . . if it can be generally adopted." Washington feared the British might restrain colonial manufactures by the same power which assumed the right of taxation, "but as a measure of this sort will be an additional exertion of arbitrary power, we cannot be worsted I think by putting it to the Test."[13]

A public association for nonimportation would provide an occasion and a justification for the colony's great gentlemen to reduce their extravagant spending. According to Washington, too many members of Virginia's gentry continued to increase expenditures for luxuries and display in an effort to convince others of their solid fortune, even if such behavior resulted in the insolvency of their estates. Washington hoped a nonimportation association, by making a patriotic duty of simple living, would allow these planters to live within their means and still maintain their social rank.[14]

Washington delivered the Maryland and Philadelphia documents along with his own thoughts on a Virginia association to George Mason who responded within a few hours. Mason also had received a copy of the Philadelphia association from a friend in Maryland, and he already was convinced a similar agreement was appropriate in Virginia. He agreed with Washington that official action should wait until the meeting of the General Court or assembly when representatives from all areas of the colony could present a united front. Before that meeting, Mason hoped to publish a newspaper article to help prepare citizens for the economic sacrifices that would be necessary. Virginia was not in a position to curtail imports as sharply as the northern colonies had done, but Mason was hopeful that nonimportation would be effective if Virginians could "retrench all Manner of Superfluitys, Finery of all Denominations." Mason also suggested Virginia might exert additional leverage by the more radical measure of halting its valuable tobacco exports, "by which the Revenue wou'd lose fifty times more than all their Oppressions cou'd raise here." Such a nonexportation scheme also would deprive British merchants of the principal payments on the Virginians' debts.[15]

[13]Ibid.
[14]Ibid.
[15]George Mason to George Washington, 5 Apr. 1769, *Papers of George Mason*, ed., Rutland, 1:99–100.

In early April Mason reported he was too ill to write anything on a proposed association, but by the eighteenth of the month he was well enough to spend four days with Washington at Mount Vernon, during which time the two men presumably discussed the final details of a proposal for nonimportation. Two days after leaving Mount Vernon, Mason sent Washington instructions for a few minor alterations in the draft of an association, a copy of which he had already sent. This was the document Washington carried to the meeting of the burgesses which convened in Williamsburg on May 8.[16]

Although the framework of the proposed association owed much to the Philadelphia agreement, its specific terms reflected the ideas shared earlier by Mason and Washington. Mason's first article asked subscribers to use their example and "all other legal ways & means in their power" to "encourage Industry & Frugality & discourage all manner of Luxury & Extravagance." The nonimportation article enumerated the wide range of British goods encompassed by the proposed boycott. Prohibited were all leather goods, including shoes and boots, food products and liquor, furniture, and all sorts of English finery. Despite the Virginians' heavy demand for imported cloth, the association proposed by Mason and Washington forbade all silks, Indian fabrics, millinery and ribbons, muslins, stockings, cotton and linens priced above two shillings per yard, woolens at more than one shilling, six pence per yard and broadcloths at more than eight shillings per yard. The exceptions for cheap cottons and woolens, although not included in the Philadelphia association, permitted Virginians to import the coarse fabrics used to clothe slaves.

Subscribers would agree to cease importing all enumerated goods immediately and stop purchasing them in Virginia after September 1, 1769. The boycott would continue until Parliament repealed the Townshend duties. Subscribers would forever refuse any goods bearing duties laid by Parliament for the purpose of raising a revenue. Mason, who was convinced slavery inhibited the diversification of Virginia's economy, also suggested a ban on all slave imports during the term of the association. Finally, Mason included a threat that if repeal were not forthcoming Virginians would halt exports of naval stores, lumber, and furs, and, without explicitly denying merchants the tobacco owed them,

[16]*The Diaries of George Washington*, eds. Donald Jackson and Dorothy Twohig, 6 vols. (Charlottesville: University Press of Virginia, 1976–79), 2:142; Mason to Washington, 23 Apr. 1769, *Papers of George Mason*, ed., Rutland, 1:102–03.

"endeavour to find some other Employment for their Slaves and other Hands than cultivating Tobacco."[17]

While the burgesses proceeded with the routine business in early May, the *Virginia Gazette* published Mason's essay in support of nonimportation. In a letter signed "Atticus," Mason elaborated on the defense that he and others had outlined in response to the Stamp Act. He argued that an unrestricted commerce between the American colonies and Great Britain was the only source of the latter's continued wealth. The recent duties thus were not only unconstitutional, but threatened to deprive Great Britain of the profits from the American trade. With the failure of petitions for redress, Mason urged Virginians to "demonstrate to them [the British] that we cannot be wounded but thro' their Sides" An association pledged to refuse British manufactures and withhold Virginia commodities would convince the inhabitants of Great Britain that the Townshend duties were injurious to them as well as to Americans.

Mason conceded that the great numbers of British factors in Virginia and the inadequacy of colonial manufactures were obstacles to the success of a commercial association, but both problems could be overcome. A boycott of all imported goods in the factors' stores would convince these traders to join the association without the use of "any Manner of Violence." Virginia's imports of British goods were so extensive and valuable that an exclusion of all but the most basic necessities would be sufficient to illustrate the value of the colony's trade. Mason also advanced Washington's argument that commercial resistance would permanently strengthen the Virginia economy. In particular, reduced tobacco cultivation and an end to slave purchases would provide the capital and labor for the development of home manufactures and induce British manufacturers to settle in Virginia.[18]

At the beginning of the second week of the assembly's session, the burgesses resumed their protest of the Townshend Acts and British enforcement policies. They unanimously adopted four resolutions, again claiming for the House of Burgesses the sole right of taxation in the colony and affirming the right of the colonists to petition the King for redress of grievances. The resolutions denounced the proposal to transport Americans to England for treason trials and called for an address to

[17]Draft printed in note accompanying George Mason to George Washington, 28 Apr. 1769, *Papers of George Washington, Colonial Series*, eds., Abbot and Twohig, 8:187–90.

[18]*Virginia Gazette* (Purdie & Dixon) and (Rind), 11 May 1769, also printed in *Papers of George Mason*, ed., Rutland, 1:106–09.

the King protesting this challenge to the right of trial by a jury of one's peers. On the following day, May 17, after the burgesses approved an address to the King, Governor Botetourt dissolved the assembly because of what he called the "ill effect" of the resolves.[19]

The governor's peremptory decision prompted Washington to bring forth his proposal for a nonimportation association. Following the governor's dissolution of the House, the burgesses hastily reconvened at Anthony Hay's Raleigh Tavern where they elected Peyton Randolph moderator and appointed a committee to draw up an association. The committee left no record, but Washington was among those who spent the evening at Hay's "upon a Committee." A later report attributed the drafting of the association to Washington, Richard Henry Lee, and Patrick Henry.[20]

The document presented before the former burgesses on May 18 was essentially Mason's draft with a few alterations. The committee decided to permit the importation of dutied paper not exceeding the cost of eight shillings per ream. The final association also made an exception for the plaid and Irish hose frequently used to clothe slaves. The committee at the Raleigh Tavern added to the association a specific article banning all imports of wine until Parliament lifted the duty applied to that commodity under the terms of the Revenue Act of 1764. In order to encourage the production of woolen cloth, the association forbade the slaughter of lambs before May 1 of any year. The agreement incorporated Mason's recommended suspension of slave imports but delayed enforcement of that article until November 1, 1769.[21]

During the debate on the proper form of commercial association, Richard Henry Lee argued that a nonexportation agreement should accompany the proposed nonimportation scheme. Commercial resistance would be more persuasive if Virginians withheld from Great Britain all shipments of "those raw Materials, from which her Trade Manufactures, Merchants, and Revenue, receive great profits; such as Tobacco, Tar, Pitch, Hemp, Flax-seed, Pot-ash &c." The necessary adjustments in Virginia's economy would result in "some temporary loss and inconvenience," but the lasting benefits would outweigh the dislo-

[19]*Journals of the House of Burgesses, 1766–1769*, eds., Kennedy and McIlwaine, 214–18.

[20]Account of proceedings and printed copy of association in *Revolutionary Virginia*, eds., Scribner and Tarter, 1:73–77; *Diaries of George Washington*, eds. Jackson and Twohig, 2:152; James Parker to Charles Steuart, 26 June 1769, Charles Steuart Papers, National Library of Scotland (Colonial Williamsburg microfilm).

[21]*Revolutionary Virginia*, eds., Scribner and Tarter, 1:73–77.

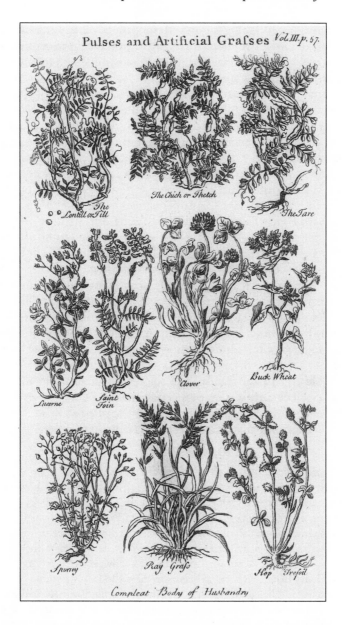

"Pulses and Artificial Grasses." Plate 57. Thomas Hale. *A Compleat Body of Husbandry.* vol. 3, London, 1758. At Mount Vernon, Washington experimented with a number of the grasses and feed crops illustrated in this popular volume which he received from London in 1761. (Library of Congress)

cation. Lee, like Washington and Mason, expected and intended that the organization of commercial resistance would help to reorient economic development in Virginia. Instead of producing crops that enriched the British, planters could begin to "raise grain, Provisions, and all Material for Manufactures, in the manufacturing of which, the rest of our labor may be employed." The final draft of the association rejected Lee's ambitious proposals, as well as Mason's threat of a future nonexportation agreement. Lee's suggestion, however, impressed the former burgesses with a sense of Virginia's potential economic influence. In his notice of the new association, Francis Lightfoot Lee assured his brother William in London that "nonexportation is to be the next step, in order to prove who is the most dependent on the other."[22]

Richard Henry Lee, like Mason, Washington, and Landon Carter, was a resident of the Northern Neck which was the center of support for commercial resistance throughout the Revolutionary era in Virginia. The peninsula between the Potomac and Rappahannock Rivers and the adjacent interior territory was the only proprietary grant in the colony and as such differed from the rest of Virginia in several ways. The Fairfax family did not administer its proprietary as a manor, but they offered unusually large grants of land with no stipulations for the settlement or improvement of a minimum portion of land. Resident agents for the proprietor patented enormous tracts and encouraged a fever for land remarkable even by the standards of colonial Virginia. Land holding in the area consequently was far more concentrated than in other areas of Virginia and pressures on eastern land appeared as early as the 1730s when marginal producers rioted against the Inspection Act.[23]

----

[22]Nineteenth-century copy of a fragment of a speech in *Lee Family Papers* (University of Virginia microfilm publication), with attribution to Francis Lightfoot Lee and dated 1774. Internal evidence proves beyond doubt that it was written in 1769. More problematic is the attribution to Francis Lightfoot Lee, who was not a member of the assembly in 1769. Another nineteenth-century copy of the fragment is in the Lee Transcripts, Virginia Historical Society. This copy contains a note saying that the original handwriting looked like that of Richard Henry Lee. This note has been crossed out and an attribution to Francis Lightfoot Lee put below it. Given his absence from the assembly, and Richard Henry Lee's known involvement in the creation of the association, it would appear the original attribution was correct; Francis Lightfoot Lee to William Lee, 22 May 1769, Brock Collection, Huntington Library (Colonial Williamsburg microfilm).

[23]Douglas Southall Freeman, *George Washington: A Biography*, 7 vols. (New York: Charles Scribner's Sons, 1948), 1:447–513; Kulikoff, *Tobacco and Slaves*, 132–34.

For some of the colony's wealthiest and most powerful families who made the Northern Neck their home, the occasional appearance of social unrest was only one of several factors reinforcing an awareness of the imperative for new economic opportunities. Local soil was not productive of the sweet-scented tobacco cultivated in lower Tidewater by large planters who wished to trade with consignment merchants in England. The distance from the regular shipping routes of consignment merchants also discouraged the large estate owners of the area who wished to maintain a prosperous correspondence with London firms. From the periphery of the consignment trade, great planters in the Northern Neck led the way in the diversification of their estates, in the initiation of new forms of plantation management, and in the pursuit of new trade routes. While the area continued to produce tobacco for both the direct and consignment trades, planters in the area also encouraged the transition to grain production. Tenantry was common in the Northern Neck not only as a necessary response to a shortage of land but as the gentry's preferred means of improving land without the investment of slaves and an overseer. The historic emphasis on western lands contributed to a keen interest not just in speculation but also the settlement and development of new territory. From practical necessity and the area's long tradition of enterprise, planters in the Northern Neck, particularly the owners of large estates, led their fellow Virginians in the search for alternatives to the British tobacco trade and traditional organization of plantations. So, too, in the movement for commercial resistance and economic independence, the gentry of the Northern Neck guided the colony not so much in opposition to the planter establishment of James River, but rather at the forefront of a response to an essential dilemma of a plantation society as it confronted the ever-more commercialized economy of the British Empire and the Atlantic world.[24]

Little division was evident at the inauguration of the association of 1769. Ninety-four of the 116 former burgesses signed the agreement on May 18, and several of the absent members added their signatures later in the summer. Shortly after the approval of the association, "Brutus" reminded *Virginia Gazette* readers that when the colony faced the Stamp Act, "a regard to our own manufactures and a resolution not to import those of Britain" insured its repeal; the present association

---

[24]James Blaine Gouger III, "Agricultural Change in the Northern Neck of Virginia, 1700–1860: An Historical Geography" (Ph.D. diss., University of Florida, 1976); Willard Bliss, "The Rise of Tenancy in Virginia," *Virginia Magazine of History and Biography* 58 (October 1950): 427–41; Lorena Walsh, "Plantation Management in the Chesapeake, 1620–1820," *Journal of Economic History* 49 (June 1989): 393–406.

would have the same effect. Other Virginians warned their London merchants that there was "no inconvenience or hardship" that they would not "submit to rather than desert the Cause," even if that meant abandoning tobacco in favor of domestic manufactures.[25]

The subscribers carried the association back to their home counties where they solicited popular support at local meetings. The *Virginia Gazette* published a model for county associations which included the full text of the Williamsburg agreement along with a preamble supporting the burgesses' resolutions and declaring "nothing but motives of particular interest" could secure "a redress of those grievances under which the trade of inhabitants of America at present labor." In Dinwiddie County alone, close to 1,000 citizens signed the local association. The *Virginia Gazette* specifically congratulated the widows who subscribed. Reports from Norfolk claimed there was "hardly a taylor or cobbler in town but what has signed it.[26]

Virginians were as enthusiastic about the intended domestic benefits of the association as they were about its political design. John Page echoed Washington's expectation that the association would clear the planters of debt even if it did not lead to a repeal. Landon Carter pointed to luxury and extravagance as the real enemies of Virginia and believed the association's discouragement of these vices would clear the colonists' debt while restoring a favorable balance of trade. Martha Jacquelin decided to observe the association because "our poor Country never stood in more need of an Effort to save her from ruin than now, not more from the taxes and want of Trayd than from our Extravagances." Other subscribers recognized the positive role of the association in developing internal resources and fulfilling Virginia's economic potential. The new emphasis on domestic manufactures, even if intended to satisfy a temporary shortage, would teach Virginians what they were capable of on their own, thereby lessening the need for commercial ties with Great Britain. Robert Beverley predicted that "we shall very shortly be able to supply ourselves with most of the useful Articles of Life, & those once established will be a perpetual Source of internal wealth to us."[27]

[25]*Virginia Gazette* (Rind), 1 June 1769; Robert Carter Nicholas to John Norton, 31 May 1769, in *John Norton & Sons, Merchants of London and Virginia, being the Papers from their Counting House for the Years 1750 to 1795*, ed., Francis Norton Mason (Richmond, 1937), 76–77.

[26]*Revolutionary Virginia*, eds., Scribner and Tarter, 1:73–77; *Virginia Gazette* (Rind), 27 July 1769.

[27]John Page, Jr. to John Norton, 27 May 1769, in *John Norton & Sons*, ed., Mason, 93–94; letter of C. R. [Landon Carter] in *Virginia Gazette* (Rind), 1

A "Private Man" from Essex County urged *Gazette* readers to diversify Virginia's economy through their observation of the association. The suspension of imports provided an impetus for local production and the cultivation of raw materials used in manufactures. Pursuit of a variety of new crops necessarily would reduce annual tobacco yields and thus raise the selling price of the traditional staple. To bring about diversification would require several years of sacrifice, but the ultimate benefits would reach beyond material security to include a more balanced, productive society. New manufactures would encourage "people of character" to immigrate to Virginia. Young men in the colony would follow "industrious pursuits," escaping the drudgery of agriculture. On individual estates, local manufactures would provide employment for older slaves and family members unable to work in the fields. The optimism of an Eastern Shore writer was less specific but seemingly boundless. "Philo Americanus" of Accomack County found the American colonies already to be the "Empire's brightest gem" and asserted that American resources could support every type of useful production, enabling the colonies to prosper without any attachments to the rest of the world.[28]

The earliest efforts toward crop diversification and internal manufacturing centered on the production of cloth for which planters were almost wholly dependent on Great Britain. Even the rough osnaburgs and coarse woolens distributed to the slaves were imported. Any attempt to curtail dependence on British manufactures necessarily began with a replacement for these basic items. Early supporters of the association recommended drawing on the colony's abundant supply of deerskins as a replacement for the laborers' coarse cloth and using available cotton and wool for fine fabrics rather than slave cloth. The association's restrictions on the slaughter of lambs was intended to contribute to local cloth production, and by the fall of 1769 Virginians engaged in various efforts to increase their flocks of sheep.[29]

June 1769; Martha Jacquelin to John Norton, 14 Aug. 1769, *John Norton & Sons*, ed., Mason, 103; Robert Beverley to John Backhouse, 25 July 1769, Robert Beverley Letterbook, Library of Congress; William Nelson to Charles Goore, 2 Sept. 1769, Nelson Letterbook, Virginia State Library.

[28]*Virginia Gazette* (Rind), 6 July 1769; *Virginia Gazette* (Purdie & Dixon), 7 Nov. 1769.

[29]*Virginia Gazette* (Rind), letter of "Buckskin," 1 June 1769; *Virginia Gazette* (Purdie & Dixon), John Wiley to Printer, 28 Sep. 1769; *Virginia Gazette* (Rind), Inhabitants of King and Queen County to the Speaker, 16 Nov. 1769.

Within a few months of the association's inception, planters reported that they were supplying homespun to their slaves and were wearing it themselves. Martha Jacquelin ordered only the cheapest linen from England and hoped soon to be dressed in Virginia cloth and moccasins. The family of William Nelson wore their own wool and linen which compared favorably to those from Yorkshire and Ireland and cost less to manufacture. Robert Wormeley Carter sent word to the slave Winey that he proudly wore a suit of clothes made by her at his father's plantation. The suit was the envy of Williamsburg where another associator offered to trade a silk suit for the Virginia product. By December 1769, plantation cloth production had expanded to a level permitting the men and women at the burgesses' ball to make a "genteel appearance . . . chiefly dressed in Virginia cloth."[30]

Francis Lightfoot Lee and John Turbeville constructed a fulling mill for the express purpose of encouraging local woolen production and extending the benefits of domestic manufactures beyond the large plantations. Lee called on his brother William to obtain some of the necessary equipment in Great Britain. By September 1769, Lee and Turbeville had the mill in operation and were advertising for customers. The mill, on Nomini River in Westmoreland County, offered no credit and expected little profit, but within six months the operator was able to reduce charges and claimed to "die and dress jeans and fustians to look as well as those from England." George Washington, who had expanded his weaving operations in reaction to the Stamp Act, by 1769 was able to hire out his weaver to farmers and tenants in the area. In the first year of the association more than thirty of Washington's neighbors hired Thomas Davis, the Mount Vernon weaver, to make linen, cottons, fustians, and a variety of other commonly used kinds of cloth.[31]

Cloth production was the most practical domestic manufacture for Virginia planters who had the labor available to divert for such work, but there were also schemes for more ambitious projects. Richard Henry

[30]Martha Jacquelin to John Norton, 14 Aug. 1769, *John Norton & Sons*, ed., Mason, 103; William Nelson to Edward Hunt & Son, 17 Nov. 1769, and Nelson to John Norton, 24 Jan. 1770, Nelson Letterbook, Virginia State Library; Robert Wormeley Carter to Landon Carter, 22 June 1770, Sabine Hall Collection, Alderman Library, University of Virginia; *Virginia Gazette* (Purdie & Dixon), 14 Dec. 1769.

[31]*Virginia Gazette* (Rind), 14 Sep. 1769, *Virginia Gazette* (Purdie & Dixon), 14 June 1770; Francis Lightfoot Lee to William Lee, 26 Sep. 1769, Edmund Jenings Lee Papers, Virginia Historical Society; George Washington, Weaving Account, Washington Papers, Library of Congress.

Lee wished to attract English glassmakers to the colony in order to begin production of that dutied article. Following his brother's instructions, Arthur Lee sought contact with tradesmen in the glassmaking
center of Bristol only to find that the tightly-controlled craft discouraged any migration from the city. Paper was another dutied item for
which Virginians depended on Great Britain, but William Rind was able
to print his *Virginia Gazette* on American paper and asked his readers to
save linen rags to support local paper manufacture. Despite these efforts and occasional shipments of American paper from Philadelphia,
associators faced shortages of domestic paper throughout the period of
nonimportation.[32]

■   ■   ■

Because the association of 1769 was voluntary and without coercive
authority, merchants joined the agreement only when their interests or
politics coincided with the boycott. From the beginning of the opposition to the Townshend Acts, colonists were perplexed by the failure of
English merchants to mobilize as they had in response to commercial
resistance to the Stamp Act. Robert Beverley was "amazed at the Su-
pineness of the mercantile People. Their Interests ought to be closely
interwoven with ours, & they should consider an Injury done to us,
must ultimately affect them." In Virginia, resident traders and Britons
unconnected with the store trade were the merchants most likely to
observe the terms of the association. William Nelson, one of the most
important native merchants, canceled some orders and reduced others.
He particularly was interested in halting the traffic in wine since it carried the most burdensome duty for Virginia traders. Harry Piper, an
Alexandria merchant who purchased tobacco for a Whitehaven firm and
was not an importer of goods, joined with the "great number" who signed
the local association in Fairfax County. He also warned his English associates that repeal was the only action that could prevent disarray in
the Virginia trade.[33]

[32]Arthur Lee to Richard Henry Lee, 15 Nov. 1769, and William Shippen
to [Richard Henry Lee], 25 Aug. 1770, *Lee Family Papers* (University of Virginia microfilm publication); *Virginia Gazette* (Rind), 31 May 1770.
    [33]Robert Beverley to John Backhouse, 25 July 1769, Robert Beverley
Letterbook, Library of Congress; William Nelson to Edward Hunt & Son, 2
June 1769 and 17 Nov. 1769, Nelson to Messrs Lamar, Hill & Bisset, 24 Aug.

British factors were more likely to ignore the association or dismiss it as the work of hypocritical and opportunistic debtors. James Parker, a Scottish merchant in Norfolk, claimed all but a few of the associators could not obtain "one shilling at any Market in England" if their actual circumstances were known. Parker, who associated almost exclusively with his fellow Scots, knew only two firms in Norfolk that subscribed to the association and of few elsewhere. He reported that the people of Northampton County (few of whom were engaged in trade with Great Britain) resisted the boycott for fear of alienating the merchants of Norfolk. One factor urged the other representatives of British firms to meet and plan a response to the association. If such a meeting took place it left no record and produced no public response. The surviving record of imports by Scottish factors suggests a complete disregard of the boycott.[34]

Although the widespread experiments in local manufactures enabled certain individuals and even entire plantations to reduce their dependence on British trade, the factors were scarcely the only ones to violate the nonimportation agreement. By the close of 1769, the association's friends and detractors on both sides of the Atlantic were commenting on the general ineffectiveness of Virginia's nonimportation agreement. The *Virginia Gazette* received complaints about one of its several advertisements that brazenly offered prohibited commodities. Landon Carter decried the "prodigious importations of British manufactures" which were "daily tempting the weakness of many to infractions." In London, tobacco merchants gossiped about planters who secretly violated the boycott. In his dismissal of the merchants' petition for a repeal of the revenue duties, Lord Hillsborough cited the increased bills of entry for every type of prohibited article. A cynical merchant like James Parker

---

1769, Nelson to Thomas Lamar, 16 Sep. 1769, and Nelson to William Cookson, 2 Sep. 1769, all in Nelson Letterbook, Virginia State Library; Harry Piper to Dixon & Littledale, 8 June 1769, Piper Letterbook, Alderman Library, University of Virginia.

[34]Parker comments on printed copy of 1769 association, in Parker Family Papers, PA 7–2, Liverpool Record Office (Virginia Colonial Records Project microfilm); James Parker to Charles Steuart, 26 June 1769, Charles Steuart Papers, National Library of Scotland (Colonial Williamsburg microfilm); Alan L. Karras, *Sojourners in the Sun: Scottish Migrants in Jamaica and the Chesapeake, 1740–1800* (Ithaca and London: Cornell University Press, 1992), 157–66; *Virginia Gazette* (Rind), 25 May 1769, letter from a "Factor"; for continued imports see Glassford Company Papers, Library of Congress.

could easily point to the many Virginians still dressing in fine clothes or drinking Madeira. Another British factor informed his London correspondent that the association, if adhered to, could procure redress, but the colonists "pay so little regard . . . that they deal with us as usual."[35]

Various measures of trade indicate the volume and worth of imports into Virginia increased throughout the first year of the association. The official value of British exports to the Chesapeake climbed from £669,523 in 1768 to £714,943 in 1769 and £997,157 in 1770. The annual volume of certain dutied items, such as tea, green glass, and Portuguese wine, declined, but imports of white glass and painters' colors, also dutied items, advanced in 1769 and again in 1770. A wide variety of nondutied British goods, including some prohibited by the association, increased in volume each year after 1768, particularly during 1770. Virginia imports in 1770 reflected orders from the first year of the association, and the increased items included linens, hosiery, leather, hats, even playing cards.[36]

The voluntary nature of the association and the haphazard organization of local agreements had left the British factors free to expand their business in Virginia. Scottish imports into Virginia alone increased at an annual rate of 14.5 percent in 1769 and 28.5 percent in 1770. The association's emphasis on nonconsumption was an effort to limit much of the market for goods from the Scottish stores, but the factors' offers of higher tobacco prices and easy credit encouraged record sales. After the initial meetings on a local level, the association provided no means of sustaining popular support or encouraging widespread observance of the boycott, let alone coercion of violators. For many yeoman planters, often without any resources to supply their own needs, the immediate

[35]*Virginia Gazette* (Rind), 2 Nov. 1769, letter from "R"; Landon Carter to Purdie & Dixon, 1769, *Carter Family Papers* (University of Virginia microfilm publication); Arthur Lee to Richard Henry Lee, 15 Feb. 1770, *Lee Family Papers* (University of Virginia microfilm publication); Perkins, Buchanan, & Brown to Thomas Adams, Thomas Adams Correspondence, Adams Family Papers, Virginia Historical Society; James Parker to Charles Steuart, 20 Oct. 1769, Charles Steuart Papers, National Library of Scotland (Colonial Williamsburg microfilm); An Associator to Rind, *Virginia Gazette* (Rind), 30 Nov. 1769.

[36]Jacob M. Price, "New Time Series for Scotland's and Britain's Trade with the Thirteen Colonies and States, 1740–1791," *William and Mary Quarterly* 3rd ser., 32 (April 1975): 307–25; Import figures for individual commodities in Public Record Office, Customs 16/1, Ledger of Imports and Exports (America), 5 January 1768–5 January 1773 (Virginia Colonial Records Project microfilm).

rewards of a booming tobacco market proved more enticing than the gentry's example of sacrifice.[37]

Despite the obvious inadequacy of the original association, supporters of commercial resistance found compelling reasons to reorganize and continue a policy of nonimportation. The architects of the original agreement continued to believe that an enforced association would compel Britain to repeal the Townshend Acts and other legislation offensive to Americans. British correspondents reassured Virginians that the colonists still possessed the leverage to pressure England's commercial classes and secure support for the repeal movement. Furthermore, the initial experiments in economic diversification, however inchoate or isolated, were tantalizing evidence of the colony's potential for economic security and moral rejuvenation.

Landon Carter recognized the "insulting contempt shewn to the Association" by merchants and others, but he also discovered a new commitment to economic responsibility and simple living. The association seemed to restore respect for what Carter called "the examples of the polite and more considerate part of the Country." "No sooner did they make their appearances apparalled in Virginia growth," he said of the gentry, "but like an extinguisher to the extravagance and folly of the middle ranks, the example convinced them of the possibility of providing an agreeable dress, by the labours of their own families." For a man like Carter, who obsessively feared the moral declension of Virginia society, this development was sufficient reason to strengthen the association.[38]

Carter believed the association would be more effective politically if it encouraged broader observation by offering concessions to the practical limitations of the Chesapeake economy. He recommended the exemption from the boycott of certain items such as slaves' shoes and tools because planters could not find sufficient replacement quantities in Virginia. Carter also wanted some provision for disciplining local tradesmen who, after the ban on British goods and the failure of northern colonies to answer Virginia's call for supplies and laborers, had raised prices as high as demand would justify. To reduce import violations, Carter suggested more frequent meetings of the association and a strict ostracism of all who ignored the agreement.[39]

[37]Price, "New Time Series," 320–21.

[38]C.R. to Purdie & Dixon, *Virginia Gazette* (Purdie & Dixon), 23 Mar. 1770; draft of this letter in Sabine Hall Collection, Alderman Library, University of Virginia; letter of "Monitor," *Virginia Gazette* (Rind), 31 May 1770.

[39]Ibid.

Receipt of Bradshaw & Davidson, 17 January 1770. Custis Papers. Even in the midst of the Nonimportation Association, large estates relied on British imports for basic supplies such as the seine twine ordered by George Washington for use on the Custis estates along York River. The whimsically illustrated receipts sent by the consignment merchants in London offered planters a direct connection with tradesmen and shopkeepers in England. (Collection of the Virginia Historical Society)

During the winter of 1769–1770, anticipation of a parliamentary repeal postponed attempts to revise the association. Several London merchants initially expressed confidence that the new Parliament would repeal the Townshend Acts. William Lee went so far as to ship a few prohibited goods from London in the expectation that they would arrive after the date of repeal. Governor Botetourt's address to the newly-convened assembly in November 1769 strongly intimated that the ministry would acknowledge the error of the recent commercial legislation and ask Parliament to repeal the duties on glass, painters' colors, and paper. This would be only a partial repeal of the disputed acts, but for Robert Carter Nicholas, who praised the popular governor, it was the first indication of the effectiveness of the association. Some associating merchants interpreted the governor's assurances as an authorization to resume imports.[40]

[40]William Lee to Richard Parker, 10 Aug. 1769, William Lee Letterbook, 1769–1771, Lee Family Papers at Stratford (University of Virginia microfilm); *Journals of the House of Burgesses, 1766–1769,* eds., Kennedy and McIlwaine,

The promise of redress, however, was short-lived. Secretary of State Hillsborough privately reprimanded Botetourt for pledging the King to repeal. William Lee reported that in the House of Commons Isaac Barré and Edmund Burke so ridiculed Botetourt's speech to the assembly that they "made every body laugh redy to dye for near an hour." Lee and merchant John Norton warned their friends in Virginia that Parliament was certain to maintain the tax on tea "as an absolute fix'd precedent." Lee also feared that Parliament would follow any partial repeal of the Townshend duties with a restraint on American manufactures or an act declaring the nonimportation association to be a felony or even treason. At the meeting of the London merchants, only Lee, his partners Dennys DeBerdt and Stephen Sayre, and John Norton argued for a general petition protesting all legislation offensive to the Americans. Other London merchants were reluctant to demand a complete redress of American grievances for fear of delaying the reopening of trade with the colonies. The final petition mentioned only the duties complained of in Virginia's association. William Lee assured Richard Henry Lee that a more emphatic association with explicit demands would be needed to motivate the North American merchants in London.[41]

The reports from London in the winter of 1769–1770 confirmed the suspicion of William Nelson and others who had concluded that a partial repeal would not satisfy American demands. A repeal of duties on glass, paper, and painters' colors would leave unsettled the contested taxes on tea, wine, and foreign cloth. By early April, Richard Henry Lee anticipated that in the absence of a full repeal the associators would revise the agreement during the May session of the assembly, while for

---

226–27; Robert Carter Nicholas to [Arthur Lee], 29 Dec. 1769, *Lee Family Papers* (University of Virginia microfilm publication); for merchant orders following Botetourt's speech see William Brown to Thomas Adams, 16 June 1770, Thomas Adams Correspondence, Adams Family Papers, Virginia Historical Society.

[41]Secretary of State to Botetourt, 18 Jan., 1770, Public Record Office, CO5/1348, ff. 23–24 (Virginia Colonial Records Project microfilm); John Norton to John H. Norton, 10 Feb. 1770, *John Norton & Sons*, ed., Mason, 23; William Lee to Richard Parker, 6 Jan. 1770, William Lee to Anthony Stewart, 5 Dec. 1769, William Lee to William Fitzhugh, 19 Jan. 1770, in William Lee Letterbook, 1769–1771, Lee Family Papers at Stratford (University of Virginia microfilm); William Lee to Richard Henry Lee, 6 Feb. 1770, Brock Collection, Huntington Library (Colonial Williamsburg microfilm).

the time being they awaited word from London to determine what changes would be appropriate.[42]

In April 1770, the colonists received word of Parliament's repeal of all of Townshend's duties except that on tea. No one greeted the announcement as an American victory. Instead the accompanying reports in the *Virginia Gazette* deplored the lack of effort on the part of America's friends in Great Britain. The failure of petitions from the London merchants convinced William Nelson of the need to organize a stronger nonimportation association. "We must work our own deliverance which is in our power," Nelson confided to several London merchants, "I think we must depend merely on our own conduct & Resolution, to import Nothing but what is absolutely necessary."[43]

The assembly convened May 21, and on the following day the associators in Williamsburg agreed to impose stronger restrictions on the import trade. George Mason was not among the burgesses in 1770, but as in 1769 he played a central role in determining the content of the new nonimportation agreement. Mason sent Richard Henry Lee a critique of the 1769 agreement and recommended modifications that corresponded closely to the revised association approved later in June. Mason admitted his policy of voluntary nonconsumption failed to reduce import levels or to convince Parliament of the seriousness of Virginia's association. Too many colonists, "even some who affect to be called Gentlemen," purchased enumerated goods as long as such items were available in the country. The revised association therefore needed to establish an effective means of restricting the importations of British factors and of securing the compliance of resident consumers. Mason believed the factors would observe the nonimportation agreement if the "Principle People" in the colony refused all business with merchants who sold enumerated goods. The factors would "hardly venture to supply their worst Customers with such Articles, at the Hazard of losing their best." In order to discourage Virginians from dealing with merchants who continued to violate the association, "the Sense of Shame &

---

[42]William Nelson to Edward Hunt & Son, 17 Nov. 1769; Richard Henry Lee to William Lee, 5 Apr. 1770, *The Letters of Richard Henry Lee*, ed., James C. Ballagh, 2 vols. (New York: The Macmillan Company, 1911), 1:41–42.

[43]*Virginia Gazette* (Rind), 26 Apr. 1770; *Virginia Gazette* (Purdie & Dixon), 24 May 1770; William Nelson to Robert Cary & Co., 20 July 1770, William Nelson to Samuel Athawes, 3 Sep. 1770, William Nelson to Edward Hunt & Son, 26 July 1770, Nelson Letterbook, Virginia State Library; *Virginia Gazette* (Rind), 26 April 1770 also contains call of "Brutus" for meeting of associators to develop more a effective method of enforcement.

the fear of Reproach must be inculcated & enforced in the strongest Manner."[44]

The shortcomings of the original association revealed that Mason, Washington, and many others had been mistaken to believe that the example of the great planters would encourage a general observation of nonimportation. The faithful compliance of the great planters had done little or nothing to curtail purchases at the factors' stores. To enforce a new association, Mason still relied on the economic and social influence of Virginia's gentry, but he hoped to institutionalize the gentry's authority through the creation of county committees. Drawing on the more successful experiments of Maryland's association, Mason proposed the creation of committees that would draw together the most important planters and merchants from one or more counties. These officers would have the authority to inspect all imported cargoes as well as the merchants' correspondence and records concerning shipments within the committee's jurisdiction. When inspectors uncovered illicit goods within any cargo, they would request that the merchant return the items to Great Britain. Refusal to comply with the committee's order would result in the publication of the merchant's name as an enemy of the country, and local associators would cease all commercial dealings with the individual or firm.[45]

Mason was convinced the association would have an impact on British merchants only if goods were reshipped rather than stored until repeal of the duties, but he was undecided whether the requirements for reexportation should be retroactive. Certainly anyone importing goods during the previous year was aware of the violation of the original association, but Mason feared an attempt to return goods already in the country would frustrate the effectiveness of the committees. Mason was most eager to halt the recent practice of shipping goods to Virginia following their rejection by associations in other colonies.[46]

The associators in Williamsburg decided at a meeting on June 1 that the success of nonimportation depended on the broader participation of the colony's merchants. They accordingly invited to a meeting on June 15 the merchants and traders who were already in the capital for the Oyer Court. James Balfour, a merchant from Hampton and Virginia agent for the Hanburys of London, persuaded other merchants in Williamsburg to attend the meeting at which Richard Henry Lee ap-

[44]*Virginia Gazette* (Rind), 3 May 1770; George Mason to Richard Henry Lee, 7 June 1770, in *Papers of George Mason*, ed., Rutland, 1:116–19.
[45]Ibid.
[46]Ibid.

parently presented some form of Mason's recommendations. Washington was in attendance until eleven o'clock at night, and one Scottish factor reported that the draft proposal underwent "some considerable amendments." One week later, on the evening of June 22, 165 people, including original associators, newly elected burgesses, and a large group of merchants, signed the Virginia nonimportation association of 1770.[47]

In the preamble of the new association, the subscribers promised "to promote the welfare and commercial interests of all those truly worthy merchants, traders and other inhabitants of this colony" who observed "the spirit of this association." Any traders who violated the nonimportation agreement would lose the patronage of loyal associators. The Williamsburg meeting approved a system of committee enforcement, much as Mason had suggested. Each county would elect five members, any three of whom would have the authority to inspect cargoes and merchants' records and to order the reshipment of prohibited goods. In addition to the boycott of enumerated goods, merchants and other associators agreed to refuse any goods which had been rejected by the associations of other colonies. Traders also pledged not to exploit shortages by raising prices for goods already in the country or for those properly imported during the association. The associating merchants also agreed to establish a committee for the investigation of commercial affairs in Virginia. The 125 member committee, including individuals of every commercial interest from native traders to the Scottish factors of Glasgow syndicates, met in June and agreed to deliver in October 1770 a report on the general state of trade in Virginia. At that time they would recommend additional British goods that might reasonably be boycotted.[48]

The merchants' public support of the new association came at a high price. The revised agreement contained enough concessions on the restrictions of imports to satisfy most merchants that their interests would not be injured by signing. James Robinson, principal agent for

[47]*Virginia Gazette* (Purdie & Dixon), 7 June 1770; *Diaries of George Washington*, eds., Jackson and Twohig, 2:247; Robert Wormeley Carter to Landon Carter, 22 June 1770, Sabine Hall Collection, Alderman Library, University of Virginia; James Robinson to David Walker, 11 July 1770, in *A Scottish Firm in Virginia, 1767–1777: W. Cunninghame and Co.*, ed., T. M. Devine, (Edinburgh: Scottish History Society, 1984), 31–33.

[48]Text of association in *Revolutionary Virginia*, eds., Scribner and Tarter, 1:79–84; account of first committee meeting and *Virginia Gazette* article, both from a now destroyed copy of 28 June 1770 newspaper, printed in *Virginia Historical Register*, (Richmond, 1850), 3:79–38.

William Cunninghame & Co., reported to another Scottish factor that "as it [the association] stands at present it will not be of great prejudice to the trading part of the Colony and you will observe an evident partiality in favor of Glasgow." The association permitted the importation of hoes, axes, sugar, pewter, cambrick costing up to six shillings per pair, men's riding saddles costing up to 25 shillings and women's up to 40 shillings—all items prohibited in the association of the previous year. The new list of enumerated goods raised the acceptable price ceiling for cotton from two shillings to three per yard, for woolens from one shilling, six pence to two shillings, and for narrow cloths from three shillings to four. Landon Carter hoped the exemptions for tools, shoes, and cheaper cloths would make it easier for the average planter to observe the association, but the revisions in the boycott also opened Virginia's trade to the exact sort of inexpensive goods that filled the Scottish stores.[49]

The new dates for enforcement of the association proved equally generous for the merchants. Although subscribers agreed immediately to stop ordering all enumerated goods, they were free until September 1, 1770, to accept any goods sent on commission from Great Britain and until December 25, 1770, to receive any goods ordered by themselves. All goods already in the country were unaffected by the association. The boycott of wine was to become effective on September 1, and the prohibition of imported slaves on November 1. The nonimportation agreement was to remain in effect only until the total repeal of the act imposing a duty on tea, paper, glass and painters' colors, whereas several of the original associators hoped to direct the boycott against a wider scope of parliamentary legislation. Indeed, shortly after signing the association, the burgesses approved an address to the King wherein they condemned the procedures of the viceadmiralty courts and the taxes on foreign cloth as well as the duties mentioned in the association. The association's moderator, Peyton Randolph, or any twenty subscribers of the association had the authority to call future meetings. A meeting of one hundred associators was necessary to revise the terms of the agreement unless Parliament met the specific demands. James Robinson hoped the association of 1770 would produce a repeal of all revenue duties, but he was more thankful that it would not interfere with the Cunninghame company's business. He confided to another Glasgow man "I am happy

[49]James Robinson to David Walker, 11 July 1770, in *A Scottish Firm in Virginia*, ed., Devine, 31–33; *Revolutionary Virginia*, eds., Scribner and Tarter, 1:79–84;. C.R. to Purdie & Dixon, *Virginia Gazette* (Purdie & Dixon), 23 Mar. 1770.

as we must have joined in a association, that the terms we have agreed to are so favorable."[50]

Washington wished the revised association were "ten times as strict," and others later complained of its inadequacies. In June of 1770, however, most subscribers were hopeful that the inclusion of the merchants would invigorate the previously ineffectual association. Richard Henry Lee found the revisions generally agreeable to the traders in the colony and expected the changes to encourage merchant participation. Harry Piper believed most of his fellow merchants would sign the association, in which case it would be observed strictly. A writer to the *Virginia Gazette* heralded the merchants' participation as the first step toward a rewarding cooperation of planters and merchants. A standing institution encouraging the collaboration of these groups, "whose real interest is the same," would overcome the impediments of Virginia's dispersed settlement and would encourage economic development by devising proper commercial legislation.[51]

Peyton Randolph and others among the original associators recognized that the participation of the merchants would contribute to an effective nonimportation agreement only if the county committees were able to supervise trade and sustain a level of popular participation that was absent from the association of 1769. By involving the local planters and encouraging a public commitment, the committees would be able to isolate any factors or planters who continued to violate the association. Shortly after the signing of the new agreement, Randolph ordered the subscribers in the House of Burgesses to carry copies of the association to their respective counties for the collection of signatures. The delegates also were instructed to publicize a meeting of all local associators to be held within two months for the purpose of electing five members to the committee of observation.[52]

---

[50]*Revolutionary Virginia*, eds., Scribner and Tarter 1:79–84; *Journals of the House of Burgesses, 1770–1772*, eds., Kennedy and McIlwaine, 27 June 1770, 101–02; James Robinson to David Walker, 11 July 1770, *A Scottish Firm in Virginia*, ed., Devine, 31–33.

[51]George Washington to Robert Cary & Co., 20 Aug. 1770, *Papers of George Washington, Colonial Series*, eds., Abbot and Twohig, 8:368–71; Richard Henry Lee to William Lee, 7 July 1770, Richard Henry Lee Correspondence, Virginia Historical Society; Harry Piper to Dixon & Littledale, 26 July 1770, Piper Letterbook, Alderman Library, University of Virginia; *Virginia Historical Register*, 3:79–83.

[52]*Virginia Historical Register*, 3:24; Norfolk signers listed in *Virginia Gazette* (Rind), 26 July 1770.

Randolph divided the counties into districts in which the burgesses circulated copies of the association. In Fairfax County, Washington added to the text of the association an oath designed for local signers. He distributed copies to Alexandria, Colchester, and five other districts encompassing almost the entire county. The 333 signers in Fairfax represented one-fifth of the adult white male population and between one-third and one-half of the regular voters in the county. The association received approval from all but two of the seventeen members of the county court as well as a majority of the vestrymen and many small landowners. In Alexandria, where the initial signing took place on July 28, almost one-half of the subscribers were Scottish merchants. In Norfolk, where the concentration of population facilitated the organization of a local association, a committee was in operation by July and 145 residents added their names to the agreement.[53]

By late summer of 1770, with only a few counties reporting the election of committees of observation, Randolph reissued his instructions to the burgesses in charge of establishing the county associations. More counties complied toward the end of the year 1770, but others were unable to hold elections until after the new year. The majority of counties failed to report altogether. In the fall of 1770, Richard Henry Lee proposed several resolutions designed to encourage the formation of more local committees and to restrict the merchants' ability to subvert the colony's commercial resistance. One of Lee's amendments would have ordered local officials to hold elections or be replaced by someone who would be willing to form a committee. Lee also wanted to require that out of the one hundred associators needed to dissolve the nonimportation agreement, seventy five be planters. Of the twenty associators required to call a meeting, Lee suggested ten be planters.[54]

The membership of the county committees represented the traditional landed gentry, with only occasional inclusion of merchants. Of the sixteen counties reporting to the *Virginia Gazette*, all but one in-

[53]Donald Sweig, "The Virginia Nonimportation Association Broadside of 1770 and Fairfax County: A Study in Local Participation," *Virginia Magazine of History and Biography* 87 (July 1979): 313–25; *Virginia Gazette* (Rind), 26 July 1770.

[54]*Virginia Gazette* (Purdie & Dixon), 6 Sep. 1770; statements concerning reports based on those appearing in *Virginia Gazette*, surviving copies of which are not complete for 1770–1771; Richard Henry Lee, Proposed resolutions for association, 1770, *Lee Family Papers* (University of Virginia microfilm publication).

cluded a burgess among its five members and in eleven of the counties both delegates to the assembly served on the committee. More than half of the men on every committee were serving or had recently served as justices of the peace. In eight counties the entire committee consisted of justices. Candidates competed for committee membership in two counties. In Spotsylvania, nineteen men were on the ballot, and in Culpeper County several polls were taken before completing the election. These contests were probably between rival planters rather than between conflicting commercial interests. Five members of the merchants' committee established in Williamsburg served on county committees and other members of the local bodies may have been traders, but the factors of British firms were conspicuously absent from the county committees.[55]

Once the widespread popular involvement evident at several county meetings abated, the enforcement of the association depended on the performance of the five-member committees. Effectiveness varied from county to county. The Norfolk committee met the first test of its authority in July 1770 when Captain Robert Speirs of the ship *Sharp* arrived in Elizabeth River with European goods which had been refused landing by the Philadelphia association. Speirs claimed his Philadelphia agent consigned the goods to William and John Brown of Norfolk, but these merchants would have nothing to do with the cargo. Norfolk's associators forbade the landing or storage of the shipment and promised to ostracize anyone who aided Speirs in the disposal of the goods. After Speirs sailed from Norfolk, the committee printed in the *Virginia Gazette* a description of the prohibited cargo as a warning for other Virginia ports. When Speirs arrived in Dumfries to load a return cargo, the local committee, in response to the *Gazette* notice, inspected the *Sharp* only to find the prohibited goods missing. Speirs had managed to unload his shipment while still in Norfolk, and the Norfolk committee finally referred the matter to the Virginia association. Shortly thereafter Speirs published a confession protesting his ignorance of the colony's association and promising never to violate the agreement of any American colony.[56]

[55]Committee members recorded in *Virginia Gazette* in 1770 and 1771; record of men serving as justices of the peace found in "Justices of the Peace in Colonial Virginia, 1757–1775," *Bulletin of the Virginia State Library* 14 (April–June, 1921): 41–149.

[56]*Virginia Gazette* (Rind), 19 July 1770, 2 Aug. 1770, 23 Aug. 1770, 6 Sep. 1770.

In Essex County the local committee forced merchants John and George Fowler to rescind an order sent to England on June 10, even though the association exempted orders placed before June 15. But when committees faced the arrival of prohibited goods that had been ordered in June, they usually acquiesced in their landing. On New Years day 1771, Caroline County's committee permitted Robert Gilchrist to accept goods that he had ordered on June 15, 1770, and that were shipped from London in mid-September. The Essex County committee three weeks later permitted local merchants to proceed with the sale of prohibited goods ordered in June 1770, since the men who had placed the orders had "not violated the true meaning and spirit of the association." Native merchants, such as Thomas Jett of Leedstown who alerted a committee to the possible violation in his own shipments, often cooperated with the local associations. The committees had less leverage with British factors, including those who signed the association.[57]

No sooner had the local committees begun their enforcement of the association in the summer of 1770 than word arrived in Virginia of attempts to rescind the nonimportation agreements in northern colonies. The effective reduction of British trade with the northern ports was injuring the local merchants who also feared the increasingly radical action of the urban enforcement committees. The announcement of Parliament's partial repeal of the Townshend duties offered these merchants an opportunity to challenge their cities' nonimportation agreements. Public meetings through the spring and summer of 1770 in New York, Boston, and Philadelphia reasserted support for a boycott to force repeal of the tea duty, but merchants in those cities continued to maneuver for a resumption of trade. When New York's merchants on July 9, 1770, claimed public support for reopening trade, supporters of nonimportation in every colony condemned the move. Nevertheless, New York's decision to import effectively broke the union of resistance, and others followed. Philadelphia merchants overcame the opposition of the city's enforcement committee and voted on September 20 to resume trade. Boston merchants agreed in October to import all British goods except the dutied tea.[58]

[57]John and George Fowler to Dobson, Daltera & Walker, 2 Aug. 1770, Dobson & Daltera vs. Fowler svg. ptr., U.S. Circuit Court, Virginia District, Ended Cases, 1798, Virginia State Library; *Virginia Gazette* (Rind), 31 Jan. 1771, 7 Feb. 1771; *Virginia Gazette* (Rind), 30 Aug. 1770.

[58]Jensen, *The Founding of a Nation*, 363–69; Schlesinger, *Colonial Merchants*, 217–33. Throughout the summer and fall of 1770, the *Virginia Gazette* carried reports of the dissolution of the northern agreements.

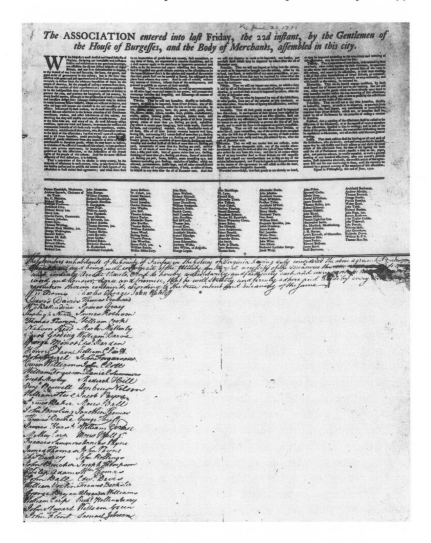

Broadside. 1770. A rare copy of the association of 1770, printed with the names of the original subscribers at a meeting in Williamsburg. The lower half of the sheet was left blank for the addition of subscriptions at local meetings. A clerk inscribed this copy with the names of associators from a section of Fairfax County. (Duke University)

The challenge to nonimportation in the Chesapeake came from Baltimore merchants who, fearing competition from importing Philadelphia merchants, declared their intention to import British goods. In late October an Annapolis meeting of the provincial association renewed the boycott, however, and pledged to cease all commerce with violators in Baltimore, thus preserving the agreement in principle if not entirely in practice. In Virginia, contributors to the *Virginia Gazette* praised Maryland's action and insisted their own colony's share of the British trade was sufficient to make a local boycott effective, but friends of nonimportation recognized that the defection of the northern colonies seriously undermined the potential impact of Virginia's association. William and Arthur Lee separately reported from London that the dissolution of the northern associations rendered repeal a dead issue, regardless of Virginia's action. Merchant Roger Atkinson of Petersburg supported nonimportation but said the second association would never have been considered if it were known the northern colonies would abandon commercial resistance. William Nelson blamed the northern defection for a decline in popular support for Virginia's association.[59]

When Peyton Randolph responded to the request of twenty associators and announced a general meeting of the association, to be held in Williamsburg on December 14, longtime supporters of nonimportation feared the action was an attempt by Virginia merchants to follow the example of the northern colonies. Richard Henry Lee believed the meeting was "a North Briton scheme for the abolition of the Association." Landon Carter also sensed a plot by merchants. Merchants had corrupted the northern associations and had entered Virginia's agreement only to serve their own interests. The traders, he insisted, had "impersonated associating" in order to collect colonial debts and then "go full handed to market with the money, as soon as the association ends." The first published attack on Virginia's association had come from a "Mercator," and Carter suspected the twenty associators requesting a

---

[59]Jensen, *Founding of a Nation*, 369; Schlesinger, *Colonial Merchants*, 233–34; report of Annapolis meeting in *Virginia Gazette* (Rind), 29 Oct. 1770; "A Virginian" to Mr. Rind, *Virginia Gazette* (Rind), 29 Nov 1770; William Lee to Dr. Charles Mortimer, 7 Nov. 1770, William Lee Letterbook, 1770-1771, Lee Family Papers at Stratford (University of Virginia microfilm publication); Arthur Lee to Richard Henry Lee, 10 Sep. 1770, *Lee Family Papers* (University of Virginia microfilm publication); Roger Atkinson to Samuel Gist, 10 Jan. 1771, Atkinson Letterbook; William Nelson to Secretary of State, 19 Dec. 1770, Public Record Office, CO5/1349, ff. 38–39 (Virginia Colonial Records Project microfilm).

meeting were also merchants. He rejected any proposals for a boycott limited to dutied articles and urged fellow associators to maintain commercial pressure on Great Britain.[60]

Carter feared a confrontation with the merchants, but the meeting in December 1770 proved to be an anticlimax. When fewer than the required quorum of 100 associators appeared, Peyton Randolph postponed the meeting until summer. The poor showing in Williamsburg reflected general apathy more than the difficulties of December travel. Even before the meeting Mason found the association to be in a "very languid state." William Nelson soon afterward predicted the boycott would "die away and come to nought." Although Francis Lightfoot Lee insisted that "the Traitors are allmost to a man merchants," he admitted that "the Country Gent[leme]n are all well inclin'd but indolent."[61]

Confusion reigned during the first six months of 1771 as planters and merchants sought to determine how the association affected their business. Scottish factors questioned whether to observe the boycott in their next orders from home. In London William Lee was unsure whether to comply with requests from Virginia planters for prohibited goods. Thomas Jefferson's orders to London in February included instructions to observe the association if there were no repeal, but by June he told Thomas Adams to ship the prohibited goods since a dissolution was likely before the articles would arrive. Harry Piper reported that the committees had stopped inspecting invoices by May and that he expected a formal dissolution.[62]

[60]Randolph's announcement in *Virginia Gazette* (Rind), 8 Nov. 1770 and (Purdie & Dixon), 22 Nov. 1770; Richard Henry Lee to William Lee, 8 Jan. 1771, *Letters of Richard Henry Lee*, 1:52–55; *Virginia Gazette* (Rind), 13 Dec. 1770, "An Associating Planter," identified as Landon Carter, *The Diaries of Landon Carter*, ed., Jack P. Greene, 2 vols. (Charlottesville: University Press of Virginia, 1965), 1:529.

[61]William Nelson to Secretary of State, 19 Dec. 1770, Public Record Office, CO5/1349, ff. 38–39 (Virginia Colonial Records Project microfilm); Francis Lightfoot Lee to William Lee, 17 Dec. 1770, Edmund Jenings Lee Papers, Virginia Historical Society.

[62]Adam Fleming to Neil Jamieson, 11 Jan. 1771, Neil Jamieson Papers, Library of Congress; William Lee to Edward Lloyd, 21 Feb. 1771, William Lee Letterbook, 1770–1771, Lee Family Papers at Stratford (University of Virginia microfilm publication); Thomas Jefferson to Thomas Adams, 20 Feb. 1771, 1 June 1771, *Papers of Thomas Jefferson*, ed., Boyd, 1:61–62, 71–72; Harry Piper to Dixon & Littledale, 13 May 1771, Piper Letterbook, Alderman Library, University of Virginia.

The committee in Fauquier County continued to report its inspection of merchant cargoes as late as June 1771. At that time the committee complained to Peyton Randolph that merchants in Falmouth and Dumfries ignored the boycott and were importing more goods than ever before. According to the Fauquier committee, merchants in these towns justified their imports by referring to the examples of Fredericksburg, Port Royal, and even Williamsburg, where traders allegedly paid the association no mind. The committee members accused the merchants in these towns of entering the association with the intent to sabotage it, and they wished all violators would be censured publicly. But Fauquier County could not maintain nonimportation by itself. If merchants throughout the colony imported without any reproach, Fauquier associators would have no choice but to conclude the boycott was terminated.[63]

Alexander Henderson, a factor for the Glasgow firm of Glassford & Co., and William Balmain, an Alexandria merchant, regularly submitted their invoices and cargo manifests for inspection by the Fairfax County committee until June 1771 when they observed such widespread disregard for the association that they declared to the committee their reluctant decision to begin imports of all but dutied British goods. The Fairfax committee confirmed the merchants' accusations of rampant violations and appealed to Peyton Randolph for a general meeting of the association in order to determine a uniform policy for the whole colony, whether it be dissolution or renewed enforcement. If the association did not respond, the Fairfax officers feared Virginia's trade would fall into the hands of the least honorable traders.[64]

The opportunity for a general meeting of the association came about as the result of a natural disaster rather than the weaknesses of the agreement or a new development in imperial relations. In May 1771, a severe storm sent flash floods down Virginia's rivers and destroyed an estimated 4,000 hogsheads of tobacco stored in public warehouses. The losses for merchants were so devastating that acting Governor William Nelson called a special session of the assembly in order to provide public compensation for the destroyed tobacco. The economic dislocation following the flood undermined the last vestiges of support for nonimportation. On July 15 the associators assembled for the burgesses session in Williamsburg dissolved the boycott agreement except as it related

[63]Fauquier Committee to Peyton Randolph, 11 June 1771, *Virginia Gazette* (Rind), 18 July 1771.

[64]Fairfax Committee to Peyton Randolph, in *Virginia Gazette* (Rind), 18 July 1771.

to tea, paper, glass, and painters' colors of foreign manufacture "upon which a Duty is laid for the Purpose of raising a Revenue in America."[65]

■   ■   ■

Virginia's second association would have proved ineffective and subsequently have collapsed regardless of the defection of the northern colonies. Although no colony by itself was likely to carry on a scheme of commercial resistance, violations of the association of 1770 began before the breakdown of nonimportation agreements in other colonies. The reorganized association never slowed the continuing expansion of British imports that began in the Chesapeake in 1769, accelerated in 1770, and reached a colonial record in 1771, when British goods valued at £1,223,726 entered Virginia and Maryland. Scottish imports into Virginia alone reached a record value of £250,401 in 1771.[66]

The pervasive dependence on British manufactures and the various exemptions in the boycott prevented Virginians from reducing imports as sharply as several northern colonies and the Carolinas did. Even the strongest supporters of nonimportation, many of whom owned large plantations capable of diversification, found it impossible to eliminate all British purchases during the association. George Washington strictly observed the associations which he helped establish, but he continued to rely on his London merchant for the supply of basic commodities needed at his several plantations. The Mount Vernon weaving operation was still not capable of producing all of the kinds and amounts of cloth required on the estate. In the early months of the association of 1769, Washington ordered from London goods costing over £77. Nearly £50 of that amount went for coarse woolens, linens, hose, and sewing supplies necessary for provisioning the slaves. During the second year of nonimportation, Washington ordered goods valued at £110, with inexpensive cloth again accounting for the bulk of his order, and much of the remainder consisted of basic tools unavailable from Virginia craftsmen. Once the association dissolved in 1771, Washington sent to London to fill the shortages that had resulted from two years of limited importations. The return shipment cost him over £350. This cargo of

[65]William Nelson to Secretary of State, 14 June 1771, Public Record Office, CO5/1349, ff. 102–03 (Virginia Colonial Records Project microfilm); *Virginia Gazette* (Purdie & Dixon) 18 July 1771.

[66]Price, "New Time Series," 320–25.

goods and the one of equal value in 1772 included some items prohibited by the associations, but the greatest costs were for large quantities
of common cloth, apparel, iron tools, equipment for the commercial
fishery at Mount Vernon, and basic plantation supplies.[67]

In 1769, John Baylor of Caroline County reduced his British orders
from the usual amount of £300 to around £100. The smaller order included necessities such as 500 ells of osnaburg, 500 yards of "Common
Negroes Cotton," 160 pair of "Negroes plaid cheap hose," sewing supplies, medicines, and tools. Baylor's request for three dozen cotton cards
indicated his expectation of producing the cheap cloth on his own plantation in the future. Although most of the great planters continued to
order goods from Great Britain, they did observe the restrictions of the
associations. As late as December 1770, Raleigh Downman of Lancaster
County was scrupulous to adhere to the terms of the association. He
instructed London merchant Samuel Athawes "You will please remember that the best of these Stockings are not to exceed 3/ pr pair & the
others I expect in proportion agreeable to our Association." Trade in
luxury goods prohibited by the association virtually ceased in Virginia
for two years. Carriages, clocks, cabinetware, expensive silks, even rac-
ing horses, disappeared from the customs records.[68]

In spite of their expensive tastes and habits, the great planters in
Virginia were in the best position to observe the boycott of goods enumerated by the associations. In addition to their renunciation of imported luxury items, the owners of large plantations controlled sufficient
labor to divert from agricultural work to experiments in domestic manufactures. The successful cloth-making operation of the Nelson family
was an example of the sort of self-sufficiency that was beyond the means
of all but Virginia's wealthiest families. The Nelsons devoted entire plantations in Albemarle County to the manufacture of clothing items while
other plantations continued the agricultural production that, along with
the family's trading business, supported the estate's income. The great

---

[67]Invoices from Robert Cary & Co., 23 Jan. 1770, 13 Nov. 1770, 3 Dec.
1771, *Papers of George Washington, Colonial Series*, eds., Abbot and Twohig, 8:295–
99, 397–400, 558–65.

[68]John Baylor to John Backhouse, 21 July 1769, Backhouse Admx. vs. Baylor
exor., U.S. Circuit Court, Virginia District, Ended Cases, 1798, Virginia State
Library; Raleigh Downman to [Samuel Athawes], 15 December 1770, Joseph
Ball Letterbook, Library of Congress; Public Record Office, Customs, 16/1,
Ledger of Imports and Exports (America), 5 January 1768–5 January 1773 (Vir-
ginia Colonial Records Project microfilm).

majority of planters did not operate on a scale that permitted this kind of division of labor.[69]

The average planter family which regularly traded with local factors and consumed few if any luxury goods found it difficult to reduce purchases of British manufactures at the same time that they maintained their regular planting activity. The easy access to Scottish stores with their inexpensive goods and lenient credit encouraged small and middling planters to concentrate all their labor on tobacco cultivation while the factors supplied a broad array of household necessities. Consequently, domestic manufacture of cloth was most common among households in the backcountry or in those that produced no crops for export, and these families had a negligible effect on import levels. With few yeoman planters producing enough cloth to supply their family and workers and with a scarcity of domestic cloth on the market, the associations' emphasis on nonconsumption was impractical for the majority of planter families in Virginia.[70]

The long-standing reliance on British manufactures and the difficulties involved in reorganizing a plantation regardless of size prevented the associators from significantly reducing the colony's annual imports from Great Britain. But during both associations Virginia's imports actually increased at unparalleled rates of growth. Virginia's first experiments with organized commercial resistance fortuitously coincided with one of the largest credit booms in Great Britain during the eighteenth century. The expansion of British credit enabled and encouraged every type of merchant in the American trade to enlarge their ventures in the colonies. In 1770, imports grew in New England and New York as well as the Chesapeake. The following year British imports reached record levels in every colony in North America.[71]

Nowhere was the expansion of imports more dramatic than in Virginia and Maryland. The recovery of tobacco prices from the depression of the mid-1760s prompted British merchants to extend generous offers of credit and goods on credit in an effort to attract the Chesapeake crop. As prices rose and tobacco exports increased in 1769 and 1770, British merchants responded with ever larger shipments of goods during the following years. The Scots led the way, expanding their outstanding credit in Virginia from £500,000 in 1766 to £1,100,000 in 1772.

---

[69]William Nelson to Edward Hunt & Son, 17 Nov. 1769; Nelson to John Norton, 24 Jan. 1770, Nelson Letterbook, Virginia State Library.

[70]Lorena S. Walsh, "Urban Amenities and Rural Sufficiency," 109–17.

[71]Price, "New Time Series," 322–25.

Direct trade merchants in England imitated the Scots' pattern. Even consignment merchants devised new enterprises to expand their business on the basis of the credit boom. The London consignment merchants, like other tobacco importing firms, entered the cargo trade in which independent Virginia merchants accepted entire store inventories on credit and an agreement to make return payments in tobacco or bills of exchange. This variation on the traditional form of the direct trade allowed consignment merchants to ship and receive larger cargoes than were manageable under the personalized service of the commission trade. In Virginia a new group of resident merchants imported large assortments of British goods with no security other than the expectation of good prices and easy credit. For example, the cargo business of one well-established consignment firm, John Norton & Sons of London, increased the company's outstanding debt from £11,000 in 1767 to £40,000 in 1773. The larger firms in London extended proportionately greater credit.[72]

The regional distribution of imports during the associations further illustrated the role of the direct trade and cargo trade in generating record shipments of British goods. The Upper James River district and to a lesser extent the Lower James district were responsible for the greatest increases, particularly among prohibited goods. This was exactly the area where Scottish traders were most influential and where yeoman planters dominated tobacco production and sold their crops through stores. At the same time, shipments of some prohibited goods actually declined in other naval districts. Among the goods that increased the most in 1770 and 1771 were linens, leather, haberdashery and millinery, hats, and hosiery, all of which were in some degree prohibited by the associations. Virginia imported 97,488 pounds of tanned leather in 1769 but in 1770 the amount rose to 232,733 pounds and reached 275,162 pounds in 1771. The Upper James district alone increased imports of leather from 10,786 pounds in 1769 to 123,862 pounds in 1770 and 148,754 the next year. Haberdashery and millinery imports followed a similar pattern, with a colony-wide increase of close to 325,000 pounds in 1770. The two James River districts accounted for 260,000 pounds of the growth. The Upper James led increases in linen and other cloths, particularly in 1770. Total imports increased during 1770 and 1771 throughout Virginia, but the absolute and proportional increases in the Upper James district, combined with the reduced shipments of luxury

[72]Jacob M. Price, *Capital and Credit*, 129–30; Allan Kulikoff, "The Economic Growth of the Eighteenth-Century Chesapeake Economy," *Journal of Economic History* 39 (March 1979): 287.

goods, indicates the degree to which direct trade merchants were responsible for the imports which destroyed the credibility of the nonimportation associations.[73]

For the majority of planter families in Virginia, the opportunities made possible by the factors' generous credit and the long-awaited rise in tobacco prices proved more persuasive than a revised association or the limited authority of the five-man committees. Despite the initial participation of British factors and the attempts to establish some mechanism of enforcement, the association of 1770, like the original agreement, found consistent support only among great planters and some resident merchants. Certainly, from the perspective of London or the northern colonies, the steady flow of goods from Great Britain to Virginia was convincing evidence that the second association was as ineffective as the first. As early as September of 1770, Arthur Lee abandoned plans for the London publication of his articles in support of Virginia's association. Lee's brother-in-law, William Shippen, reported that his fellow Philadelphians assumed Virginians were unable to establish "any associations that will be of any efficacy from the nature of their commerce & the number of Scotch factors &c."[74]

■   ■   ■

For the great planters, the failure to reduce imports during the association confirmed their worst apprehensions about the factors' influence in Virginia society. The size and nature of this increase were irrefutable evidence of the British merchants' nearly unchecked influence over Virginia's domestic economy and external trade. The fear that the Scots' extensive economic activity in Virginia would erode the great planters' political authority was no longer hypothetical. The factors' commercial connection with yeoman planters effectively undermined the gentry's ability to organize popular support for the associations. The example of the "gentlemen," which George Washington, George Mason, Landon Carter, and others had expected to inspire a general obser-

[73]Ledger of Imports and Exports (America), 5 January 1768–5 January 1773, Public Record Office, Customs, 16/1 (Virginia Colonial Records Project microfilm).

[74]Arthur Lee to Richard Henry Lee, 10 Sep. 1770, William Shippen to [Richard Henry Lee], 25 Aug. 1770, *Lee Family Papers* (University of Virginia microfilm).

vation of the nonimportation agreement, was no match for the factors' lucrative offers. Clearly, an effective association in Virginia required stricter regulation of merchants' business activity, a concerted effort to sustain popular participation, and domestic manufactures on a scale that would permit all planter families to reduce their purchases of British manufactures.

By the end of 1770, George Mason conceded that his proposals for commercial resistance had been unrealistic for the Chesapeake economy. Mason realized he had been too ambitious to expect that a boycott of British goods would produce a repeal of the Townshend Acts within one or two years. The variety of goods encompassed by the nonimportation agreement had been impractical; few Virginians could continue to operate their estates and abide by the agreement even for one year. The coincidental rise in demand for British goods in Europe and the inconsistencies among the agreements in different colonies canceled out whatever effect Mason hoped the associations might otherwise have had. In the event commercial resistance was necessary in the future, Mason suggested a single association for all the colonies, with the boycott covering "only Articles of Luxury & Ostentation together with the Goods at any Time taxed." Such an association, "in the Nature of a Sumptuary Law," would cost the government "more in one year on two Articles only (manufactured Tobacco & Malt Liquors) than it wou'd gain in ten by the American Revenue Act." Mason recommended that future associations should place more emphasis on long-term plans for the development of domestic manufactures and the encouragement of immigration by skilled workers from Europe. As the colonies became capable of producing more consumer goods at home, they would reduce their dependence on British trade. Although Mason hoped further commercial resistance would be unnecessary, he confessed that a plan like his own was "now in Contemplation."[75]

The nature of the associations' failure suggested that some type of commercial resistance would be necessary if Virginians were to achieve any measure of economic independence from Great Britain and the tobacco merchants. The lessons of the associations, and particularly the role of the factors in subverting the schemes for nonimportation, provided fresh evidence of the dangers that resulted from Virginia's reliance on British manufactures and the commercial services of British merchants. The experience that led to a better understanding of the

[75]George Mason to [George Brent?], 6 Dec. 1770, *Papers of George Mason*, ed., Rutland, 1:127–30.

limitations of Virginia's colonial economy also contributed to a greater awareness of the possibilities for independent economic development. The immediate legacies of the associations were additional schemes, both public and private, for the diversification of agriculture and manufactures, a continued campaign to restrict the slave trade and attract skilled laborers to the colony, and broader interest in the kind of commercial development that would allow native merchants to compete with the British factors.

Yet neither Mason nor any of the other principal architects of nonimportation grasped the fundamental inadequacy of a plan of commercial resistance that relied on the example and conduct of the great planters. The design of the associations, the selection of goods to be prohibited and exempted, and the methods of enforcement all reflected the experience and expectations of wealthy planters rather than the smaller households that accounted for the bulk of imports in Virginia as well as the largest share of tobacco produced for export. The owners of Virginia's largest estates, in fact, by and large complied with the terms of the association. Throughout the duration of the association, the gentry planters and their families filled their correspondence with self-congratulatory remarks about a general reorganization of plantation management that seemed to promise a diversified, independent, and integrated provincial economy. These same planter families seemed genuinely bewildered when their own enterprise and sacrifice did not translate into broader support for the long-term goals of the association. The secure political authority of the gentry and the popular affirmation of their culture blinded the great planters to the division of interests among tobacco producers which arose in the wake of the transformation of British trade. When the leading planters and burgesses tested the limits of their influence during the association, the deference of the yeoman planters dissolved in the face of generous offers from British factors. For the time being, however, the great planters continued to believe that economic independence would emerge from their own efforts to make their plantations more competitive and productive in the commercial system of the Atlantic economy.

"A Source of Ignorance and Vice": The Slave Trade and Economic Development in Virginia

However compelling the cultural proscription against public dialogue on the institution of slavery, no ambitious effort to redirect Virginia's economy and curtail the influence of the British tobacco trade could long ignore the principal source of labor in the colony. The system of slavery that developed in Virginia did more than any other single factor, tobacco included, to define the economy and society of the eighteenth-century colony. As a labor system, slavery was central to the perpetuation of staple agriculture and the organization of plantations. The institution of racial slavery, moreover, was the basis of the hierarchical and stable social structure of Virginia in the half-century preceding Independence. The capital investment in slavery, the shortage of alternative labor supplies, and the significance of racially-defined social distinctions all restricted the options available to planters intent on diversification at the same time that they made more urgent the goals of economic independence.

Any ideal of economic independence confronted the labor system that British merchants introduced and helped to perpetuate in the Chesapeake. The size and extent of the colonial investment in slave labor affected every choice about plantation management, commercial development, domestic manufactures, internal improvements, and the use of natural resources. The prohibition of slave imports under the associations of 1769 and 1770 was a rare and reluctant public acknowledgment on the part of gentry planters that they considered their commitment to chattel slavery an impediment to the full realization of the colony's economic potential. For several years on either side of the associations, the House of Burgesses conducted a quieter but determined campaign to halt or at least to reduce sharply the further importation of slaves into the colony. The assembly's repeated approval of a prohibitive slave duty was the most important governmental effort to guide the growth of Virginia's economy in the decade and a half before the Revolution.

But slavery, as the burgesses learned, was never an exclusively provincial matter. The institution was central to the Atlantic economy and particularly to the commercial structure of the British Empire. Any local attempt to interfere with the slave trade challenged the mercantilist principles of the British government and the interests of British traders. On no other economic issue did the intent of the Virginia assembly so sharply conflict with imperial regulations and ministerial policy. The burgesses' attempts to curtail or close off the commerce in slaves repeatedly provoked the direct intervention of the Crown. Ultimately the colonists' determination resulted in a British prohibition on all provincial legislation regulating this integral aspect of the Virginia economy.

■   ■   ■

Through much of the eighteenth century, white Virginians eagerly purchased large numbers of black slaves brought to the colony from Africa and to a lesser extent the West Indies. In certain areas, demand for imported slaves continued nearly unabated until the 1770s. Although slavery had existed in Virginia as long as tobacco had been a major export, slaves became an important part of Virginia's labor force in the 1690s when privateers first arrived with large numbers of enslaved blacks to replace the dwindling supply of indentured servants from England. The opening of the slave trade to all shippers after the expiration of the Royal African Company's monopoly in 1698 accelerated the transition to slave labor as Virginia planters received increasing numbers of slaves directly from Africa. The colony's black population of 16,930 in 1700 advanced to 23,118 in the century's first decade. The largest slave shipments were between 1727 and 1769 during which time 45,440 slaves arrived in Virginia. Volume was highest during the 1730s and 1740s, although slave imports reached a record annual high of 3,975 in 1752. After 1740 South Carolina surpassed Virginia as a slave importer, but the steady shipment of slaves and a healthier climate in the Chesapeake made Virginia's the largest slave population among the British mainland colonies on the eve of the Revolution. One-hundred-eighty-seven thousand blacks, constituting 40 percent of the total population, lived in Virginia in 1770. All but a small percentage of them were held as slaves.[1]

Virginia's wide-scale adoption of slavery coincided with and was made possible by Great Britain's ascendancy as the premier slave-trading nation in the Atlantic world. Although the English were comparatively late to enter the slave trade, they were the major shippers from West Africa by 1700. By the 1730s, they controlled the largest share of the slave trade from all of Africa and maintained that dominance until the early nineteenth century. British advancement in the trade provided Virginia planters with access to the African slaves that they preferred to import. The colonists no longer needed to rely on the irregular West Indian slave trade which had been incapable of filling the demand for bound laborers in the Chesapeake. By the 1720s, the majority of slaves imported into Virginia were from Africa. The following years of heavy importations were largely the story of British traders shipping African slaves directly to Virginia. West Indian slaves, whom white Virginians considered too savvy and rebellious, accounted for only 12 percent of slave imports after 1727. The slave trade from the islands was always ancillary to the commodities trade with the West Indies.[2]

As valuable as the labor of slaves was for colonial planters, Virginians gained little from the slave traffic which remained in the hands of British traders and drained the colony of always scarce specie and bills of exchange. The profits from Virginia's slave trade went primarily to English merchants and ship owners who carried 89 percent of the slaves from Africa to the colony. Although American shipping was more involved in slave importations from the West Indies, English capital supported a large share of this trade as well. During the entire colonial period, Virginia ships carried only nine slave shipments from Africa,

---

[1]*Historical Statistics of the United States: Colonial Times to 1970*, part 2 (Washington: U.S. Department of Commerce, Bureau of the Census, 1975), 1168; K. G. Davies, *The Royal African Company* (London: Longmans, Green, 1957), 43, 125–43; *Virginia Slave Trade Statistics 1698–1775*, eds., Walter Minchinton, Celia King, and Peter Waite (Richmond: Virginia State Library, 1984), xv; Herbert S. Klein, "Slaves and Shipping in Eighteenth Century Virginia," *Journal of Interdisciplinary History* 5 (Winter 1975): 385–86, 409.

[2]James A. Rawley, *The Transatlantic Slave Trade: A History* (New York: W. W. Norton, 1981), 149,164, 333; Klein, "Slaves and Shipping," 384–87, 394–95; *Virginia Slave Trade Statistics*, eds., Minchinton, et al., xv.

accounting for 920 of the 70,524 slaves recorded as imported into the colony. Virginia ships did not carry a single slave from Africa during the years of heaviest imports, 1727–1751, and they carried only small shipments, usually ten or fewer slaves per voyage, from the West Indies. Planters and local merchants in Virginia frequently acted as sales agents for slave shipments or sold smaller lots within the colony, but they did not manage the entire venture. The high operating costs of the complicated network of the slave trade and the efficient specialization of Bristol and Liverpool merchants precluded the competition of colonial purchasers in the financing or operation of the trade between Africa and the Chesapeake. Like the commerce in tobacco, the slave trade enabled many individual planters to grow rich in Virginia but did little to encourage the development of commercial centers in the colony or a native class of merchants.[3]

The staple trade and British mercantilism were as responsible for the structure of Virginia slavery as were the avarice of the planters and the demands of tobacco culture. The volume of slave imports as well as their destination roughly corresponded with the fortunes of the tobacco market. Bristol merchants were most active in the Virginia slave trade and focused their shipments in the York River area during the first four decades of the eighteenth century when the large planters of that region dominated tobacco production. Liverpool traders preferred the Rappahannock River for their slave sales. After 1740 the Bristol slave merchants maintained their command of the Virginia market by concentrating their shipments in the Upper James River district where the expansion of tobacco cultivation generated a demand for slave labor. Few slave ships sold their cargoes on the Eastern Shore of Virginia or in the Southside area of the Lower James where tobacco was never an important money crop.[4]

Annual fluctuations in the volume of slave imports reflected the price of tobacco and the ease of British credit. The high volume of slave importations during the 1730s and 1740s coincided with the influx of

[3]Klein, "Slaves and Shipping," 404–06; Rawley, *The Transatlantic Slave Trade*, 404, chs., 8 and 9; *Virginia Slave Trade Statistics*, eds., Minchinton, et al.

[4]Rawley, *The Transatlantic Slave Trade*, 190; Lorena Walsh, "Slave Life, Slave Society, and Tobacco Production in the Tidewater Chesapeake, 1620–1820," in *Cultivation and Culture: Labor and the Shaping of Slave Life in the Americas*, eds., Ira Berlin and Philip D. Morgan (Charlottesville: University Press of Virginia, 1993), 170–81; Klein, "Slaves and Shipping," 396; *Virginia Slave Trade Statistics*, eds., Minchinton, et al.

credit through the direct trade and enabled Virginia planters to expand their slave holdings and increase tobacco production in the Piedmont region. The British ships from Africa, specializing in the transport of slaves, were most likely to land in the several upriver areas where they could sell their large cargoes of slaves. Ship captains from the West Indies generally landed their much smaller slave cargoes in the Lower James district and disposed of the slaves as a sideline to their trade in West Indian produce.[5]

Virginia's slave imports decreased sharply in the 1750s as the French and Indian War disrupted trade and then revived during the short boom following the end of hostilities. The depression of the mid-1760s reduced the shipments of slaves and almost completely discouraged the trade from Africa. The return of more favorable tobacco prices in 1769 once again attracted large cargoes from Africa. Petersburg merchant Roger Atkinson in 1770 was confident that a slave trader would find a ready market in the James River "where all Guineamen come now." After mid-century the majority of slaves imported into the colony were settled in the Piedmont region of the Upper James. The slaves entering the colony between 1769 and 1772, the last sizable importations into Virginia, arrived almost exclusively in this region that was at the center of the Scottish factors' trade in tobacco.[6]

The overall demand for new slaves declined in Virginia after mid-century while the British traders carried a higher proportion of their North American-bound slaves to South Carolina. In contrast with the high mortality rates for the slave populations of South Carolina and the British West Indies, a remarkable rate of natural increase among Virginia slaves provided an expanding labor force without imports. This natural population increase, however, occurred only after the number of native-born slaves was sufficient to offset the high mortality and low fertility rates suffered by African immigrants in Virginia. The increase in a native-born slave population also corrected the gender imbalance

[5]Klein, "Slaves and Shipping"; Kulikoff, *Tobacco and Slaves*, 65–66; Walsh, "Slave Life, Slave Society and Tobacco Production," 170–71; Philip D. Morgan and Michael L. Nicholls, "Slaves in Piedmont Virginia, 1720–1790," *William and Mary Quarterly* 3rd ser., 46 (April 1989): 215–17.

[6]*Virginia Slave Trade Statistics*, eds., Minchinton, et al.; Roger Atkinson to Lionel and Samuel Lyde, 28 May 1770, Atkinson Letterbook, Alderman Library, University of Virginia; Morgan and Nicholls, "Slaves in Piedmont Virginia."

of the early years of the eighteenth century when two-thirds of the African immigrants were males. The slave population of Virginia grew from 60,000 in 1740 to 101,000 in 1750 and 187,000 in 1770, with imports accounting for less than 15 percent of the growth after mid-century. This large resident labor force combined with changes in agricultural practices to eliminate much of the demand for new slaves, particularly the market for Africans who, though skilled in the agricultural methods required of tobacco, were unfamiliar with the supporting crafts of Virginia's plantations. The tobacco planters of the Piedmont and the southwestern counties still paid good prices for "New Negroes" during advancing tobacco markets, but many other Virginia planters, especially the gentry of the Northern Neck and Tidewater, needed few new slaves. Indeed, many of these planters found compelling reasons to discourage the importation of slaves into the colony.[7]

■   ■   ■

After living in England, Robert Beverley returned to his native Essex County in 1761 and was overwhelmed by his "Aversion to Slavery." "'Tis something so very contradictory to Humanity, that I am really ashamed of my Country whenever I consider it, & if ever I bid adieu to Virginia, it will be from that Cause alone." Yet Beverley personified the dilemma of the planters' involvement in slavery when, in the same letter to an English merchant, he announced that he was sending 50 slaves to an unimproved western tract in order to cultivate tobacco. Beverley was hardly alone in his decision to extend slavery and the plantation system of agriculture in order to increase the value of western landholdings. Nathaniel Burwell assured John Norton in 1770 that he could better than double his annual shipments of tobacco by sending more slaves to his mountain estates. William Fitzhugh of Stafford County was so "overstocked" with slaves in 1772 that he borrowed £400 to purchase land on which he could employ the extra slaves. In response to the surplus of slaves in Tidewater and the availability of cheap, productive land to the west, as many as 17,000 slaves may have been transported from Tidewater plantations to the Piedmont between mid-century and the close of the Revolutionary War. Many of these slaves were moved west by

[7]*Historical Statistics*, part 2, 1168; Klein, "Slaves and Shipping," 385–86; Kulikoff, *Tobacco and Slaves*, 64–76.

Slaves stringing and rolling tobacco amidst a fanciful pairing of American flora and fauna. Pierre Pomet. *A Compleat History of Drugs.* London, 1737. Third edition. (Collection of the Virginia Historical Society)

slaveowners who held western lands. Others were sold by Tidewater planters.[8]

Tidewater planters and settled Piedmont planters also confronted the need to compensate for the declining productivity of slaves cultivating tobacco. Although a familiar system of land rotation restored soil fertility, recycled lands were never as productive as virgin soil. The increased reliance on women and children for field work further reduced output per worker. Many planters maintained income by introducing grain cultivation and by finding a greater variety of work for their slaves at the same time that they continued to grow the tobacco necessary for access to British markets. An exclusive commitment to grain cultivation, with its requirements for more intensive labor and plow culture,

[8]Robert Beverley to Edward Athawes, 11 July 1761, Robert Beverley Letterbook, Library of Congress; Nathaniel Burwell to John Norton, 3 Sep. 1770, *John Norton & Sons*, ed., Mason, 146–47; William Fitzhugh to Stuart & Campbell, 3 Apr. 1772, American Loyalist Claims, Public Record Office, T. 79/12 (Virginia Colonial Records Project microfilm); Morgan and Nicholls, "Slaves in Piedmont Virginia," 221–27.

was beyond the means of most Virginia planters. And the lack of a steady export market with the financial services of the tobacco trade frustrated the transition to grain. Consequently the surplus of slaves on large estates remained a challenge for gentry planters in the late-colonial period. William Lee feared that he had more slaves at his Green Spring plantation than ever could be employed profitably in agriculture. He urged his steward to train the surplus slaves to work in manufactures and produce the supplies needed for the plantation. Advocates of the various proposals for nonimportation commonly recommended domestic manufacturing schemes not only as a means of replacing British goods, but also as a way of finding additional work for slaves.[9]

As long as natural increase and continued imports resulted in an ample supply of slave labor, Virginia planters would be tempted to extend plantation agriculture to western lands. An agricultural system that relied on field rotation and consumed large quantities of land, population pressures on eastern and even Piedmont lands, the shortage of free laborers willing to toil in fields, and the presence of a mobile, unfree labor force all combined to drive tobacco culture and the plantation system further and further west. Landless young men waiting to inherit their fathers' lands, families unable to purchase land in settled areas, and gentry planters with more slaves than they could employ on their eastern estates all found reason to settle new lands and there put slaves to work.[10]

Yet the seductive combination of western lands and slave labor ultimately carried a high price. For some there could be a risky, even desperate quality to the settlement of western lands with slaves. Already in debt to his London merchant, John Page went to great expense to open up estates for his slaves to work and, he hoped, extricate himself from his indebtedness. In 1773 after the collapse of tobacco markets, his lack of credit forced him to purchase supplies for the slaves at expensive local stores, and the venture threatened to drive him deeper and deeper into debt. The extension of slavery also presented broader social and

---

[9]Walsh, "Slave Life, Slave Society, and Tobacco Production," 179–87; William Lee to Francis Lightfoot Lee, 13 July 1770, William Lee Letterbook, 1769–1777, Lee Family Papers at Stratford (University of Virginia microfilm); William Lee to Cary Wilkinson, 22 May 1771, William Lee Letterbook, 1769–1772, Virginia Historical Society.

[10]Kulikoff, *Tobacco and Slaves*, 64–77.

economic risks for the colony. In the decade preceding Independence, the use of slaves to establish additional tobacco plantations appeared to many, especially gentry planters in the Northern Neck and Tidewater, as a foolish repetition of the type of agriculture that already imposed limitations on the great estates of Virginia and tied planters ever closer to the commercial services of British merchants.[11]

■   ■   ■

After mid-century, a growing number of Virginians argued that slave labor, whether skilled or unskilled, inherently restricted the growth of a diversified economy and that the continued importation of Africans would perpetuate the colony's economic dependence on Great Britain. Notwithstanding the personal discomfort of Robert Beverley and many other slaveholders, the public critique of slavery centered not on the institution as it existed within Virginia but rather on the external slave trade. What unified the opposition to the slave trade and tied it to the broader interest in economic diversification was the fear that unrestricted slave importations would threaten Virginia's economic preeminence among the North American colonies. Many Virginia planters had accumulated and were continuing to accumulate great fortunes through the exploitation of slave labor, but after the mid-eighteenth century, some Virginians became convinced that the predominance of slave labor limited the colonists' ability to compete in the changing markets of the Atlantic economy. By the 1760s, a majority of the House of Burgesses were committed to reversing that reliance on slavery.

The principal argument in opposition to the slave trade was enunciated most articulately and insistently by Richard Henry Lee. As early as 1759 Lee called attention to neighboring colonies which, "though much later than ourselves in point of settlement, are now before us in improvement." The explanation appeared obvious to Lee: "with their whites they import arts and agriculture, whilst we, with our blacks ex-

---

[11]Robert Beverley to Edward Athawes, 11 July 1761, Robert Beverley Letterbook, Library of Congress; Nathaniel Burwell to John Norton, 3 Sep. 1770, *John Norton & Sons*, ed., Mason, 146–47; William Fitzhugh to Stuart & Campbell, 3 Apr. 1772, and John Page to Campbell, 14 June 1773, American Loyalist Claims, Public Record Office, T. 79/12 (Virginia Colonial Records Project microfilm).

clude both. Nature has not partially favoured them with fertility of soil nor do they enjoy more of the sun's cheering and enlivening influence; yet greatly have they outstript us." In fact, no northern colony had "outstript" Virginia in trade or personal wealth, but the rapidity of growth and the economic diversification of places like Philadelphia greatly alarmed those in Virginia who were concerned about the restrictive character of a staple economy and its relatively inflexible labor system.[12]

Twelve years later, following the collapse of the association of 1770, a writer to the *Virginia Gazette* echoed Lee in urging Virginians to establish a permanent ban on slave imports. "Let us endeavour to discourage a Practice which must for ever prevent our Country from flourishing as the northern Colonies have done. A Practice which is a never failing source of ignorance and Vice, of Indolence and Cruelty, amongst us." Slavery was not the only characteristic distinguishing the Chesapeake economy from that of the northern colonies, but as the major source of labor and a significant capital investment, it precluded the flexibility required in manufactures, the production and marketing of food crops, and commercial development. The reliance on slavery also discouraged whites from cultivating the skills and work habits that would contribute to a diversified, commercially competitive economy. The large supply of slave labor might continue to be a source of wealth, but if free, white Virginians were to maintain the colony's economic strength and exploit the full potential of its resources, they needed to curtail the importation of slaves.[13]

During the assembly's debate on slave import duties in 1759, Richard Henry Lee argued that the introduction of new labor through the slave trade prevented Virginia from attracting the skilled European immigrants required for economic diversification. Lee's argument and its various formulations over the next fifteen years became the most frequent case for ending the slave trade in the colony. The House of Burgesses repeated Lee's claim in the 1772 address to the King requesting

[12]Richard Henry Lee, *Memoir of the Life of Richard Henry Lee and His Correspondence*, ed., Richard Henry Lee, 2 vols. (Philadelphia: H. C. Carey and I. Lea, 1825), 1:17–18.

[13]"Associator Humanus," *Virginia Gazette* (Purdie & Dixon), 18 July 1771; *Memoir of Richard Henry Lee*, 1:17–19; Richard K. MacMaster, "Arthur Lee's 'Address on Slavery': An Aspect of Virginia's Struggle to End the Slave Trade, 1765–1774," *Virginia Magazine of History and Biography* 80 (April 1972): 141–57.

authority to impose restrictions on the colony's slave traffic. The slave trade, according to the assembly's petition, "greatly retards the Settlement of the Colonies." This line of thought was so widespread by the summer of 1774 that various county committees, in meetings following the dissolution of the assembly, recommended the nonimportation of slaves as a means of encouraging skilled, free laborers to settle in Virginia. In language first drafted at a meeting in Prince George County, the committees declared the "African Trade is injurious to this Colony, [and] obstructs our Population by Freemen, Manufacturers, and others who would emigrate from Europe and settle here."[14]

In the midst of the Stamp Act Crisis, George Mason argued that slavery was linked inextricably with economic decline. Recalling the example of ancient Rome, he reminded Virginians that "one of the first signs of the Decay, & perhaps the primary cause of the Destruction of the most flourishing Government that ever existed was the Introduction of great Numbers of Slaves." Mason anticipated that legislative impediments to the slave trade would encourage a more productive use of land than was possible with slave-based agriculture and thereby accelerate the pace of westward settlement.[15]

Mason and others expected a cessation or reduction of slave imports would contribute to the expansion of tenantry in the colony. The increased incidence of tenantry in the years before Independence had several sources, one of which was the advantage it held as a system of land management for large planters who formerly supervised the cultivation of their estates by their own slaves. Renting to tenant families allowed these planters to improve new lands more rapidly and more economically than was possible with their own labor supply and the necessary hiring of overseers. Tenants with sufficient income offered the added advantage of hiring the landowners' surplus slaves. Richard Henry Lee rented out much of his land as well as most of his slaves. In addition to personal advantages for large planters, Mason and Richard Henry Lee believed "that the Custom of leasing lands is more beneficial

[14]*Memoir of the Life of Richard Henry Lee*, ed., Lee, 1:17–18; *Journals of the House of Burgesses, 1770–1772*, eds., Kennedy and McIlwaine, 283–84; Proceedings of the committees of Caroline, Culpeper, Nansemond, Prince George, Princess Anne, and Surry Counties in *Revolutionary Virginia*, eds., Scribner and Tarter, 1:116, 119, 146, 151, 162.

[15]George Mason, "Scheme for Replevying Goods and Distress for Rent," 23 Dec. 1765, *Papers of George Mason*, ed., Rutland, 1:61–62.

to the Community than that of settling them with Slaves." Lee urged others to rent land as a way of distributing the advantages of property to all white Virginians. George Washington, who rented an increasing portion of his eastern estates to tenants, planned to settle his western bounty lands with German redemptioners and Scots-Irish immigrants who would sit as tenants, thereby freeing himself and new settlers from a deepening commitment to slavery. Following Dunmore's Proclamation in 1775, William Lee, from the safe distance of London, went so far as to suggest the slaves themselves might be freed and made tenants.[16]

The critique of slavery and the slave trade in Virginia was only occasionally and peripherally humanitarian in origin. Petersburg merchant Robert Pleasants and other Quakers kept their Philadelphia brethren informed about anti-slavery activity in Virginia, but they had only a fringe audience in the colony and made no impact on the efforts to restrict the slave trade. Isolated individuals like Arthur Lee publicly opposed the institution on moral grounds, though Lee was more concerned about the effects on whites than on blacks whom he considered "abominable objects." Humanitarian arguments, like references to the security threats posed by a large slave population, were most common in appeals to royal officials and Parliament. Although humanitarian rhetoric became more common in the years immediately preceding the Revolution, few advocated any interference with the institution of slavery within Virginia. The argument against the slave trade remained essentially one of political economy, and the campaign to restrict slave imports paralleled commercial resistance and the broader search for economic independence.[17]

■   ■   ■

[16]George Mason, "Scheme for Replevying Goods and Distress for Rent," 23 Dec. 1765, *Papers of George Mason*, ed., Rutland, 1:61–62; George Washington to James Tilghman, Jr., 17 Feb. 1774, George Washington to Henry Riddell, 22 Feb. 1774, Washington Papers, Library of Congress; Freeman, *George Washington*, 3:327–28, 343; "Rusticus" [Richard Henry Lee] to Rind, [176–], *Lee Family Papers* (University of Virginia microfilm publication); William Lee to Robert Carter Nicholas, 6 Mar. 1775, William Lee Letterbook, 1774–1775, Virginia Historical Society.

[17]Robert Pleasants to Anthony Benezet, 22 Feb. 1774, Robert Pleasants Letterbook, Library of Congress; Arthur Lee to Richard Henry Lee, 20 Mar.

"A new and accurate map of Virginia." By John Henry. Engraved by
Thomas Jeffrys, geographer to the King. London. February 1770. In
the midst of the House of Burgesses' efforts to impose a prohibitive
duty on slave imports, the engraver of John Henry's map of the colony
illustrated British assumptions regarding the correlation between slave
labor and the agricultural bounty of Virginia. (Library of Congress)

As long as Virginia was a colony of Great Britain, the House of
Burgesses was unable to close the slave trade, but the assembly was able
to regulate the flow of slave imports in the colony through its imposition of duties. Throughout the eighteenth century the burgesses enacted a series of import duties that served variously as a source of revenue
and a means of regulating the trade. The first duty, established in 1699,
was a 20 shilling levy on each imported slave. The assembly allocated
the proceeds to help finance construction of the new capitol building in
Williamsburg. The burgesses renewed this duty several times before
1710 when they replaced it with a substantial £5 duty on new slaves.
The higher duty, twice renewed before its expiration in 1718, was a
valuable source of revenue for public projects, but the assembly also
intended it to act as a curb on the rush of slaves imported into the colony.
Rumors of slave insurrections had raised fears about the colony's ability

---

1765, *Lee Family Papers* (University of Virginia microfilm publication);
MacMaster, "Arthur Lee's 'Address on Slavery,'" 141–57.

to assimilate safely the large importations of Africans. The burgesses wanted a duty that permitted slave imports but at a pace that better assured the security of whites in the colony. The slower rate of importation also would provide planters an opportunity to reduce the often reckless debts accumulated in their frenzied purchase of slaves. Governor Spotswood feared the duty might prove prohibitive, but demand was so strong that over 4,000 slaves entered Virginia between 1710 and 1718.[18]

Twice in the 1720s, the House of Burgesses attempted without success to secure another slave duty that would operate as something more than a source of revenue. These efforts were the clearest precedent for the movement to restrict the slave trade in the 1760s. Large tobacco crops and slackening demand for the commodity in Europe made the depression of the 1720s a serious economic crisis for Virginia planters. In response to these pressures, a group of planters in the assembly argued that Virginians could avoid the dangers of periodic depressions only if they reduced their dependence on tobacco as the sole export crop. In 1723, these burgesses gained approval of a discriminatory duty of 40 shillings on imported slaves as part of a broader program to discourage the expansion of tobacco production. Despite approval by the assembly and the reluctant consent of Governor Drysdale, many slaveholders in Virginia opposed the duty, and the Crown disallowed the act. As overproduction and low prices continued to plague the tobacco market through the 1720s, the assembly in 1728 again approved a 40 shilling duty on imported slaves, this time with the full support of Governor William Gooch. The ministry, unwilling to approve any measure that might lower revenues from tobacco duties or limit the interests of British traders, disallowed the second duty as well.[19]

In 1732, the Virginia assembly succeeded in overcoming the British government's resistance to any duty paid by merchants or shippers and won approval for a five percent *ad valorem* duty on imported slaves, to be paid by the purchaser. The revenue measure had no discernible effect on the record slave imports of the 1730s and 1740s. With the ex-

[18]Darold D. Wax, "Negro Import Duties in Colonial Virginia: A Study in British Commercial Policy and Local Public Policy," *Virginia Magazine of History and Biography* 79 (January 1971): 32–35.

[19]Ibid., 35–36; Hemphill, *Virginia and the English Commercial System*, 66–71, 88–91; *Documents Illustrative of the History of the Slave Trade to America*, 4 vols., ed., Elizabeth Donnan (Washington, 1935), 4:102–17, 122–27.

ception of a six-month lapse in 1751, regular extensions by the assembly maintained this base duty of five percent until 1773.[20] The success of the duty in raising revenue without disturbing the slave trade persuaded the House of Burgesses to increase periodically the duty in order to answer temporary financial demands. Between 1740 and 1744, an additional duty of five percent helped defray the costs of establishing defenses and enlisting troops for the war against Spain. Another five percent duty in 1754 provided security for a £10,000 loan the assembly used to encourage settlement along the waters of the Mississippi. This added income proved so useful that the burgesses, even after abandoning their support for western settlement, continued the additional five percent duty until 1771, thereby raising to ten percent the base levy paid on slaves imported after 1754.[21]

When faced with the unprecedented requirements of financing its part in the French and Indian War, Virginia's assembly again turned to the slave duty to help meet the costs of military preparation. An act of 1755 raising £20,000 for protection against the French included the imposition of an additional ten percent *ad valorem* duty on imported slaves. Two years later the assembly approved another slave duty of ten percent. The accumulated duties, now totaling 30 percent and coinciding with the wartime disruption of shipping, effectively closed Virginia's

---

[20]Text of the Act of 1732 in *Hening's Statutes*, 4:317–24. The act was continued in 1734, *Hening's Statutes*, 4:394; in 1738, *Hening's Statutes*, 5:28–31; in 1742, *Hening's Statutes*, 5:160–61; in 1745, *Hening's Statutes*, 5:318–19. After expiring on 31 July 1751, the act was revived by the assembly in April 1752, *Hening's Statutes*, 6:217–21; and continued in 1753, *Hening's Statutes*, 6:354–55; in 1759, *Hening's Statutes*, 7:281; in 1766, *Hening's Statutes*, 8:193–94; in 1769, *Hening's Statutes*, 8:336–37; and finally in 1772, *Hening's Statutes*, 8:530–32.

[21]*Hening's Statutes*, 5:92–93. The assembly renewed this duty in June 1742, but the governor withheld his approval. Philip Ludwell moved to revive the duty of 1740 in October 1744, but the motion failed. Carter Burwell suggested another five percent increase in December 1748, and this motion also failed. *Journals of the House of Burgesses, 1742–1747, 1748–1749*, eds., Kennedy and McIlwaine, 62, 69, 139, 322–25. The act for the duty of 1754 is printed in *Hening's Statutes*, 6:419. Acts continuing this duty in 1755, *Hening's Statutes*, 6:468–70; in 1759, *Hening's Statutes*, 7:282–83; in 1763, *Hening's Statutes*, 7:639–42; and in 1769 when it was included in "An Act for the better support of the contingent charges of government," *Hening's Statutes*, 8:342–48.

slave trade. No African slaves arrived in 1756, 1757, or 1759; total registered imports for the years 1756–1759 amounted to only 60 slaves.[22]

The assembly received reports of more slaves being brought illegally into Virginia through Maryland and North Carolina, and in 1759 it imposed a 20 percent duty on all slaves imported into Virginia from Maryland, the Carolinas, or the West Indies for a planter's own use. Without slave imports, of course, the levies did not serve the purpose of raising revenues, and so the assembly as early as March 1759 considered reducing the slave duties. In 1760, citing the discouragement to western settlement and the increased custom abuses as well as the lack of significant revenue, the House of Burgesses repealed the ten percent duty established in 1755. The following year they eliminated the ten percent duty from 1757.[23]

The increased duties of 1755 and 1757 were desperate revenue measures, but their prohibitory effect encouraged those who subsequently wished to reduce Virginia's reliance on slave labor. The debate in 1759 on the motion for repeal of the duties marked the first time since the 1720s that the assembly discussed slave duties in terms of restricting the trade. Richard Henry Lee, who had entered the House only one year earlier, argued for continuing the higher duties as a means of limiting Virginia's involvement with the institution of slavery. In one of the strongest public attacks on slavery in Virginia during the late colonial period, Lee ignored the issue of revenue and focused on the questions of political economy and morality that he associated with slavery.[24]

When the motion for repeal of the duty of 1755 came up again in 1760, the assembly approved the measure only by a single vote. Governor Francis Fauquier feared the sharp political division produced by this issue would continue during the following session when the assembly discussed repeal of the duty of 1757. Fauquier considered the debate on slave duties representative of a broader conflict between opposing economic interests in the colony. "The Contest on this Occasion is between the old Settlers who have bred great Quantity of Slaves, and would

[22]*Hening's Statutes*, 6:461–68; *Hening's Statutes*, 7:81; annual imports in *Virginia Slave Trade Statistics*, eds., Minchinton et al., 157–59.

[23]*Hening's Statutes*, 7:338–40, 363, 383; *Journals of the House of Burgesses, 1758–1761*, eds., Kennedy and McIlwaine, 95–96.

[24]*Memoir of the Life of Richard Henry Lee*, ed., Lee, 1:17–19.

make a Monopoly of them by a Duty which they hope would amount to a prohibition; and the rising Generation who want Slaves, and don't care to pay the Monopolists for them at the price they have lately bore, which was exceedingly high." Fauquier conceded that "these reasons . . . are not urged in the arguments on either side; but I believe are the true foundation of the Squabble." Certainly Tidewater planters were willing to take advantage of any such opportunities (Richard Henry Lee, to the dismay of his brothers in London, negotiated for a cargo of Africans while he campaigned for an end to the slave trade), but the potential for profits from an internal slave trade at this time was too limited and too short-lived to explain the depth of support for restricting slave imports. Advocates of a prohibitive slave duty consistently maintained that an end to slave imports would result in an overall reduction in the reliance on slave labor. The political division was not based on the narrowly-defined self-interests described by Fauquier, however, a real antagonism did exist between the proponents of a limited slave trade and those who believed more slaves would improve the economic status of small planters.[25]

Following the repeal of the duty of 1755, the assembly received and rejected a petition from "sundry inhabitants" of the Northern Neck asking for a reduction of the 20 percent duty on slaves imported from Maryland, the Carolinas, and the West Indies. This appeal presumably came from small planters or tenants along the Potomac who purchased slaves in Maryland rather than from gentry planters in the area, most of whom supported limitations on the slave trade. Fauquier had his own doubts about the legality of this duty which he reluctantly approved only after the Council assured him that it imposed no additional duty, rather it enforced a standing act. Matthew Lamb, the legal counsel for the Board of Trade, found no objection to the levy. The heavier duty on the intercolonial slave trade remained in effect because it served the interests of several powerful groups. Advocates of a restricted slave trade welcomed any duty that might limit the arrival of new slaves. Planters of the Upper James district hoped the duty would encourage the importation of African slaves rather than those from the West Indies whom they considered less desirable. And the Board of Trade approved of any

[25]Francis Fauquier to the Board of Trade, 2 June 1760, *The Official Papers of Francis Fauquier*, ed., Reese, 1:372.

measure that discriminated in favor of British shippers in the African trade.[26]

The return to a ten percent duty on slaves and the economic resurgence of the early 1760s attracted to Virginia slave traders who brought 4,931 slaves between 1761 and 1763. With the onset of another depression, slave imports dropped to 974 in 1764 and to a negligible 180 in 1765. Opposition to the slave trade, however, did not disappear in the face of reduced imports. The resistance to the Stamp Act in 1765 called fresh attention to the limitations of an agricultural economy reliant on slavery and the production of a staple crop. Various proposals for reducing British imports at this time included suggestions for the more productive use of slave labor in domestic manufactures. Private interest in developing a skilled labor force and reducing dependence on tobacco cultivation continued after the repeal of the Stamp Act in 1766. By 1767, a majority of the burgesses were convinced that a prohibitive duty on slave imports would contribute to a diversification of the economy and greater self-sufficiency.[27]

In 1763, the assembly renewed the five percent duty of 1754 under a new "Act for continuing and appropriating the additional duty upon slaves." This act, together with the renewal in 1766 of the original five percent duty from 1732, extended to 1770 a base slave import duty of ten percent. Then on March 23, 1767, the House of Burgesses ordered Henry Lee and John Bolling to prepare a bill for establishing an additional duty on slaves imported into Virginia. The bill that Henry Lee reported to the House on March 28 called for a ten percent duty, to be paid by the purchaser, "over and above the several duties already laid upon slaves imported or brought into this colony." The bill stated that such a duty was the only possible import or export levy that would not be an oppressive burden. The assembly reserved the right to apply the revenue from the new duty to a reduction in the poll tax or to any other

[26]*Journals of the House of Burgesses, 1758–1761*, eds., Kennedy and McIlwaine, 211; Fauquier to the Board of Trade, 1 Sept., 1760, in *The Official Papers of Francis Fauquier*, ed., Reese, 1:404; Francis Fauquier to the Board of Trade, 2 June 1760, in *Documents Illustrative of the History of the Slave Trade*, 4:145; Wax, "Negro Import Duties in Colonial Virginia," 39–40; Arthur Lee to Richard Henry Lee, 14 Feb 1773, *Lee Family Papers* (University of Virginia microfilm publication); William Lee to Richard Henry Lee, 23 Feb. 1773, Richard Henry Lee Correspondence, Virginia Historical Society.

[27]Import figures in *Virginia Slave Trade Statistics*, eds., Minchinton, et al., xv.

purpose on which it later determined. The publication on March 19 of Arthur Lee's address to the House of Burgesses, calling for an end to the slave trade, suggests the bill was far more than a revenue measure and that the burgesses in Williamsburg had been discussing the merits of limiting the importation of slaves.[28]

The burgesses recognized that the prohibitive level of the proposed duty might meet objections in London. The third article of the act as passed by the House on April 9 and approved by the council and governor suspended enforcement of the duty pending the Crown's assent. Although the Board of Trade and the King's Privy Council had consented to earlier duties providing revenue, Fauquier's refusal to approve any new duty in 1759 raised doubts about London's reaction to this act. The burgesses' committee of correspondence directed its agent, Edward Montague, to use his best abilities to secure the King's approval. When the Board of Trade referred the act to Matthew Lamb, he questioned whether the act conflicted with the governor's instructions to withhold approval from any slave duties which fell on the shipper. He also was disturbed by the act's preamble which declared all other duties to be oppressive. The Board of Trade too found the preamble disturbing, and it recommended disallowance of the act. At this time the board held "no particular objection" to the substance of the act, but in the midst of the American protest of the Townshend duties it was hesitant to approve a colonial law that asserted the provincial assembly's reluctance to submit to other revenue measures. If the board permitted such an act it would "only operate to restrain and deter the Legislature of Virginia from making further Provisions if such shall be required of them in future cases of Emergency." The board's report made no reference to the duty's potential effect on the slave trade. The Privy Council accepted the board's recommendation, and on August 18, 1768, John Pownall informed Governor Botetourt of the disallowance of the act which never had gone into effect.[29]

---

[28]*Hening's Statutes*, 7:639–42; *Hening's Statutes*, 8:193–94, 237–38; *Journals of the House of Burgesses, 1766–1769*, eds., Kennedy and McIlwaine, 92, 101; text of Lee's address in MacMaster, "Arthur Lee's 'Address on Slavery,'" 153–57.

[29]*Journals of the House of Burgesses, 1766–1769*, eds., Kennedy and McIlwaine, 119, 123, 125, 129; *Hening's Statutes*, 8:237–38; Lamb's report in Public Record Office, CO5/1332, ff. 35–36; Board of Trade to His Majesty, 29 July 1768, Public Record Office, CO5/1368, ff. 184 (Virginia Colonial Records Project microfilm).

During the first session of the assembly following the disallowance of the act of 1767, the burgesses renewed their effort to establish an additional duty on imported slaves. On May 17, 1769, the day Governor Botetourt dissolved the assembly and one day before the creation of the nonimportation association that included a prohibition of slave importations, the House of Burgesses ordered the committee on propositions and grievances to prepare a bill to lay an additional duty on slaves. When the assembly reconvened in November 1769 the House repeated the order, this time to the committee of trade. The bill enacted on December 20 imposed an additional ten percent duty similar to that in the act of 1767. This time the burgesses omitted the offending preamble and promised to direct the new revenue to cover the expense of colonial government. This act also contained a clause suspending enforcement until the King granted his approval.[30]

At the November session the burgesses reorganized the existing legislation covering slave duties so as to make the renewal of duties simpler and to protect the base duty on slaves imported from Africa. The original five percent duty, dating form 1732, and the 20 percent duty on slaves brought from Maryland, the Carolinas, and the West Indies were now combined in a single act and extended until April 1773. The other five percent duty on imported slaves, originally part of "An Act for the encouragement and protection of settlers upon the waters of the Mississippi," and more recently included in "An Act for continuing and appropriating the additional duty on slaves . . ." was now encompassed by "An Act for the better support of the contingent charges of government" which was to be in effect until October 1771. These alterations may have eased matters for the burgesses, but they further complicated the maze of slave duty legislation and dangerously confused the Board of Trade.[31]

In Great Britain, slave traders and government officials reacted to the prohibitory intent of Virginia's new duty legislation. Merchants from Liverpool, Bristol, and Lancaster petitioned the Board of Trade for disallowance of the additional duty which they claimed was actually a tax on the importer and would operate to the discouragement of British trade. The Liverpool merchants argued that the colonial slave trade was valuable for all Britons because it encouraged the cultivation of cash

---

[30]*Journals of the House of Burgesses, 1766–1769*, eds., Kennedy and McIlwaine, 217, 289, 350; *Hening's Statutes*, 8:337–38.

[31]*Journals of the House of Burgesses, 1766–1769*, eds., Kennedy and McIlwaine, 289, 302, 310; *Hening's Statutes*, 8:336–37, 342–48.

crops and promoted the nation's foreign trade. Richard Jackson, legal counsel for the Board of Trade, found the act for an additional duty to be legally proper but questioned the commercial wisdom of allowing a high duty on so valuable an article of British trade. Jackson recommended the board members approve the additional duty only if they found Virginia to be populated sufficiently with slaves or if they wished to redirect slave shipments to the West Indian islands recently ceded to Great Britain under the terms of the Treaty of 1763. The Board of Trade, which had considered the additional duty of 1767 solely as a question of revenue laws and imperial sovereignty, now believed the possible interference with the slave trade to be so important a matter that it delayed its decision for four months after receiving the merchants' petitions and Jackson's legal report.[32]

In November of 1770, the Board of Trade advised the King and his Council to disallow Virginia's act imposing an additional duty on imported slaves and to forbid the continuation of the "Act for the better support of the contingent charges of government." The board mistakenly believed the latter act created a new duty which would increase to 25 percent the total charge on imported slaves. According to the Board of Trade, Virginia's assembly intended to prohibit absolutely the slave trade. Such an action, in the board's opinion, would damage the economy of Great Britain and the colony. The lack of new slaves necessarily would limit tobacco production which would in turn raise prices, reduce consumption, and ultimately diminish the Crown's revenue from the tobacco trade. In support of its recommendations, the board also transmitted a 1728 report that another board had prepared following an earlier attempt to establish a prohibitive slave duty in Virginia.[33]

The Privy Council accepted the board's recommendation and accompanied its disallowance with additional instructions to Virginia's

[32]Petition to the Board of Trade from Merchants of Lancaster, 2 June 1770, Public Record Office, CO5/1332, f. 192; Petition to the Board of Trade from Merchants of Liverpool, 7 June 1770, Public Record Office, CO5/1332, f. 193; Board of Trade to His Majesty, 23 November 1770, Public Record Office, CO5/1336, ff. 182–85 refers to petitions from Lancaster, Liverpool, and Bristol; Richard Jackson to Board of Trade, 18 July 1770, Public Record Office, CO5/1332, ff. 203–04; John Pownall to Bamber Gascoyne, 20 July 1770, Public Record Office, CO5/1368, ff. 19 (Virginia Colonial Records Project microfilm).

[33]Board of Trade to His Majesty, 23 Nov. 1770, Public Record Office, CO5/1369, ff. 26–28; Board of Trade to His Majesty's Council, 23 Nov. 1770, Public Record Office, CO5/1369, ff. 5–54 (Virginia Colonial Records Project microfilm).

governor, ordering him to withhold approval from a renewal of the "Act for the better support of the contingent charges of government" and from any act that increased the original duty of ten percent or interfered with the importation of slaves. The insistence on a duty no greater than ten percent suggests that the council might have disallowed the additional duty even if it had understood that the "Act for the support of the contingent charges . . ." did not impose a new duty. In any case, the additional instructions had the effect of lowering Virginia's import duty on slaves to the lowest level since 1753 and barred the assembly from further regulating the slave trade in the colony. Acting Governor William Nelson, in a letter to the secretary of state, attempted to clarify the confusion over Virginia's recent duty legislation but to no avail. The colony's new governor, Lord Dunmore, arrived in September 1771 with orders to reject any additional duties on slave imports.[34]

The associations' prohibitions of slave imports was ineffective in the face of renewed demand for imported slaves in 1770 and 1771. The availability of British credit and the rising tobacco market encouraged planters in the Upper James River district to invest in newly-arrived slaves. In both 1770 and 1771, more slaves were brought to the colony than in any year since 1764. In the early months of 1772, before the credit collapse in Great Britain, Virginia imported more slaves than in the two previous years combined. Support for closing off the slave trade, however, continued after the dissolution of the association of 1770 and after the Privy Council refused to permit higher duties. The burgesses maintained their opposition to the unrestricted slave trade during the years from 1769 to 1772 when Virginia enjoyed a favorable balance of trade. In July 1771, "Associator Humanus," a contributor to the *Virginia Gazette*, suggested that the association's article forbidding the im-

---

[34]Disallowance on 9 Dec. 1770, Privy Council Register, Public Record Office, PC2/114, 653; Additional Instructions to Virginia's Governor, 10 Dec. 1770, Public Record Office, PC2/114, 653–54. The Board of Trade wrote to Botetourt (who in fact had died previously) on 5 Dec. 1770 informing him of their recommendation for a disallowance of the slave duty act and for not continuing the "Act for the better support of the contingent charges of government," Public Record Office, CO5/1369, ff. 28–30. On 11 Dec. 1770, Hillsborough sent acting Governor William Nelson the Orders in Council for the disallowance and the Additional Instructions, Public Record Office, CO5/1375, ff. 55–56; Copy of additional instructions in CO5/1375, ff. 82–83; Dunmore's Instructions regarding future slave duties, 30 Jan. 1771, Public Record Office, CO5/1369, ff. 124–25 (Virginia Colonial Record Projects microfilm).

portation of slaves be made "perpetual, and most strictly obligatory." A coercive association was the only way to overcome the objections of a ministry which endeavored to increase the number of slaves in the colony and would never approve an additional duty. Some plan for ending slave imports was necessary, the writer argued, if the Virginians were to maintain ideological consistency and encourage economic development.[35]

The special assembly of July 1771, called to provide public relief for losses in the spring flood, did not take any action regarding the slave trade or the disallowed duties. When the next assembly convened in February 1772, it attempted to reinstate the long-standing ten percent duty. The bill presenting "An Act for continuing and amending several acts, and reviving one act, for laying duties" with the five percent duty from the recently expired and now forbidden "Act for the better support of the contingent charges of government," passed in 1769. In an attempt to convince the Board of Trade that the new bill was not for an additional duty or a limitation on the slave trade, the text of the act explained the history of the second duty from its inception in 1754. The burgesses also included in the bill a continuation of the duty on slaves imported from Maryland, the Carolinas, and the West Indies, although they changed the rate from 20 percent *ad valorem* to a flat £5 per slave. Finally, the act created a new collection procedure by which the burgesses hoped to end fraud and smuggling.[36]

Before passing the act for a slave duty on March 21, the House agreed to send an address to the King asking for permission to limit the slave traffic to Virginia. The burgesses appointed a committee composed of Benjamin Harrison, Archibald Cary, Edmund Pendleton, Richard Henry Lee, Robert Carter Nicholas, and Richard Bland to draw up the address which was unanimously approved and presented by the assembly on April 1, 1772. The Virginians acknowledged the value of the slave trade for some merchants in Great Britain, but they argued that the prohibition of the trade would encourage the settlement of the colonies "with more useful inhabitants" to the eventual benefit of the whole Empire. The burgesses' appeal also emphasized the inhumanity of the trade and the potential threat that unchecked importations might present to the security of the American colonies. In the hope "that the Interest of a few will be disregarded when placed in Competition with the Security and Happiness of such Numbers," the burgesses requested

[35]*Virginia Slave Trade Statistics*, eds., Minchinton, et al., xv; "Associator Humanus," *Virginia Gazette* (Purdie & Dixon), 18 July 1771.

[36]*Journals of the House of Burgesses, 1770–1772*, eds., Kennedy and McIlwaine, 246, 248, 263; *Hening's Statutes*, 8:530–32.

that the King "remove all Restraints on your Majesty's Governors of this Colony, which inhibit their assenting to such laws as might check so very pernicious a Commerce."[37]

Governor Dunmore agreed to support the burgesses' address, although for his own particular reasons. After six months in Virginia, Dunmore had an exaggerated fear of the colony's blacks (whom he thought outnumbered whites by two to one), and his argument against the slave trade rested on his own considerations of security. With ironic prescience, he suggested an enemy army might draw support from Virginia's slaves and "encourage them to revenge themselves; by which means a conquest of this Country would inevitably be effected in a very short time." The secretary of state, Lord Hillsborough, referred Dunmore's supporting letter and the burgesses' address to the Privy Council, but he gave Dunmore little reason to expect satisfaction. The council initially directed the address to its committee for plantation affairs and five months later passed it off on the Board of Trade. In January of 1773, the board read the appeal and Dunmore's letter but recorded no further action on the matter.[38]

Virginia's new slave duty act fared as badly as the address to the King. The Board of Trade considered the revival of the duty from the earlier "Act for the better support of the contingent charges of government" to be a direct violation of the governor's instructions. The board's report to the King repeated its earlier arguments about the dangers to the "commerce & manufactures of this Kingdom" that would result from prohibitive slave duties, and it recommended disallowance of the entire act of 1772. The Privy Council agreed and in April 1773 Lord Dartmouth, the new secretary of state, transmitted to Dunmore news of the disallowance, along with the report of the Board of Trade. Dunmore defended his support, insisting that the act only restored the traditional ten percent duty rather than create a prohibitive tax, but the board adhered to its position and sent Dunmore additional instructions to reject any further duties.[39]

[37]*Journals of the House of Burgesses*, 1770–1772, eds., Kennedy and McIlwaine, 256–57, 283–84.

[38]Dunmore to Hillsborough, 1 May 1772, Public Record Office, CO5/1350, ff. 46–47; Hillsborough to Dunmore, 1 July 1772, Public Record Office, CO5/1350, ff. 472–73; Privy Council Register, 31 July 1772, and 19 Dec. 1772, Public Record Office, PC2/116, p. 395–96, 524; Journal of the Board of Trade, 25 Jan. 1773, Public Record Office, ff. 8–9 (Virginia Colonial Records Project microfilm).

[39]Board of Trade to His Majesty, 11 Mar. 1773, Public Record Office, CO5/1350, ff. 217–21; Privy Council Register, 5 Apr. and 7 Apr. 1773, Public Record

When the last slave duties expired in April 1773, the economic collapse of the previous year had quieted what remained of a demand for new slaves in Virginia. The issue of the slave trade returned, however, in the spring and summer of 1774 when various county committees and the provincial association demanded a prohibition of slave imports. The assembly of May 1774 considered a revival of the duty act of 1769, but the governor's dissolution prevented a vote on the bill. In the final session of June 1775, the burgesses again reported a bill to reestablish the original five percent duty, along with the duty on slaves imported from neighboring colonies and the West Indies. The House later included these measures and another five percent duty in a bill for appointing commissions to settle the accounts on the militia. Dunmore, who already had withdrawn to the safety of a British naval vessel, refused to approve the bill on the grounds that it was contrary to his instructions forbidding prohibitive slave duties. The House replied that ten percent duties were never considered prohibitive, but the ordinance as enacted by the assembly omitted the duties, probably because the collapse of the customs service prevented enforcement. Although the colonial assembly never had another opportunity to limit the slave trade, its repeated efforts finally reached fruition in 1778 when the assembly of the Commonwealth of Virginia became one of the first legislative body in the Americas to abolish the slave trade.[40]

■   ■   ■

During the Virginia ratifying convention of 1788, George Mason referred to the royal disallowance of prohibitive slave duties as "one of the great causes of our separation from Great Britain." Allowing for the hyperbole of political debate, this statement reflected a widely held belief that was most clearly articulated by Thomas Jefferson in the *Summary View* and in his draft of the Declaration of Independence. The

---

Office, PC2/117, p. 131–32, 160–62; Dartmouth to Dunmore, 10 Apr. 1773, Public Record Office, CO5/1351, ff. 18–19; Dunmore to Dartmouth, 9 July 1773, Public Record Office, CO5/1351, ff. 63–65; additional instructions sent to Dunmore by the Board of Trade on 27 October 1773, Public Record Office, CO5/1351, (the latter does not contain the exact text of the instructions but refers to the Board as having been correct on the matter of the additional duty.) (Virginia Colonial Records Project microfilm.)

[40]*Journals of the House of Burgesses, 1773–1776,* eds., Kennedy and McIlwaine, 85, 91, 201, 208, 278–80; *Hening's Statutes,* 9:61–71, 471–72.

royal government, Jefferson charged, had forced slavery upon the colonies in their "infant state"; more recently George III had exacerbated the wrongs of his predecessors by rejecting colonial attempts to halt the slave traffic, "thus preferring the immediate advantages of a few British corsairs to the lasting interests of the American states."[41]

British responsibility for the introduction and subsequent support of colonial slavery was a comforting fact for Americans trying to reconcile slaveholding with republican political principles. Jefferson's charges would become a central myth in the southern defense of slavery in the nineteenth century. The involvement of the British in the development of American slavery, of course, was no absolution of the white Virginians who purchased the Africans and made the decision to perpetuate the bondage of slaves and their descendants. Yet, in the 1770s, Jefferson's remarks contained an accurate critique of imperial policy. The British had protected slavery because the institution was essential to a mercantilist policy that encouraged colonial production of raw goods and restricted the development of manufacturing in the colonies. The continued vitality of the slave trade also strengthened British shipping interests and was an important contribution to Great Britain's balance of trade. White landholders in Virginia had benefited as well from the British-supplied labor during the years of expanding tobacco production, but by the third quarter of the eighteenth century many Virginians considered the state-supported trade to be one of several obstacles to the development of the economic potential of the colony. The failure of the various efforts to prohibit the trade heightened frustrations with the British government and made more ironic Virginia's deepening commitment to slavery in the decades following the Revolution.[42]

---

[41]George Mason in the Virginia Ratifying Convention, 17 June 1788, *Papers of George Mason*, ed., Rutland, 3:1086; Thomas Jefferson, Draft of Instructions to the Virginia Delegates in the Continental Congress (MS text of *A Summary View*) and draft of the Declaration of Independence, in *Papers of Thomas Jefferson*, ed., Boyd, 1:129–30, 317–18.

[42]Rawley, *The Transatlantic Slave Trade*, ch. 11; Richard S. Dunn, "Black Society in the Chesapeake, 1776–1810," in *Slavery and Freedom in the Age of the American Revolution*, eds., Ira Berlin and Ronald Hoffman (Charlottesville: University Press of Virginia, 1983), 49–83.

COMMERCIAL DEVELOPMENT AND THE CREDIT CRISIS OF 1772

Iℕ ᴛʜᴇ ᴍɪᴅsᴛ ᴏꜰ ᴛʜᴇ ᴀssᴏᴄɪᴀᴛɪᴏɴ ᴏꜰ 1769, Virginia merchants Hartwell Cocke and Alexander Trent ordered from London a large assortment of goods, some of which were in violation of the terms of the nonimportation agreement. Their London agent, fellow Virginian Thomas Adams, was reluctant to ship the large cargo before a repeal of the Townshend duties or word of a revision of the association. A correspondent of Adams' in Virginia, however, assured him that no one would challenge a cargo of goods for Cocke or Trent. "The country seems inclined to indulge these Gentlemen as much as possible as they are great champions to oppose the Scotch Interest & it would be a Sin to leave them to Combat on unequal terms." The desire to supplant the Scottish factors and develop a native commercial establishment, it would seem, took precedence over the immediate goals of the nonimportation associations.[1]

The organization of commercial resistance in Virginia demonstrated anew the difficulty of establishing any measure of economic independence in a colony with few commercial resources of its own. Virginians attempting to reduce imports and develop domestic manufactures gained a keen awareness of the limited options available in an economy for which the tobacco trade with Great Britain remained the only regular source of substantial credit. As early as the Stamp Act crisis, supporters

---

[1] William Brown to Thomas Adams, 16 June 1770, Perkins, Buchanan, & Brown to Thomas Adams, 9 Apr. 1770, Thomas Adams Letters, Adams Family Papers, Virginia Historical Society.

of commercial resistance recognized that an effective defense against interference from Parliament or the demands of British merchants would require an ongoing effort to restructure certain aspects of the colony's plantation economy. The campaign against the slave trade was one manifestation of this attempt to provide a greater variety of opportunities for Virginia planters. The organization of commercial resistance also inspired a broad array of proposals and experiments designed to enhance the commercial flexibility of Virginia's economy. In the late 1760s and early 1770s, Virginians explored various means of expanding the indigenous commercial community in the hopes of competing in the tobacco trade and tapping other markets. The related interest in the diversification of produce available for export was intended to allow Virginians to take advantage of varied opportunities throughout the Atlantic economy. Without challenging the essential agricultural orientation of the colony's economy, the proper degree of commercial development would enable planters to maintain the viability of their estates at the same time that they curtailed their reliance on British merchants.

■   ■   ■

The failure to reduce imports during the associations of 1769 and 1770 called particular attention to the need for an independent commercial establishment in Virginia. In contrast to Virginia, the northern colonies with thriving merchant communities of their own and more diversified economies effectively reduced British imports during the observation of their local associations. The best efforts of Virginia's great planters, however, had been insufficient to establish a substitute for the credit and essential commodities supplied by British merchants. The influence of British factors operating in the colony overwhelmed the planters and resident merchants who adhered to the nonimportation agreements.

Throughout 1770, several writers in the *Virginia Gazette* recognized that Virginians would not be able to control their own economic affairs until the colony established certain commercial advantages beyond the scope of the current association. The prosperity of a nation's commerce determined its wealth, according to one writer, but Virginia did not enjoy the benefits of any significant commercial activity. "The tobacco trade cannot so properly be called the trade of this colony as of Great Britain, in as much as the merchants concerned therein mostly reside there, where the profits centre." Another writer cited the rise of

Glasgow's merchant class in recent years as an indication of "what wealth is lost to the colony by inhabitants not having a greater interest in the commerce of the country." Great Britain achieved her preeminence through a strict regard for trade and commerce, and Virginia needed to follow her example if the colony were to secure economic prosperity.[2]

"A Friend to Virginia" realized that the absence of a strong merchant community, like the dependence on slave labor, deprived Virginia of the economic benefits that several northern colonies appeared to enjoy in the third quarter of the eighteenth century. Virginia possessed the greatest of natural advantages, yet the northern colonies "have supplied by industry and trade ... what their natural situation denies." Philadelphia, "though but of yesterday as to us," was a city comparable to those of Europe. Trade from that port as well as from New York and Newport extended the cities' influence to Europe and Africa. The commercial success of northern ports also threatened to absorb a share of Virginia's own trade. The ports traded without the supposed advantage of a staple crop, but "they have outdone those that boast a certain and dependable one and even from the very shores of such colonies, they gather wealth." Virginia's export and import trade remained the most valuable of all the mainland British colonies, but the recent and rapid expansion of trade in the port cities of the northern colonies offered opportunities unavailable in the Chesapeake. Only an encouragement of similar trading interests in the colony would allow Virginians to build on its natural riches and maintain its leading position among the American colonies.[3]

These writers understood that the development of commercial options for Virginia would require more than a nonimportation association, but they believed the effort would be "worth a few years inconvenience." The encouragement of trade would solve several economic problems in the colony including the scarcity of cash and the low price of lands. A manufacturing base for trade would result in a more productive employment of labor and the introduction of new crops. The

[2]C. R., *Virginia Gazette* (Purdie & Dixon), 22 Mar. 1770; Letter to Purdie & Dixon, *Virginia Gazette* (Purdie & Dixon), 14 June 1770, Supplement.

[3]"A Friend to Virginia" to Mr. Rind, *Virginia Gazette* (Rind), 14 June 1770; the commercial development of the colonies to the north was a concern for many Virginians during the 1760s and 1770s, see e.g. "Associator Humanus," *Virginia Gazette* (Purdie & Dixon), 18 July 1771; "To Mr. Printer," *Virginia Gazette* (Purdie & Dixon), 22 Mar. 1770; and "A Virginian to the Printer," *Virginia Gazette* (Purdie & Dixon), 3 Mar. 1774.

political conflict between Great Britain and the American colonies added to the imperative for an independent colonial trade. William Lee, writing from London in 1771, warned one wealthy Chesapeake planter that Americans ought "strenuously to endeavour to bring everything forward so as to enable you as soon as possible to live without the assistance of this country, for it does not require the gift of prophecy to forsee that it is a contingency that you must be put to the tryal of before many years."[4]

In the years following the Stamp Act crisis and with greater frequency after 1769, Virginians interested in commercial development appealed to the provincial assembly for public support. The scores of petitions and proposed bills presented to the House of Burgesses were significant less for their immediate impact or practical effect than for their demonstration of the urgent support for economic diversification and greater independence. The House of Burgesses considered proposals for bounties for new crops, governmental funding of internal improvements, the regulation of trade in various commodities, and for other legislation favoring local commerce. Parliament and the colonial assemblies frequently had offered bounties for the cultivation of crops unavailable in Great Britain and had established favorable trade arrangements for these desired commodities. Various petitioners to the House of Burgesses hoped that body would offer similar aid to the ambitious schemes that were beyond the means of any individual. Hemp was one crop that Virginians hoped would complement tobacco cultivation and coincide with the mercantilist goals of British policy. Parliament itself in 1764 offered a bounty for colonial-grown hemp which the British navy and merchant fleet used for roping. Virginia's assembly acknowledged this encouragement in an act in 1767 for the erection of warehouses for the storage of hemp before shipment. A similar system of warehouses for tobacco had facilitated the export of large cargoes. In 1770, the burgesses added their own enticement for hemp production with a bounty of four shillings for every gross hundred weight of hemp made in the colony. Hemp production increased during the decade preceding the Revolution, but even with bounties, the costs of labor and

---

[4] "A Private Man in Essex," *Virginia Gazette* (Rind), 6 July 1769, and *Gazette* articles cited above; William Lee to Edward Lloyd, 8 Apr. 1771, William Lee Letterbook, 1770–1771, Lee Family Papers at Stratford (University of Virginia microfilm).

shipping prevented Virginia hemp from competing with European imports on the British market.[5]

Since the days of the Virginia Company, recurring schemes for economic diversification had included suggestions for the production of wine, a commodity thought suitable for Virginia's climate and useful for reducing Virginia's dependence on foreign imports. In 1770, the House of Burgesses answered the petition of French émigré Andrew Estave with £450 for the establishment of a vineyard. The burgesses appointed a board of trustees, made up of the assembly's most prestigious members, to purchase for Estave's use one hundred acres near Williamsburg. They also built him a house, bought three slaves for his use, and appointed three apprentices to be trained in the art of viniculture. If Estave within six years produced "ten hogsheads of good merchantable wine," the trustees would convey to him the land and slaves as a reward. Two years later, Estave had established vines and was ready to train apprentices presented by the trustees. At this time, the burgesses also offered him additional financial assistance. After frost killed the season's grapes in 1774, Estave petitioned for more money and equipment, but the burgesses had not acted on his request when the governor dissolved the house in May.[6]

Robert Bolling expected the production of wine to solve several of Virginia's persistent economic problems. Vineyards provided a family income on a relatively small acreage and would allow many of the colony's poor to remain in settled areas rather than migrate to the frontier. Wine-making required the assistance of craftsmen, such as glass-makers, and would foster the development of towns filled with the supporting services of traders and artisans. Successful viniculture in Virginia would benefit Great Britain by reducing the price of Madeira and increasing the colony's power to purchase British goods. When Bolling in 1773

[5]For Parliament's bounty, see *The Statutes at Large*, 9, (London, 1770), Cap. XXVI, 185; "An Act for erecting warehouses for the reception of Hemp," *Hening's Statutes*, 8:253–55; "An act for encouraging the making of Hemp," ibid., 363–64; George Melville Herndon, "The Story of Hemp in Colonial Virginia" (Ph.D. diss., University of Virginia, 1959), Ch. 4–5, 82–153.

[6]*Journals of the House of Burgesses, 1770–1772*, eds., Kennedy and McIlwaine, 17, 19, 96, 240, 265; *Journals of the House of Burgesses, 1773–1776*, eds., Kennedy and McIlwaine, 111; *Hening's Statutes*, 8:364–66.

petitioned for public assistance in the establishment of a winery in the hills of Buckingham County, the assembly granted him £50.[7]

The assembly, however, proved of limited value in the advocacy of economic diversification. At the same time that the burgesses offered premiums for the production of commodities in demand in Great Britain and endorsed other schemes which coincided with the traditional mercantilist goals of the Board of Trade and Parliament, they rejected appeals for the support of manufactures that would reduce Virginia's dependence on British imports. The assembly was reluctant to promote any scheme that might contribute to a restructuring of Virginia's trade or otherwise challenge the interests of British merchants. The burgesses' repeated efforts to establish a prohibitive slave duty was the exception that proved the rule, and their failure confirmed the assembly's unwillingness to challenge directly British commercial policy. The members of the assembly feared that public encouragement of manufactures or trade outside the Empire might convince Parliament to prohibit colonial manufactures altogether. Even in instances when a majority of burgesses favored a proposed measure, in their official capacity they would reject any plans that might displease the Board of Trade or provoke the interference of Parliament. In December 1769, the assembly failed to approve a bounty for Virginia-made cloth, in spite of the burgesses' near unanimous support of domestic manufactures in the association of the previous May. The assembly in May 1769 also rejected a petition from leather manufactures in the colony calling for a ban on the exportation of unfinished hides.[8]

■   ■   ■

[7]*Journals of the House of Burgesses, 1773–1776*, eds., Kennedy and McIlwaine, 16–17; *Virginia Gazette* (Purdie & Dixon), 25 Feb. 1773; Bolling and Estave carried on a debate on various aspects of viniculture in *Virginia Gazette* (Purdie & Dixon), 18 Mar., 29 July, and 2 Sep. 1773.

[8]For governmental role in the colonial economy see Dickerson, *The Navigation Acts and the American Revolution*, Chs. 1–2; and Robert Johnson, "Government Regulation of Business Enterprise in Virginia, 1750–1820" (Ph.D. diss., University of Minnesota, 1958), Ch. 4. On 12 Dec. 1769, the House ordered James Mercer and Lemuel Riddick to prepare a "Bill for giving a Bounty on Woolen, Cotton, and Linen Cloths, made in this Colony," but a vote for the

Requests for the kind of governmental regulation that already supported the trade in tobacco were subject to similar concerns about the reaction of British officials as well as the constraints on the public treasury. An Augusta County petition in 1769 was the first of several requests for an inspection system for hemp, similar to that in operation for tobacco. Certificates of inspection would grant credibility to the marketing of a crop which varied widely in quality. The use of inspection notes as local currency also would extend to western counties the same advantages enjoyed in tobacco-growing counties east of the Blue Ridge. Despite these requests, Virginia's assembly did not institute any such hemp inspection until the Revolutionary War years, when demand for rope increased the market for the crop. The burgesses moved more quickly to regulate further the uniform size and quality of barrels for foodstuffs important in the West Indies trade. Flour, which with bread grew to "become a very advantageous article of commerce," required more detailed regulation in 1772. The burgesses instructed inspectors, who were required to have no interest in the flour trade, to guard carefully the quality of flour, the condition of shipping casks, and the honest weighing of filled barrels. In the Northern Neck, George Washington and others established a successful trade in salted fish, which they shipped to the West Indies for provisioning slaves. In 1774, residents of Fairfax County petitioned the assembly for a uniform regulation of this new trade. The request, however, arrived too late for the House of Burgesses to act before its dissolution.[9]

Between 1769 and 1774, Alexandria merchants and inhabitants of several counties petitioned for the removal of duties on West Indian rum. The trade in several commodities dependent on West Indian mar-

---

measure never came up, *Journals of the House of Burgesses, 1766–1769*, eds., Kennedy and McIlwaine, 332; Petition of leather manufacturers: *Journals of the House of Burgesses, 1766–1769*, eds., Kennedy and McIlwaine, 203, 206, 247, 288. The House declared the petition reasonable when it was submitted in May of 1769 but rejected it after being resubmitted in November.

[9]*Journals of the House of Burgesses, 1766–1769*, eds., Kennedy and McIlwaine, 210; *Hening's Statutes*, 11:412–14; "An act to amend so much of an act of assembly, intituled An act for the inspection of pork, beef, flour, tar, pitch, and turpentine, as relates to the inspection of flour," *Hening's Statutes*, 8:511–14; Freeman, *George Washington*, 3:243, 263, 267, 287; petition sent through Fairfax burgesses George Washington and John West, see Robert Adam to George Washington, 16 May 1774, Washington Papers, Library of Congress; *Journals of the House of Burgesses, 1773–1776*, eds., Kennedy and McIlwaine, 123.

kets suffered from Virginia's rum duties which diverted much of the West Indian trade into duty-free Maryland. Robert Carter Nicholas, treasurer of the colony, wanted to encourage new trade but explained that the "Duties on Liquors offered the principal Part of the Revenue appropriated for discharging the current expences of the Country."[10]

Similar fiscal concerns limited, although they did not eliminate, the colonial government's appropriations for internal improvements. Virginia's commercial development, whether it involved new products in the trade with Great Britain or new markets elsewhere in the Atlantic world, required a reliable transportation system extending into the interior beyond the tidewater of the colony's principal rivers. For many years the assembly ordered the clearing of Virginia's streams and established ferries or roads, but the expansion of tobacco, grain, and hemp cultivation into western areas demanded a broader governmental support of internal improvements. Augusta County's petition for roads over the mountains were supported by residents of Fairfax and other eastern counties who hoped to secure the western trade that otherwise might fall into the hands of merchants from Pennsylvania or Maryland. In 1772, the assembly responded with funding for a road from Warm Springs to Jenning's Gap in Augusta County and another one over South Mountain in Botetourt County to Crow's ferry on the James in Bedford County.[11]

During the same session, the assembly approved measures encouraging two ambitious proposals for opening the James and Potomac Rivers to navigation. The first act, authorizing a company of subscribers to build a canal around the falls of the James, would allow the growing merchant community around Richmond and Manchester to expand its trade into the Piedmont counties to the west. The other act, establish-

---

[10]*Journals of the House of Burgesses, 1766–1769*, eds., Kennedy and McIlwaine, 251; *Journals of the House of Burgesses, 1770–1772*, eds., Kennedy and McIlwaine, 242; *Journals of the House of Burgesses, 1773–1776*, eds., Kennedy and McIlwaine, 119–120; Alexandria petition presented 10 Nov. 1769 and 13 Mar. 1772; similar petition presented by Berkeley, Loudoun, and Frederick Counties on 21 May 1774; To Mr. Printer, *Virginia Gazette* (Purdie & Dixon), 22 Mar. 1770; for the Treasurer's defense of the rum duties, see Robert Carter Nicholas to George Washington, 9 April 1774, Washington Papers, Library of Congress.

[11]*Journals of the House of Burgesses, 1766–1769*, eds., Kennedy and McIlwaine, 253, 259; *Hening's Statutes*, 8:546–49.

"A Map of the British and French Dominions in North America. . . ."
(detail) Jno. Mitchell, London, 1755. In this cartouche, hogsheads
await loading at one of the many small warehouse communities that
served as shipping points in the Chesapeake tobacco trade. (Collection of the Virginia Historical Society)

ing a similar company and permitting a lottery to finance a canal above
the falls of the Potomac, would enable Alexandria and other Virginia
towns to capture the trade of areas currently falling under the influence
of Baltimore and Philadelphia. Canals also offered the potential for the
development of commercial centers in established areas of Virginia.
The House of Burgesses in 1772 approved construction of a canal, "for
the navigation of boats . . . with heavy burthens," between York and
James Rivers, by way of Williamsburg. Deep-water access would be "of
great advantage" to the capital city, and "promote the improvement of
navigation in other parts, which would make a great addition to the
commerce and riches of this country."[12]

After the assembly established the two canal companies, all plan-
ning and financing were the responsibility of the private individuals who
subscribed. George Washington invested in the Potomac canal out of a
conviction that the project would make the "Potomack the Channel of

[12]*Hening's Statutes*, 8:556–79; *Journals of the House of Burgesses*, 1770–1772,
eds., Kennedy and McIlwaine, 251.

Commerce between Great Britain and that immense Tract of Country which is unfolding to our view the advantages of which are too great, & too obvious I shoud think to become the Subject of serious debate." The subscribers to the canal projects commissioned John Ballendine to tour the canal sites of England and to investigate possible designs for Virginia. Ballendine returned to the colony in 1774 with forty "ingenious mechanicks" trained in the construction of canals, but the Revolution delayed the initiation of work on these waterways.[13]

When the assembly was unwilling or unable to support ambitious commercial ventures, domestic manufactures, or agricultural diversification, other types of private associations and community partnerships attempted to fill the void. The one hundred founding members of a "Society for advancing useful knowledge" established in 1773 intended their sponsorship of scientific research to produce commercial advantages for Virginia. The study of natural resources in the colony would "yield the greatest emoluments" to Virginians by providing new articles for trade. The encouragement of mechanical innovations would be particularly valuable in a colony with a scarcity of skilled labor.[14]

"Academicus" hoped the society would provide the exchange of ideas that in other colonies took place in cities and that was a necessary prerequisite to advancement in the sciences or letters. By improving technical skills and expanding knowledge of agricultural sciences, the society would extend benefits to the entire population. One immediate goal would be the discovery of alternatives to tobacco, a crop that "Academicus" found "completely adapted for restraining the Progress of Population, and national wealth." The search for alternative trade commodities led a group of Virginia's wealthiest and most influential citizens to finance the Italian Philip Mazzei in his attempts to make silk, wine, and olive oil in the colony. Although this scheme of 1774 proved no more successful than earlier experiments with silk and wine, Governor Dunmore and men like Washington, Jefferson, Benjamin Harrison, and Thomas Nelson joined in the hope of finding new products for export crops that would reduce the colony's dependence on tobacco.[15]

[13]George Washington to Thomas Johnson, 20 July 1770, *Papers of George Washington, Colonial Series*, eds., Abbot and Twohig, 8:357–60; *Virginia Gazette* (Purdie & Dixon), 7 July 1774.

[14]*Virginia Gazette* (Purdie & Dixon), 13 May, 22 July 1773.

[15]*Virginia Gazette* (Purdie & Dixon), 5 Aug. 1773; Mazzei's "Outline of a Plan for Introducing into the Colonies of Great Britain in North America the Different Products of Europe" and list of subscribers in Thomas Adams Cor-

The emphasis on new export commodities and the development of internal transportation networks offered few commercial advantages for Virginia as long as external markets and foreign credit sources continued to dominate the colonial economy. What commercial successes Virginians achieved in the decade before Independence owed more to fortuitous developments in British finance and Atlantic markets than to the limited promotions of the assembly or recurrent private efforts to cultivate new commodities. The expansion of British credit and the proliferation of new marketing arrangements in the late 1760s enabled a growing number of Virginia merchants and planters to participate directly in the Anglo-American trade. At the peak of the tobacco boom, Virginia traders opened stores that imitated the organization of the largest Scottish firms. The demand for Virginia foodstuffs both in southern Europe and in the West Indies encouraged local merchants to expand their operations in those markets. The new opportunities, coinciding with the nonimportation associations, briefly offered Virginia merchants a partial fulfillment of their goal of economic independence. By the time the British withdrew the generous credit, Virginia merchants had enlarged the size and scope of their businesses and permanently raised their expectations.

The influx of credit available to Virginia merchants most frequently came through the "cargo trade," in which British merchants consigned wholesale shipments of manufactured goods to the colonial trader who in turn sold the goods through a retail store. The Virginia merchant usually accepted the goods on twelve-months credit and paid for them with purchased tobacco or with bills of exchange received in other trading operations. The British merchant, who purchased the goods for the cargo from wholesalers and shopkeepers on twelve-months credit, profited from the large "advance," or mark-up, on the articles exported and from the remittances of tobacco shipments sent from local merchants in Virginia as well as from the five percent interest applied to all accounts outstanding after one year. The credit extensions from British tradesmen to British merchant, from British merchant to Virginia trader, and from local storekeepers in Virginia to their customers substantially raised the costs of British goods (the advance in the colonial store alone was often as high as 80 percent above the Virginia merchant's costs), but

respondence, Adams Family Papers, Virginia Historical Society; see also Dumas Malone, *Jefferson the Virginian* (Boston: Little, Brown, 1948), 164–65.

the availability of credit in Great Britain during the late 1760s and early 1770s and the simultaneous rise in tobacco prices encouraged Virginia merchants to accept cargoes from every kind of British merchant.[16]

As early as the middle of the century, some specialized firms in Glasgow began shipping wholesale cargoes to Virginia merchants. After 1765, tobacco merchants throughout Great Britain imitated the arrangement. During the boom years before the credit collapse of 1772, even consignment merchants joined with direct traders to ship cargoes in an effort to secure more tobacco and a higher, quicker return on their investments. Beginning in the late 1760s, firms like Robert Cary & Co., John Norton & Sons, and that of merchant James Russell, all of which previously had catered to the largest consigning planters, added commercial accounts to their business in the colony. The scattered stores of Glasgow firms such as William Cunninghame & Co. and John McCall & Co., which dealt with the smallest tobacco planters, also advanced goods to resident merchants.[17]

The generous extensions of credit from British merchants allowed George Fowler and his brother John to establish their own business in Virginia in 1769. In August 1769, George Fowler, an assistant of merchant Thomas Tabb in Petersburg, ordered close to £1,000 worth of goods on his own account from his employer's Liverpool correspondent. Three months later, John Fowler, a former assistant with the Virginia firm, Field & Call, joined with his brother to order more goods from the Liverpool merchants, Dobson, Daltera, & Walker. The Fowlers used the goods to open a new store at Bowlers, along the Rappahannock River in Essex County, where they planned to specialize in high-volume goods such as osnaburgs and Irish linens. In their initial proposal for a correspondence with Dobson, Daltera, & Walker, the Fowlers stated their intention to make their payments in bills of exchange rather than tobacco or other commodities. John Fowler, who

[16]Price, *Capital and Credit*, 127–30, 149–51.

[17]Jacob M. Price, "Buchanan & Simson, 1759–1763: A Different Kind of Glasgow Firm Trading to the Chesapeake," *William and Mary Quarterly* 3rd ser., 40 (January 1983): 3–41; cargo interests of Russell and Norton discussed in Price, *Capital and Credit*, 129–30; commercial debts of Robert Cary & Co. listed in Claims of Wakelin Welch for Debts Owing Cary, Moorey, & Welch, Public Record Office, T. 79/3, ff. 446–48; List of Debts due John McCall & Co., T. 79/4; William Cunninghame & Co., T. 79/1 (Virginia Colonial Records Project microfilm).

had experience purchasing goods in England and Ireland, was disappointed with the quality of goods they received and with the confused shipping instructions, but the brothers continued to order more cargoes from the firm. By the end of 1770, they had received over £4,000 in goods from Liverpool. Despite a remittance of only £500 from the Fowlers in 1770, Dobson, Daltera, & Walker sent another £1,100 in goods in 1771, and in the first half of 1772 they forwarded nearly £4,500 more. Landon Carter believed the prices at Fowlers' store were the most reasonable in the area, as well they might have been with such abundant credit from England. The store attracted a diverse business which allowed the Fowlers to remit a few more bills in 1771 and, in the spring of 1772, to ship a cargo of 236 hogsheads of tobacco along with pig iron, copper, flax seed, and snake root. In the summer of 1772, however, the Fowlers still owed over £4,500 to Dobson, Daltera, & Walker.[18]

The cargo offers allowed merchants who previously restricted their business to the West Indies trade to profit from the current tobacco boom. Occasionally individuals with little or no commercial experience were able to open stores on the basis of new British credit. Robert Beverley found that many of the recipients of cargoes could scarcely be called merchants. They were actually "people possessed of very little more than an ideal Property, & who in general depend upon the Profits, which they expect from the Sale of those Goods, w[hic]h the Merchts of England have sent them to make even their first remittances." British merchants were so eager to enter the cargo trade that Virginia merchants could obtain credit and goods from several sources at a time. Alexander and Peterfield Trent by 1775 owed commercial debts to British direct traders, London consignment merchants, and several Scottish stores in the colony. The Fowlers in their relatively small business had established a correspondence with at least one other British company besides Dobson, Daltera & Walker. The entrance of so many Virginians into the cargo trade contributed to the record levels of Chesapeake imports from Great Britain in the years 1769–1771 and undermined the nonimportation associations. Writing to his Whitehaven correspondents, Harry Piper of Alexandria found "the people to be run-

---

[18]George Fowler to Dobson, Daltera, & Walker, 12 Nov. 1769, 30 Feb. 1770, 10 Jun. 1770; and Accounts of Fowlers with Dobson, Daltera, & Walker in Dobson & Daltera vs. Fowler, svg. ptr., U.S. Circuit Court, Virginia District, Ended Cases, 1798, Virginia State Library; *Diary of Landon Carter*, ed. Greene, 1:524.

ning mad here, it would amaze you the number of ships and stores we have in Town." By November 1771, Piper counted twenty stores and shops in Alexandria, and he expected more to open soon.[19]

During these few hectic years before 1772, Virginians for once appeared to have an opportunity to assume the commercial advantage. When merchant Thomas Adams returned to Virginia in 1770, he wrote his London business associates, with slight exaggeration, that "the principal planters from the great Prices they have lately got for their Commodities are entirely out of Debt & choose to be their own Bankers or to leave their Money in the hands of Men of more permanent Property," rather than keep it with British merchants. Prosperity allowed the Virginians to become merchants in their own right. Adams warned the Londoners that "no considerable consignments can in future be received at your Port but by sending Cargoes of Goods." Adams recognized that the cargo trade provided Virginians with an opportunity to challenge the pervasive and resented influence of the Scottish stores. "The Virginians seem to be gaining ground fast on the Glasgow Men in the Tobo Trade," he reported to London, and then added, "the latter were never in such low credit since their first Settlement in this Country." The Scots had demonstrated that the tobacco trade was most profitable when carried out through a system of stores that sold goods on credit, in expectation of receiving future tobacco crops as payment. The offer of cargoes from British merchants provided Virginia merchants their first opportunity to duplicate the Scottish store organization, and they expected their involvement in the trade to counter the Scots' influence. Yet at the same time that the cargo trade provided opportunities for Virginia merchants to participate in the tobacco trade, the general expansion of credit and the rise in crop prices enabled the Scots to absorb an unprecedented share of Virginia's trade with Great Britain. The suc-

[19]Robert Beverley to Samuel Athawes, [Feb. 1773], Robert Beverley Letterbook, Library of Congress; Trent accounts in Claim of Wakelin Welch for Debts Owing Cary, Moorey, & Welch, Public Record Office, T. 79/3, ff. 446–48; List of Debts due Speirs, Bowman & Co., T. 79/16 (Virginia Colonial Records Project microfilm); William Lee to Francis Lightfoot Lee, 5 Sep. 1774, *Lee Family Papers* (University of Virginia microfilm publication); Fowlers to Dobson, Daltera, & Walker, 25 Oct. 1774, U.S. Circuit Court, Virginia District, Ended Cases, 1798, Virginia State Library; Harry Piper to Dixon & Littledale, 30 Aug. 1771, Piper to Dixon & Littledale, 27 Nov. 1771, Piper Letterbook, University of Virginia.

cess of the cargo trade was limited further by the traditional dependence on British credit, albeit in a new form.[20]

Attempts to promote commercial enterprises fully independent of Great Britain or British merchants met with more frustration than success. During the association of 1770, Richard Henry Lee and Landon Carter attempted to establish a "Patriotic Store" that would carry on trade to Great Britain without any participation from British merchants. Lee and Carter found popular support for their project but not the financial backing they needed to replace British capital. A writer calling himself "Benvolus" urged other Virginians to follow the lead of the men from the Northern Neck and create the same type of cooperative stores in order to halt the collusion of Scottish factors. This contributor to the *Virginia Gazette* accused the British factors of secretly advancing the price of goods more than 30 percent above the tremendous advances to which they admitted. The alleged exploitation of captive consumers reinforced fears of the political subjugation of the colonies. "Benvolus" insisted that the increased costs created such debts among the planters that "it is unnecessary to send troops here, for the people are already made captives with the ledger." The writer suggested that planters from two or three counties might contribute the money needed to import the goods ordered by a group of subscribers. The goods would be sold only with the charges involved in importation and the operation of the store. Investors would receive ten percent interest and the satisfaction of witnessing the "change from universal distress to universal happiness, from a state of debt and thraldom to one of ease and independence."[21]

Several months after the dissolution of the second association in 1771, a "Planter" in the *Virginia Gazette* suggested another form of planter cooperation that would restrict if not eliminate the influence of British merchants in the tobacco trade. In this writer's view the merchants' advantage arose from the regular meetings held during the General Court. "Do they not meet twice a year in Williamsburg to consult and plan schemes to enslave us, by setting their own price on our tobacco, and what per cent we must give them for goods?" The planters

[20]Thomas Adams to Perkins, Buchanan, & Brown, 22 Mar. 1770, Thomas Adams Letters, Adams Family Papers, Virginia Historical Society.
    [21]For Lee's criticism of store trade see draft of "Rusticus" to William Rind, [176–], *Lee Family Papers* (University of Virginia microfilm publication); Richard Henry Lee to Landon Carter, 18 Apr. 1771, Richard Henry Lee Correspondence, Virginia Historical Society; *Diary of Landon Carter*, ed., Greene, 1:536; *Virginia Gazette* (Rind), 7 Feb. 1771.

could challenge the merchants' control by organizing meetings at the local courthouses and establishing their own prices, below which they would not sell tobacco. Planters might also refuse to sell tobacco without the promise of a "reasonable" advance on the merchants' goods. The "Planter" reminded readers that they could not rest easy from the suppressed tyranny of the British government when "we are slaves to the power of the merchants."[22]

The increased demand for grain exports after 1765 offered Virginia merchants one area of commercial growth where they neither relied on British credit nor competed with British merchants. Throughout the eighteenth century Virginia merchants had carried wheat and corn to the West Indies and occasionally to southern Europe. Wheat exports from Virginia reached as high as 48,028 bushels in 1739, but wars and droughts interrupted the trade and forced exports back to around 10,000 bushels a year in the late 1740s and again in the late 1750s. During the decade after 1765, a steadier demand for American grain made wheat the second most important export from Virginia, and in certain regions of the colony it rivaled tobacco. In 1768, Virginia shipped 140,252 bushels and in 1773 the figure reached 254,517, making the colony the third largest exporter of wheat behind Pennsylvania and New York. Virginia already exported the largest amount of corn of any mainland colony, 566,672 bushels in 1773, and processed bread and flour further boosted the value of the grain trade in the colony. The foreign demand for grain was so strong in the early 1770s that in Alexandria, local merchants hurried to the edge of town to solicit incoming wagon loads of wheat and flour.[23]

The value of annual grain exports from Virginia in the years 1768–1772 was still only about one-tenth of the value of the record tobacco exports of the period, but for many Virginians wheat appeared to be the surest foundation for future economic growth. Roger Atkinson of Petersburg was euphoric in his expectations for wheat production. In 1772 he wrote to the London merchants Lionel and Samuel Lyde:

> We shall in a few years make more wheat in Virginia than in all the Province of Pennsylvania put together, altho' it is their staple com-

[22]"A Planter" to Rind, *Virginia Gazette* (Rind), 31 Oct. 1771.
[23]Bergstrom, *Markets and Merchants*," Ch. 5, esp. table on 136; see also Gill, "Wheat Culture in Colonial Virginia," 380–93; Price, "Economic Function and the Growth of American Port Towns in the Eighteenth Century," 165; Harry Piper to Dixon & Littledale, 27 Nov. 1771, Piper Letterbook, University of Virginia.

modity . . . our poorest lands will produce it in great abundance . . . but the richer Lands will still produce it in greater Abundance. I do not believe there is a finer Country under the Sun, take it altogether, the rich and & the poor, for any grain.

Articles in the *Virginia Gazette* echoed Atkinson's optimism about the future of Virginia's wheat trade.[24]

Virginia merchants who hoped to profit from the expanding wheat trade confronted a persistent limitation on commercial development in the colony. A successful wheat trade depended on urban centers for milling facilities, for storage of the bulky cargoes, and for the ease of loading ships, but the development of port towns had been retarded in an economy where the British-controlled tobacco trade held sway. Although a few Virginia towns such as Norfolk and Alexandria grew after 1750 as entrepôts of the wheat trade, most areas of the colony did not have easy access to local shipping centers. One writer to the *Virginia Gazette* in 1770 complained that "great numbers of our farmers labour under the necessity of carrying their wheat and flower to Baltimore Town, and even to Philadelphia, for want of a sufficient market on our rivers." If grain or hemp were to become viable alternatives to tobacco, the first thing "necessary is to have towns erected near the heads of those rivers which penetrate farthest into the colony and are most contiguous to our fertile back counties." Even along the tidewater reaches of the Rappahannock, Francis Lightfoot Lee in 1773 remarked on the need to ship Virginia wheat to Baltimore "for want of a market here." Virginia also lacked the shipping capacity to carry increased exports of wheat and foodstuffs. Much of the new trade fell into the hands of merchants like Willing & Morris of Philadelphia who purchased wheat along the Potomac River to supplement their Pennsylvania supply.[25]

■   ■   ■

[24]Roger Atkinson to Lyonel and Samuel Lyde, 25 Aug. 1772, Atkinson Letterbook, University of Virginia; "A Traveller to Mrs. Rind," *Virginia Gazette* (Rind), 3 Mar. 1774; To Mr. Printer, *Virginia Gazette* (Purdie & Dixon), 22 Mar. 1770.

[25]To Mr. Printer, *Virginia Gazette* (Purdie & Dixon), 22 Mar. 1770; For relationship of wheat trade and urban developments see Carville Earle and Ronald Hoffman, "Urban Development in the Eighteenth-Century South," *Perspectives in American History* 10 (1976): 7–80; Price, "Economic Function

The unusual and ambitious merchant career of William Lee encompassed the range of commercial opportunities available in the Virginia trade during the decade preceding 1776. One of the few Virginians to establish a trading firm in Great Britain, Lee was in a unique position to understand the difficulties of developing independent commercial interests in the colony. Lee entered the consignment trade in 1769 and soon attempted to expand his business by advancing cargoes to Virginia merchants and soliciting new trade commodities in the Chesapeake. During his years in London, Lee also became involved in radical politics, and among the merchant community there, he was a chief defender of American rights. His political activity, culminating in his election as alderman in the City of London in 1755, further acquainted him with the limitations imposed on the colonial economy and with the interplay of imperial politics and colonial trade. Lee had come to London to find a personal career, but he always believed his own success might coincide with and contribute to the improvement of Virginia's trading advantages. An early and persistent advocate of the nonimportation associations, Lee shared his lessons in trade and politics with his Virginia clients, many of whom were friends and relatives. The course of Lee's business and his correspondence with Virginians help to explain many of the pressures on colonial trade in the years immediately preceding the Revolution.

William Lee was born in 1739 to one of the wealthiest and most influential families in Virginia, yet upon reaching his majority he owned no land and held few resources. When Councillor Thomas Lee died in 1750, he left the great house and estate at Stratford to his eldest son, Philip Ludwell Lee. Three of the younger sons, Richard Henry, Thomas Ludwell, and Francis Lightfoot, each received land and slaves, but to his youngest sons, William and Arthur, Thomas Lee left only money and instructions that the boys should be trained in a profession. Philip Ludwell Lee, as executor of his father's will, further restricted the opportunities of his two youngest brothers by withholding the money due them from Thomas Lee's estate.[26]

---

and the Growth of Port Towns in the Eighteenth Century," 123–186; Francis Lightfoot Lee to William Lee, 20 Nov. 1773, Francis Lightfoot Lee Correspondence, Virginia Historical Society.

[26]Burton J. Hendrick, *The Lees of Virginia: Biography of a Family* (Boston, 1935), 89, 158; "Executors of the late Honble Thomas Lee of Virginia, Deceased, in Acct Currt with William Lee," Lee Family Papers, Virginia Historical Society.

Even without his patrimony William Lee was heir to a family legacy that would shape his private life and public career. The Lee family heritage had an important influence on William and others of his generation who, in a manner more typical of Virginia families in the nineteenth century than the colonial period, chronicled their genealogy and the achievements of their ancestors. One result of this emphasis on family history was an awareness of the need for each generation to renew the family's wealth and reestablish its social influence. The Lee's collective experience also taught the Stratford children that economic success was predicated on public service and political involvement. The ability of Thomas Lee and his predecessors to adjust to Virginia's shifting economy and to exploit the advantages of public office had allowed them to expand their estates in unison with the growth of the colonial economy. And the Revolutionary generation of Lees, perhaps more than any family in the colony, identified their own well-being with the future prosperity of Virginia.[27]

Philip Ludwell Lee, who inherited his father's seat on the governor's council as well as his plantation, had the easiest task of maintaining his family's influence. Richard Henry Lee explored new methods of plantation management and applied for various imperial appointments in an effort to emulate his father's career and amass an estate for his own children. All of the Lee brothers invested in western land companies in the hope of connecting their fortunes to regions with the greatest potential for economic development. William Lee, however, was the only brother in this land-rich family who found it necessary to concentrate on the possibilities of a commercial career.[28]

After William Lee completed schooling with a tutor at Stratford Hall, he was uncertain how to support himself. While his brother Arthur, also without an estate, went to study medicine in Scotland, William Lee worked at various positions which taught him about plantation operations and Virginia's trade. He served as steward and manager of the plantation at Stratford during Philip Ludwell Lee's frequent trips to Council meetings in Williamsburg. Returning from a trip to England

---

[27]William Lee's genealogical studies in Edmund Jenings Lee Papers, Virginia Historical Society. For history of earlier generations of Lee family in Virginia see Hendrick, *The Lees of Virginia*, Chs. 1–2; related discussion of Richard Henry Lee in Pauline Maier, *The Old Revolutionaries: Political Lives in the Age of Samuel Adams* (New York: Alfred A. Knopf, 1980), Ch. 4.

[28]Hendrick, *The Lees of Virginia*, Chs. 1–2; Maier, *The Old Revolutionaries*, Ch. 4.

in 1761–1762, William became involved in scattered trading activity and may have served as an agent for the London merchant James Russell. He became the secretary of the Mississippi Company in 1763. Three years later, he was among the subscribers to Richard Henry Lee's Westmoreland Association. William Lee's various experiences in the 1760s exposed him to a broad range of economic ventures, but without his inheritance he found no real opportunities in Virginia. In 1768, he decided to accompany Arthur to London where each of them hoped to find a career.[29]

Upon arriving in England, William Lee arranged to go to India as a merchant, but his plans and opportunities changed in March 1769 when he married Hannah Ludwell. The Virginia-born Hannah had lived in London for almost a decade and, with her sister Lucy Ludwell Paradise, was heir to the estate and fortune of Philip Ludwell of Green Spring in Virginia. At the division of the Ludwell estate in 1770, William Lee found himself the master of Green Spring plantation with its 7,030 acres, 164 slaves, and valuable livestock. Within two weeks of his wedding, Lee decided to remain in London and enter the tobacco trade, provided he found support from his friends in Virginia. He noted at the time that consignments from his family alone would probably be sufficient to inaugurate the business.[30]

A handful of friends and relatives, most of them from Lee's native Westmoreland County, consigned small cargoes of tobacco to William in the spring of 1769. The forty hogsheads carried by Captain Aderton

---

[29]Cazenove Gardner Lee, Jr., *Lee Chronicle: Studies of the Early Generations of the Lees of Virginia*, compiled and edited by Dorothy Mills Parker (New York, 1951), 195. Between 1763 and 1766 William Lee traded West Indian goods for grain with Richard Lingan Hall, Peckatone, Westmoreland Co., Va. Papers, Virginia Historical Society; James Russell account with Dr. Richard Lingan Hall signed by William Lee suggests Lee was agent for Russell. When William Lee began his London business he referred to his "being a good deal conversant in collecting Debts in Virga," James Russell account with Dr. Richard Hall, Peckatone Papers, Virginia Historical Society; William Lee to Francis Lightfoot Lee, 5 Dec. 1769, William Lee Letterbook, 1769–1771, Lee Family Papers at Stratford (University of Virginia microfilm).

[30]Background of Hannah Ludwell in Archibald Bolling Shepperson, *John Paradise and Lucy Ludwell of London and Williamsburg* (Richmond: The Dietz Press, 1942), Ch. 1–2; division of Ludwell estate in Lee Family Papers, Virginia Historical Society; William Lee to Richard Lee, 20 Mar. 1769, Richard Bland Lee Papers, Library Congress.

of Northumberland County included twenty from John Tayloe who was eager for Lee to stay on in London rather than go to India. The other shippers were interested in improving the return they regularly got from the established English merchants James Russell and William Molleson. Upon receiving the tobacco, Lee advanced goods by return voyage in order to encourage his Virginia shippers. At the same time, he called on friends in Virginia and Maryland to advise him on the wisdom of establishing a full-scale consignment business. Richard Henry Lee assured his brother that in normal years he could easily fill a small ship with tobacco consignments and that this would provide a foundation for a more extensive business. Francis Lightfoot Lee suggested that if William was to "vary at all from practice it should be in favor of planters & in those particulars where they think themselves imposed upon." The Annapolis merchant Anthony Stewart was more cautious. Beyond the immediate disruptions of the imperial dispute, Stewart feared that the changes in the tobacco trade would render a consignment business unprofitable. The returns from the cargo trade were unpredictable, and the costs of credit extensions so high that a new merchant could not afford to send goods to Chesapeake merchants. Even when London merchants established their own stores for the purchase of tobacco, they could not compete with the advantages of the Glasgow men. Stewart warned Lee that once a merchant engaged creditors and customers he could not easily draw back.[31]

By the early fall of 1769, William Lee had decided to enter the consignment business on terms that he hoped would avoid the potential risks for merchants and planters. He proposed to sell tobacco for a flat commission of 25 shillings per hogshead rather than the customary 2 ½ or 3 percent. He would advance money to no one and returns for the tobacco would be made in goods or bills for the exact amount of the sales. When Lee began to solicit consignments, he agreed to allow shippers to draw bills of exchange on tobacco before it reached market, but only under certain conditions. After the tobacco sailed, the shipper could

---

[31][Francis Lightfoot Lee] to William Lee, 9 Mar. 1769, Brock Collection, Huntington Library (Colonial Williamsburg microfilm); Richard Henry Lee to William Lee, 17 Dec. 1769, Richard Henry Lee Correspondence, Virginia Historical Society; [Francis Lightfoot Lee] to William Lee, 9 Mar. 1769, Brock Collection, Huntington Library (Colonial Williamsburg microfilm); Anthony Stewart to William Lee, 24 Jul. 1769, William Lee Correspondence, Virginia Historical Society.

draw bills at 60 days sight for the amount at which tobacco was selling on the river of origin. Lee demanded immediate notification of such drafts and full insurance on the consigned cargo. He hoped to discourage early drafts by promising to sell the drawer's crop immediately upon receipt rather than wait for the best market.[32]

The current boom in tobacco markets convinced Lee that a London business could bring him success. He found many merchants in the city who "cleared more in one year by the tob. trade than any man ever did by a Virga estate in seven." Within two years of "tolerable trade," he expected "more money may be made . . . than all my Estate is now worth." His knowledge of Virginia's trade would also benefit the consigning planters and, possibly, the colony's economy. Lee understood from experience the many complaints against the consignment trade, but he was convinced that his plan of operation would guarantee the planters a better price than they could receive in Virginia. A consignment business run from a Virginian's point of view would be Lee's public service to the colony. Virginia needed patriots in England as well as at home, and he was convinced he could "serve her as a Mercht here, much more effectually than in any office I can ever possibly expect to fill there."[33]

On the recommendation of Philip Ludwell Lee, William Lee negotiated with Captain James Walker to manage a voyage to Virginia in the spring of 1770. Lee was debating whether to charter a small ship for Walker or obtain space on the large vessel of another captain when he decided to limit his own risks and enter a trading partnership with Dennys DeBerdt and Stephen Sayre. DeBerdt, his son Dennis, and Sayre were merchants with extensive American connections through their trading ventures to the New England and Middle Colonies. The elder DeBerdt was colonial agent for Massachusetts and Delaware, while the New York-born Sayre had represented the firm on business in the colonies. Both men were noted supporters of colonial rights.[34]

[32]William Lee to Anthony Stewart, 2 Oct. 1769, William Lee Letterbook, 1769–1771; William Lee to Philip Ludwell Lee, 3 Feb. 1770, William Lee Letterbook, 1770–1771, Lee Family Papers at Stratford (University of Virginia microfilm).

[33]William Lee to Richard Henry Lee, 5 Dec. 1769, William Lee Letterbook, 1769–1771; William Lee to Philip Ludwell Lee, 5 Dec. 1769, William Lee Letterbook, 1769–1771; William Lee to Richard Corbin, 26 Jan. 1770, William Lee to Col. Henry Lee, 27 Jan. 1770, William Lee Letterbook, 1770–1771, Lee Family Papers at Stratford (University of Virginia microfilm).

Stratford Hall, the birthplace of William Lee, as it appeared in 1930. (Colonial Williamsburg Foundation)

In January of 1770, the partnership of DeBerdts, Lee, & Sayre purchased the 350-hogshead ship *Liberty* for Walker's spring voyage. Lee, who enjoyed access to the personal contacts on which a successful consignment business depended, remained the principal director of the *Liberty*'s adventure to Virginia. He took advantage of his Virginia connections by engaging his brother, Philip Ludwell Lee, and his cousin, Richard Lee, collector for the South Potomac Naval district, to organize the collection of consignments in the colony. Philip Ludwell Lee assured his brother that, given full control over the ship's business in Virginia, he could gather consignments from the largest shippers in the Northern Neck and along the York River.[35]

William Lee made his own solicitations for tobacco from dozens of acquaintances and relatives along the Potomac and Rappahannock Riv-

[34]William Lee to Capt. James Walker, 29 Oct. 1769, William Lee to Philip Ludwell Lee, 5 Dec. 1769, William Lee Letterbook, 1769–1771, Lee Family Papers at Stratford; "Dennys DeBerdt" in *Dictionary of American Biography*, 3:180; John Alden, *Stephen Sayre* (Baton Rouge: Louisiana State University Press, 1983).

[35]William Lee to Francis Lightfoot Lee, 16 Jan. 1770; William Lee to Philip Ludwell Lee, 5 Dec. 1769; William Lee to Francis Lightfoot Lee, 9 Dec. 1769, all in William Lee Letterbook, 1769–1771, Lee Family Papers at Stratford; Philip Ludwell Lee to William Lee, 4 Dec. 1769, Letters of Philip Ludwell Lee, Virginia Historical Society.

ers. To each potential shipper, Lee explained his business operation and suggested various advantages of dealing with a Virginian in London. With the assistance of his friends, Lee hoped to correct the worst abuses of the tobacco trade and expand the commerce of the Northern Neck. He promised a reasonable commission rate, an honest accounting of all shipping charges, and a full discount on duties for any planter who deposited money with him. Lee's knowledge of the "particular tastes of the Gentl[me]n in Virginia" would improve the quality of goods shipped to the consigning planters. Hannah Lee planned to assist in the purchase of fineries for the Virginia women. During this period of imperial conflict and nonimportation associations, Lee hoped that Virginians would support a countryman of sympathetic political beliefs. He emphasized that his partners were "almost the only real Friends to America amongst all the American Merchts."[36]

Lee was sufficiently familiar with the tobacco trade not to depend entirely on consignments to load his first ship. He enlisted the assistance of his brothers, Francis Lightfoot Lee and Richard Henry Lee, to carry out whatever contingency plans might be necessary to return the *Liberty* in time to meet the best tobacco market in London. These two brothers understood the importance of allowing the vain Philip Ludwell Lee to manage affairs in name, but they became William's actual agents during each venture to the colony. For this voyage, William Lee instructed Francis Lightfoot Lee to purchase as many as 150 hogsheads on his own account if they were needed to fill Walker's ship in time for a profitable return trip. He suggested that Francis Lightfoot Lee observe the purchasing activity of the London merchants and their agents. If those men were buying in the James and York River areas, the price would remain high and Walker should prepare to sail with purchased tobacco. William Lee set ceilings on the prices for various types of tobacco and recommended specific warehouses from which tobacco usually fetched the highest prices in London. A less preferable but acceptable alternative would be to load planters' tobacco "on liberty of consignment" and collect the freight charges. If tobacco purchases were not feasible, Lee planned to send the ship to Annapolis where his friend

[36]See general correspondence with Virginia planters in William Lee Letterbooks, 1769–1771 and 1770–1771 for the winter of 1769–1770. Particular reference to William Lee to George William Fairfax, 19 Jan. 1770, William Lee Letterbook, 1769–1771; William Lee to Landon Carter, 26 Jan. 1770; William Lee to George William Fairfax, 27 Jan. 1770, William Lee Letterbook, 1770–1771, Lee Family Papers at Stratford.

Anthony Stewart would load her with grain for Oporto. As a final option, Lee preferred that Walker load available space with barrel staves rather than remain in Virginia too long.[37]

Captain Walker sailed from England in mid-February of 1770 with instructions to land the *Liberty* in York River where he could collect tobacco from Green Spring and contact planters at the General Court in Williamsburg before sailing to Yeocomico in Westmoreland County. By the time Walker reached the Virginia Capes, Lee's partnership with the DeBerdts and Sayre had dissolved because of the death of the elder DeBerdt. Lee was well rid of DeBerdt's heavily indebted firm, but his purchase and outfitting of the *Liberty*, at a cost of £1,450 placed new pressures on his inaugural venture. Now Lee insisted on remittances from everyone who owed him for goods shipped in 1769. He also asked Philip Ludwell Lee for £1,000 of his inheritance to keep the business in operation.[38]

Walker managed to load a full cargo of tobacco only after annoying the several agents in Virginia and delaying the return voyage. His failure to collect important consignments that had been solicited by Philip Ludwell Lee forced the latter to add 155 hogsheads on liberty of consignment to the tobacco consigned to William Lee. Francis Lightfoot Lee, who criticized Walker for ignoring his instructions, helped salvage the venture by loading 80 hogsheads of purchased tobacco. The *Liberty* also carried 24 hogsheads from William Lee's plantation at Green Spring. Of special pride to William Lee was the consignment from several Marylanders of a single hogshead of tobacco, the proceeds of which were directed to England's political radical, John Wilkes. Ballast of barrel staves and twenty tons of pig iron from John Tayloe's foundry completed the *Liberty*'s cargo.[39]

When Walker reached England in September 1770, William Lee had set up a household at 33 Tower Hill in London and, with his assis-

---

[37]William Lee to Francis Lightfoot Lee, 5 Dec. 1769, 9 Dec. 1769, and 16 Jan. 1770, in William Lee Letterbook, 1769-1771; William Lee to Francis Lightfoot Lee, 10 Feb. 1770; William Lee to Philip Ludwell Lee, 3 Feb. 1770; William Lee to Messrs. James Dick & Stewart, 10 Feb. 1770, William Lee Letterbook, 1770–1771, Lee Family Papers at Stratford.

[38]William Lee to James Walker, 15 Feb. 1770, 20 Apr. 1770, William Lee to Francis Lightfoot Lee, 15 Apr. 1770, 20 Apr. 1770, in William Lee Letterbook, 1770–1771, Lee Family Papers at Stratford.

[39]William Lee to Francis Lightfoot Lee, 7 Sep. 1770, William Lee Letterbook, 1769-1771, Lee Family Papers at Stratford; Philip Ludwell Lee

tant Edward Browne, had established an office at the same address. Lee was disappointed with Walker's late sailing which cost him £3 per day and with the large number of hogsheads on consignment to others, but the returns from the *Liberty*'s cargo were sufficient to encourage an expanded voyage during the next season. For the *Liberty*'s second adventure to Virginia, Lee hoped to solicit larger consignments from fewer planters. He made a special appeal to his godfather, Landon Carter, who was reportedly angered with his London merchant, William Molleson. Lee hoped to pick up substantial consignments from Edward Lloyd of Maryland, also dissatisfied with his regular London merchant. John Tayloe agreed to transfer his business from James Russell to William Lee in return for Lee's promise of freight-free shipment of pig iron. In his instructions to Walker and his Virginia agents, Lee emphasized the importance of cultivating other large shippers like William Nelson, Richard Corbin, and Robert Carter of Nomini Hall.[40]

Larger and fewer consignments from Virginia made it easier for Lee to market the tobacco in London and secure freight payments. Lee was especially anxious about freight charges in the winter of 1770–1771 when the threat of war with Spain and the impressment of sailors raised the costs of hiring a crew. In order to cover the costs of the outbound voyage, Lee needed to load a full freight of British goods. He solicited cargoes from John Glassford & Co. and other Glasgow firms that ex-

---

to William Lee, 3 May 1770, 21 Jan. 1771, Letters of Philip Ludwell Lee, Virginia Historical Society; William Lee had solicited the tobacco for Wilkes through William Fitzhugh. William Lee to Fitzhugh, 19 Jan. 1770, William Lee Letterbook, 1769–1771; William Lee to Abraham Barnes, 30 Jan. 1770, William Lee to William Fitzhugh, 25 Jan. 1770, William Lee Letterbook, 1770–1771; reference to iron shipment in William Lee to John Tayloe, 31 Oct. 1770, William Lee Letterbook, 1770–1771, Lee Family Papers at Stratford.

[40]William Lee to Edward Browne, 1 Aug. 1770; William Lee to Francis Lightfoot Lee, 7 Sep. 1770, William Lee Letterbook, 1769–1771; William Lee to Philip Ludwell Lee, 31 Oct. 1770, William Lee Letterbook, 1770–1771, Lee Family Papers at Stratford; Richard Henry Lee to William Lee, 7–9 July 1770, Richard Henry Lee Correspondence, Virginia Historical Society; William Lee to Landon Carter, 30 Oct. 1770; William Lee to Edward Lloyd, 7 Nov. 1770; William Lee to Francis Lightfoot Lee, 9 Nov. 1770, William Lee Letterbook, 1770–1771, Lee Family Papers at Stratford; John Tayloe to William Lee, William Lee Correspondence, Virginia Historical Society; William Lee to Richard Henry Lee, 9 Nov. 1770; William Lee to James Walker, 28 Nov. 1770, William Lee Letterbook, 1770–1771, Lee Family Papers at Stratford.

ported many of their store goods from London. He also expected his own involvement in the cargo trade to cover freight costs as well as insure larger remittances of tobacco. Lee's first advance of goods to a Virginia merchant was to John Gordon in Lancaster County. In November of 1770, he offered Gordon a cargo with no interest charged if remittances of tobacco were made for the full amount within twelve months. Lee made a similar offer to William Carr of Dumfries and shipped £570 worth of goods on his own account to be sold by Francis Lightfoot Lee. William Lee wanted to use these goods, the cost of which included shipping charges, to attract tobacco sellers if the crop were small. If tobacco were plentiful, Francis Lightfoot Lee could sell the goods for cash which was always needed to cover the expenses of loading the ship.[41]

Walker's management of the second venture again threatened the success of Lee's business in Virginia. The *Liberty* left London in November but was still at Falmouth in January. By April when the ship reached Virginia, Francis Lightfoot Lee could not sell the cargo of winter goods until the fall, and many consigning planters had sent their tobacco on James Russell's ship in expectation of a favorable early market. Walker was ill during much of his stay in the colony and spent the rest of his time socializing. The loading of the *Liberty* was principally the work of Richard Henry Lee on the Potomac and Francis Lightfoot Lee on the Rappahannock. Walker remained four months in Virginia, which prevented the *Liberty's* cargo of 347 hogsheads of tobacco from reaching a satisfactory market in London. William Lee was still trying to sell some of the consignments in the early months of 1772.[42]

---

[41]William Lee to Richard Henry Lee, 9 Nov. 1770, William Lee Letterbook, 1770–1771; William Lee to John Glassford, 11 Oct. 1770, William Lee Letterbook, 1769–1771; William Lee to John Gordon, 30 Oct. 1770; William Lee to William Carr, 31 Oct. 1770; William Lee to Francis Lightfoot Lee, 9 Nov. 1770, William Lee Letterbook, 1770–1771, Lee Family Papers at Stratford.

[42]William Lee to Francis Lightfoot Lee, 4 Feb. 1770, William Lee Letterbook, 1770–1771, Lee Family Papers at Stratford; Francis Lightfoot Lee to William Lee, [ ] Apr. 1771, Edmund Jenings Lee Papers, Virginia Historical Society; Philip Ludwell Lee to William Lee, 18 June 1771, Letters of Philip Ludwell Lee, Virginia Historical Society; William Lee to Francis Lightfoot Lee, 9 Aug. 1771, 13 Aug. 1771; William Lee to Richard Lee, 31 Aug. 1771, William Lee Letterbook, 1770–1771, Lee Family Papers at Stratford; William Lee to Richard Henry Lee, 9 Aug. 1771, 16 Feb. 1772, Richard Henry Lee

Lee determined that a reorganization of his business would over-come the problems of personality and management that plagued his first two ventures to Virginia. In the fall of 1771, he fired James Walker and made Captain Charles Rayson a part owner of the *Liberty*. Rayson sailed in December to load consignments exclusively on the Potomac River under the direction of Richard Henry Lee. William Lee char-tered space for 200 hogsheads on Captain William Outram's ship which Francis Lightfoot Lee would fill with consignments and purchases from Rappahannock and the York River areas. Because London tobacconists were prejudiced in favor of any tobacco from York River, Lee suggested Outram's ship clear out from the York River Naval district. For the outvoyage of the *Liberty*, William Lee obtained the freight of goods for several Scottish stores on both shores of the Potomac. He also advanced cargoes to the merchant firms of William Carr and Hipkins & Tomlin.[43]

By the completion of this venture in 1772, William Lee had devel-oped an extensive clientele of regular consignors in Virginia ranging from Frederick County in the west, through the Northern Neck, and south to the York River. The success of his business brought with it a more realistic awareness of the limitations on the consignment trade. Lee had hoped to reform the tobacco trade, but practical experience soon taught him that institutional obstacles prevented an individual from changing the operation of the trade and thereby effectively promoting the interests of Virginians. Lee would have to control a dominant share of the market if he were to challenge the schedule of charges that re-duced a planter's receipts. He agreed with Landon Carter on the use-lessness of London brokers, but he could not sell tobacco without paying the fees of these long-established middlemen. Lee also found the con-signment system to be the least efficient method of marketing tobacco in London, even when the leaf was of top quality. The separate sale of small parcels was more time-consuming than the commissions warranted,

---

Correspondence, Virginia Historical Society; Cargo of the *Liberty* recorded in Naval Office Returns, South Potomac district, Public Record Office, CO5/ 1349, f. 20 (Virginia Colonial Records Project microfilm).

[43]William Lee to Richard Henry Lee, 4 Oct. 1771, 31 Dec. 1771, Richard Henry Lee Correspondence, Virginia Historical Society; William Lee to Rich-ard Henry Lee, 20 Jan. 1772; William Lee to Francis Lightfoot Lee, 17 Feb. 1772, *Lee Family Papers* (University of Virginia microfilm publication); Accounts of goods shipped in William Lee Letterbook, 1769–1771, Lee Family Papers at Stratford.

and when the tobacco was poor, as it often was, disposal of the parcel took twice as much effort.[44]

Lee's activity as a London agent for his consignment customers was troublesome and unrewarding. In the summer of 1771, after searching for skilled servants requested by several clients, Lee swore he would reject future requests in this "reproachful business." The expectations of special service from a Virginian exacerbated Lee's problems with the consignment business. After two years of trading, William Lee complained to Richard Henry Lee that the Virginians "have the same expectations from me that Jews have from a Messiah—that is, I am to make them all rich & Princes over the Earth." Lee's friends in the colony wanted reduced freight rates, the highest prices for their tobacco, unlimited power to draw bills of exchange, and goods shipped with no commission charges. These unreasonable demands were particularly irksome in light of the weak support Virginians offered their countrymen in trade. All too often Virginians shipped their crop to British merchants connected with tobacco manufacturers or the agents for foreign markets, "when common sense will tell us that it is the common interest of these sets of men to keep down the price of Tobo." Until Lee's fellow colonists recognized their true interests in Great Britain, they would never challenge the dominance of the Scottish firms and the large merchants of London. He reminded Landon Carter that "the Virginians have one principal in general diametrically opposite to the most warrantable, if not the only one for which the N. Britons are remarkable. The Virginians by their conduct seem always to think any unprincipled, beggarly stranger, can & will do them more justice than a Countryman, & one too who they know has Property to answer for any effects they trust in his hands."[45]

---

[44]William Lee to Landon Carter, 30 Oct 1770; William Lee to Squire James Davenport, 25 Feb. 1771, William Lee Letterbook, 1770–1771, Lee Family Papers at Stratford (University of Virginia microfilm).

[45]William Lee to Samuel Washington, 17 July 1771, William Lee to John Turbeville, 17 July 1771, William Lee Letterbook, 1770–1771, Lee Family Papers at Stratford; William Lee to Richard Henry Lee, 4 Oct. 1771, Richard Henry Lee Correspondence, Virginia Historical Society; William Lee to Edward Lloyd, 21 Feb. 1771, William Lee Letterbook, 1769–1771; Lee and his brothers repeatedly commented on the Virginians' unwillingness to support each other in trade, see e.g. William Lee to Robert Wormeley Carter, 18 Jan. 1770, William Lee Letterbook, 1769–1771, Lee Family Papers at Stratford; Francis Lightfoot Lee to William Lee, 17 Dec. 1770, Edmund Jenings Lee Papers, Virginia Historical Society; William Lee to Landon Carter, 30 Oct. 1770, William Lee Letterbook, 1770–1771, Lee Family Papers at Stratford.

Lee's frustration with the consignment trade often focused on the influence of the Scottish traders, who by the 1770s affected even the London tobacco market. When Glasgow merchants flooded the London market in 1771, Lee found that prices for all kinds of tobacco fell, notwithstanding the destruction of much of Virginia's crop in the flood of that year. The low price at which Scots regularly sold tobacco to the French further deflated London's market and confounded Lee. Lee, however, could do nothing to counter Scottish domination of the tobacco trade which he attributed to unethical business dealings in Glasgow and a Virginia inspection system that facilitated the sale of bulk cargoes of mediocre tobacco. His chronic suspicion of Scottish business practices was justified in the spring of 1772 when he warned his Virginia correspondents not to accept Scottish bills of exchange unless they were at a lower exchange rate than bills for the same amount drawn on London. After June 1772, and the credit collapse that began in the overextended businesses of Glasgow, Lee refused all Scottish bills.[46]

The credit crisis of 1772 soon affected every aspect of British–American trade, bringing bankruptcy to some London tobacco markets and forcing others, like James Russell, to restrict their affairs in order to stay in business. Lee faced no immediate threat from the collapse of credit, and although he understood the need for caution, he also believed he was in a position to take advantage of the disruption in Virginia's trade. While his consignment business now insured a full load of the *Liberty* and was as extensive as he cared to handle, his cargo trade might successfully expand in the wake of Scottish credit failures. Lee gambled that the Scottish factors would reduce their sales of goods on credit and curtail cash purchases of tobacco. If Lee advanced cargoes to more Virginia merchants, he could fill the demand for goods and procure shiploads of tobacco as remittances.[47]

[46]William Lee to James Mills, 24 Sep. 1770, William Lee Letterbook, 1769–1771; William Lee to John Tayloe, 6 Aug. 1771; William Lee to Landon Carter, 26 Aug. 1771; William Lee Letterbook, 1770–1771, Lee Family Papers at Stratford; William Lee to Francis Lightfoot Lee, 24 Apr. 1772, 23 Jun. 1772, *Lee Family Papers* (University of Virginia microfilm publication).

[47]Jacob M. Price, "One Family's Empire: The Russell–Lee–Clerk Connection in Maryland, Britain, and India, 1707–1857," *Maryland Historical Magazine* 72 (Summer 1977): 186–190; William Lee to Richard Henry Lee, 18 Nov. 1772, 30 Jan. 1773, Richard Henry Lee Correspondence, Virginia Historical Society.

During the first six months of 1773, Lee made his largest cargo advances to date: £800 of goods to William Triplett and George Thornton, £900 to Hudson Muse, almost £3,000 to the Trents and their various partners, and to Daniel Muse alone enough goods to produce a return of 200 to 300 hogsheads of tobacco. Lee preferred to advance cargoes to resident merchants in Virginia rather than to operate his own store, the fixed costs of which proved a burden to many direct trade merchants in London. Yet he was confident the Virginians managing their own stores would profit from the cargo trade. "The Glasgow men this year will hardly send anything from hence," Lee wrote from London in January 1773, "so these young men have it in their power to make a great beginning." After the *Liberty* returned with 372 hogsheads of consigned tobacco in the summer of 1773, Lee needed to charter a special ship to collect tobacco from his merchant correspondents.[48]

Despite warnings from Richard Henry Lee and early indications of the merchants' inability to repay the value of the cargo advances, William Lee shipped cargoes to more merchants in the early months of 1774. Merriwether Smith and John Mills each received goods worth £1,500. By the summer of 1774, Lee was aware that neither he nor his mercantile correspondents in Virginia were immune from the effects of credit restrictions and falling tobacco prices. From that time forward, he advanced goods only to a few merchants who posted securities for the full value of the cargo. Other merchants, such as the Trents, were so remiss in payments that Lee ordered suits against them. Lee's advances had been so large, in such a short period of time, that remittances of 200 hogsheads failed to reduce some of the debts by half.[49]

William Lee's late entry into the cargo trade and his steady consignment business saved him from the near ruin faced by other merchants who advanced cargoes during the boom cycle of the early 1770s. Yet during the final year of trade before the Revolution, Lee's major business concern was the collection of debts from his commercial cli-

---

[48]William Lee to Richard Henry Lee, 30 Jan. 1773, Richard Henry Lee to William Lee, 4 July 1773, Richard Henry Lee Correspondence, Virginia Historical Society; William Lee to Francis Lightfoot Lee, 30 Jan. 1773, *Lee Family Papers* (University of Virginia microfilm publication).

[49]William Lee to Francis Lightfoot Lee, 30 Jan. 1773, *Lee Family Papers* (University of Virginia microfilm publication); Richard Henry Lee to William Lee, 4 Jul. 1773, 27 Sep. 1773, Richard Henry Lee Correspondence, Virginia Historical Society.

ents in Virginia. Like many consignment merchants, Lee had hoped the cargo trade would advance his business to the level of London's biggest direct traders, with importations of several thousand hogsheads a year. As a Virginian, he had the added incentive of promoting colonial merchants in competition with the Scottish factors. The cargo trade had enlarged the scope of Lee's business and temporarily boosted the fortunes of Virginia merchants, but neither he nor they were any freer of British credit than the consigning planters or the patrons of the factors' stores. Lee could advance cargoes only so long as he received credit from the London warehousemen and tradesmen who supplied the goods. And the ability of Virginia merchants to make remittances, thereby keeping open Lee's access to credit, depended on a steady market for goods and tobacco, neither of which continued after 1772. Lee's trading experience in the years before Independence proved that the disadvantages associated with Virginia's tobacco planters were not to be explained simply by the corruption or collusion of British merchants. The promise of Lee's entry into the consignment trade and his later encouragement of cargo merchants raised expectations of commercial arrangements favorable to the colonists, but the collapse of credit reminded Lee and his correspondents that the foundation of Virginia's tobacco trade had changed very little. The impact of William Lee's intended reforms would be inconsequential as long as Virginians depended on Great Britain for the financing and marketing of their agricultural produce.

■   ■   ■

In varying degrees, the credit crisis of 1772 affected every Virginian who traded in the Atlantic economy and brought to an abrupt halt the recent commercial advancements in the colony. Consigning planters once again faced the shortages of credit and bills of exchange that accompanied the periodic depressions in the tobacco market. By June 1773, John Tayloe believed that Virginia "can equal any part of the Globe in want of money and credit." The crisis was particularly severe for the planters who had borrowed money to finance the expansion and diversification of their plantation operations. Falling tobacco prices limited their ability to reduce outstanding debts, while the lack of further credit extensions suspended the improvement of recently purchased lands. The fortunate planters, like George Washington and Robert Carter, who had established alternatives to tobacco production found this depression less severe than others, but even these men continued to depend on the tobacco trade and the financial services of London merchants.[50]

For the resident Virginia merchants who had entered the cargo trade, the collapse of credit put an end to their opportunity to compete directly with the Scottish factors and London agents. During the three years before the Revolutionary War and the enforcement of a nonexportation agreement, the cargo merchants struggled to reduce the debts they had accumulated in the boom market before 1772. A glut of British goods, falling tobacco prices, and the scarcity of British bills of exchange in the colony made it difficult for the Virginia merchants to procure remittances of any kind. When they collected a shipload of tobacco, whether through the exchange of undervalued goods or purchases with local currency, the proceeds were not likely to cover their British debts. The inability to pay for cargoes within twelve months added interest charges to the merchants' debts.[51]

As early as the fall of 1772, the credit collapse endangered the business of John and George Fowler. At the October General Court in Williamsburg, the Fowlers could not purchase any bills of exchange to send to their Liverpool correspondents. The Scottish factors, who supplied many of the bills in the colony, were unable to draw a shilling, according to the Fowlers, and the exchange rate was up to 30 percent. Within the next few months, the Fowlers traveled to Alexandria and Norfolk just to purchase bills "at a dear price." In November 1772, their store at Bowlers was selling goods at prices lower than the original costs in Liverpool. Dobson, Daltera, & Walker, hoping to keep their debtors in business, agreed to send small spring and fall cargoes in 1773, but the Fowlers' remittances over the next twelve months barely covered the value of those goods. In February 1774, the Fowlers announced the closing of their store and began to press their own debtors for payments. Their troubles, however, were far from over. Interest charges of £253 in 1774 and £360 in 1775 increased their debts, while the closing of Virginia's courts in the summer of 1774 prevented the Fowlers from suing their customers for their debts. In the spring of 1775, John Fowler sailed to Jamaica to sell his sloop and a cargo of grain, but, with the

---

[50]John Tayloe to William Lee, 15 June 1773, William Lee Correspondence, Virginia Historical Society; Price, *Capital and Credit,* 135–36.

[51]Price, *Capital and Credit,* 136–37.

beginning of hostilities, the Fowlers did not send their English creditors the proceeds of this venture. At the opening of the Revolution, the
Fowlers owed over £7,000 to Dobson, Daltera, & Walker.[52]

The severity of the credit restrictions in Scotland directly affected
Virginia's small planters who had been immune from the worst effects
of earlier depressions. The financial resources of the large Glasgow firms
and the steady demand for cheap tobacco on the continent allowed Scottish factors to offer their Virginia customers a relatively steady supply
of goods, credit, and marketing outlets, even during the market
fluctuations to which consigning planters were so susceptible. The
financial collapse of 1772, however, threatened the great Scottish houses
with bankruptcy. These trading firms survived the crisis only by immediately curtailing their Virginia operations. On July 1, 1772, a week after the first bank failure in Scotland, William Cunninghame & Co. issued
new instructions to its factors in Virginia. The company ordered an end
to the factors' liberal drafts and limited future bills drawn to a fraction
of the value of tobacco shipped. For the next year, the factors would
receive "very Scanty Supplys" in order to clear out old goods and to
encourage the collection of tobacco in payment for old debts rather
than to use goods to attract new accounts. For the future, factors were
permitted to order only those goods that would find immediate sale or
were necessary to round out the assortment on hand. The company also
ordered the factors to close out the accounts of all customers who were
not tobacco producers. The impact of the credit collapse soon appeared
in the prices offered for tobacco at the local stores of the Glasgow firms.
Throughout the first six months of 1772, the Dumfries store of John
Glassford & Co. paid 20 shillings Virginia currency for a hundred weight
of tobacco. By August the price fell to 18 shillings, and for the next year
the factors offered no more than 12 shillings 6 pence.[53]

---

[52]Fowlers to Dobson, Daltera, & Walker, 20 Oct. 1772, 14 Nov. 1772, 9
Feb. 1773, 28 Feb. 1774, 25 Oct. 1774, and 1 June 1775; Account of John and
George Fowler with Dobson, Daltera, & Walker, Dobson & Daltera vs. Fowler,
svg. ptr., U.S. Circuit Court, Virginia District, Ended Cases, 1798, Virginia
State Library.

[53]William Cunninghame & Company to James Robinson, 1 July 1772,
Cunninghame of Lainshaw Muniments, 1761–1778 (Virginia Colonial Records
Project microfilm); Ledgers of Boyds Hole and Dumfries stores, Glassford
Company Papers, Library of Congress.

Cunninghame & Co. and other Glasgow firms seldom sued for the recovery of their debts, most of which were for less than £10, but the retraction of their businesses after 1772 had a disastrous effect on their customers, many of whom had nowhere else to go for credit, household goods, or the sale of their tobacco crop. In areas where Scottish factors dominated trade, frustrated planters supported various cooperative schemes to import goods and market tobacco on their own. In the fall of 1773, a Louisa County "Planter," angered by the low price of to-bacco and the high price of imported goods, blamed the merchants for his distress and that of his fellow tobacco growers. He feared that the estates of Virginia planters were likely to fall into the hands of merchant creditors if the planters did not organize for their defense. This "Planter" recommended that tobacco growers in every county appoint four men from among their number to represent them in negotiations with to-bacco purchasers. A planter from Caroline County wrote the *Virginia Gazette* about the support in his county for a similar association "to frustrate the ingenious Designs of the merchants." From Bedford County in the west came a more elaborate proposal. Local agents would be ap-pointed for the marketing of tobacco and the procurement of imported goods. Agents from the various counties would determine a minimum price for tobacco sold in the country. The proposals for planter associa-tions and cooperative stores often betrayed a misunderstanding of or ignored the substantial costs of credit extensions in the Chesapeake trade, but they focused new attention on the inflexibility of tobacco culture and heightened anti-Scottish sentiment. They were also evidence of support for voluntary associations and commercial resistance among exactly the sort of tobacco growers who largely ignored the nonimpor-tation associations of 1769 and 1770. By 1773, more planters than ever before were determined to play a more direct role in the operation of colonial trade.[54]

The credit crisis and falling tobacco prices put an end to the brief hopes of commercial independence that had flourished during the non-importation associations and the economic prosperity at the opening of the decade. By the latter months of 1773, the pervasive nature of the depression had united the interests of small tobacco producers with those

[54]"A Planter to the Tobacco Planters of Virginia," *Virginia Gazette* (Purdie & Dixon), 21 Oct. 1773; "A Planter in Caroline to the Planter in Louisa County," *Virginia Gazette* (Purdie & Dixon), 4 Nov. 1773; *Virginia Gazette* (Purdie & Dixon), 25 Nov. 1773.

of the gentry planters and resident merchants who tried to establish some degree of economic independence from Great Britain. The suffering and disappointment after 1772 contributed to the ferocity of colonial opposition to British policy in the spring of 1774 and prompted widespread calls for a renewal of commercial forms of resistance.

THE RENEWAL OF COMMERCIAL RESISTANCE

IN THE MIDST OF THE DEPRESSION THAT FOLLOWED the collapse of British mercantile credit, Parliament unwittingly provoked the most severe imperial crisis to date with its approval of legislation intended to encourage American importation of dutied tea. For many Virginians, already alarmed by the severity of the economic depression and Great Britain's repeated attempts to secure revenue from the colonies, the new legislation and Parliament's extreme reaction to American protests were incontrovertible proof of a design to fix the colonists' absolute dependence on both parliamentary authority and British commerce. Again and again in 1774, Virginians defending American prerogatives drew the connection between economic dependence and the political subservience that surely ensued, all the while emphasizing that commercial independence would bring its own material rewards for Virginia. The imposition of parliamentary restrictions on American trade, following in quick succession the withdrawal of British credit and the drop in tobacco prices, offered a compelling logic for the renewal of commercial resistance as

> the only possible Means of avoiding that dependent commercial connexion which hitherto subsisted between the Colonies and Great Britain, [and] which hath induced an arbitrary and designing Administration to attempt the Total Destruction of our Rights and Liberties.

The search for economic independence and the struggle to secure political rights fully merged in 1774 in the face of the challenge from a

173

British policy that appeared to deprive the colonists of both. Emboldened by a sense of the colony's worth to the British economy and confident of the potential for economic development in Virginia, an unprecedented number of Virginians, great planters and yeoman farmers alike, joined in demands for the most far-reaching commercial associations yet proposed in America.[1]

■   ■   ■

The legislation that precipitated the final imperial crisis originated in Parliament's reform of the East India Company and the tea trade rather than as part of the recurring efforts to collect more revenue from the American trade. In an effort to salvage the near-bankrupt company, Parliament set out to increase tea imports in America and to grant the East India Company the profits from that expanded trade. In the Tea Act of May 1773, Parliament approved a refund of all duties paid on tea landed in Great Britain upon the reexportation of such cargoes to America. To reduce further the price of tea, Parliament allowed the East India Company to circumvent colonial middlemen and sell the tea through the company's own agents in Boston, New York, Philadelphia, and Charleston. This legislation reduced the price of tea to a level competitive with smuggled Dutch tea, but the arrangement, with its connotations of monopoly and imperial patronage, aroused immediate opposition in the designated port cities. Even fiercer protests greeted the actual arrival of the tea which carried the sole duty remaining from the Townshend revenue acts and which in principle the colonial nonimportation agreements still forbade. Popular political organizations, often with the support of local merchants, prevented the landing or sale of the tea in each city and in Boston destroyed the Company's cargo in the famous Tea Party of December 1773.[2]

Although immediately unaffected by the Tea Act, Virginia political leaders kept abreast of the protests through a recently established network of intercolonial and transatlantic communication. The assembly's committee of correspondence, created in March 1773, provided the

[1]Quotation from resolves of Chesterfield County meeting, 14 July 1774, *Revolutionary Virginia*, eds., Scribner and Tarter, 1:116–18

[2]Benjamin Woods Labaree, *The Boston Tea Party* (New York: Oxford University Press, 1964), 58–145; Jensen, *Founding of a Nation*, 434–60.

burgesses with intelligence regarding developments in other colonies and in Great Britain. The committee's London correspondent, tobacco merchant John Norton, offered the first warning of the Tea Act and its implications for trade throughout the American colonies. In July 1773, Norton informed the committee of Parliament's "Strides toward Despotism . . . with respect to the East India Company as well as America." The Company, according to Norton, was to be but "a Cat's paw" used to establish a tea duty of three pence per pound. From the committees of Massachusetts and Connecticut came defenses of colonial rights and assurances of effective opposition to the landing of the East India Company tea. The private correspondence between Virginia committee member Richard Henry Lee and Samuel Adams provided the House of Burgesses with additional information regarding the organization of commercial resistance in Massachusetts.[3]

Articles in the *Virginia Gazette* further publicized the northern protests against the Tea Act and emphasized the commercial and economic implications for Virginia. A report from Charleston claimed that the establishment of tea warehouses in the four cities was "intended to pave the Way for introducing large Factories for other Goods at all the principle Ports, and then bring in an Honourable Board of Excise." The announcement of revived associations in New York carried appeals for similar organizations in all colonies. Soon the Virginia press carried a new round of local debates on the proper commercial organization of the Empire. In the fall of 1773, two contributors to the *Virginia Gazette* dared to justify Parliament's latest commercial legislation for the colonies. "Corporal Trim" of Suffolk in Nansemond County argued that parliamentary duties were the proper price for British protection of American commercial and military security. A certain "Landon Honduras" of "Cosmopoli" attacked the resolves of Philadelphia, New York, and Boston as a dangerous provocation of the British government. If Americans refused to accept the East India Company's ships, he warned

---

[3]Peyton Randolph, Robert Carter Nicholas, and Dudley Digges to John Norton, 6 Apr. 1773, John Norton to Randolph, et al., 6 July 1773, *Revolutionary Virginia*, eds., Scribner and Tarter, 2:20–21, 37–38, 44–47, 51–52; Richard Henry Lee to Samuel Adams, 4 Feb. 1773, 24 Apr 1774, in *The Letters of Richard Henry Lee*, Ballagh, ed., 1:82–83, 106–08; Samuel Adams to Richard Henry Lee, 10 Apr. 1773, in *Lee Family Papers* (University of Virginia microfilm publication).

176 A PLANTERS' REPUBLIC

the British might cease buying colonial goods. "Honduras" urged the colonists to rest content with the advantages of cheap tea.[4]

These isolated defenses of Parliament, almost certainly the contributions of British factors in the colony, quickly exposed the depth of opposition to the Tea Act in Virginia. A letter signed by "Thousands" challenged "Honduras's" description of the northern resolves and dismissed his suggestion of threats to American export trade. The northern colonies were virtuously adhering to an association which remained in effect for Virginians as well. "Thousands" contended that the Tea Act was "part of the abominable plan" that began with the Stamp Act and continued with the Declaratory Act and Parliament's betrayal of its promise to repeal the Townshend duties. "Landon Honduras" defended himself with warnings of the likely alienation of British merchants and incitement of "the lower class, with who it may be sufficient to make use of the Term Liberty to make them believe a mere Question of Trade or Expediency has anything to do therewith." "Thousands" countered that Virginia's "Tobacco Trade is so extremely profitable to our Friends beyond the Water" that the British never would obstruct commerce with the colony. Landon Carter reminded "Honduras" that Parliament's duty, not the cheapness of tea, was the crucial issue. Carter admitted that Virginians made a mistake of importing tea during recent years, but the dutied article was accepted in good faith while other events in Great Britain had suggested a possibility of reconciliation.[5]

The nonimportation associations of 1769 and 1770 had reduced Virginia's tea imports from a level of 23,804 pounds in 1768 to 20,076 pounds in 1770 and 11,104 pounds in 1771. Although the prohibition on tea remained in effect after the association's dissolution in July 1771, Virginians imported over 44,000 pounds of tea in 1772. Only a few devoted adherents to the nonimportation associations refused to accept tea while it carried a duty. Tea imports declined in 1773 as a result of the general depression in Chesapeake trade rather than from any observance of the old association.[6]

---

[4]*Virginia Gazette* (Purdie & Dixon), 25 Nov., 2 Dec., 16 Dec., 1773, 13 Jan. 1774.

[5]*Virginia Gazette* (Purdie & Dixon), 23 Dec. 1773, 20 Jan. 1774, 3 Mar. 1774; Landon Carter to Purdie & Dixon, 14 Feb. 1774, Sabine Hall Collection, University of Virginia.

[6]Import figures for tea in Ledger of Imports and Exports (America), 5 Jan. 1768–5 Jan. 1773, Public Record Office, Customs 16/1 (Virginia Colonial Records Project microfilm); for example of continued refusal to import dutied

By January of 1774, the American protest of the Tea Act prompted Virginians to call for a strict observation of the moribund boycott. "A Lady's Adieu to her Tea Table" announced in verse that some Virginia families already had rejected the popular drink. The poem in the *Virginia Gazette*, bidding "Farewell to the Tea Board, with its gaudy Equipage" and vowing allegiance to the "Goddess" Liberty, marked a new awareness of the importance of mobilizing the support of women in any political strategy that rested on nonconsumption. Other articles in the *Virginia Gazette* described the allegedly unhealthy effects of tea, particularly that from the East India Company, and offered suggestions for herbal substitutes. In February the newspaper refused to print a letter from King William County criticizing the destruction of the tea in Boston and warning of the dangers from an enraged ministry. Editors Alexander Purdie and John Dixon denied that the British would seek revenge or retribution because the "Ministry, from past Experience are too wise to attempt any Thing against America which may affect its commercial Intercourse with the Parent State, whose Prosperity so much depends on that Cement of Nations."[7]

The editors of the *Virginia Gazette* accurately assessed the value of the American trade but not the wisdom of the British Ministry. Lord North insisted on a plan to punish Boston and exact compliance with the Tea Act through a series of measures that confirmed the most exaggerated suspicions of American colonists. The Port Act, first of the four Coercive Acts directed against Massachusetts, closed Boston to all shipping except for a restricted coastwise trade in foodstuffs and fuel. The port was to remain shut until the city paid for the destroyed tea and compensated customs officers for losses sustained during several riots.

The Lee brothers in London immediately informed their Virginia friends that Parliament's drastic interference with the trade of Massachusetts presented a threat against the rest of America. During the parliamentary debate on the Port Bill, Arthur Lee warned Richard Henry Lee that Boston might be the direct target of British retaliation, but all America would suffer. Lord North, having destroyed the opposition,

---

tea see invoice inclosed in George Washington to Robert Cary & Co., 26 July 1773, Washington Papers, Library of Congress.

[7]*Virginia Gazette* (Purdie & Dixon), 6 Jan. 1774, 13 Jan. 1774, 20 Jan. 1774, 10 Feb. 1774; *Virginia Gazette* (Rind), 16 Dec. 1773 printed an article from Newport claiming that the East India tea had been infected by a flea–like insect "which renders it more pernicious to health than usual."

"made the vast revenue & territory of India in effect a royal patronage" and now intended to do the same with America. The only effective defense, according to Arthur Lee, would be a "general resolution of the Colonies to break off all commercial intercourse with this Country." As difficult as such a cooperative agreement might be, Arthur Lee assured his brother "you would be amply repaid not only in saving your money & becoming independent of these petty tyrants the Merchants, but in securing your general Liberties." William Lee advocated a similar response with an emphasis on nonexportation. Withholding the exports of the Chesapeake and Carolina colonies, he maintained, would be sufficient to bring repeal of the offensive acts within one year. A suspension of all commerce with Great Britain would also "in the end tend to the particular pecuniary advantage of each colony."[8]

Even before receiving word of the Port Act or his brothers' advice, Richard Henry Lee prepared for the assembly's official response to any potential parliamentary retaliation against Boston. The session of the Virginia assembly scheduled for early May would be the first to convene since the announcement of the Tea Act and the subsequent protests in other colonies. Lee wanted to insure that the gathering of the burgesses would be an opportunity for the Virginia legislature to condemn the Tea Act and take a lead in defending the colonies against any further parliamentary interference with trade or local political rights. In anticipation of harsh measures against Boston, Lee asked Samuel Adams to forward any relevant news directly to Williamsburg in time for the opening of the assembly. He also suggested that communications from the Massachusetts committee of correspondence would have the most effect if they arrived while the burgesses were in session.[9]

As the assembly proceeded with its routine business during the first two weeks of the session that opened on May 5, the *Virginia Gazette* printed various reports of proposals for punitive measures against the colonies and of military preparations in Great Britain. When George Mason arrived in Williamsburg on private business, he "found every body's attention . . . entirely engrossed by the Boston affair." In private, burgesses discussed possible resolutions in support of Boston, and most

[8]Jensen, *Founding of a Nation*, 453–60; Arthur Lee to Richard Henry Lee, 18 Mar. 1774, 2 Apr. 1774, *Lee Family Papers* (University of Virginia microfilm publication).

[9]Richard Henry Lee to Samuel Adams, 24 Apr. 1774, *The Letters of Richard Henry Lee*, ed., Ballagh, 1:106–08.

assumed the colony's response to any parliamentary threat would be the revival of some form of commercial resistance. After the *Virginia Gazette* of May 19 published an official report of the Boston Port Act, the burgesses immediately began preparations for a specific plan of commercial association. One member of the assembly reported on May 20 a "universal determination to stop the exportation of tobacco, pitch, tar, lumber, &c., and to stop importation from Britain while this act of hostility continues." The calls for commercial resistance came from outside the capital as well. William Carr in Dumfries learned of plans to end all imports and exports as well as proposals to close the county courts to debt cases.[10]

The expiration of a routine administrative statute fortuitously presented the House of Burgesses with a justification for suspending the courts of justice if a majority so desired. The Fee Act provided for the payment of over 200 levies for services of the provincial government including all court costs associated with civil cases. Since 1745 the assembly had included a date of termination in each renewal of the Fee Act, and the most recent lapsed in April 1774. Members of the General Court sitting at that time ruled that they could continue the existing fee schedule for the remainder of the term in expectation of a renewal of the law when the assembly met the following month. Local courts also proceeded with routine business. During the first week of the May session of the House of Burgesses, however, Richard Henry Lee, as chairman of the committee responsible for renewing any administrative statutes which may have expired during the recess of the assembly, presented a report that pointedly omitted any reference to the Fee Bill. Lee, known to be a supporter of an aggressive commercial resistance including nonexportation, presumably meant to establish the administrative technicality that would justify a suspension of the courts of jus-

---

[10]*Virginia Gazette* (Purdie & Dixon), 5 May, 12 May, 19 May 1774; William Aitchison to Charles Steuart, 16 May 1774, Charles Steuart Papers, National Library of Scotland (Colonial Williamsburg microfilm); George Mason to Martin Cockburn, 26 May 1774, *Papers of George Mason*, ed., Rutland, 1:190–91; *Diary of Landon Carter*, ed., Greene, 2:812; "Member of the Virginia Assembly to his correspondent in London," 20 May 1774, in *American Archives, Fourth Series*, ed., Peter Force (Washington, 1837), 1:340; William Carr to James Russell, 26 May 1774, Russell Papers, Coutts & Co., London (Virginia Colonial Records Project microfilm). (Carr was writing from Dumfries where he would have had no knowledge of the dissolution of the assembly on the same date.)

tice just as the lack of stamps had provided the excuse for closing the courts to debt recovery suits during the Stamp Act crisis. Lee, however, had moved too fast or too far for the comfort of some of the burgesses. The whole House ordered Lee and his committee to report a renewal of the Fee Bill. The bill was then referred to another committee before consideration by the burgesses.[11]

On May 25 Richard Henry Lee drafted resolutions which he agreed to withhold from formal consideration until the burgesses completed the country's business lest they provoke the governor's dissolution as in 1769. Lee's seven resolutions included defenses of the colonial assemblies' exclusive right of taxation, a condemnation of the blockade of Boston harbor, and a pledge to boycott East India Company tea. The precise terms of a commercial association endorsed by Lee were left to a proposed congress of deputies from each colony who would determine the most effective means of stopping exports and would adopt "other Methods as shall be most decisive for securing the Constitutional rights of America against the Systimatic plan formed for their destruction." Two days before writing these resolves, Lee joined with several burgesses including Thomas Jefferson, Patrick Henry, and Francis Lightfoot Lee to prepare a resolution for a day of fasting on June 1 to mark the enforcement of the Port Act. The fast-day resolution, submitted by Robert Carter Nicholas and approved by nearly the whole House, declared the assembly's solidarity with the citizens of Boston and prayed for an avoidance of the civil war that surely would follow a continued disregard for American rights. The burgesses intended the fast to alert the public to the danger from the Port Act and to prepare the colony for the sacrifices necessary under a strict commercial association.[12]

Governor Dunmore interpreted the fast solely as a "determined resolution to deny and oppose the Authority of Parliament." He accordingly dissolved the House on May 26, two days after the burgesses'

[11]Frank L. Dewey, *Thomas Jefferson, Lawyer* (Charlottesville: University Press of Virginia, 1986), 94–106; George M. Curtis III, "The Role of the Courts in the Making of the Revolution in Virginia," in *The Human Dimensions of Nation Making: Essays on Colonial and Revolutionary America*, ed., James Kirby Martin (Madison: The State Historical Society of Wisconsin, 1976), 121–46; A. G. Roeber, *Faithful Magistrates and Republican Lawyers: Creators of Virginia Legal Culture, 1680–1810* (Chapel Hill: University of North Carolina Press, 1981), 160–62.

[12]Text of fast-day resolution and Jefferson's comments in *The Papers of Thomas Jefferson*, ed., Boyd, 1:105–07.

approval of the fast-day. The burgesses had anticipated a dissolution, but the surprise of the timing prevented the assembly from completing the country's business, including passage of the Fee Bill or consideration of Richard Henry Lee's more far-reaching resolutions.[13]

With Dunmore's abrupt dismissal of the assembly, the burgesses followed their precedent established at the dissolution in 1769 and quickly reconvened at an extra-legal meeting in the Apollo Room of the Raleigh Tavern. There they accepted an association which was signed on May 27 by eighty-nine of the former burgesses. This initial agreement urged all Virginians to oppose the "Determined system . . . formed and pressed for reducing the inhabitants of British America to slavery" but stopped well short of the detailed program of commercial resistance that many members expected and preferred. A "tender regard" for the interests of British merchants and manufacturers temporarily prevented the burgesses from entering into a more radical agreement, although the association recognized that a suspension of all commerce with Great Britain would be necessary if Parliament persisted in its unconstitutional taxation of the colonies. For the time being, the former burgesses reaffirmed their boycott of dutied tea and recommended a prohibition of all East India Company imports with the exception of saltpeter and spices which were necessary for medicinal preparations. The boldest measure of the association was Richard Henry Lee's proposal for an annual convention of deputies from all the American colonies. In his original draft for the assembly's resolves, Lee recommended that this congress adopt a uniform strategy of commercial resistance.[14]

[13]Governor Dunmore to Lord Dartmouth, 29 May 1774, Public Record Office, CO5/1352 (Virginia Colonial Records Project microfilm); *Journals of the House of Burgesses, 1773–1776*, eds., Kennedy and McIlwaine, 132; George Washington to George William Fairfax, 10 June 1774, *Writings of Washington*, ed., Fitzpatrick, 3:223; Richard Henry Lee to Samuel Adams, 23 June 1774, *Letters of Richard Henry Lee*, ed., Ballagh, 1:111–13.

[14]*Revolutionary Virginia*, eds., Scribner and Tarter, 1:97–98; Lee's original resolutions printed with Richard Henry Lee to Arthur Lee, 26 June 1774, *Letters of Richard Henry Lee*, ed., Ballagh, 115. The former burgesses assumed theirs was the first official suggestion for a general congress, but Delaware's committee of correspondence had issued the same call on 26 May, *Revolutionary Virginia*, eds., Scribner and Tarter, 2:82–84. The idea of a general congress had been discussed regularly since the fall of 1773, see *Virginia Gazette* (Purdie & Dixon), 11 Nov 1773, and Jensen, *Founding of a Nation*, 461.

If the burgesses had been hesitant to repeat the unhappy experience of the association of 1770 and enter into a commercial boycott without the full cooperation of other colonies, their reluctance vanished on May 29 when Peyton Randolph received copies of the recent resolves from Boston, Philadelphia, and Annapolis. Confronted with the enforcement of the Port Act, Boston's town meeting had concluded that the surest defense as well as the "Salvation of North America & her Liberties" would be a joint colonial agreement to refuse all imports from Great Britain and to halt all exportations to Great Britain and the West Indies. In a cautious response to Boston's appeal, the Philadelphia city committee resisted a commercial association for the time being but accepted the idea of a general congress. Annapolis's town committee endorsed the proposal for nonimportation and nonexportation and distributed the Boston resolves to every part of Maryland. The Annapolis committee suggested public meetings be called to discuss the strategy for nonintercourse and the possibility of closing the courts to all debt cases.[15]

Randolph gathered the burgesses remaining in Williamsburg and presented them with the letters from Massachusetts, Philadelphia, and Annapolis. The twenty-five members who met on May 29 and 30 unanimously agreed to support whatever measures were decided on by a congress of all the colonies. They hoped that any joint agreement would include a nonimportation association, but they divided on the issue of nonexportation. Randolph, Thomas Nelson, and Paul Carrington believed exports should continue so that planters could reduce the private debts they owed to British merchants. Robert Carter Nicholas led those who believed that an effective association must curtail all commerce. This small gathering refused to make a final decision on the enlargement of their recent association but recommended a general meeting of all former burgesses. On May 31, Randolph and the others attending the rump meeting sent their fellow burgesses a summary of their reaction to the Boston resolves and an invitation to a convention in Williamsburg on August 1. The intervening two months would allow

---

[15]Samuel Adams to Virginia Committee of Correspondence, 13 May 1774, with enclosure of Boston Town Meeting's resolution of the same date, *Revolutionary Virginia*, eds., Scribner and Tarter, 2:71–73; Philadelphia City Committee to Peyton Randolph, with enclosures, 21 May 1774, in ibid., 2:75–77; Annapolis Town Committee to Virginia Committee of Correspondence, 25 May 1774, in ibid., 2:80–81.

the former burgesses time to ascertain "the Sense of their respective Counties." Already the citizens of Williamsburg had "most cheerfully acceded to the Measures" adopted.[16]

Opposition to the Port Act was so widespread in Virginia that merchant William Carr of Dumfries predicted "the sense of their constituents" would force the burgesses into a more radical association. In fact, the decision to consult popular opinion in the summer of 1774 was among the most momentous of the Revolutionary era in Virginia. Already communities were demanding some form of commercial resistance that went beyond anything proposed in 1769 and 1770. Carr was convinced at least two-thirds of the inhabitants would support a complete cessation of commerce with Great Britain. A town meeting in Dumfries, held before announcement of the burgesses' association, responded to the resolves of the Boston town meeting with a resolution favoring nonintercourse with Great Britain and the West Indies. When Fredericksburg's town committee received the resolves of Boston and other cities to the north, it convened a town meeting which approved a general commercial association of the colonies. A joint committee of Norfolk and Portsmouth on May 31 called on the citizens of Charleston and other commercial cities "to fix upon such expedients in the regulation of Trade, as may be most productive of relief to our suffering Brethren in Boston."[17]

As George Washington understood, the Port Act was only the most dramatic in a series of events contributing to the pervasive sense of crisis in Virginia. In June of 1774 Washington observed that "since the first Settlement of this Colony the Minds of People in it never were more disturbed, or our Situation so critical as at present." On every front, the colony seemed besieged. The frontier faced attacks from an Indian confederacy and the likely prospect of war, "whilst those from whom we have a right to seek protection are endeavouring by every

[16]Instructions for August convention and reference to meeting in Williamsburg in *Revolutionary Virginia*, eds., Scribner and Tarter, 1:101–02; Williamsburg Town Meeting, 30 May 1774, ibid., 7:730.

[17]William Carr to James Russell, 26 May 1774, 30 May 1774, Russell Papers, Coutts & Co., London (Virginia Colonial Records Project microfilm); Dumfries Town Committee to Virginia Committee of Correspondence, with enclosure, 31 May 1774; Norfolk and Portsmouth Joint Committee to the Inhabitants of Charleston, S.C., 31 May 1774; Fredericksburg Town Committee to Peyton Randolph, with enclosure, 1 June 1774, all in *Revolutionary Virginia*, eds., Scribner and Tarter, 2:92–96.

piece of Art and despotism to fix the Shackles of Slavery upon us." The
failure to pass the Fee Bill and the indefinite suspension of the assembly
closed the county courts while a shortage of currency further disrupted
business affairs. Nature conspired to worsen matters with a freakish
snowstorm and frost that destroyed at least half of the colony's wheat
crop in May.[18]

The lingering effects of the British credit collapse complicated the
misfortunes described by Washington. Throughout the first six months
of 1774 tobacco prices remained so low that planters refused to sell
their crops. The rate of exchange between Virginia currency and British sterling continued well above par, thus making it costly if not impossible for Virginians to purchase bills of exchange or to reduce their
sterling debts. The accumulation of economic hardships and disruptions in the normal process of government laid the foundation for the
popular reaction to the Port Act. Great Britain's arbitrary restrictions
on colonial commerce, the disregard for the rights of the government
of Massachusetts, and the dissolution of their own legislative assembly
appeared to Virginians as evidence of a determination to secure the permanent and absolute dependence of the colonies. The sequence of events
involving the passage of the Tea Act, Boston's protest, and Parliament's
approval of the Port Act had special significance in Virginia at a time
when every planter and native merchant recognized the vulnerability of
a colonial economy largely dependent on British merchants and their
credit. Not since the Stamp Act had a measure of the British government provoked such protests from all ranks of free Virginians.[19]

In the early summer of 1774, few observers doubted the serious
intent of the numerous calls for commercial resistance. Merchant Harry
Piper warned his English partners that this time the "Americans will
undergo many hardships before they will part with their libertys." William Reynolds assured a friend in England that the fate of earlier associations was no indication of the unanimous support a new one would
receive. Yet, however widespread popular opposition appeared in June
1774, the burgesses and other members of the gentry were determined
to cultivate and organize anti-British sentiment in order to avoid the

---

[18]George Washington to George William Fairfax, 10 June 1774, *Writings
of Washington*, ed., Fitzpatrick, 3:221–26.

[19]William Carr to James Russell, 10 May 1774, Russell Papers, Coutts &
Co., London (Virginia Colonial Records Project microfilm); exchange rates in
John J. McCusker, *Money and Exchange in Europe and America, 1600–1775*
(Chapel Hill: University of North Carolina Press, 1978), 212.

shortcomings of the associations of 1769 and 1770 and at the same time to sustain their own authority in the face of unprecedented popular participation in public affairs. Only popular support and an appearance of unanimity could legitimate the proceedings of the August convention that was in effect a House of Burgesses operating outside the jurisdiction of royal authority.[20]

The fast day was the first effort to organize and direct the popular opposition to the Boston Port Act. "The effect of the day," according to Jefferson, "was like a shock of electricity arousing every man & placing him erect and solidly on his centre." A more direct type of public appeal came a week later when Landon Carter appeared at the Richmond county court to persuade the gathered crowd that a commercial association would be the most effective defense against the British assault on American rights. Carter cleverly exploited the prejudice against Scottish merchants, many of whom were the leading opponents of any commercial resistance. He argued that the Scots favored submission to British taxation because "they were strangers to Liberty themselves and wanted the rest of Mankind to live under the same slavish notions, that they have ever done, that is from a tendency to be arbitrary themselves they wanted to set the example to others." The image of Scots depriving Virginians of their independence was all too plausible to the many Virginians who stood indebted to the factors' stores and had suffered from the Scots' restricted credit policy after 1772. Carter also argued that stopping all commerce with Great Britain and closing the courts to debt cases would be an effective and deserved response to the failure of the British people to oppose "this Arbitrary Proceeding of their Parliament." After his speech, Carter was convinced the people of the county would be "Pretty unanimous" in support of nonimportation and nonexportation. Carter's friend Dr. Walter Jones found that public gatherings also provided an opportunity to cultivate support among those who persisted in the belief that commercial resistance was only of interest to the gentry. Following a meeting at Farnham in Richmond County, Jones reported the "Many people who came there with an opinion, too common among the Vulgar, that the Law affecting Tea alone, did not concern them, because they used none of it had their prejudices removed."[21]

---

[20]Harry Piper to Dixon and Littledale, 9 June 1774, Piper Letterbook, University of Virginia; William Reynolds to George Flowerdew Norton, 3 June 1774, William Reynolds Letterbook, 1771–1796, Library of Congress.

[21]*Diary of Landon Carter*, ed., Greene, 2:821–22; Dr. Walter Jones to Landon Carter, 17 June 1774, Sabine Hall Collection, University of Virginia.

■   ■   ■

Virginians developed a specific strategy of commercial resistance through a series of county meetings called to elect and instruct delegates to the August convention. During June and July of 1774, at least forty-one of Virginia's sixty-one counties held meetings and announced their recommendations for the convention. The late burgesses' association of May and the resolves of the Boston town meeting served as starting points for the county proposals which also attempted to correct the inadequacies of Virginia's earlier nonimportation agreements. The county resolves ranged from cautious statements of support for an intercolonial congress to demands for a radical break with all British commerce. Some counties immediately entered into an association while most waited for the results of the Virginia convention. The overwhelming majority of counties favored some form of nonimportation.[22]

Attended by large numbers of "Freeholders and other inhabitants," the county meetings in effect expanded the franchise and were an important device for translating the popular opposition to the Tea Act and the Port Act into an effective scheme of commercial association. In 1769 and 1770 county meetings served as a ratification of the agreement formulated by the burgesses in Williamsburg rather than as a means of collecting proposals from every area of the colony and from a wide range of citizens. Through the process of instructing delegates in 1774, the burgesses and the county gentry acknowledged that the freeholders' support and participation were prerequisites for the success of this unprecedented political mobilization.

The public gatherings also provided the local gentry with an opportunity to demonstrate their intention to participate fully in the program of austerity. At the opening to the York County meeting, Thomas Nelson, one of the county's wealthiest merchant-planters, announced that "we must resign the Hope of making Fortunes." Repeated assurances of a strict regulation of business activity, expressions of support for the poor in Boston, and the renunciations of extravagance became the gentry's formulaic pledge that all ranks of society would share in the burdens of economic sacrifice. By taking the lead in the organization of

[22]Extant proceedings of county meetings printed in *Revolutionary Virginia*, eds., Scribner and Tarter, 1:111–68, 7:733–38. At least eight counties submitted to the *Virginia Gazette* resolutions that were never published.

commercial resistance and often directing the proceedings of the county meetings, burgesses, members of the county courts, and others from among the gentry maintained their local authority by incorporating popular opposition to the British government into their own long-standing efforts to achieve a greater degree of economic and political independence.[23]

The Dumfries town committee called for the first county meeting in Virginia even before it received a copy of the Williamsburg association or the announcement of the August convention. By the time the meeting for Prince William County convened at Dumfries on June 6, the assembled citizens had received reports of the proceedings in Williamsburg and found the recent association disappointing. The former burgesses had "not fallen upon means sufficiently efficacious to secure us the enjoyment of our civil rights and liberties." Prince William County's meeting was fully prepared to accept the Boston town meeting's recommendation for complete cessation of imports from and exports to Great Britain and the West Indies. The meeting also advocated closing the colony's courts to all civil cases until the acts directed against Boston were repealed. On June 8 a meeting in Frederick County in the west echoed the Boston resolves in their call for a joint resolution of all the colonies to halt imports and exports. Frederick's meeting imitated the Williamsburg association in declaring an immediate boycott of East India Company imports and also suggested a network of local committees of correspondence that would insure the uniformity of a general association. Loudoun County's meeting on June 14 resolved to suspend all commerce with Great Britain until the repeal of the Port Act and until such time as "the right of regulating the internal policy of N. America by British Parliament shall be absolutely and positively given up."[24]

In Westmoreland County, where Richard Henry Lee was elected a deputy and undoubtedly influenced the resolves, the meeting agreed to join a nonimportation–nonexportation association that included a majority of the continental colonies. The Westmoreland resolves of

---

[23]*Revolutionary Virginia*, eds., Scribner and Tarter, 1:165–66.

[24]Dumfries Town Committee, 31 May 1774, *Revolutionary Virginia*, eds., Scribner and Tarter, 2:92–93; Prince William County Committee meeting, 6 June 1774, ibid., 1:152–53; Frederick County meeting, 8 June 1774, ibid, 1:135–36; Loudoun County meeting, ibid. 7:733–34.

June 22 offered several suggestions for the successful execution of a broad commercial association. No court action for the recovery of debts should be allowed, "it being utterly inconsistent with a Non-exportation Plan that Judgement should be given against those who are deprived of the Means of paying." During the period of nonexportation, no one should carry their produce to warehouses or shipping wharves unless it be grain intended for other parts of Virginia or for other colonies operating under the association. The storage of crops at individual plantations would prevent "a few designing Persons" from hoarding commodities in expectation of a rising market when the ports reopened. The Westmoreland citizens also declared that anyone who agreed to the association and later disregarded its terms would be censured by the community.[25]

Prince George County, in a set of resolutions that served as a model for several other counties, offered more proposals to encourage the observance of a nonimportation agreement and to make economic independence a reality. As in 1769 and 1770, some Virginians feared the colony could not expect realistically to exclude all British manufactures. Prince George's resolves suggested exemptions for tools, coarse fabrics used to clothe slaves, medicines, and paper, all items for which demand exceeded the production of colonial manufactures. Culpeper and Hanover Counties recommended exemptions for these items as well as for the saltpeter, lead, and powder required for defense. Chesterfield County wanted permission to import wool and clothiers' cards and other "Implements necessary for the manufacturing of Woolens and Linen." Albemarle and Hanover asked that "the necessary tools and implements for the handycraft arts and manufactures" be excepted "for a limited time." Jefferson's resolves for Albemarle County also recommended the free importation of books and printed paper.[26]

In an effort to reduce the colonies' dependence on Great Britain for basic supplies, Prince George became the first of several counties to propose subscriptions for the encouragement of local manufactures. Public support of sheep raising and cultivation of hemp and flax would

---

[25]Westmoreland County meeting, 22 June 1774, *Revolutionary Virginia*, eds., Scribner and Tarter, 1:163–65.

[26]Prince George County meeting, June 1774, *Revolutionary Virginia*, eds., Scribner and Tarter, 1:150–52; Culpeper County meeting, 20 July 1774, ibid., 1:118–20; Hanover County meeting, ibid., 20 July 1774, 1:139–41; Chesterfield County meeting, 14 July 1774, ibid., 1:116–18; Albemarle County meeting, 26 July 1774, ibid., 1:112–13.

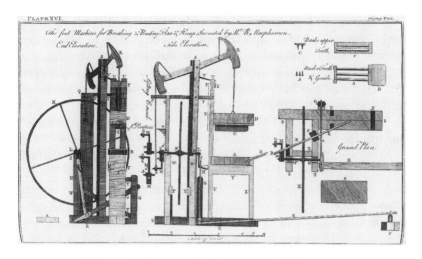

"The Foot Machine for Breaking & Beating Flax & Hemp. Invented by Mr. R. McPherson," printed in *The Complete Farmer; or, A General Dictionary of Husbandry*. London, 1767. This volume included among the collection at Mount Vernon demonstrated a new machine for processing the hemp and flax that Washington and many Virginia planters hoped would become staple crops in the colony. (Library of Congress)

increase the production of the coarse fabrics for which Virginians seldom were able to find sufficient local replacements. The Prince George County meeting elevated cloth manufactures to a matter of civic duty when it declared that "to be clothed in Manufactures fabricated in the colonies ought to be considered as a Badge and Distinction of Respect, and true Patriotism." The authors of Chesterfield County's resolves recommended subscriptions for the promotion of "Manufactures amongst the Inhabitants" as the only guarantee of the economic independence that was a necessary foundation for political liberty.[27]

A consideration of Virginia's scarcity of manufactures led once again to a discussion of the effects of slave labor on the colony's economy. Repeating the familiar argument used in support of prohibitive slave duties, the Prince George resolutions declared the African trade was an impediment to the settlement in Virginia of freemen, "Manufacturers

[27]Prince George County meeting, *Revolutionary Virginia*, eds., Scribner and Tarter, 1:150–52; Chesterfield County meeting, 14 July 1774, ibid., 1:116–18.

and other useful Emigrants from Europe," as well as the source of the annual increase in the colony's unfavorable balance of trade. Seven other counties repeated this condemnation of the slave trade and recommended extending the association to prohibit slave imports in Virginia. Culpeper, Princess Anne, and Surry Counties' resolves proposed a prohibition on the importation of convict servants as well as slaves.[28]

Despite the obvious seriousness of the county's support for a non-importation association, the Prince George resolves made no mention of nonexportation. This was the first indication on a county level of the debate that had divided the twenty-five former burgesses in Williams-burg. At least seven more of the county meetings omitted all reference to nonexportation, while other counties pronounced their objections or qualifications to this more radical form of commercial resistance. The Henrico and Hanover County meetings admitted nonexportation might be necessary if the British government persisted in its measures against Massachusetts, but "A Love of Justice, and the tender Regard" for the British merchants and manufacturers convinced them to limit their sup-port to a nonimportation agreement. James City County offered a pos-sible point of compromise with the suggestion for delaying the effective date of a nonexportation association. The Albemarle and Fairfax re-solves recommended that exports continue uninterrupted until the fall of 1775. Norfolk's meeting, with a large representation of merchants, wanted to allow "Time for the discharge of British Debts" before enter-ing a nonexportation association.[29]

Throughout July various county meetings offered further refine-ments of the general outline for a commercial association. Essex County's meeting insisted that merchants pledge not to advance the price of goods above the general level in effect "for some time" before the association. Citizens of Elizabeth City County and the town of Hampton concurred and promised to withhold all business from anyone who attempted to extort higher prices. Stafford County's meeting wanted to broaden any nonexportation agreement to encompass all shipments of "wheat, flour, provisions, and lumber, to any part of Europe." Richard Henry Lee feared that the free exportation of grain to Southern Europe would pro-

[28]*Revolutionary Virginia*, eds., Scribner and Tarter, 1:151, 119, 154, 162; Caroline, Fairfax, and Hanover Counties also recommended an end to slave importations, ibid., 116, 132, 140.

[29]*Revolutionary Virginia*, eds., Scribner and Tarter, 1:150–52, 142, 140, 143, 112, 132, 149.

vide an opportunity for unscrupulous ship captains to smuggle their cargoes into the West Indies. The meeting of Princess Anne County endorsed nonimportation and nonexportation with regard to British trade but instructed its delegates to oppose any restrictions on the West Indies trade which was so important to lower Tidewater.[30]

Most of the county meetings intended the commercial association to remain in effect until Parliament repealed the Coercive Acts. Many also demanded a withdrawal of the tea duty. In his Albemarle County resolves Thomas Jefferson appealed for far more extensive concessions from the British government. In addition to the usual demand for the repeal of the Port Act, Albemarle's resolves called for continuing nonimportation and nonexportation until Parliament lifted all restraints on American manufactures, removed all commodity duties payable in America, and repealed all other restrictions on American trade. After Parliament agreed to these terms, Jefferson suggested, the colonies might consider granting "Great Britain such privileges in commerce as may amply compensate their fraternal assistance, past and future." Jefferson's adherence to his recently-formulated theory of Empire and his insistence on such unlikely concessions from a government that never considered the Empire a union of equal partners raises questions about how seriously he expected or, perhaps, even desired a reconciliation.[31]

Fairfax County, long a center of support for commercial resistance and economic diversification, produced the most comprehensive and influential of all the resolves and instructions approved by county meetings in the summer of 1774. Ever since the Stamp Act crisis, individuals in the county had supported nonimportation and domestic manufactures as a means of pressuring British merchants and simultaneously strengthening the local economy. In 1769 George Mason, a Fairfax justice and prominent planter, wrote the draft of the colony's nonimportation association, and a Fairfax burgess, George Washington, presented the plan in Williamsburg. During the association of 1770, Fairfax County's committee organized a broad-based popular subscription to the provincial agreement. The economic interests of the county's planters and merchants, still actively involved in the tobacco trade but also leaders in the diversification of plantation organization and the devel-

---

[30]*Revolutionary Virginia*, eds., Scribner and Tarter, 1:126, 124, 160, 154; Richard Henry Lee to Samuel Adams, 23 June 1774, *Letters of Richard Henry Lee*, ed., Ballagh, 1:111–13.

[31]*Revolutionary Virginia*, eds., Scribner and Tarter, 1:112–13.

opment of non-British trade routes, placed them in a favorable position to define a commercial association for Virginia. Of all the county proposals for commercial resistance in 1774, the final document issued by the Fairfax County meeting most convincingly combined a legal justification for American resistance and a workable plan of nonintercourse designed particularly for Virginia with a regard for the long-term requirements for economic development outside the confines of Anglo-American commerce.

After waiting for Washington to return from Williamsburg and his York River estates, the inhabitants of Fairfax County held their initial meeting on July 5. The demands of the wheat harvest prevented many people from attending, but those present subscribed £272 sterling, 38 barrels of flour, and 150 bushels of wheat for the relief of the poor in Boston. The meeting also appointed a committee to draft resolves such as "the Circumstances of the County would permit us to go into." Within six days the committee completed a draft of resolves that was either circulated through the county or distributed at the election of the burgesses on July 14. A general meeting of the "Freeholders & Inhabitants" on July 18 approved the resolves with a few revisions. Membership of the drafting committee was not recorded and authorship of the resolves, long attributed to George Mason, is uncertain. If the committee elected on July 18 reflected the membership of the earlier group, the resolves were written by leading members of the county gentry and the resident merchant community of Alexandria. The text of the resolves strongly suggests that Mason and Washington were, if not the principal authors, leading contributors to this most ambitious of all plans for commercial association.[32]

Fairfax County prefaced its specific proposals for an association with a justification of commercial resistance against the acts of Parliament. Recalling the petitions drafted by Virginians during the Stamp Act crisis, the Fairfax resolves reminded the British that compliance with the Navigation Acts had never represented an acknowledgment of Parliament's sovereignty over the colonies. Virginians had accepted the Navigation Acts, "altho in some degree repugnant to the principles of

---

[32]Text of Fairfax resolves in *Revolutionary Virginia*, eds., Scribner and Tarter, 1:127–33; see "Extract of a Letter to a Gentleman in Boston," in *American Archives, Fourth Series*, ed., Force, 1:517–18, for account of meeting of July 5; George Washington to [   ], 11 July 1774, in Donald M. Sweig, "A New-Found Washington Letter of 1774 and the Fairfax Resolves," *William and Mary Quarterly* 3rd ser., 40 (April 1983): 289–91.

the Constitution," as a convenient means of promoting trade within the Empire. As long as the colony retained control over internal affairs and all revenue legislation, Virginians did not wish to challenge policy that mutually benefited the commerce of Great Britain and her colonies. Virginians, however, could not accept the recent series of parliamentary acts that interfered with the colonists' established constitutional rights and jeopardized the commercial benefits of the imperial connection. Before the July 5 meeting, George Washington decided that evidence of a "systematic plan" against the colonies necessitated some form of commercial retaliation as a defense against the ministry's and Parliament's design.[33]

The first step in the colonial defense recommended by the Fairfax resolves was a congress at which representatives from all the colonies could agree upon a "General & uniform plan." The plan suggested by Fairfax County was a nonimportation association that would prohibit goods shipped from Great Britain after September 1, 1774. Inexpensive woolens and linen, some sewing and weaving supplies, nails, saltpeter, and medicines from Great Britain would be exempt from the prohibition until September 1, 1776. Throughout the period nonimportation was in effect, no colony would import slaves, a restriction that the Fairfax meeting hoped to make permanent. Lumber exports to the West Indies would cease as soon as nonimportation became effective.[34]

The authors of the Fairfax resolves agreed with the Williamsburg associators on the need to boycott the East India Company which they called the "Tools and Instruments of Oppression," but they insisted on recognizing the private property rights of the company. Following a satisfactory redress of American grievances, Fairfax County was willing to contribute to a reimbursement of the East India Company for the tea destroyed in Boston harbor. In the meantime all tea in Virginia and that imported before September 1 was to be burned publicly. If no subscription paid for the tea, it would be stored at the risk and expense of the owners until Parliament lifted the duty.[35]

Under the terms of the Fairfax resolves, merchants in Virginia would be required to swear a special oath testifying to their willingness to abide by the nonimportation agreement. The colony's experience with the

---

[33]*Revolutionary Virginia*, eds., Scribner and Tarter, 1:127–33; Sweig, "A New-Found Washington Letter"; George Washington to Bryan Fairfax, 4 July 1774, 20 July 1774, in *Writings of Washington*, ed., Fitzpatrick, 3:227–34.

[34]*Revolutionary Virginia*, eds., Scribner and Tarter, 1:127–33.

[35]Ibid.

associations of 1769 and 1770 demonstrated that no plan of nonimportation could succeed without the participation of all merchants in the colony. Fairfax County's resident merchants, who supported nonimportation in the past, were particularly concerned that British factors not carry on business as usual. According to the prescribed oath, anyone who received goods shipped after September 1, 1774, was bound to return the shipment or store the goods in a warehouse under the supervision of the respective county committee. Merchants and storekeepers were also to agree to sell goods at the same price that had been in effect through the previous year. County committees would certify all traders who took the oath and publicly announce the names of those who refused. A "Solemn Covenant and Association" to be sworn to by the inhabitants of every colony would be further assurance of a uniform observation of the association of the general congress. Committees in the counties or communities of each colony would publish a list of all who violated the association, "That such Traitors to their Country, may be publickly known & detested."[36]

Washington was reluctant to endorse a nonexportation scheme when Virginians owed so many debts to British merchants. He feared that withholding remittances would lessen the credibility of colonial demands for justice. "Nothing less than the last extremity," he felt, "can justify it." The question was whether the colony had reached that extreme. The Fairfax drafting committee was willing to wait one year and schedule nonexportation to go into effect in September 1775 if Parliament had not repealed by that time the Coercive Acts and all revenue duties. The general meeting for Fairfax County on July 18, 1774, voted to delay nonexportation until November 1, 1775. In preparation for a nonexportation agreement, subscribers to the Fairfax resolves agreed not to plant tobacco after the harvest of the current crop. If the general congress of the colonies decided upon a nonexportation association, the Fairfax resolves recommended immediately closing the courts to all judgments on debts cases.[37]

Throughout the Fairfax resolves the committee offered assurances of the County's desire to restore the prosperous relationship that once had served both Mother Country and colony. One resolve specifically denied the rumors that the American colonies intended to establish an independent union. "While we are treated upon an equal footing with

[36]Ibid.
[37]Ibid; George Washington to Bryan Fairfax, 4 July 1774, *Writings of Washington*, ed., Fitzpatrick, 3:227–29.

our fellow Subjects, the motives of self interest and preservation" would persuade Virginians to contribute to the costs of defending the Empire, "But tho we are its Subjects, we will use every means, which Heaven hath given us, to prevent our becoming its slaves." Fairfax County recommended to the general congress that it prepare a petition to the King explaining the colonies' desire to remain under his authority but warning of their determination to resist the unconstitutional acts of his Parliament. The Fairfax meeting suggested that the petition remind the King "that from our Sovereign, there can be but one Appeal."[38]

The cumulative effect of the Fairfax resolves was to balance a radical challenge to parliamentary authority and British domination of colonial commerce with a careful regard for the internal order of Virginia society. The denial of parliamentary sovereignty was followed by an extended legal justification of colonial resistance and an affirmation of the gentry's leadership in the local community. Proposals for diminishing the colony's reliance on British capital and credit were accompanied by a recognition of the rights of private property and a protection of private debts through the postponement of nonexportation. Here was an outline of the ideal economic society as envisioned by the men who drafted the resolves. The principal men of the colony would direct the development of a more independent economy through their personal example and their financial encouragement of manufacturers and smaller planters. The proposed association fully incorporated the local merchants and regulated their commercial activity according to the needs and welfare of the planter community. The long-range results of such a commercial association would be an integrated economy in which merchants, manufacturers, and skilled free laborers supported the dominant agricultural interests of the planter gentry.

■   ■   ■

Only a few county meetings dissented from the general support for a commercial association. Middlesex County's meeting condemned the Port Act and Parliament's attempts to raise a revenue in the colonies but was quick to disassociate itself from the destruction of the tea in Boston. The Middlesex resolves approved the boycott of East India goods and the prohibition of British luxury items but dismissed the proposals for a more extensive nonimportation–nonexportation association as "in-

[38]*Revolutionary Virginia*, eds., Scribner and Tarter, 1:127–33.

jurious to the Commerce, and fatal to the Credit, of this Colony." Subscribers to the Middlesex resolves were more interested in instructing
their deputies to avoid any course of action that might result in another
dissolution of the assembly. Dinwiddie County's meeting also criticized
"the Outrages committed by the People of Boston in destroying the
private Property of the East India Company," although it was equally
critical of Parliament's excessive reaction. The Dinwiddie resolves, like
those of Accomack County, supported the August convention but omitted all reference to a commercial association.[39]

Isolated individuals who supported a cautious opposition found it
difficult to influence the county meetings. Robert Beverley went to the
Essex County meeting of July 9 with a draft of resolves that stopped
short of a commercial association. The meeting rejected Beverley's suggestions and appeared to go out of its way to refute those who coun-
seled moderation. The approved resolves of Essex County declared that
any censure of the Boston Tea Party was "inimical to American Liberty" and rejected any reimbursement of the East India Company unless it be a condition for the repeal of all offensive legislation. If the
Essex County meeting made any concession to Beverley it was in the
resolve acknowledging that the recommended nonexportation association would unfortunately injure merchants and manufacturers who had
supported the trade of America. "Nothing but the Desire of preserving
our Rights and Liberties could induce [the Essex County meeting] to
adopt a Measure big with such melancholy Consequences."[40]

The strength of public opinion favoring a commercial association
persuaded Bryan Fairfax that he could not stand for election as a deputy
when he opposed nonimportation. Fairfax's critique of the radical stance
of his county's resolves never even entered the public debate. When he
received a copy of the proposed resolves for Fairfax County, Bryan Fairfax
wrote Washington of his objections to the denial of parliamentary sovereignty and his preference for a petition to the King rather than an
immediate endorsement of a nonimportation association. Washington
received the letter in the midst of the county's July 18 meeting, read

---

[39]Middlesex County meeting, July 1774, Dinwiddie County meeting, 15
July 1774, Accomack County meeting, 27 July 1774, in *Revolutionary Virginia*,
eds., Scribner and Tarter, 1:143–45, 120–22, 111–12.

[40]Robert Beverley to Landon Carter, 17 July 1774, Sabine Hall Collection, University of Virginia; Essex County resolves in *Revolutionary Virginia*,
eds., Scribner and Tarter, 1:125–27.

Fairfax's objections, and circulated the letter among the other officers at the meeting, whereupon they agreed that it was useless to present the letter to a general meeting which already was nearly unanimous in support of the proposed resolves. The same insistence on a public appearance of unanimity was evident at Norfolk's meeting where reluctant merchants found their names added to the roster of the county committee.[41]

During the month preceding the August convention, two other opponents of nonimportation presented their case in the public press. Thomson Mason, a lawyer from Stafford County and brother of George Mason, considered a commercial association an inappropriate and possibly counterproductive form of protest against Parliament. Mason, a steady opponent of Parliament's recent acts, doubted that Virginians were capable of the sacrifices that would be necessary during a complete boycott of British goods. In questioning the potential for self-sufficiency on Virginia's plantations, he offered a sarcastic vision of half-clothed planters huddled in log cabins together with naked slaves. In a series of letters printed in the *Virginia Gazette* and signed by a "British American," Mason argued that the strategy of commercial resistance was ill conceived because it injured the merchants and manufacturers who were not responsible for ministerial policy. Mason was even more disdainful of the proposals for nonexportation which he considered dishonest as well as misdirected. If the nonexportation of tobacco were intended to reduce government revenues, the British would counter the effect by creating new taxes on other commodities. Nonexportation as a means of withholding debt payments again hurt merchants who were friends of the colonists and would alienate future sources of credit throughout Europe.[42]

John Randolph, attorney general for Virginia and brother of the Speaker of the House of Burgesses Peyton Randolph, published his objections to the association proposals in the anonymous pamphlet *Considerations on the Present State of Virginia*. Randolph's derision of public

---

[41]Bryan Fairfax to George Washington, 17 July 1774, George Washington to Bryan Fairfax, 20 July 1774, Washington Papers, Library of Congress; James Parker to Charles Steuart, 16 July 1774, in Charles Steuart Papers, National Library of Scotland (Colonial Williamsburg microfilm).

[42]"The British American," No. 8, in *Revolutionary Virginia*, eds., Scribner and Tarter, 1:187–93; originally published in *Virginia Gazette* (Rind), 21 July 1774.

opinion and his sardonic tone made this tract more an indulgence in self-justification than an attempt at political persuasion. A new nonimportation association would prove no more viable than earlier ones, said Randolph, who even doubted the Virginians' ability to surrender their tea habit. Nonexportation would unjustly hurt the innocent men who produced crops for external markets and the merchants who had advanced credit to the colonies. Neither form of commercial resistance would have any effect on a powerful British government that could easily compensate for the loss in trade. Randolph anticipated that the most likely result of American opposition would be further restrictions on American commerce and government.[43]

Thomson Mason and John Randolph, like Robert Beverley, Bryan Fairfax, and earlier opponents of commercial resistance, represented the same political and economic interests, indeed the same families, as some of the leading architects of the associations. What separated these individuals from the popular support for nonimportation was their faith in the responsiveness of the British government, their identification of Virginia's economic development with the imperial connection, and their doubts about the efficacy of commercial resistance. The sacrifices and disruptions of a commercial association appeared unnecessary to these men who were confident that the King and Parliament would respond favorably to a rational presentation of American grievances. They likewise saw the proposals for nonimportation and nonexportation as dangerous threats to the trade that formed the most important of mutually advantageous bonds between the Mother Country and the American colonies. Ultimately these Virginians considered the commercial ties of Empire as valuable for the cultural identity they imparted as for any material benefits they might have offered. Randolph in particular feared that a dissolution of commercial ties would precipitate the decline of Great Britain as a world power and bring America under the dominion of a less benevolent, more autocratic nation. At a time when most of Virginia's political leaders emphasized the limitations of economic dependence on Great Britain and popular opinion distrusted the motivations of Parliament, these opponents of nonimportation and defenders of the old imperial order found themselves isolated and politically irrelevant.[44]

[43]John Randolph, *Considerations on the Present State of Virginia*, in *Revolutionary Virginia*, eds., Scribner and Tarter, 1:206–18.
[44]Ibid.

■   ■   ■

The central debate in Virginia during the summer of 1774 was not over the advisability of a commercial association but focused instead on how ambitious such an agreement should be. By July individuals throughout the colony informally and enthusiastically had adopted the nonconsumption agreement regarding tea and other East India Company goods. The county resolves published in the *Virginia Gazette* announced the widespread support for an extended nonimportation association. These same resolves indicated that the principal sources of division among supporters of a commercial association were the related issues of withholding exports and closing the courts to civil cases. Advocates of nonexportation intended the wider association to place added pressure on the British government by reducing revenue from import duties in Great Britain, curtailing merchants' profits from the American trade, and suspending the principal means of payment on outstanding debts. Nowhere was the issue of nonexportation and debt repayment more complicated than in the Chesapeake colonies where by 1774 per capita debts owed to British merchants reached unprecedented levels and were substantially higher than in other colonies. Because even the announcement of a future nonexportation association was likely to produce a flood of suits for debt recovery by British creditors, the proposals to halt exports usually included provisions for shutting the courts to all debts cases in order to protect indebted tobacco planters who would have no alternative means of making remittances during an association. No one suggested that nonexportation might be initiated without this protection for debtors. In addition to shielding planters, the suspension of legal actions on debt cases would perhaps mobilize British merchants as it had during the Stamp Act crisis.[45]

Many of the planters who supported a nonexportation agreement at the same time were anxious to avoid any appearance of debt evasion and attempted to maintain the colonists' credit with British merchants.

[45]Rejection of tea discussed in Philip Vickers Fithian, *The Journals and Letters of Philip Vickers Fithian*, ed., Hunter Dickinson Farish (Williamsburg: Colonial Williamsburg Inc., 1943), 147; County meetings that recommended closing the courts included Prince William, Westmoreland, Richmond, Essex, Gloucester, Fairfax, and Stafford, in *Revolutionary Virginia*, eds., Scribner and Tarter, 1:153, 164, 156, 126, 138, 132, 161; Price, *Capital and Credit*, 12–16.

Washington was particularly reluctant to endorse any nonexportation scheme that had the appearance of negating private obligations to creditors. Fairfax County's proposal for delaying the nonexportation agreement was an effort to allow time for making remittances on outstanding accounts in Great Britain. The proposal also was an announcement to those indebted to their fellow Virginians that an association would not be an occasion for debt repudiation. In their private correspondences, Washington and other wealthy planters assured their British merchants that they would make every effort to find some means of remittance and would eventually pay all their debts. John Tayloe fully supported nonexportation as a means of reducing the Crown's revenue from tobacco, but he promised merchant Duncan Campbell that he would meet the payment on his London debts. Tayloe expected his iron forge to fill increased local demands during an association and produce the money for payments to Campbell. For the majority of planters who had no such manufacturing interests on which to rely, however, nonexportation effectively would eliminate every means of making remittances to Great Britain.[46]

Throughout the summer debate on the wisdom and practicality of nonexportation, the courts of Virginia by and large were already shut to suits from British creditors. Although county courts commonly followed the lead of the General Court in the spring of 1774 and continued to operate after the expiration of the Fee Act, most closed completely or suspended all but administrative and criminal proceedings after the dissolution of the House of Burgesses. In the weeks between the end of the assembly's session and the opening of the August convention, a dialogue in the public press and among the colony's lawyers examined the theoretical implications of the expiration of the Fee Bill and, more important, the merits of closing the courts to debt cases. Jefferson denied that the General Court or any other judicial body could usurp the legislative prerogative of establishing the fee schedule for government officials. Edmund Pendleton on the other hand saw no reason why the courts could not continue to operate on the assumption that the assembly would renew the Fee Bill once it met again. Although Pendleton agreed to support whatever commercial association the convention

---

[46]Emory G. Evans, "Planter Indebtedness and the Coming of the Revolution in Virginia," 529–30; John Tayloe to Duncan Campbell, 20 July 1775, American Loyalist Claims, Public Record Office, T. 79/12 (Virginia Colonial Records Project microfilm).

adopted, he feared that the closure of the courts at a time of such unrest would "introduce anarchy & disorder & render life & property here precarious." The conservative minority that opposed any sort of commercial association raised even more alarming visions of life without the stabilizing influence of courts of justice.[47]

As British merchants in the colony well understood, the debate on closing the courts had little do to with theoretical considerations of Jefferson or regard for the maintenance of social order. A frustrated and suspicious merchant like James Parker of Norfolk, who claimed that "calling a man a Patriot here is saying he is in bad Circumstances," was convinced that the court closings and debate on nonexportation were excuses for the evasion of debts. More reasonable merchants were reluctant to impugn the personal integrity of the Virginians but recognized the court closures as largely political in motivation. James Robinson of William Cunninghame & Company reported to Glasgow that the Coercive Acts were the true reason the courts in Virginia were closed. William Allason assured English correspondents that the courts' refusal to proceed on debt cases was part of a political strategy despite public pronouncements about the expiration of the Fee Act. In fact no county suggested that county courts and their officers suspend routine administrative duties which might also come under the terms of the Fee Bill.[48]

Although the merchants in Virginia stood the most to lose from a suspension of the civil courts, most of them did not have the political influence to challenge advocates of nonexportation. The merchants' meeting in Williamsburg during the first week of June petitioned Governor Dunmore for a new assembly to renew the Fee Bill, but the governor had assured the Ministry that he would postpone another gathering of the burgesses. Of greater influence were planters like Councillor Robert Carter whose business affairs in the colony were jeopardized by their inability to sue for debts. Throughout the summer, Carter complained of tenants who refused to pay rents, but he was reluctant to

---

[47]Dewey, *Thomas Jefferson, Lawyer*, 94–106; Curtis, "The Role of the Courts," 121–46.

[48]James Parker to Charles Steuart, 7 June 1774, Charles Steuart Papers, National Library of Scotland (Colonial Williamsburg microfilm); James Robinson to William Cunninghame and Co., William Cunnighame and Co., Letterbook of Colonial Agent, 1772–1774, National Library of Scotland (Colonial Williamsburg microfilm); Allason quoted in Dewey, *Thomas Jefferson, Lawyer*, 102.

criticize publicly the popular association proposals. A week after the merchants' meeting in June, Carter and the other members of the council unanimously recommended that the governor issue writs for the election of a new assembly in order to pass a new Fee Bill and prepare an adequate defense of the frontier. The governor again protested that a meeting of the assembly would run counter to his reports home as well as present the opportunity for more "violent resolves." After consulting with the council on the following day, Dunmore reluctantly issued writs for a new assembly to meet on August 11. The writs were quickly followed by a secret letter to Dartmouth in which Dunmore assured the secretary that he had no intention of allowing the assembly to meet without permission from the Ministry. Many counties held assembly elections, often in conjunction with the approval of resolves from the August 1 convention, but Richard Henry Lee suspected the governor's plans and urged all his fellow representatives to attend the earlier convention since it was likely to be the only opportunity for a general meeting in the colony. On July 8, as he prepared a military expedition for the west, Dunmore prorogued the assembly until November. The fate of the courts would thus be determined by the convention's decision on nonexportation. Few doubted what that decision would be. A week before the convention, Edmund Pendleton confided to Ralph Wormeley that the majority of delegates wanted to keep the county courts shut. At the same time, James Robinson learned that the convention was likely to approve an immediate nonimportation association, with nonexportation to commence at a later date and with the courts to remain closed to civil business for the duration.[49]

In the public debate preceding the August convention, Landon Carter sought to have the last word with the publication of a defense of the strategy of withholding exports and suspending the courts of jus-

[49]*Executive Journals of the Council of Colonial Virginia*, ed., H.R. McIlwaine, 6 vols. (Richmond, 1925–66), 6:574, 577–78; Dunmore to Dartmouth, 29 May 1774, 6 June 1774, Public Record Office, CO5/1352 (Virginia Colonial Records Project microfilm); Richard Henry Lee to Arthur Lee, 26 June 1774, *The Letter of Richard Henry Lee*, ed., Ballagh, 1:165; Robert Carter Letterbook, 1772–1775, v.2, May 1774–May 1775, passim., esp. Carter to Gildart & Busigny, 12 Sep. 1774, Duke University (Colonial Williamsburg microfilm); Edmund Pendleton to Ralph Wormeley, 28 July 1774, Ralph Wormeley Letters, University of Virginia; James Robinson to William Cunninghame and Co., 26 July 1774, in *A Scottish Firm in Virginia*, ed., Devine, 143–46.

tice. Carter dismissed the self-interested criticisms from merchants, but he was concerned by others "truly worthy in their social Conduct" who questioned the justice of halting exports when debts were owed to British merchants. Carter's *Virginia Gazette* article signed "Experience" asserted that the merchants and other creditors in Great Britain were responsible for ministerial policy, if only by their indifference to the fate of America, and these were the men who owed their entire livelihood to the American trade. To those who claimed that nonexportation would prevent individuals from fulfilling personal obligations, Carter answered that the commercial arrangements between planters and merchants were always something more than private transactions, that they had a public dimension. Besides, Carter asked with some justification, if these Virginians were so worried about the safety of British debts, why had they not previously made greater efforts to pay their own accounts. Nonexportation would just be another and worthwhile postponement. Privately Carter urged his son Robert Wormeley Carter and Francis Lightfoot Lee, both delegates from Richmond County, to insist that the convention keep the courts closed to all action on the recovery of debts due, the suspension of justice "being the only expedient to compell the creditors in that great ballance w[hi]ch must be forever ag[ain]st us from the very situation of our trade with G.B."[50]

■   ■   ■

When the Virginia convention met at the capitol in Williamsburg on August 1 with Peyton Randolph as moderator, the gathering had all the appearances of the House of Burgesses and enjoyed even greater popular authority than the regular assembly. Attendance of delegates at the six-day meeting was more complete than at any assembly in memory and contributed to the legitimacy of the extra-legal session. The detailed proceedings for most of the convention, like the burgesses' regular sessions, were not recorded, although Landon Carter later learned that the debates were "warm." During the first day in session, the delegates approved the proposal for a general congress of the colonies sched-

[50]"Experience," *Virginia Gazette* (Purdie & Dixon), 28 July 1774; Alexander Purdie to Landon Carter, 3 Aug. 1774; Landon Carter to Robert Wormeley Carter and Francis Lightfoot Lee, 1774, Sabine Hall Collection, University of Virginia.

uled for Philadelphia. On Friday, August 5, the convention elected Peyton Randolph, Richard Henry Lee, George Washington, Patrick Henry, Richard Bland, Benjamin Harrison, and Edmund Pendleton to represent Virginia at the general congress.[51]

In the course of the convention, Peyton Randolph presented the delegates with suggested resolves from Thomas Jefferson who had fallen ill on the road to Williamsburg. When Jefferson turned back to Monticello, he forwarded to Randolph and Patrick Henry copies of his proposal which soon after the convention was published as *A Summary View of the Rights of British America*. In the *Summary View*, Jefferson's radical interpretation of the Empire as a union of various parliaments and colonial assemblies, completely independent of one another and voluntarily offering their allegiance to the King, led to the broadest assertion yet offered in Virginia of the commercial rights of the American colonies. According to Jefferson, Parliament's regulation (he called it "tyranny") of American commerce was an infringement of the colonists' natural right to free trade with all nations. Since the mid-seventeenth century, Jefferson wrote, Parliament's Navigation Acts had restricted American trade with the sole design of protecting British commercial profits. Colonial imports and exports carried unfair duties; Americans were not allowed to ship to northern Europe produce that the British did not want, nor were they able to purchase European goods that the British could not supply; Parliament denied the Americans the right to sell their own tobacco on the valuable continental markets; and British monopoly of the carrying trade to American doubled and tripled the price for British manufactures. Nothing was so foolish or unjust, Jefferson thought, as the regulation of iron manufacturing by which Parliament required the colonists to ship unfinished pig and bar iron, so "necessary in every branch of husbandry," to Great Britain and then pay for the reshipment of finished tools and nails. The act of 1732 subjecting American lands to the demands of British creditors while British lands were protected provided Jefferson with further evidence "that Justice is not the same in America as in Britain." He recommended that the Virginia convention and the general congress declare these acts of Parliament void.[52]

[51]Proceedings of the Convention in *Revolutionary Virginia*, eds., Scribner and Tarter, 1:223–24, 229; George Washington to Thomas Johnson, Jr., 5 Aug. 1774, *Writings of Washington*, ed., Fitzpatrick, 3:235–36; *Diary of Landon Carter*, ed., Greene, 2:847.

[52]Text of *Summary View* in *Papers of Thomas Jefferson*, ed., Boyd, 1:121–35.

The Virginia convention devoted most of its time to the task of devising the proper form of commercial association. The final agreement signed on August 6 owed most of its provisions to the Fairfax resolves. The colonial agreement incorporated suggestions from other counties in an effort to achieve the most acceptable and effective method of commercial resistance. First among the convention's resolutions was an agreement not to import any British goods, whether from Great Britain, the West Indies, or other colonies, nor to purchase such goods imported by others after November 1, 1774. British medicines were the single exemption in the nonimportation agreement. The associators pledged themselves not to import or purchase slaves from Africa, the West Indies, or any other place. Otherwise, the import trade in West Indian goods would continue as usual. Tea was of such symbolic importance in the British assault on American rights that the deputies prohibited the importation of any type of tea and resolved not to use any on hand in the colony. The convention refused to accept Fairfax County's suggestion that the tea destroyed in Boston might be paid for after the imperial dispute reached a settlement, declaring instead that if Boston were coerced into paying the East India Company for the value of the tea, Virginians would boycott all East India Company commodities until the company reimbursed Boston. The ban on British goods would continue until such time as the British government satisfied American demands according to terms that the general congress would determine. Virginia's association avoided tying the agreement to specific complaints against Parliament, citing only "certain ill advised Regulations, as well of our Trade as internal Polity."[53]

Resolution of the debate over exports and British debts came with an agreement to delay nonexportation until August 10, 1775. If the British government had not met American demands by that date Virginia's associators would ship no more tobacco or other produce to Great Britain nor sell any goods to any person who thereafter might export them to Great Britain. The convention intended the delay to allow "as quick and full Payment as possible of our Debts to Great Britain." The delegates also decided that immediate enactment of nonexportation would cause too much hardship for the many Virginians who had invested all their resources in the current crop of tobacco, "by which Means they have been prevented from pursuing other Methods of clothing and sup-

[53] Text of Convention Association, *Revolutionary Virginia*, eds., Scribner and Tarter, 1:231–35.

porting their Families." After the planters "made what profit they could of the crops they had raised," the initiation of a nonexportation association would encourage them "to turn their farms to some other article of produce and deprive the exchequer of that immense revenue it receives from that article."[54]

The controversial question of whether to close Virginia's courts during a nonexportation agreement provoked the expected debate in the convention. The association ended by omitting all reference to the subject. A "great majority" of the delegates voted to keep the courts shut, but they decided that a public announcement of the suspension of civil justice was unnecessary and potentially dangerous. The lack of a Fee Bill and the unlikelihood of a new assembly were sufficient guarantees that debtors would be free from court judgments during the observance of the association. In early September, members of the General Court, wishing to avoid any contribution "to the Uneasiness of the present Times," announced that they too would hear only criminal cases during their upcoming session.[55]

As in the Fairfax resolves, the convention's association suggested that Virginians prepare for nonexportation by turning their attention from tobacco to crops that might form the basis of colonial manufactures. The specific resolve by which the Associators promised to increase their sheep herds and sell surplus stock to the "poorer Sort of People" was the first step toward establishing colonial cloth manufactures. "The greatest Industry, the strictest Economy and Frugality, and the Exertion of every Publick Virtue" on the part of the gentlemen of the Colony would further encourage the people to develop home manufactures and abide by the terms of the association.[56]

The provisions for the enforcement of the association closely followed the suggestions of Fairfax County and reflected the lessons of the association of 1770. Each county was to establish a committee which would invite merchants to sign the association and subsequently issue a certificate affirming the merchants' cooperation. Merchants who refused

[54]Ibid.; William Davies [Norfolk–Portsmouth Joint Committee] to Baltimore Committee of Correspondence, 13 Aug. 1774, *Revolutionary Virginia*, eds., Scribner and Tarter, 7:740–41.

[55]James Parker to Charles Steuart, 14 August 1774, Charles Steuart Papers, National Library of Scotland (Virginia Colonial Records Project microfilm); announcement of General Court in *Virginia Gazette* (Purdie & Dixon), 8 Sep. 1774.

[56]*Revolutionary Virginia*, eds., Scribner and Tarter, 1:231–34.

to sign risked losing their business in the local community. The association's specific regulations for merchants bound them to sell goods at the price in effect for the past twelve months. In a concession designed to encourage merchant participation, the association permitted the local committees to authorize price increases if exchange rates rose. Merchants or anyone else importing goods after November 1, 1774, were obligated to reship the cargo or accept the cost and risk of public storage during the observance of the association. Refusal to cooperate would result in the local committee's publication of the violator's name and details of the infraction. Associators would "thereafter consider such Person or Persons as inimical to this Country, and break off every Connection and all Dealings with them." Anyone exporting commodities after August 10, 1775, would receive similar treatment from the respective local committee.[57]

The convention's instructions for the delegates to the general congress enumerated specific grievances against Great Britain, even if they fell short of Jefferson's grand proposals. Like Jefferson, the delegates affirmed their allegiance to the King while denying the authority of Parliament "in all cases whatsoever." The colonies had acquiesced in the Navigation Acts as an appropriate price for British military and commercial protection, but recent legislation restricted American rights in ways that far exceeded the benefits of the imperial connection. The convention instructed the delegates to demand a repeal of the acts for raising a revenue in America, the act extending the jurisdiction of the courts of the admiralty to allow the transportation of accused criminals in America to trial in Great Britain, and the several coercive acts regarding Massachusetts. The instructions allowed the delegates to negotiate the terms of an intercolonial association except for the date of a nonexportation agreement, which was not to go into effect before August 10, 1775.[58]

While the convention was still in session, a published address "To the People of Virginia" called for popular support of a nonimportation and nonexportation agreement along with public subscriptions for the promotion of local manufactures. The author contended that a commercial association, bringing forth "the virtue of *America*, and the cries of British merchants and manufacturers," was the surest way to avoid

[57]Ibid.

[58]Instructions to the Deputies, *Revolutionary Virginia*, eds., Scribner and Tarter, 1:236–39.

the bloodshed that otherwise would follow Parliament's continued infringement of colonial rights. During the week after the convention,
Peyton Randolph helped to cultivate that popular support by holding a
meeting of the inhabitants of Williamsburg at which time the citizens
voiced their approval of the association and signed the agreement.[59]

Even before other communities held similar meetings, the widespread approval of the association was apparent. In Yorktown, William
Reynolds "never knew people more unanimously resolute than every
Class of people here are." The Norfolk–Portsmouth committee reported
that "the merchants that are natives are unanimous" in their support for
the new association. Thomas Nelson and Robert Beverley both reported
to London merchants of the Virginians' determination to adhere to the
association "with the most scrupulous Exactness." Nelson's letters to
Samuel Athawes and Thomas and Rowland Hunt, written just one day
after the signing of the association, explained the Virginians' hope that
the association would prompt British merchants and manufacturers to
demand parliamentary repeal of the objectionable legislation. The determination to cut off exports to Great Britain was not, Nelson insisted,
an attempt to end commercial relations which he hoped could resume
along mutually satisfactory terms. Although the conservative Beverley
had resisted any form of commercial resistance and still opposed
nonexportation, he admitted that the association might provide internal benefits for Virginia. The colony was fully capable of developing
manufactures to satisfy most needs, and the decreased reliance on Great
Britain would "be a means of extricating many People from their present
Distresses." Beverley, however, continued to believe that America's long-
term interests would be served best by cultivating agricultural products
in return for British manufactures.[60]

Before the convention met, Robert Carter Nicholas responded to
John Randolph's pamphlet with an extended defense of Virginia's opposition to parliamentary authority. When Nicholas's rebuttal was published in late August under the title *Considerations on the Present State of*

[59]"To the People of Virginia," 4 Aug. 1774, *American Archives, Fourth Series*, ed., Force, 1:685–86; *Virginia Gazette* (Purdie & Dixon), 11 Aug. 1774.

[60]William Reynolds to George Flowerdew Norton, 18 Aug. 1774, William
Reynolds Letterbook, Library of Congress; Thomas Nelson to Samuel Athawes,
7 Aug. 1774, idem. to Thomas and Rowland Hunt, 7 Aug. 1774, Nelson
Letterbook, Virginia State Library; Robert Beverley to Samuel Athawes, 6 Sep.
1774, Robert Beverley Letterbook, Library of Congress.

Virginia Examined, it served as a persuasive justification of the new association. Nicholas dismissed as illegitimate all objections to a nonimportation association; the Americans were free to purchase or not purchase British manufactures as they chose. He admitted that nonexportation unfortunately would injure British creditors, but considerations for the "Safety of the Community" could in extreme cases justify withholding exports. Americans who were struggling for basic liberties could not be expected to devote their energies to paying debts to creditors who made no effort to relieve their suffering. Nor were the merchants of Great Britain entirely innocent of the creation of the large Virginia debts. They had offered numerous "Solicitations and Allurements" for Virginians to expand tobacco cultivation despite the likelihood of prolonged indebtedness during depressed markets. Nicholas did not believe the closing of the courts would be as socially disruptive as Randolph predicted. As far as he could tell, the officials in every county had agreed to serve without fee "for that Part of their Office which is necessary to preserve the Peace and good Order of Society."[61]

"A Contrite Debtor" writing in the *Virginia Gazette* expected the nonconsumption agreements of the association to relieve the private indebtedness that inhibited diversified economic development in Virginia. His own experience illustrated that an individual debtor, particularly among the colony's gentry, had ramifications for all levels of society. This debtor had wanted to purchase fine linen manufactured by an Irish family living in Virginia, but his lack of ready cash forced him to buy other linen on credit from a merchant. An association encouraging gentlemen "to appear simply in Publick and frugally in private" would break the cycle which forced debtors to go deeper into debt. The rejection of finery and vanity would secure individual estates, promote local manufactures, and develop a sense of public spirit.[62]

Most critics of the association remained silent, whether out of support for the general aim of the agreement or out of fear of public censure. When Jefferson received a copy of the association, he privately noted his several disappointments with the agreement. Although the association allowed Virginians to purchase British goods imported before November 1, 1774, Jefferson regretted that it did not permit the importation of tools necessary for manufactures. The agreement failed

[61]*Considerations on the Present State of Virginia Examined*, in *Revolutionary Virginia*, eds., Scribner and Tarter, 1:259–85.
[62]*Virginia Gazette* (Purdie & Dixon), 18 Aug. 1774.

to ban West Indian and European goods that carried a British duty and left open the commerce with the West Indies and other parts of the British Empire that did not support a commercial association. Jefferson feared that these shortcomings, along with the inadequate explanation of American grievances and the restrictions on the negotiating position of Virginia's delegates to the general congress, would undermine the effectiveness of the colonies' commercial resistance. Landon Carter thought the professed regard for debts owed to British merchants and the delay in nonexportation were a "Hypocrisy to America." At the opposite extreme from Jefferson and Carter, many British merchants resident in Virginia criticized the association because it was so comprehensive, but, like James Parker of Norfolk, they only expressed their contempt in private conversations or in letters home. Parker and others hoped that by refusing to participate merchants could nullify the effect of the association. John Randolph, the severest Virginia critic of commercial resistance, spoke out against early proposals but declined to venture forth from his house in Williamsburg during the convention.[63]

■   ■   ■

Following the earliest discussions of a commercial association in 1774, Virginia merchants and planters attempted to reorganize their business affairs in preparation for the impending restrictions on trade. The prolonged economic depression with its low tobacco prices and shortages of credit and currency combined with the shifting proposals for association to frustrate many of these efforts to protect private interests. The Dumfries merchant William Carr responded to the early rumors of nonexportation and court closings with a scheme to ship the largest possible cargo of tobacco to his London merchant James Russell. By the time Carr procured sufficient tobacco, much of it of indifferent quality and at inflated prices, he learned that the convention would probably delay the start of the nonexportation agreement. The threatened suspension of civil justice persuaded other merchants to collect large remittances before the start of a Virginia association. The planters' re-

[63]Jefferson's Observation on the Convention Association, in *Papers of Thomas Jefferson*, ed., Boyd, 1:143; *Diary of Landon Carter*, ed., Greene, 2:847; James Parker to Charles Steuart, 14 Aug, 1774, 29 Sep. 1774, Charles Steuart Papers, National Library of Scotland (Colonial Williamsburg microfilm).

luctance to sell their tobacco in the spring and early summer months of 1774, however, made it difficult for merchants to purchase cargoes on acceptable terms. Even before hearing of the Coercive Acts or possible associations, many planters refused to sell their tobacco at current prices because the poor returns they had received the previous year convinced them to wait for a rise in the market. By early June, the supporters of a commercial association were refusing to sell their tobacco until they learned the full details of the acts against Massachusetts and the plans for a Virginia association.[64]

When merchants did find tobacco on the market, it was often difficult to purchase. Merchants still suffered from a shortage of currency, and their bills of exchange rated at 30 to 30 1/2 percent were unacceptable to most planters. With the likelihood of some form of nonimportation in the near future, planters were reluctant to ship on consignment for fear of having no means of receiving goods in return. The planters' hesitancy to sell and the merchants' determination to buy inevitably raised the price of tobacco as the summer progressed. After a year of tobacco prices remaining at ten shillings sterling and twelve shillings, six pence Virginia currency for a hundred weight, Potomac tobacco was by August selling at fifteen shillings for the most ordinary sort and eighteen shillings sterling for superior quality leaf. The late-summer arrival of an uncommonly large number of London ships kept the prices up and injured the resident merchants who relied on cash purchases.[65]

In April 1774, Charles Yates complained that he spent as much as £10 on the travel expenses, court costs, and assistants' wages involved in the collection of ten shillings worth of old debts. When the courts closed in June of 1774, merchants did not even have the more expensive alternative of legal suits for the collection of outstanding debts. Several Westmoreland County merchants decided to sell goods only for cash in

[64]William Carr to James Russell, 30 May, 15 June, 28 June, 6 July 1774, Russell Papers, Coutts & Co., London (Virginia Colonial Records Project microfilm); Harry Piper to Dixon & Littledale, 27 Apr. 1774, and through spring and summer, Piper Letterbook, University of Virginia; reluctance to ship tobacco mentioned in *The Journals and Letters of Philip Vickers Fithian*, ed., Farish, 150, 156,

[65]Price and exchange levels from Harry Piper Letterbook, University of Virginia; Charles Yates Letterbook, University of Virginia; and Russell Papers, Coutts & Co., London (Virginia Colonial Records Project microfilm).

the future, but while this policy might protect them from further losses it did nothing to collect the large amounts due most merchants. After the chaotic and unproductive June meeting of the merchants in Williamsburg ("a parcell of People Gaping at one another"), William Carr realized that few debts would be collected and that bills of exchange sent to England were likely to be returned protested. The principal agent for William Cunninghame & Company left the same meeting with the faint hope that the "Honor & Honesty of the Debtor" would protect the company's accounts. By early July the company's factors were finding it impossible to collect from "some of the worthless kind" who became "very impudent and daring" in the absence of court enforcement. As Carr discovered while traveling around Westmoreland County in July, personal application to the indebted planters yielded few payments. Yates found that by early fall the decision to withhold payments from British merchants and their factors had led "by a strange mode of reasoning" to the conclusion that it was "Patriotism not to pay anybody."[66]

During the period between the August convention and the approval of a general association by the Philadelphia congress, the local committees had few occasions to govern the merchants' business. The arrival in the Chesapeake Bay of the brigantine *Mary and Jane*, laden with tea, prompted the committees in several Maryland and Virginia counties to alert neighboring counties of the vessel's cargo. In Norfolk where the tea was consigned to three merchant firms, the borough committee resolved that the tea should be returned. A delegation from the committee carried the decision to each of the merchants. The three firms readily acceded to the committee's decision and later received public acknowledgment of their cooperation. Caroline County's committee chastised and demanded a public apology from Andrew Leckie, a merchant in Port Royal who had ridiculed the association and falsely accused Walker Taliaferro of violating the agreement. Such committee actions, however, were relatively infrequent before the enforcement of the nonim-

[66]Charles Yates to Dixon & Littledale, 2 Apr. 1774, idem to Samuel and William Vernon, 5 Oct. 1774, Yates Letterbook, University of Virginia; William Carr to James Russell, 15 June, 22 July 1774, Russell Papers, Coutts & Co., London (Virginia Colonial Records Project microfilm); James Robinson to William Cunninghame & Company, 7 June 1774, in *A Scottish Firm in Virginia*, ed., Devine, 141–43; James Bartlett to James Robinson and William Henderson, 8 July 1774, Cunninghame of Lainshaw Muniments, 1761–1778, Scottish Records Office (Virginia Colonial Records Project microfilm).

portation agreement and as long as most merchants publicly approved of the association. The absence of committee interference convinced some traders that they might avoid the full effect of commercial restrictions. William Cunninghame & Company instructed its factors to sign any association on the assumption that a temporary nonimportation agreement would help reduce standing debts and that the Virginians would never interfere with the company's shipping of exports from the colony. Charles Yates, also assuming that enforcement measures would be as ineffective as in 1770, sent his British merchant instructions for smuggling in the goods that he ordered after the convention. As late as the end of September, James Parker noted that many British factors had avoided signing the association. In Petersburg only one factor signed before September, and others prepared orders for goods from Great Britain.[67]

■   ■   ■

The full implications of the trading restrictions became apparent only after October when newly-instituted local committees began to enforce the association of the Continental Congress. What was clear well before that intercolonial congress met in Philadelphia was the dramatic evolution of commercial resistance in Virginia in the decade since the strategy was first devised as a response to the Stamp Act. What had begun as an individual and often disparate campaign in 1765 and remained largely the focus of the gentry in 1769 and 1770, now united the great majority of free Virginians in an effort to secure the economic independence and political sovereignty of the colony. The proposed commercial association, with its goal of a diversified economy and re-

[67]Charles County, Maryland Correspondence Committee to Fairfax, Virginia Committee, 9 Aug. 1774, Washington Papers, Library of Congress; *Revolutionary Virginia*, eds., Scribner and Tarter, 2:159–62; William Cunninghame & Company to John Turner, 18 July 1774, Cunninghame of Lainshaw Muniments, Scottish Record Office (Virginia Colonial Records Project microfilm); Charles Yates to Gale & Fearon, 27 Aug. 1774, Yates Letterbook, University of Virginia; James Parker to Charles Steuart, 29 Sep. 1774, Charles Steuart Papers, National Library of Scotland (Colonial Williamsburg microfilm); Thomas Irving to Neil Jamieson, 28 Aug. 1774, Neil Jamieson Papers, Library of Congress.

strictions on the British mercantile community in Virginia, was the centerpiece of the organized resistance to all claims of parliamentary authority over the colonies. In the county meetings and at the convention in August, the architects of commercial resistance in 1774 prepared for a prolonged association that would restructure the economy of Virginia in order to gain for its residents the full value of the colony's wealth and a proper defense of their political liberties.

VIRGINIA AND THE CONTINENTAL ASSOCIATION

T HE ASSOCIATION THAT EMERGED FROM the collective proposals of the county meetings and the August convention provided a persuasive model for the delegates at the Continental Congress. There Virginians for the first time took the lead in the formulation of an intercolonial plan of commercial resistance. During the Stamp Act crisis and in response to the Townshend Acts, Virginia's assembly and the colony's supporters of nonimportation had deferred to political organizers in the trading centers of colonies to the north. The concentration of native merchant communities in port cities like Boston and Philadelphia facilitated the establishment of effective associations, while Virginians, however eager to initiate similar agreements in their own colony, were forced to wait for a gathering of burgesses and merchants in Williamsburg. After nearly ten years' experience with the particular demands of organizing commercial resistance in the Chesapeake, Virginia's political leadership, supported at last by broad popular participation, in 1774 developed the most elaborate and sophisticated strategy of commercial resistance yet proposed in the colonies. The alliance of the colony's political elite with the yeoman planters who attended the local organizational meetings helped to produce a viable plan of commercial association for the united colonies. Virginia's valuable trade with Great Britain, furthermore, enhanced the influence of the colony's congressional delegates and their plan of commercial resistance. No continental association, after all, could succeed without the full participation of the wealthiest and most populous of North American colonies. At the First Continental Congress

Virginians succeeded in determining the shape of a united agreement at the same time that they saw a joint association dilute the focus on the unique goals of economic independence in the Chesapeake.

■   ■   ■

During the opening days of the Continental Congress, which convened in Philadelphia on September 5, 1774, the more radical delegates gained approval for demands that ranged from the choice of a meeting place to endorsement of the Suffolk Resolves which affirmed Massachusetts' right to resist British authority. The vote on these early measures indicated the likely support for an aggressive and comprehensive commercial association. Only the precise terms of commercial resistance would be subject to debate. The expectation of nonimportation was so widespread that the Congress, even before discussing the terms of an association, published a recommendation that all merchants countermand orders for goods from Great Britain.

The debate that followed Richard Henry Lee's motion for a nonimportation agreement centered on the question of a starting date rather than the wisdom of an agreement itself. Virginia's association had fixed November 1 as the date to initiate nonimportation. Thomas Mifflin of Pennsylvania agreed that no honest man had ordered goods after June and therefore should receive no goods after the first of November. Some of the Massachusetts delegates insisted the boycott begin immediately, while Richard Bland, following the example of the Fairfax resolves, wanted the starting date to apply to the shipment of cargoes from Great Britain rather that the date of their arrival in America. The motion accepted by the Congress on September 27 established December 1, 1774, as the date on which Americans would cease to import all manner of British goods (including the medicines exempted from the Virginia association), whether they be from Great Britain, Ireland, or any other port of origin. The resolution also forbade the purchase of any British goods imported after December 1, 1774.[1]

---

[1]David Ammerman, *In the Common Cause: American Response to the Coercive Acts of 1774* (Charlottesville: University Press of Virginia, 1974), 53–87; Jensen, *The Founding of a Nation*, 483–507; *Journals of the Continental Congress, 1774–1789*, 34 vols. (Washington: U.S. Government Printing Office, 1904), 1:41, 43; John Adams, *Diary and Autobiography of John Adams*, ed., L. H. Butterfield, 2 vols. (New York, 1964), 2:137–40.

Despite Thomas Jefferson's suggestion that Americans also prohibit the importation of dutied items from non-British ports, the Virginia association and the original resolution of Congress ignored the subject of dutied commodities and the West Indies trade in general. Thomas Mifflin moved to exclude imports of dutied articles, and this motion raised the question of whether the Americans were protesting all duties or only those devised for revenue. On October 6, the Congress amended the nonimportation resolution with a further prohibition of molasses, coffee, and pimiento from the West Indies, wine from Madeira, and foreign indigo, all commodities carrying a British revenue duty. During the final debate on the association, Congress agreed to add syrups and paneles (a type of brown sugar) to the list of forbidden imports.[2]

After the easy approval of nonimportation, Virginia's demand that the current crop of tobacco reach the British market complicated the debate on nonexportation. The proposed delay of nonexportation until the summer of 1775 was the one major issue separating the Virginia delegates from the radicals representing the northern commercial colonies. Delegates from Massachusetts, Pennsylvania, and Connecticut, assisted by Samuel Chase of Maryland and Christopher Gadsden and Edward Rutledge of South Carolina, argued that only immediate nonexportation would compel the British to rescind all oppressive legislation. As delegates from various colonies listed the importance of their exports, from the New England lumber used for masts to the naval stores of the Carolinas and the enumerated commodities of the plantation colonies, Eliphalet Dyer of Connecticut remarked on how dependent the British economy and military were on the continued exports of the North American colonies. Surely, a year of nonexportation, coming upon Great Britain "like a Thunder Clap," would secure a redress of American grievances.

But the instructions to the Virginia delegates were unequivocal and fixed. The insistence on a year's delay before the enforcement of nonexportation reflected the anticipated reorientation of Virginia's economy as well as the relatively greater debt owed by the colony's planters. Richard Henry Lee, who privately preferred an earlier date for nonexportation, defended his colony's demand by reminding Congress that tobacco went to market the year after its harvest, whereas other colonies were already shipping their crops produced in 1774. The in-

---

[2]*Revolutionary Virginia*, eds., Scribner and Tarter, 1:112; *Diary and Autobiography of John Adams*, ed., Butterfield, 2:138–40, 147–49; Ammerman, *In the Common Cause*, 81; *Journal of the Continental Congress*, 1:54.

transigence of Virginia convinced Gadsden that nonexportation should begin without the participation of the principal tobacco colony, but this proposal prompted the Maryland delegation to announce that their colony could not withhold tobacco exports while Virginia continued to ship. In the end the influence of Virginia and the value of the tobacco trade resulted in the postponement of nonexportation until September 10, 1775. If the British government had not satisfied American demands before that date, the colonists would withhold all exports to Great Britain, Ireland, and the West Indies. Although Rutledge and Gadsden had spoken in favor of immediate nonexportation, the South Carolina delegation refused to accept the agreement unless Congress made some provision for the rice trade. Rice, as an enumerated commodity, could be exported legally only to Great Britain, and the low country areas of rice cultivation were suitable for few other crops. Congress accordingly revised the nonexportation resolution to permit the exportation of rice to Europe, thereby nullifying Parliament's trade restriction.[3]

Following approval of the nonimportation, nonconsumption, and nonexportation resolutions, Congress appointed Richard Henry Lee, Thomas Cushing, Isaac Low, Thomas Mifflin, and Thomas Johnson as a committee to prepare the draft of an association. Twelve days later, the committee reported a draft which was then subject to several sessions of debate, revision, and amendment. The delegates signed the final Continental Association on October 20, 1774. The language, the provisions, and the enforcement procedures of the Continental Association all paralleled the association endorsed by Virginia's convention. In addition to the nonintercourse agreements adopted by the Congress, the final draft of the association incorporated Virginia's prohibition of the slave trade and extended this provision to prevent associators from leasing vessels or selling produce to anyone engaged in the commerce of slaves. The terms of the nonconsumption agreement followed Virginia's example by forbidding the use of tea, although the Continental Association limited this restriction to East India Company tea and other kinds on which a duty was paid, rather than accept Virginia's unqualified rejection of the beverage. In an article recommended by several county meetings in Virginia but omitted from the August association, Congress resolved to end all connection and commerce with

[3]*Diary and Autobiography of John Adams*, ed., Butterfield, 2:138–40; *Journals of the Continental Congress*, 1:51–52; Ammerman, *In the Common Cause*, 82–83.

any North American colony that refused to join the Continental Association or later violated its terms.[4]

Delegates to the Congress agreed with the Virginia convention that Americans needed to develop sheep herds as a source of wool rather than meat and added a proposal to halt all sheep exports to the West Indies. Another article promoting "Agriculture, Arts, and the Manufactures" stressed the particular importance of woolen production for the colonies. The Virginia convention's general statements about the need for industry, economy, and frugality expanded into article eight of the Continental Association which prescribed specific regulations of entertainment and dress. In a measure that would find frequent application in Virginia, the associators pledged to discontinue all horse races, cock fights, and every form of gambling. They likewise would discourage shows, plays, "and other expensive Diversions and Entertainments." The same article restricted the observation of mourning to a black ribbon and necklace for women and an armband for men in place of the more elaborate succession of mourning clothes worn by the wealthiest rank of colonists.[5]

The Continental Association repeated Congress's earlier recommendation, now more of a command, that merchants notify as soon as possible their British correspondents and cancel all orders for goods. For merchants who received shipments from Great Britain after December 1, 1774, the Continental Association offered the options of reshipment, responsibility for the storage costs during the term of the nonimportation agreement, or a public sale of the goods from which the owners of the cargo would receive payment for the costs. All profits from the sale would go to the relief of Boston's poor. After February 1, 1775, all goods arriving from Great Britain would be returned without being unloaded. As in the Virginia association, the congressional agreement required merchants to sell goods at the same prices in effect during the previous year. In expectation of scarcities, Congress also ordered that new manufactures of the colonies sell "at reasonable prices."[6]

Enforcement of the association was the responsibility of local committees to be elected in counties and cities by citizens eligible to vote for representatives in the provincial assemblies. According to the in-

[4]*Journals of the Continental Congress*, 1:53, 62, 74–80; *Revolutionary Virginia*, eds., Scribner and Tarter, 1:112, 132–33, 147, 152, 160.

[5]*Journals of the Continental Congress*, 1:75–80.

[6]Ibid.

structions of Congress, these committees would "attentively . . . observe the conduct of all persons touching this Association." The majority of any committee could determine if an individual violated the association, in which case the committee was required to publish the circumstances and name of the offender so that any transgressors "may be publicly known and universally contemned as the Enemies of American Liberty." Signers of the Continental Association agreed to break off all dealings with any individual censured by a committee, just as they pledged to end commercial connections with any merchant who violated the trade regulations. In addition to these few, albeit far-reaching, instructions, the Congress recommended that the local committees and provincial conventions establish additional regulations that might facilitate the execution of the association. Without any explicit challenge to royal government, the association created in these local committees institutions that would soon become the *de facto* authority in every community.[7]

The Continental Association cited the parliamentary legislation passed since 1763 that the Congress believed was evidence of a calculated design "for enslaving these colonies." Whereas the Virginia Convention had deferred a summary of American grievances to the decision of the general meeting of the colonies, the Continental Congress now made repeal of the objectionable legislation the single condition for a dissolution of the association. The catalog of parliamentary acts included the familiar subjects of American protests over the previous decade: the duties on tea, wine, sugar products, coffee, pimiento, indigo, foreign paper, glass, and painters' colors; the extension of the admiralty court's jurisdiction; the interference with the right to a trial by jury; the provisions for transporting to trial in Great Britain individuals accused of offenses in the colonies; and the "Coercive Acts" depriving Massachusetts of its liberties. The most recent legislation included in the association's demands was the Quebec Act which established an arbitrary government and thereby discouraged "the Settlement of that wide-extended Country." The preamble of the Continental Association explained that a plan of commercial resistance was "the most speedy, effectual, and peaceable Measure" by which Americans might obtain a repeal of the objectionable parliamentary acts.[8]

[7]Ibid. According to the terms of the Continental Association, the only supervisory institution above the local committees would be the provincial committees of correspondence, which would oversee the customs operations in their respective colonies.
[8]Ibid.

In a series of addresses and petitions issued after October 20, 1774, Congress offered further justification for the commercial boycott and outlined its intended effects. The address to the people of Great Britain recounted the imperial policies that had forced Americans into a posture of radical resistance. Before the French and Indian War, Great Britain had been content to receive the wealth produced by colonial commerce. Since 1763, the ministry had determined to increase revenue from the colonies at the expense of constitutional principles. The interests of self-preservation demanded that Americans unite against individual friends in Great Britain. Congress called on "the magnanimity and justice of the British Nation" to force Parliament to overturn the ministry's policy and restore a mutually beneficial commerce between Great Britain and the American colonies. An address to the inhabitants of British North America also chronicled the recent policies of the ministry. According to Congress the interference with American rights and excessive demands for revenue warranted a stronger, though unspecified, form of resistance than that prescribed in the association. For the time being, however, the delegates in Congress preferred commercial opposition because it made reconciliation possible. The address urged Americans to accept the temporary inconveniences and sacrifices entailed in a suspension of trade as a small price for the defeat of arbitrary power. A petition to the King, with no concession to Parliament's sovereignty over the colonies, contained the formal presentation of American grievances.[9]

Since early summer Richard Henry Lee had expected the general Congress to convey to British merchants and manufacturers a special address expressing regret that a commercial association would materially injure innocent traders. Although the Continental Congress was content with the single message to the British people, Lee's draft of a memorial to the "Gentlemen, Merchants & Manufacturers" of Great Britain reflected the commercial assumptions that underlined the association, particularly for Virginians with their complicated, historical connections to British merchants. As a gesture of reconciliation, Lee assured the British that the colonists did not desire independence and were willing to abide by the traditional regulations of the Navigation Acts. British restrictions on commerce and manufactures, however, were all the concessions Americans would be willing to offer in return for military and maritime protection. Lee reminded the merchants and

---

[9]Ibid., 82–121; draft of Richard Henry Lee's address, 1774, *Lee Family Papers* (University of Virginia microfilm publication).

manufacturers that colonial exports of resources and the colonial market for finished goods provided employment for "multitudes of people," increased the value of British lands, and contributed to the national wealth in innumerable other ways. American compliance with the Navigation Acts, in turn, cost the colonists the full benefit of their own labor and stifled the manufacturing potential of various colonies. The revenue acts of recent years were an added burden that Americans could not bear. Lee urged the merchants and manufacturers to press for repeal of the objectionable acts and thereby restore the mutual benefits of Anglo-American commerce.[10]

■   ■   ■

By the time the *Virginia Gazette* printed the text of the Continental Association on November 3, 1774, the popular determination to enforce commercial resistance was evident throughout the colony. As William Carr awaited news from Congress, he noticed "a spirit of opposition & resistance . . . amongst all sorts of People" and concluded that Virginians would "go naked rather than have any commerce or connection with Great Britain after the time Congress agrees on for stopping the imports." During October and early November in counties that had established committees to enforce the August association, merchants and other dissenters faced increasing pressure to support the trade boycott or risk public censure and a loss of business. James Parker found that the Glasgow factors were the principal targets of resentment; a fact which he attributed to the great sums owed to those merchants. Whatever the source of the public anger, the treatment accorded James Dunlop of Port Royal indicated that the current association would elicit a degree of compliance unknown in 1769 or 1770. After Dunlop refused to sign the August association, a mob attacked his house and offered him the options of being hanged, having his storehouse and record boxes burned, or signing the agreement. Dunlop predictably accepted the final choice. Other counties made less dramatic but equally persuasive demands on those who dared to criticize the association.[11]

[10]Richard Henry Lee to [Arthur Lee], 26 June 1774, in *The Letters of Richard Henry Lee*, ed., Ballagh, 114–118; draft of Memorial, [1774], *Lee Family Papers* (University of Virginia microfilm publication).

[11]William Carr to James Russell, 23 Oct. 1774, Russell Papers, Coutts & Co., London (Virginia Colonial Records Project microfilm); James Parker to

Four days after the publication of the Continental Association in Virginia, an attack on the ship of a prominent London merchant signaled that no one would be immune from the restrictions of the nonimportation agreement. The ship *Virginia* with Captain Howard Esten arrived in the colony in early November, carrying 154 pounds of tea consigned by John Norton of London to shopkeeper John Prentis of Williamsburg. Norton, aware of the resolution against tea consumption, had ordered Esten to report the nature of the cargo as soon as he reached Virginia. A committee of former burgesses met in Williamsburg at eight o'clock on the morning of November 7 to determine what should be done with the tea. A crowd from Yorktown boarded the *Virginia* at ten o'clock the same morning and waited for a decision from the Williamsburg meeting. When the former burgesses failed to answer a messenger from the Yorktown crowd, the assembled group tossed the tea into the York River. The committee of Gloucester County, accompanied by a crowd of local residents, also headed toward the *Virginia* on the afternoon of the seventh with similar intentions but arrived to find "the Tea had met its deserved Fate."[12]

When the Gloucester County committee reconvened on the evening of November 7, it censured Norton, Prentis, and Esten and asked that a "publick Example" be made of Prentis. The most serious reprimand was ordered against Norton, who had "lent his *little Aid* to the Ministry for enslaving America." The committee ordered the *Virginia* to leave within twenty days without loading any tobacco. The committee further resolved that no one in the county would thereafter consign tobacco or any other commodity to the Norton house until "satisfactory concessions" were made. The York County committee meeting two days later also condemned the action of the three parties involved and ordered the *Virginia* to clear out with only ballast on board within 18 days.[13]

John Prentis recovered his public reputation on November 24 when he offered the Gloucester and York committees his fullest apologies for not countermanding the order for tea. As soon as John Norton learned

Charles Steuart, 26 Oct 1774, postscript, 1 Nov., Charles Steuart Papers, National Library of Scotland (Colonial Williamsburg microfilm); *Revolutionary Virginia*, eds., Scribner and Tarter, 2:163–64, 218–19.

[12]*Revolutionary Virginia*, eds., Scribner and Tarter, 2:163–64, 218–19.

[13]Ibid., 165–66; James Parker to Charles Steuart, 6 Dec. 1774, Charles Steuart Papers, National Library of Scotland (Colonial Williamsburg microfilm).

of the incident, he sent the two committees a lengthy explanation of his own actions. Norton insisted that he had always been uneasy about the order and waited for an expected countermand. Soon after the *Virginia* cleared from London in September, Norton received one of the earliest notices of the August association. Customs regulations would not allow Norton to stop the ship and remove the cargo, but he did send word to Captain Esten to consult with the Virginia committee of correspondence and return the tea if necessary. After receiving word of his censure by the Gloucester and York committees, Norton wrote another letter assuring all Virginians that his violation was unintended and that he continued to oppose any parliamentary attempts to tax the American colonies.[14]

Norton's apology, printed in the *Virginia Gazette* in May 1775, arrived too late to save him from damaging losses in trade. James Parker noted that the 700 hogsheads intended for the *Virginia* would have paid a great many tradesmens' bills in London. Charles Yates predicted that a continuing reluctance to consign tobacco to Norton & Sons could cost the London firm much of the £40–50,000 advanced to Virginians by the firm. Yates assured his British associates that he would heed the lesson of the Norton affair and avoid any provocation of public opinion. The loss for Norton was all the more alarming to other merchants because of his standing in the colony. Perhaps no other British merchant was as well-connected in Virginia as was John Norton. He had lived in Yorktown for over twenty years, during which time he married a Virginian and served in the House of Burgesses. After returning to London, Norton carried on his Virginia business through the representation of his son in Yorktown and the informal assistance of Robert Carter Nicholas, the Treasurer of the colony. In addition to his business affairs, Norton provided Virginians with important political information from London and in 1773 became the official agent of the colony's committee of correspondence. These connections in Virginia, however, yielded no leniency in November 1774 when men as prominent as Councillor Thomas Nelson were among the group that insisted on returning the *Virginia* in ballast.[15]

---

[14]*Revolutionary Virginia*, eds., Scribner and Tarter, 1:218–29.
[15]*Virginia Gazette* (Dixon & Hunter), 6 May 1775; James Parker to Charles Steuart, 27 Nov. 1774, Charles Steuart Papers, National Library of Scotland (Colonial Williamsburg microfilm); Charles Yates to Gale & Fearon, 2 Dec. 1774, Yates Letterbook, University of Virginia; see also *John Norton & Sons*,

Even those who sought to defend Norton came under public criticism. William Reynolds, after speaking in favor of Norton when the York County committee inspected the ship, found himself accused of partiality and voted off the committee at the following election. Robert Carter Nicholas, who by 1774 was related to Norton by marriage as well as by friendship and business, presented the merchant's case to the York County committee. An early and steady advocate of commercial resistance, Nicholas condemned Norton's shipment of tea but questioned whether the committee's censure was proper under the terms of the Continental Association. Nicholas's appeal for moderation had no effect on the committee and prompted a printed attack that accused him of hypocrisy and several specific violations of the association. As Richard Henry Lee later recognized, the reprisals against Norton, "a much favored Merchant here," were a clear indication of the popular support for a strict enforcement of the association as well as an absolute regulation of all commercial activity in Virginia.[16]

The regular enforcement of the Continental Association began in mid-November as counties throughout Virginia formed new committees or reorganized old ones along the guidelines set forth by the Congress. Following the *Virginia Gazette*'s publication of the association text and its large-print notice of the instructions for committee selection, at least twenty-nine of Virginia's sixty-one counties along with the cities of Williamsburg and Norfolk established new committees for the administration of the commercial agreement. Most of these counties selected their committees by January 1775, but in a few counties such as Westmoreland and Lancaster existing committees enforced the association until the gathering of freeholders at the election of convention delegates could vote for a new board. Augusta, Bedford, and Mecklenburg counties formed committees only in May 1775 after the Virginia convention ordered the creation of local militia units. The

---

ed., Mason, 379–87; Jacob M. Price, "Who was John Norton? A Note on the Historical Character of Some Eighteenth–Century London Virginia Firms," *William and Mary Quarterly* 3rd ser., 19 (July 1962): 400–07.

[16]William Reynolds to George Flowerdew Norton, 25 May 1775, William Reynolds Letterbook, Library of Congress; "Queries from An Associator," *Virginia Gazette* (Purdie & Dixon), 8 Dec. 1774, supplement; reply of Nicholas in "A Real Associator," *Virginia Gazette* (Purdie & Dixon), 15 Dec. 1774; Richard Henry Lee to Samuel Adams, 4 Feb. 1775, *The Letters of Richard Henry Lee*, ed., Ballagh, 1:127–30.

Bedford County committee subsequently regulated commercial activity as well as military affairs in the county.[17]

The size of the committees ranged from as few as 12 members in Warwick County to as many as 45 in Spotsylvania, although most counties elected between 20 and 30 members. The committeemen were the familiar leaders of the county communities. In many counties, former burgesses served, often as chairmen, and the majority of members had been justices of the peace. Most of the men who served on the inspection committees during the association of 1770 also were elected under the Continental Association. Planters dominated the committees, although resident merchants were frequently represented. Because the size of the committees was generally larger than the county courts, the association offered broader opportunities for officeholding. This expansion of the political base reinforced rather than challenged the traditional county leadership. Committee members were consistently among the wealthiest men in their respective counties, and the wealthiest members of the committees generally dominated proceedings. In addition to political experience and wealth, the committees reflected a geographical balance within the counties. Landon Carter noted that the twenty-eight members of the Richmond County committee were "convenient in their Situation to inspect the attention paid to the Association through the whole county." Northampton's committee divided the county into seven districts and appointed three members from each area to "observe the conduct of all persons therein, touching the association."[18]

---

[17]*Virginia Gazette* (Purdie & Dixon), 3 Nov. 1774; *Revolutionary Virginia*, eds., Scribner and Tarter, vols. 2 and 3 passim; another eighteen Virginia counties had enforcement committees operating in the months after November 1774. Some of these committees were established after the August association, while others may have been new committees which did not publish their selection proceedings in the *Virginia Gazette*. For overview of enforcement of the Continental Association, see Ann Fairfax Withington, *Toward a More Perfect Union: Virtue and the Formation of American Republics* (New York and Oxford: Oxford University Press, 1991), 217–50.

[18]*Revolutionary Virginia*, eds., Scribner and Tarter, 2:174–75, 195, 202; "Justices of the Peace in Colonial Virginia, 1757–1775," *Bulletin of the Virginia State Library* 14 (April–June 1921): 41–149; Dale E. Benson, "Wealth and Power in Virginia, 1774–1776: A Study of the Organization of Revolt" (Ph.D. diss., University of Maine, 1970), ch. 3; Landon Carter, Notes on County meeting, 5 Dec. 1774, Sabine Hall Collection, University of Virginia.

The committee election meetings were the first and most important step in consolidating popular support of the Continental Association. Freeholders and other residents gathered much as they would for the election of burgesses and listened to readings of the association, after which they subscribed to the agreement. Following the elections, the committees circulated copies of the association in order to collect signatures from individuals who were unable or unwilling to attend the general meeting. In Albemarle County where over 200 freeholders participated in the election, the committee sent copies to each of 13 militia captains who garnered signatures in their own localities. Southampton's committee divided the county into ten districts for the distribution of the association.[19]

■   ■   ■

As Virginians had learned in 1769 and 1770, commercial resistance could not succeed without the merchants' acquiescence and a recognition of the local committee's authority. In the early months of the Continental Association, the Virginia committees were absorbed in their determined effort to compel the merchants' faithful observance of the nonimportation agreement. The influence of the committee members and the weight of public opinion, not to mention the examples presented by James Dunlop and John Norton, convinced most merchants, including Scottish factors, to sign the association. At a meeting of the merchants in Williamsburg during early November, between 400 and 500 traders, "sensible of the need to preserve Peace & Harmony not only between different colonies, but also among all Ranks and Societies in each colony," presented Peyton Randolph with the association, "voluntarily and generally signed." In Spotsylvania County the committee appointed members to wait on individual merchants and secure their subscriptions to the association. In the city of Norfolk, where a concentration of Scottish merchants might have presented an obstacle to the execution of the association, the organizers of the committee election persuaded inhabitants from the surrounding country to participate in

[19]*Revolutionary Virginia*, eds., Scribner and Tarter, 2:167, 177–78, 319–20; Albemarle County election and notes on distribution in Thomas Jefferson Account Books, 1774, p. 167, Account Books, 1775, p. 214, photostatic copies, University of Virginia.

the election. Once in power, the Norfolk committee prevented the sale of goods owned by merchants who had yet to sign the association.[20]

In the few instances when merchants resisted the committees' demand for public assent, popular reaction was so swift and strong as to exact compliance. In Williamsburg, the committee placed a barrel of tar, a bag of feathers, and a tar mop at the spot near the Capitol where reluctant merchants were asked to sign the association. Under these intimidating arrangements the committee required several people to recant earlier criticisms of the association. The committee, chaired by Archibald Cary, also called on the merchants Anthony Warwick and Michael Wallace to account for the tea cargoes they had recently imported. Norfolk's committee initially demanded the tea of Warwick and Wallace who claimed that the cargo had to be landed at Milners in Nansemond County. The merchants never reported the tea to the Nansemond committee, but while in Williamsburg a Nansemond committee member called the merchants before Cary's committee. The crowd was so angered at the apparent attempt to elude the committee and smuggle the tea that only the intercession of Peyton Randolph, Robert Carter Nicholas, Edmund Pendleton, and Richard Bland saved the merchants from physical assault. Warwick and Wallace returned to the Nansemond committee, to which they promised to deliver the tea. They then "voluntarily signed" the Continental Association.[21]

William Allason and other merchants from Falmouth in King George County met in January 1775 to establish their own town committee for the purpose of evading the authority of the county committee. Faced with this challenge, members of the King George committee appealed to Richard Henry Lee for his opinion of Congress's intention in the association's article eleven calling for committees in counties and towns. Lee assured them that the mention of towns applied only to the cities of the northern colonies and the few population centers in the

---

[20]*Virginia Gazette* (Purdie & Dixon), 10 Nov. 1774; *Revolutionary Virginia*, eds., Scribner and Tarter, 2:197; James Parker to Charles Steuart, 6 Dec. 1774, Charles Steuart Papers, National Library of Scotland (Colonial Williamsburg microfilm).

[21][James Parker] to Charles Steuart, 27 Nov 1774, Charles Steuart Papers, National Library of Scotland (Colonial Williamsburg microfilm); William Atchison to James Parker, 14 Nov. 1774, Parker Family Papers, Liverpool Record Office (Virginia Colonial Records Project microfilm); *Revolutionary Virginia*, eds., Scribner and Tarter, 2:172–73.

"The Alternative of Williams-burg." Printed for R. Sayer & J. Bennett, London, February 16, 1775. With the threat of tar and feathers hanging above them, reluctant merchants sign "The Resolves of the Congress" in this satirical English print, while a statue of the late Virginia governor, Lord Botetourt, watches over the scene. The English depiction of patriots includes women, children, a knife-wielding cook, and a lone African American. The signing of the association takes place upon a hogshead of tobacco consigned to John Wilkes. (Library of Congress)

southern colonies rather than "small knots or collections of interested Traders." The merchants of Falmouth already had the opportunity to participate in the election of the King George committee; any further division of the county would produce "endless confusion" and lead "to the utter destruction of the Association." If the other communities followed Falmouth's example, committees would appear in every village where the "foreign Traders are generally collected." Lee urged the King George committee to assert its authority over Falmouth, "and as a Trading Place that their attention to it should be particularly careful."[22]

On February 3, 1775, the King George committee, accompanied by the committee of Stratford County and a crowd of 150 people, confronted the merchants from Falmouth. After interrogating each merchant about the formation of the separate committee, the King George committee voted to censure the individuals according to the terms of the Continental Association. A portion of the crowd hoped to expose the merchants to public mockery, but the merchants escaped with only the reprimand of the committee. The following day William Allason learned that the Fredericksburg assemblage, angry at the merchants' failure to sign either an apology or the association, planned to attack the Falmouth traders if ever they entered the nearby town. "From motives of self-preservation," Allason and the others agreed to sign. James Robinson, the Falmouth agent for William Cunninghame & Company, later testified that he signed the association only to insure his personal safety.[23]

For two months after December 1, 1774, the association permitted the importation of goods ordered before the meeting of Congress on the condition that the county committees administer a public sale of the goods. After a merchant or planter delivered up the goods, the committee published a notice of the sale and announced whatever conditions were attached. In some counties importers were able to purchase the cargo for the exact amount indicated by the invoice and thereby avoid

[22]William Allason to Thomas Bryan Martin, 31 Jan. 1775, Allason Letterbook, Virginia State Library; Richard Henry Lee, Opinion for Committee of King George County, 1774, *Lee Family Papers* (University of Virginia microfilm).

[23]William Allason to Thomas Bryan Martin, 6 Feb 1775, Allason Letterbook, Virginia State Library; testimony of James Robinson in claims of William Cunninghame & Co., Public Record Office, AO 12/56 (Virginia Colonial Records Project microfilm).

paying the surplus which the association appropriated for the relief of Boston's poor. Under these conditions the importer was restricted only by the demand for payment in ready money or the competitive bidding of another. In other counties, committees ordered the goods to be sold in smaller batches. The King George County committee restricted the goods to lots valued at £5 to £20 and determined the exchange rate in January 1775 to be 35 percent. In Henrico County the committee sold 3,500 bushels of salt in lots of 500 bushels. The profits from these sales were generally small or nonexistent, although in King George County the sale of £357 worth of goods produced a profit of over £19, and in Spotsylvania County the committee collected a profit of more than £21 on a cargo worth £258.[24]

Dr. Alexander Gordon offered the single instance of defiance to the public sale of imported goods when he refused to hand over £200 of medicines on the grounds that the provincial association exempted that classification of goods. When the Norfolk Borough committee protested that they were governed by the Continental Association, Gordon replied that he preferred to store the goods according to the provision of the association rather than offer them for public sale. Gordon also appealed to Peyton Randolph for an opinion on his right to import medicines. After Randolph reaffirmed the committee's decision, Gordon refused to deliver the medicines for sale or storage. A reluctant committee, abandoning its effort to provide the medicines to the community, published a notice of Gordon's violation.[25]

After February 1, 1775, any goods imported into Virginia met with the committees' demand for immediate reshipment. The authority of the committees and the jealous scrutiny of citizens was such that few individuals attempted to challenge the nonimportation agreement. Occasionally the inspection of a merchant's books would yield evidence of a violation. When a ship carrying slaves from Jamaica arrived in Norfolk, consigned to John Brown, the merchant denied that he ordered the slaves. A committee review of Brown's letterbook revealed that he had asked for all remittances from Jamaica to be made in slaves. Fur-

---

[24]For example of a planter's delivery of imported goods, see Thomas Jefferson to Archibald Cary, 9 Dec. 1774, in *Papers of Thomas Jefferson*, ed., Boyd, 1:154–55; *Revolutionary Virginia*, eds., Scribner and Tarter, 2:213–14, 237–40, 264–65.

[25]*Revolutionary Virginia*, eds., Scribner and Tarter, 2:258–60, 272, 278.

thermore, he had warned the Jamaican shippers to watch out for the enforcement committees. The Norfolk committee condemned Brown for "willfully and perversely" violating the association.[26]

In June 1775, the same committee investigated the arrival of the ship *Molly* loaded with goods for Eilbeck, Ross & Co. of Norfolk. The ship's invoice indicated that the cargo was sent by Walker Chambre of Whitehaven without an order from Eilbeck or Ross. The committee nevertheless ordered a reshipment on board the same vessel and asked the merchants to obtain a certificate from Whitehaven verifying the cargo's relanding in England. When the committee received the certificate in August, it published the name of Chambre as an enemy of America. Essex County's committee chose the strictest enforcement of the nonimportation agreement, even in ambiguous cases. In 1773, Captain Joseph Richardson had imported into Virginia a cargo of osnaburg cloth that he could not sell at the time. He carried the cloth to Antigua, but on a recent trip to the island, finding the cloth unsold, brought it back to Essex County. The Essex committee did not censure Richardson, who was unaware of the association when he returned from Antigua, but insisted that he return the osnaburg.[27]

After demanding the merchants' public assent to the Continental Association and imposing the terms of the nonimportation provisions, the county committees maintained a surveillance of the traders' business affairs. By December Dunmore reported to London that the committees had assumed the right to inspect merchants' records and publicly censure any who violated the association. William Carr complained of unprovoked investigations of traders' accounts, and Charles Yates warned others that the committees would censure merchants "for the smallest deviation." Carr also urged the prominent London merchant, James Russell, to be cautious in all his dealings with Virginians because "some People here are watching every opportunity to render your solicitations fruitless."[28]

[26]*Revolutionary Virginia*, eds., Scribner and Tarter, 3:186–88.

[27]*Revolutionary Virginia*, eds., Scribner and Tarter, 3:190, 483, 2:306–07

[28]Dunmore to Earl of Dartmouth, 24 Dec. 1774, Public Record Office, CO5/1353 (Virginia Colonial Records Project microfilm); William Carr to James Russell, 24 Jan. 1775, Russell Papers, Coutts & Co., London (Virginia Colonial Records Project microfilm); Charles Yates to Samuel Martin, 6 Feb 1775, Yates Letterbook, University of Virginia.

Some committees encouraged local inhabitants to report any violations of the association, while others actively searched for possible infringements. Prince William County's committee announced in December that it would summon any merchants suspected of a violation to appear before the committee and to present their daybooks and invoices. Refusal to appear would be considered an admission of guilt. In December Caroline County's committee, followed by the Charlotte committee in February, ordered the inspection of local merchants' records even without receiving any specific accusations. Charlotte County's committee hoped the examination of the "day books, invoices, &c. of the several merchants, or storekeepers within this county" would allow local residents to discriminate between honest merchants and those who subverted the intention of the association. Christopher McConnico refused the request of the Charlotte committee and found himself cut off from the business of the community. Only in November 1775, nine months after the original demand, did McConnico deliver his books to the committee and receive a retraction of its censure. The Caroline County committee also recommended a public boycott of the Port Royal merchants who denied the committee access to their financial records. The censured merchants published a statement asserting their innocence but failed to persuade Edmund Pendleton, who as chairman of the Caroline committee offered the merchants a final opportunity to cooperate. On January 13, 1775, one day after receiving Pendleton's assurance that no bodily harm would come to them if they attended the meeting, the six Port Royal merchants presented their books and apologies to the Caroline County committee.[29]

At the courthouse and every other public place in the county, the Isle of Wight committee posted copies of the association's ninth article which prohibited price increases in the face of shortages. Other committees inspected merchants' records for possible price violations. The Gloucester County committee boarded the sloop of John Blatt and discovered that his employers ordered him to sell goods at an advance of 100 percent. The committee extracted a public apology from Blatt and from his Scottish ship captain who had challenged the right of the committee to regulate prices. Two weeks later the Richmond County committee found Blatt continued to sell goods at an enormous mark-up. Because Blatt was a young man in the employ of John and George Fowler of Alexandria, the Richmond County committee expelled him from the

[29]*Revolutionary Virginia*, eds., Scribner and Tarter, 2:210, 232–34, 145–46.

area and asked the Fairfax County committee to take action against the Fowlers. In Surry County the committee censured Robert Kennan for selling salt at three shillings rather than his usual price of two shillings and six pence; an advance far below Blatt's 100 percent. In addition to the regulation of prices for merchants' goods, the Caroline County committee established limits on the prices for raw cotton and wool produced in the colony.[30]

During the early months of 1775, several committees suggested refinements and amendments to the regulations of the association in order to make its enforcement more effective in Virginia. The Richmond County committee feared that small vessels trading within the colony might subvert the nonimportation agreement by smuggling goods from British ships waiting offshore. Beginning in early February the committee required all shipmasters and supercargoes selling goods to provide a certificate attesting that the items were imported in accordance with the association. The certificates, to be issued by committees in the counties from which the traders came, would also provide a license to sell the cargo. The Westmoreland County committee similarly was concerned with the "itinerant or casual vendor of goods" who might carry illicit imports from one county to another. Before traveling vendors sold goods in Westmoreland County, they needed to provide the county committee with proof of importation before February 1, 1775.[31]

Virginia's committees were uniformly rigorous in their application of the association, particularly the commercial restrictions on merchants, and intolerant of all dissent. They were careful, however, to maintain their credibility and public respect by clearing the innocent of false accusations. The Brunswick County committee published a vindication of merchant Allan Love who stood accused of speaking against the American resistance to Great Britain. Witnesses before the committee denied the reports, and Love offered assurances by signing the association. After declaring his belief that Parliament had no right to tax the colonies, Love asked the committee to publish an exoneration of his name. A subcommittee in Spotsylvania County inspected the daybook and journal of merchant William Triplett on a suspicion of his selling goods for an unreasonable price. Although the committee members attested to the "good ground for the accusation," they found no evidence

---

[30]*Revolutionary Virginia*, eds., Scribner and Tarter, 2:200, 206, 277, 282–83, 290; 4:449.
[31]*Revolutionary Virginia*, eds., Scribner and Tarter, 2:262–64, 281–83.

of price hikes and published their acquittal of Triplett. Landon Carter as chairman of the Richmond County committee personally investigated two merchants who allegedly hoarded goods during the first weeks of the association. When Carter was convinced of their innocence he presented the evidence to the bearer of the accusation. Carter ordered an account of the case to be printed in the *Virginia Gazette* "in order to discourage and stifle such ungenerous, as well as unjust Accusations." The Norfolk Borough committee demanded to know the name of all accusers "as it is obvious to every one that aspersions of this nature should be well founded before they are made public."[32]

■   ■   ■

As successful as they were in regulating merchant activity and ensuring a compliance with the policy of nonimportation, the enforcement responsibilities of the county committees often overwhelmed the association's other objectives, such as the promotion of domestic manufactures and the diversification of agricultural production. The encouragement of local manufactures would be as essential to the success of the various goals of commercial resistance as the supervision of traders. Virginians needed to establish domestic supplies of essential goods and commodities if they were to bring pressure to bear on British merchants and manufacturers. Local manufactures also were a prerequisite for the achievement of any degree of economic independence. From his perspective in England, Arthur Lee assured his friends in Virginia that the association would be effective only if the colonists managed to supply their own needs. Planting grain crops and "Great quantities of Cotton" would convince the British that the threat of nonexportation was serious and would enable the Virginians to survive without British trade. Lee also urged Virginians to grow every kind of crop that would produce the alcoholic beverages so in demand among "the Common Planters." If the organizers of the association failed to satisfy the needs of the average planter, Lee feared the Scots would exploit popular resentments. The nonimportation provisions of the association already met with great derision from Dunmore, who, like many British officials, believed the Virginians were incapable of furnishing their own manufactured goods. The governor dismissed the threat of the association. "The people of

[32] *Revolutionary Virginia*, eds., Scribner and Tarter, 2:256–57, 274–75, 278–79.

Virginia are very far from being naturally industrious," and even if they reformed their work habits Dunmore assured Lord Dartmouth that "times of anarchy and confusion" would not provide the foundation for improvements in manufacturing.[33]

Whether as a result of the indolence cited by Dunmore or the more likely consequence of a long commitment to staple agriculture in a colonial economy, Virginians in the fall of 1774 did not have the manufacturing capacity to replace even a fraction of their usual British imports. Of critical necessity were the coarse clothes worn by slaves and which the British produced more cheaply than was possible in Virginia. As during earlier associations for commercial resistance in Virginia, communities sought to consolidate resources in order to establish the basic manufactures that were beyond the scale possible on most individual plantations. The committee of Henrico County sought to satisfy the demand for domestic cloth by offering subscriptions for the "encouragement of all kinds of husbandry and manufactures" within the county. Chesterfield County also raised a subscription for the establishment of cloth manufacturing in the county. Household production of cloth depended on the availability of wool and cotton cards usually imported from Great Britain. Isle of Wight County's committee offered £20 to the first person who made 1,000 "merchantable" cotton or wool cards. Gloucester County's committee offered £50 for just 60 of the same. In Essex County the committee provided a bounty and offered to purchase the cards. The bounty of £40 from Northampton's committee was conditional on the card-maker settling in the county. The Northampton committee regretted its bounty was not larger but proposed joining with other counties to present higher premiums for new manufactures. The committee of Caroline County suggested a similar joint scheme for the manufacture of linen.[34]

As during earlier boycotts of British goods, promises of public support inspired experiments in manufacturing. Elisha and Robert White hoped to meet the demand for cloth with the establishment of a "Woolen and Worsted Manufactury" in Henrico County. After receiving encour-

---

[33]Arthur Lee to [Francis Lightfoot Lee], 13 Dec. 1774, *Lee Family Papers* (University of Virginia microfilm publication); Governor Dunmore to Earl of Dartmouth, 24 Dec. 1774, Public Record Office, CO5/1353 (Virginia Colonial Records Project microfilm).

[34]*Revolutionary Virginia*, eds., Scribner and Tarter, 2:189, 231–32, 287; 3:34–35, 60, 117, 306–07.

agement from the Virginia convention, the Whites solicited subscriptions for the support of their project. They promised investors the security of repayment in the form of finished cloth. More frequently, the complete cessation of the British import trade forced planters to concentrate on collecting the basic provisions immediately required by their families before they could turn their attention to the ambitious schemes recommended by Arthur Lee or proposed by the Whites. Robert Carter Nicholas, who refused to buy anything from England after May 1774, was unable to gather in Virginia more than one-third of his usual supplies. Nicholas was fortunate enough to own an estate capable of producing some of these goods. By December 1774, Nicholas had ordered his plantation steward to reorganize the estate for greater self-sufficiency. In place of tobacco, Nicholas turned the land over to wheat, hemp, flax, cotton, and pasture for sheep. He also provided a building on his plantation to accommodate slave women working in the preparation and weaving of cloth. "Instead of reaping the Advantages of an Estate hitherto somewhat profitable to me," Nicholas expected only to "cloath and feed my numerous Family and my Slaves."[35]

Robert Carter of Nomini Hall had abstained from the debate on commercial resistance through the summer of 1774, but by October he recognized the need to make provisions for the supply of his extensive estates. He informed an overseer that all future management of the plantations would be governed by Congress's announcement of nonimportation and nonexportation. Carter ordered enough flax and hemp seed to employ 100 slaves in the preparation of these crops. He also chose ten slave women, "the most expert Spinners belonging to me," to work solely in the preparation of cloth. What formerly served as a tobacco house at one of Carter's plantations in February 1775 became the spinning workshop.[36]

While large planters diverted slaves to the work of cloth production, the majority of Virginians faced severe shortages, particularly of cloth. By March of 1775, William Allason reported such scarcities "of all kinds of course Goods" that he could not imagine "how the poorer

---

[35] *Virginia Gazette* (Pinkney), 27 Oct. 1774; "A Real Associator," [Robert Carter Nicholas], *Virginia Gazette* (Purdie & Dixon), 15 Dec. 1774.

[36] Robert Carter to Fielding Lewis, 28 Oct. 1774, 14 Nov. 1774, Robert Carter to William Mathis, 14 Nov. 1774, Robert Carter to William Taylor, 21 Feb. 1775, Robert Carter Letterbook, 1774–1775, Duke University (Colonial Williamsburg microfilm).

sort of People & Negroes are to be provided with Cloathing & Linnen in future." Two months later Allason could find no osnaburg at all. Robert Pleasants hoped to locate "Negro Cloth" in the West Indies since it would be some time before the local manufacturing schemes were "brought to perfection." In the fall of 1775 a British soldier reported that cloth was not available "for money at any rate, there being none in the country."[37]

The Virginia convention of March 1775 endorsed a series of resolutions designed to encourage manufacture of goods that by that time were in scarce supply. The delegates urged local magistrates and church officials to find employment for vagrants and the poor within their communities. The perennial problem of drifters and the indigent might now become an advantage in the establishment of manufactures if officials enforced the poor laws. The convention intended several of its resolves to promote the manufacture of increasingly scarce cloth. The association's encouragement of sheep raising expanded into a prohibition of the butchering and marketing of all sheep under the age of four years old. The convention further recommended that families in need of mutton kill those sheep "least profitable to be kept." In order to expand the potential for home manufactures, the convention requested large landholders to offer their flax, hemp, and cotton on moderate terms to their neighbors. Cloth was the commodity most in demand during nonimportation, but the convention also promoted the manufacture of iron for nails and wire, steel, paper made from rags, salt, saltpeter and sulphur for gunpowder, glass, and the cards and heckles used in the preparation of hemp and flax for weaving. The construction of fulling mills and mills for processing hemp and flax would permit manufacturing on a larger scale than was possible on individual plantations. The cultivation of hops and barley would encourage the brewing of liquors in Virginia and thereby lessen the dependence on imported alcoholic beverages. The convention had no means to finance these recommended developments, but the delegates hoped premiums from local commit-

---

[37]William Allason to Thomas Bryan Martin, 10 May 1775, William Allason to Edward Snickers, 22 May 1775, William Allason Letterbook, Virginia State Library; Robert Pleasants to Thomas Applethwaite, 5 May 1775, Robert Pleasants Letterbook, Library of Congress; James Freeland to John Taylour, 20 Oct. 1775, intercepted letter, Committee of Safety, in *Revolutionary Virginia*, eds., Scribner and Tarter, 4:246–47.

tees and a preference among consumers for American-made goods would provide the material encouragement for diversifying the colonial economy.[38]

■   ■   ■

In contrast to the hardships created by nonimportation, the scheduled nonexportation agreement provided Virginia planters with an opportunity to demand higher prices for their tobacco crops. Once the merchants began to speculate in expectation of an unusually high market in London, the planters held out for the highest reported prices. James Robinson, agent for William Cunninghame & Company, recognized the dangers of speculative buying and recommended that the factors concentrate on collecting tobacco from debtors. Robinson also organized a merchants' agreement to limit the price of tobacco to fourteen shillings per hundredweight. The informal plan for a price restriction was ineffective in the face of the pressures to ship as much as possible and the reluctance of the planters to part with their crop at such a low price. Planters also refused to ship on consignment or exchange tobacco for goods at the factors' stores. Merchants who hoped to get tobacco to the most favorable British market had no choice but to compete for cash purchases. By February Charles Yates reported that a great deal of tobacco was bought and resold in the colony by merchants. Even the Cunninghame factors began to make cash purchases.[39]

The speculative frenzy and the frequent advances of bills from London satisfied the planters' hope for higher prices. From a price of sixteen shillings currency per hundredweight in November 1774, Potomac River tobacco was fetching as much as twenty-five shillings sterling in February 1775, and planters were refusing twenty shillings sterling. Prices continued to climb throughout the spring months, especially in May when the threat of an earlier starting date for the nonexportation

[38]Proceedings of the Second Virginia Convention in *Revolutionary Virginia*, eds., Scribner and Tarter, 2:381–83.

[39]James Robinson to Wm. Cunninghame & Co., 16 Nov. 1774, 8 Jan. 1775, in *A Scottish Firm in Virginia*, ed., T. M. Devine, 165–68, 169–74; Charles Yates to John Baynes, 22 Feb. 1775, Yates Letterbook, University of Virginia; William Carr to James Russell, 24 Jan. 1775, Russell Papers, Coutts & Co., London (Virginia Colonial Records Project microfilm).

agreement convinced merchants to make extravagant offers. The rush to buy and ship was so strong that William Carr in Dumfries could not locate sufficient loading craft. James Robinson complained that the planters' demands exceeded the price ceilings established by company directors in Scotland in the aftermath of the credit crisis of 1772. The regular offers of twenty shillings sterling and more appeared to Cunninghame factor James Likly as the highest prices could go. But by July merchants on James River repeatedly paid as much as twenty-seven shillings and six pence for a hundredweight of tobacco.[40]

The merchants' generous offers for tobacco through the first half of 1775 were one indication of how thoroughly the Continental Association determined business activity in Virginia. The committees' careful observation of all shipping, the popular determination to refuse imports and halt exports, and the closure of the courts forced merchants to meet the planters' demands or return their company's ships in ballast. The Virginia convention that met in March 1775 explicitly sanctioned the first convention's tacit agreement to close the courts to all debt cases. The announcement of March 25, 1775, recommended that no one proceed with civil suits at the April General Court. The delegates also advised the county courts not to hear civil cases other than such "amicable proceedings as may become necessary for the Settlement, Division, or Distribution of Estates." In the meantime, they could only hope that creditors would be indulgent and debtors attempt to pay to the best of their abilities. Any private disputes incapable of resolution should be decided by "judicious Neighbours." With no access to courts for the recovery of outstanding debts, the British merchants in the spring of 1775 could only hope to secure tobacco from indebted planters and ship it to what everyone agreed would be inflated markets in Great Britain. The merchants who had come to play so influential a role in the colony now found themselves with no protection for their investments and credit extensions in the colony.[41]

[40]Price quotations from Piper Letterbook, University of Virginia, and Yates Letterbook, University of Virginia; Russell Papers, Coutts & Co., London; and *A Scottish Firm in Virginia*, ed., T. M. Devine. William Carr to James Russell, 6 Feb. 1775, 14 May 1775, Russell Papers; James Robinson to William Cunninghame & Co., John Likly to James Robinson, 23 May 1775, William Cunninghame & Co. Papers, Virginia Historical Society.

[41]*Revolutionary Virginia*, eds., Scribner and Tarter, 2:381–83.

■   ■   ■

From their inception, the county committees in Virginia assumed an authority that extended well beyond this strict regulation of all commerce. At the election of the James City committee on November 25, 1774, freeholders agreed that the resolutions of the Continental Congress would be "the *sole rule of their conduct*, in all matters respecting their *present political engagements.*" By January, William Carr reported that many county committees exceeded the instructions of the Continental Association, and in Norfolk James Parker complained that "Every thing is Managed by Committee."[42]

The committees in Virginia quickly became far more than local boards for the administration of the association; they became the principal institutions of local government. The formation of committees at the same time that the county courts relinquished many of their most important powers allowed the local political elites to maintain their authority in the counties at the same time that they isolated and subverted royal government. By Christmas, Governor Dunmore was denouncing the assumption of power by committees that supervised every aspect of merchants' business and raised independent militias "for the avowed purpose of protecting" the committees' authority. When the governor tried to cultivate appointed officeholders on the local level he discovered that nearly every justice of the peace was also a committee member and that by closing the county courts, the local political leadership united itself with the yeoman planters. Dunmore was convinced the arbitrary proceedings of the committees and the scarcity of basic supplies would breed popular dissent. Until his wishful predictions were fulfilled, however, the governor could only recommend that Parliament aggravate existing shortages by blockading ports and shutting off all American commerce.[43]

[42]*Revolutionary Virginia*, eds., Scribner and Tarter, 2:177, 193; William Carr to James Russell, 24 Jan. 1775, Russell Papers, Coutts & Co., London (Virginia Colonial Records Project microfilm); James Parker to Charles Steuart, 27 Jan. 1775, Charles Steuart Papers, National Library of Scotland (Colonial Williamsburg microfilm).

[43]Governor Dunmore to Earl of Dartmouth, 24 Dec. 1774, Public Record Office, CO5/1353 (Virginia Colonial Records Project microfilm).

As the central institutions uniting county communities during a political crisis, the county committees inevitably assumed more and more responsibilities unrelated to the commercial boycott. Committees played a crucial role in unifying public opinion and silencing the opposition through the enforcement of noncommercial provisions in the Continental Association. For instance, violators of article eight's prohibition of gambling occasionally received a public censure from their local committee, but frequently the committees preferred to use the gamblers' contrition as an example for others to emulate. The Cumberland County committee concluded that John Scruggs, though guilty of gambling, "exhibited such Marks of true Penitence, that it is resolved that the said Scruggs be again considered a worthy Member of the Community." Public testimonials offered committees the opportunity to demonstrate popular assent to the association's calls for sacrifice as well as deferral to the authority of the committee itself. When four men voluntarily appeared before the Southampton County committee, confessed to gambling, and agreed to refund their winnings, the committee members asked the public to "join with them in not considering them as enemies to American liberty." Orange County's committee explained that its decision not to censure an apologetic gambler "proceeds from a desire to distinguish penitent and submissive from refractory and obstinate offenders."[44]

In a decision that would dramatically expand the committees' power and legitimacy at the same time that it undermined the commercial objectives of the association, the Virginia convention of March 1775 called on local committees to reorganize and strengthen the colonial militia. Since the fall of 1774, some committees had managed military matters ranging from the organization of independent companies to the manufacture of gunpowder. In the months following the March convention, military business became more important and eventually would eclipse most of the commercial functions of the county committees. Initially the outbreak of hostilities in Massachusetts, the governor's removal of the gunpowder from Williamsburg, and the preparations for defense in Virginia had important commercial implications for the local committees and the Continental Congress. The threat of further British military action necessitated some restriction on the open coastwise trade that allowed merchants to carry provisions to British troops in Boston. Once Governor Dunmore retreated from Williamsburg in June and

[44]*Revolutionary Virginia*, eds., Scribner and Tarter, 2:302; 3:42, 115.

later fortified himself near Norfolk, the internal trade of Virginia also required protection against the British interception of supplies.[45]

Various county committees in Virginia responded to military preparations with a closer supervision of trade within their respective jurisdictions. In addition to their establishment of a system of authorization certificates for all incoming and outgoing cargoes, the committees investigated charges of merchants' complicity with the British military. Traders found guilty of these accusations faced the most severe reprisals of the local community. Anthony Warwick, who had shipped a large quantity of pork to Gage's troops in Boston and smuggled gunpowder into North Carolina, evaded the summons of the Nansemond County committee only to face a determined mob from Isle of Wight County. The crowd, which Warwick branded "a rabble" but the *Virginia Gazette* characterized as "a number of respectable inhabitants," overcame Warwick and carried him ten miles to the town of Smithfield. There Warwick received the only coat of tar and feathers recorded during the operation of the county committees. The crowd subsequently planted Warwick on a horse and chased him out of town with "a shower of eggs."[46]

The deterioration of relations between the British and the colonists aroused demands for an immediate halt to all commercial connections with British ports. As early as March, Robert Pleasants had identified support in Virginia for an accelerated enforcement of nonexportation in order to counter the Scottish factors who were contriving to prolong the period of free exportation. The general expectation of a revised association in the aftermath of military conflict led the Gloucester County committee on May 2, 1775, to prohibit all tobacco exports to Great Britain, pending a further determination by the Continental Congress. Within ten days of Gloucester's ruling, Virginians learned that the Maryland convention had suspended all exports from that colony to Boston or to any continental colonies not subscribing to the association. That same month, George Mason wrote to William Lee of the possibility that exports would end "much sooner" than September 10, 1775. Mason was among the Virginians who found several reasons to hasten the commencement of the nonexportation agreement. He believed that an earlier observance of nonexportation would be the most effective response to Parliament's Restraining Acts. The New

[45]Dunmore to Dartmouth, 24 Dec. 1774, Public Record Office, CO5/1353 (Virginia Colonial Records Project microfilm).

[46]*Revolutionary Virginia*, eds., Scribner and Tarter, 3:485–86.

England Restraining Act of March 1775 closed off all trade in and out of the New England colonies and blocked the colonists' access to off-shore fishing grounds. A second Restraining Act, approved by the King in April, applied similar restrictions to the trade of Pennsylvania, New Jersey, Maryland, Virginia, and South Carolina. Mason hoped that a nonexportation association, commencing before the enforcement of these acts, would "have the Appearance of Reprizal."[47]

When the Second Continental Congress met in Philadelphia in May 1775, the delegates approved several resolutions designed to adjust the commercial association to the demands of military defense. Congress ordered an immediate halt to all exports to the British continental colonies not subscribing to the association. The resolution specifically banned the shipment of any provisions to the British fisheries off the New England coast. Congress also forbade the shipment of any provisions to British troops in Massachusetts or to British vessels transporting troops or supplies to America. After a debate on the merits of an earlier observance of nonexportation, the delegates voted to maintain the starting date of September 10. A secret resolution permitted a limited export trade to continue after September as a means of paying for the return shipments of military supplies. In addition to these revisions in the commercial regulations of the association, Congress added the Restraining Acts to its list of legislation which must be repealed before a resumption of Anglo-American trade.[48]

After the decision of Congress to wait until September for the initiation of nonexportation, George Mason remained convinced that Virginia's security required further trade restrictions. At the provincial convention convened at Richmond in July, Mason submitted a proposal to end all exports of grain and other provisions from the colony on August 5, 1775. As protection against British raids, the resolution ordered inhabitants living in towns and along navigable waters to store only those provisions which they needed for their own use. The resolution as approved by the convention on July 24 also recommended that

[47]*Revolutionary Virginia*, eds., Scribner and Tarter, 3:78–79; George Mason to William Lee, 20 May 1775, *Papers of George Mason*, ed., Rutland, 1:234; Robert Pleasants to John Thomas, 12 Mar 1775, Robert Pleasants Letterbook, Library of Congress; Jensen, *Founding of a Nation*, 582; George Mason to Richard Henry Lee, 31 May 1775, *Papers of George Mason*, 1:235–36.

[48]*Revolutionary Virginia*, eds., Scribner and Tarter, 3:383–88; *Journals of the Continental Congress*, 3:313–15.

"The Congress, or The Necessary Politicians." London, 1775. British mockery of the Continental Association found no more sardonic expression than this print depicting a politician tearing up the resolutions of the Congress for use in the privy. The figure seated to the right intently reads a reply to Samuel Johnson's attack on the American patriots. The walls of the necessary feature a portrait of John Wilkes and the image of an individual tarred and feathered. (Library of Congress)

anyone living within five miles of the shoreline should thresh out only the amount of wheat needed at a given time.[49]

This late alteration in the trade regulations of Virginia's association provoked immediate opposition from those merchants who depended almost entirely on the grain trade for their business. The Norfolk Borough committee asked their convention delegates to consider the hard-

[49]*Revolutionary Virginia*, eds., Scribner and Tarter, 3:338–39; George Mason to Martin Cockburn, 24 July 1775, *Papers of George Mason*, ed., Rutland, 1:241–42.

ships imposed on local merchants who had entered contracts for grain shipments in August and already held unusually large quantities in their warehouses. The committee's request for repeal of the resolution warned of the probable erosion of popular support for the association if this amendment went into effect. A group of powerful merchants in Norfolk and Portsmouth sent a similar protest to their convention delegates, although their language was considerably less conciliatory than the petition from the borough committee. The traders were particularly critical of a resolution "which was adopted with great haste, and without even allowing time or opportunity for the trading interest of the colony to know that such a measure was in agitation." A third appeal from the Northampton County committee requested an exemption for the local traders who had negotiated cargoes of Indian corn for export to the West Indies. The committee assured the convention that no cargoes would sail northward near the British installations.[50]

The convention dismissed the merchants' petition which it considered insolent and inflammatory, but was more sympathetic toward the appeals from the two committees. The delegates could not make an exception for grain shipments from Norfolk, however, because many of the delegates who voted for the resolution also had personal interests in the grain trade. They did make an exception, however, for traders who already had negotiated shipments of Indian corn from last year's crop. The whole debate on Mason's resolution became moot on August 8 when the convention received word of the Maryland convention's refusal to join in the early nonexportation agreement. Matthew Tilghman explained that the Marylanders saw no advantage to stopping exports of commodities that would continue to flow from the ports of other colonies. The adjournment of Congress prevented any further consideration of the issue until after the commencement of nonexportation of all commodities on September 10.[51]

When exports finally ended in September, the local committees enforced the trade restrictions much as they did with the import trade. Yet export violations were infrequent and notoriously difficult to prosecute since both the offender and the evidence slipped out of the colony. Infractions of the nonexportation agreement seldom appeared on the agenda of the committees. The presence of British ships enforcing the Restraining Acts ironically served to enforce the association as well. Some

[50]*Revolutionary Virginia*, eds., Scribner and Tarter, 3:364–67, 371–72.
[51]*Revolutionary Virginia*, eds., Scribner and Tarter, 3:396–98, 405–06.

smuggling occurred — grain to the West Indies and tobacco to continental markets— but for nearly all of the merchants and traders in Virginia, September 1775 brought an end to opportunities for external trade. Once exports ended in September, many merchants had no reason to remain in Virginia despite uncollected debts. Just two weeks after the beginning of nonexportation, James Parker found that many of the factors in Norfolk had left, and more were preparing for home. One of those who remained sent word to Glasgow that "business is Scarcely now talked of." Factors in the colony relied on the dubious process of personal application for the collection of debts and found, as James Gilchrist complained, that the people "are not so ready to pay as when the compulsive Power of the Law can be exerted behind them" At the cost of depriving themselves of the imports that provisioned their estates and the export markets that long had brought them wealth, Virginians had at last determined the terms of business with the British merchants.[52]

■   ■   ■

In the organization of resistance to Great Britain and in the maintenance of a striking degree of internal political order, the Continental Association proved to be a great success in Virginia. The local committees helped to unify communities, distribute limited resources, and organize defenses at the same time that they monitored the business of the merchants and isolated potential loyalist support. As Virginia moved closer and closer to effective independence from Great Britain, the committees established under the Continental Association proved to be remarkably functional institutions for the preservation of local political authority. This largely unexpected utility of the committees stood in contrast to the failure of the association to achieve some of its principal

---

[52]For enforcement of nonexportation see, *Revolutionary Virginia*, eds., Scribner and Tarter, 4:159; James Parker to Charles Steuart, 25 Sep. 1775, Charles Steuart Papers, National Library of Scotland (Colonial Williamsburg microfilm); Robert Shedden to John Shedden, 10 Nov. 1775, intercepted letter, Committee of Safety, in *Revolutionary Virginia*, eds., Scribner and Tarter, 4:366–67; James Gilchrist to Isaac Robely, 12 Oct. 1775, Original Correspondence, Secretary of State, Post Office, Public Record Office, CO/134 (Virginia Colonial Records Project microfilm).

objectives, particularly in Virginia where the strategy of commercial resistance embodied such ambitious expectations.

The association's unprecedented success in regulating the business activity of British merchants resident in Virginia failed to translate into the intended political mobilization of merchants resident in Great Britain. Rather than respond to the cessation of trade with concessions to American demands, the British government, with little domestic pressure to do otherwise, offered only further restrictions on American trade. In part this was a result of the Virginians' insistence that nonexportation be delayed a year. As soon as they learned of the terms of the Continental Association, Arthur and William Lee warned their fellow Virginians that the postponement of nonexportation would in the minds of merchants in London undermine the credibility of the new scheme of commercial resistance. In fact, many British merchants saw it as a welcome opportunity to reduce the outstanding debts owed by so many Virginia planters. A coincidental rise in demand for British goods in other markets compensated for the loss of the valuable Chesapeake markets and offered further reason for merchants to ignore the Continental Association. In August 1775 a Glasgow merchant informed an associate in Virginia that demand for manufactures was so great and prices so inflated that "the greatest peace & harmony is everywhere to be seen. . . . In short these disturbances have happened at a very lucky time."[53]

William Lee, now active in radical London politics, easily discerned the merchants' feeble and often feigned support for America. As the North American merchants met in January to prepare a petition, Lee predicted that "they will not go any further than the Ministers choose for there is a good understanding between them." A friend of Virginia merchant Thomas Adams also found "the Majority of the Merchts in the American Trade are very Cold & indifferent." From Liverpool, Gildart & Busigny urged Robert Carter to disregard the petition from their own port "as we have reasons to believe many have put their hands to papers much against their inclinations, and did it for fear of losing their Commissions from America."[54]

---

[53]William Lee to Francis Lightfoot Lee, 24 Dec. 1774, William Lee Letterbook, 1774–1775, Virginia Historical Society; Arthur Lee to [Francis Lightfoot Lee], 13 Dec. 1774, *Lee Family Papers* (University of Virginia microfilm publication); Henry Ritchie to James Dunlop, 31 Aug. 1775, James Dunlop and Family Correspondence, Library of Congress.

[54]William Lee to Richard Lee, 9 Jan. 1775, William Lee Letterbook, 1774–1775, Virginia Historical Society; Thomas Hill to Thomas Adams, 31 Jan. 1775,

When Gustavus Wallace arrived in Scotland from Virginia in March 1775 he confidently assured his brother in the colony that the Glasgow merchants actively supported the American cause. After two months in the country, he realized that Virginia had "few real friends" among the Scottish merchants. In London, William Lee learned that the Glasgow merchants, following their public petitions in vague support of the colonies, delivered to Lord North a private message assuring him that they intended no real opposition. By the time armed hostilities broke out in the colonies, no one could escape the recognition that, in disappointing contrast to the experience during the Stamp Act crisis nearly a decade earlier, a cessation of trade and the popular consensus in favor of resistance had failed in its central political objective of cultivating British support for the American patriot cause.[55]

■   ■   ■

The strict observation of the Continental Association in Virginia was no more successful at prompting economic development than it was at applying political pressure in Great Britain. A strategy of resistance that prepared Virginia for political independence proved unable to lay a comparable foundation for economic independence. All too often the magnitude of the task of regulating commerce and preserving order in the absence of the courts overwhelmed all other objectives of the association as the local committees assumed responsibility for governing the counties. Later the demands of military preparation displaced schemes for the promotion of agricultural diversification and manufactures. The challenges of provisioning colonial soldiers and protecting local commerce from British interception took precedence over the county committees' initial support for agricultural and manufacturing experiments. The severe shortages of all goods and inevitable dislocations of military defense further limited the ability of individual planters to reorganize their estates and farms.

Adams Family Papers, Virginia Historical Society; Gildart & Busigny to Robert Carter, 20 Feb. 1775, Robert Carter Correspondence, Virginia Historical Society.

[55]Gustavus Brown Wallace to Michael Wallace, 11 May 1775, Wallace Family Papers, University of Virginia; William Lee to Thomas Adams, 18 Mar. 1775, William Lee Letterbook, 1774–1775, Virginia Historical Society.

For all these practical complications of a resistance movement that soon evolved into revolution, the collapse of the ambitious schemes for economic independence had roots far deeper than the unforeseen exigencies of defense. More than any previous plan of commercial resistance, the Continental Association as it was enforced in Virginia exposed the incompatibility of a strategy devised for immediate political goals with one designed to inaugurate a long-term reorientation of the colony's economy. The very success of this association in organizing popular resistance to British authority stood in marked contrast to its inadequate response to the challenges of establishing a measure of economic independence in Virginia. The abrupt cessation of trade, despite its usefulness in rallying citizens and awakening a sense of crisis, forced colonists to devote all their energies and means to gathering essential provisions rather than to the necessarily gradual process of investing in new production. All the determination of spirit and dedication of resources evident in 1774 and 1775 could not within a few months or even a year and a half restructure a colonial economy.

The near obsessive focus on the regulation of merchant activity in Virginia revealed more serious flaws in a critique of the colonial economy that emphasized commercial conspiracy and individual corruption. A campaign against factors and other British merchants in the colony received great support among a population that long resented its reliance on British traders and remembered all too well the factors' role in the subversion of earlier nonimportation associations. Yet the public rebuke of merchants and a strict enforcement of price controls was not the foundation of an independent commercial community. The Continental Association's dramatic step toward effective independence offered Virginians the first of many realizations that neither political autonomy nor restraints on British merchants in themselves would abolish the limitations on diversification and commercial development. As Virginians entered a war to defend their political liberties and supplant imperial authority, they confronted the full magnitude of the obstacles to economic independence.

COMMERCIAL DEVELOPMENT IN
AN INDEPENDENT VIRGINIA

INDEPENDENCE IMMEDIATELY BESTOWED UPON the new government of Virginia the capacity to regulate the commerce and economy of the former colony. After years of relying on appeals to imperial officials and a decade of voluntary associations designed to achieve a measure of economic independence within the framework of Empire, Virginia's elected government now had the means to prescribe the formal structure of trade. The effective displacement of imperial authority at once freed Virginians from the Navigation Acts that had directed the flow of American trade and protected the investments and property of British tobacco merchants. With the dismantling of the institutions of royal administration, British revenue officers no longer collected levies on the exports of the chief staple or monitored the entrance and clearance of every mercantile vessel in Virginia's waters. The provisional convention and the state government formally constituted in 1776 soon replaced imperial regulations with their own conditions on trade. In the most dramatic reversal of British policy and with a characteristic lack of public discussion of the subject, the assembly in 1778 prohibited the further importation of slaves. In other trade-related legislation of the war years, the state government expelled British merchants and factors from the state, reopened trade with all nations but Great Britain, closed the courts to the recovery of British-held debts, and established a state naval office for the closer supervision of commerce.[1]

[1]John E. Selby, *The Revolution in Virginia, 1775–1783* (Williamsburg, Va.: The Colonial Williamsburg Foundation, 1988), 149–50, 158.

The independence that secured Virginia's legal authority over trade also led to a more profound and sobering understanding of the obstacles to the development of the state's economy. Stripped of the Navigation Acts and the formal ties of Empire, Virginia's economic reliance on Great Britain appeared more entrenched and problematical than ever. When the repeal of British regulations and the enforcement of the assembly's own legislation failed to attract traders from other European nations or to stimulate the diversification of the domestic economy, Virginians began the difficult process of identifying the extent to which their own tastes and habits, and, more important, the economic imperatives of a planter society impeded their successful competition in the trade of the Atlantic world. Peace and the resumption of trade offered additional evidence of the distinct character and interests of Virginia and the other southern states where slave labor and the production of staple export crops dominated the economy. Individual Virginians responded to the persistence of economic dependence in very different ways which contributed to the divisive state politics of the years between the end of the Revolutionary War and the adoption of the Federal Constitution, but all recognized that the colonial economy and the pervasive influence of British merchants had survived the surrender of the British military and the establishment of political independence. From various political positions, Virginians in the 1780s sought to free the state from its residual ties to Great Britain and lay a true foundation for independent economic growth.

■   ■   ■

In the early years of Independence, the exigencies of war determined the contours of Virginia's trade. As the most valuable export commodity in the United States, Virginia's tobacco served the needs of a state and nation with armies confronting the formidable might of Great Britain. Contractors for the state government and the Continental Congress purchased tobacco in Virginia, seeking to exchange the prized commodity for military supplies abroad. Private merchants also carried tobacco to European ports in search of the basic manufactured goods Virginians previously bought from Great Britain. The success of contractors and merchants in gaining access to European ports depended on the willingness of those nations to risk alienating Great Britain for the opportunity of selling tobacco on the Continental market. Military considerations also shaped the trade of other Virginia commodities. State contractors shipped goods to the West Indies and other states in exchange for saltpetre and military supplies. The overwhelming demand for provisions in the army compelled the state to prohibit the export of many items in demand in the West Indies or Southern Europe where the exports might have provided the foundation for new trade routes. What trade continued between Virginia and Europe or the foreign West Indies often encountered the British blockades which forced shippers to use more expensive routes and increased freight charges on armed vessels. Much of the coastal trade was diverted to costly overland routes, while the consequent reliance on Philadelphia and Baltimore merchants added the price of middlemen to the importation of the scarce foreign goods that arrived in wartime Virginia. For some, the interruptions of commerce were too expensive and troublesome to allow them to remain in business. Charles Yates announced to a friend in Scotland that he had retired to his farm outside of Fredericksburg and was "No longer a Mercht but a Farmer." Like many other merchants as well as planters during the war, Yates had abandoned commercial crops and converted his estate to the production of basic supplies that were no longer available from overseas.[2]

As much as the military conflict distorted the commerce of Virginia during the Revolutionary War and delayed the exploration of opportunities in new markets, these early years of trade outside the confines of the British Empire portended many of the challenges Virginia planters and merchants would confront after the return of peace. Even without the obligations of debt or the prospect of credit and goods from British merchants, Virginia planters could not escape the dominance of tobacco in the state's export trade. Although the absolute quantity of all exports declined during the Revolution, tobacco's share of exports actually increased. Tobacco proved to be the most valuable commodity of exchange for the supply of manufactures, whether it be military provisions or basic household goods. As the American commissioners discovered in France, Chesapeake tobacco was also the most powerful enticement for the establishment of trading ties with that nation which had purchased one third of the American crop before the war.[3]

[2]Robert Walker Coakley, "Virginia Commerce during the American Revolution" (Ph.D. diss., University of Virginia, 1949); Selby, *The Revolution in Virginia*, 170–83; Price, *France and the Chesapeake*, 684–717; Charles Yates to George McCall, 2 Sep. 1778, Charles Yates Letterbook, University of Virginia; Walsh, "Plantation Management in the Chesapeake," 400–01.

[3]Coakley, "Virginia Commerce," c.3–5; Price, *France and the Chesapeake*, 681–727.

The continued attraction of tobacco frustrated those in Virginia who hoped that the suspension of trade with Great Britain would stimulate commerce in other commodities and encourage the growth of a native merchant community. In Orange County, 105 planters, including James Madison and his father, petitioned the assembly in 1777 to urge the imposition of limits on the cultivation of tobacco. Citing the need to improve internal resources, the petition expected restraints on tobacco to encourage "the raising and Manufacturing of those Articles necessary for the Army," but the House of Delegates ignored the plea. Merchants who expected planters to abandon the traditional staple in favor of crops in demand in the West Indies also were disappointed. George Webb of Williamsburg found that the wheat crop of 1778 to be of the highest quality ever, but little was to be had, "our Farmers having discontinued making it, in order to increase their quantities of Tobacco which has late been much more profitable."[4]

Tobacco in itself need not inhibit commercial development if Virginians were able to open new markets and gain greater control over the processing and shipping of the crop. Colonial patterns, however, persisted in the organization of the trade throughout the war. For all the hopes and money invested in the promise of a direct trade with France, that nation proved unable to approximate the role formerly played by Great Britain. French manufactures did not meet the tastes or needs of American consumers, and French merchants offered few of the financial services that had enabled the British to expand their trade in the American colonies, particularly in Virginia. Nor did French merchants employ the kind of fleet necessary to establish a regular trade with the Chesapeake.[5]

Virginia merchants also discovered that they were woefully unprepared to establish themselves as entrepreneurs in new tobacco trade routes. Few had the necessary capital, and for those who did, the depreciation of currency encouraged investment in land or slaves, not risky trading ventures. Richard Adams hoped to overcome the shortage of capital by combining the investments of the "Principal Gentlemen" in order to establish trading companies with stores at the heads of the main rivers in Virginia. Such a scheme would "supply the People at large on

[4]James Madison, *The Papers of James Madison*, eds., Hutchinson and Rachal, 1:213–14; George Webb to Thomas Adams, 26 June 1778, Adams Family Papers, Virginia Historical Society.

[5]Price, *France and the Chesapeake*, 681–727; Coakley, "Virginia Commerce."

the best Terms" and "prevent Foreigners as much as Possible from En-
grossing the Trade as Heretofore." Unfortunately the plan attracted
few investors and by Adams own admission would probably depend on
the support of wealthy Philadelphia merchants like Robert Morris.[6]

Just as the mercantile community in Virginia was unable to absorb
the tobacco trade formerly carried by British merchants, so too did the
dearth of supporting artisans and laborers discourage ambitious commercial ventures. As early as 1776, Richard Henry Lee identified the
lack of a native merchant marine as one of the most serious impediments to commercial development, and he proposed to indenture or-
phans and poor children for training in the trades of the sea. In France
during the Revolutionary War, William Lee advised that nation's merchants not to expect any ships for charter or sailors for hire when they
reached the Chesapeake. When Richard Morris considered establishing a trading business in Virginia in 1778, he discovered that the necessary pilot boats would be prohibitively expensive and carpenters to build
new ones "very scarce." The shortage of smaller loading craft in a state
with few ports and the near absence of free seamen in a society that
relied largely on slave labor for the loading and unloading of ships remained a serious barrier to the encouragement of new commercial ventures.[7]

The void left by the withdrawal of British merchants was filled more
frequently by traders from Philadelphia or other ports to the north than
by resident Virginia merchants. The apprehensions voiced by Richard
Henry Lee in the years preceding the Revolution came closer to reality
during the war for independence as Virginia planters relied more heavily
on Philadelphia merchants for the marketing of their produce, the purchase of manufactured goods, and the extension of credit. Soon after
the cessation of British trade in the Chesapeake, Philadelphia merchants
bought tobacco for export through their home port and acted as agents
for the direct shipment of the crop from Virginia to Europe. By the
final years of the war, James Madison found the balance of trade with
Philadelphia "so much against Virginia that on every application for

[6]Coakley, "Virginia Commerce," 335–37; Richard Adams to Thomas
Adams, 1 June 1778, Adams Family Papers, Virginia Historical Society.
[7]Richard Henry Lee to Thomas Jefferson, 3 November 1776, in *Lee Family Papers* (University of Virginia microfilm); [Richard Morris] to [James Maury],
10 Dec. 1778, Richard Morris Papers, University of Virginia; Price, *France and
the Chesapeake,* 706.

money on a Draught we are answered 'we want no draught on Virginia, we want money from thence.'" Edmund Randolph found it "lamentable to behold the produces of our labour, remitted to Philadelphia."[8]

The prospect of a prolonged war and the indefinite suspension of British trade inspired various manufacturing schemes even more ambitious than those begun under the commercial associations of the previous decade. Many centered on the production of cloth which always had been the most important of British imports for all ranks of Virginians. The Manufacturing Society of Williamsburg hoped to establish a spinning and weaving facility large enough to accept "a Number of Boys & Girls as apprentices." The enterprise would care for the poor of the state while it met the demand for household goods. Yet, the Williamsburg manufacturers as well as fulling mills, weaving workshops, and private estates throughout the state faced the same shortage of capital, scarcity of skilled labor, and competition from cheaper imported goods that inhibited the promotion of domestic industry in the late colonial period. Within months of advertising for young white apprentices, the Williamsburg Manufacturing Society shifted its search to slave youths to be bought for labor at the cloth works. A hemp and flax manufacturer in Fredericksburg hoped to solve the shortage of skilled workers by training planters' slaves in the production of cloth in return for six months labor. A wealthy planter like Landon Carter, with more than sufficient labor to divert to domestic manufactures, resorted to newspaper notices in his search for an experienced spinner and weaver to instruct his workers. The competition for skilled manufacturers was so great by 1777 that the Williamsburg Manufacturing Society, in extending a conditional invitation to visit its works, requested that "no Person would wish to do it so much Injury as to take any Steps that may induce the People employed there to leave it." Although some individual planters were able to meet their estates' need during war years, the commercial cloth manufacturing schemes never filled the market demand nor laid a foundation for peacetime industry. The success of manufactures was limited to iron and lead, both of which enjoyed state patronage and neither of

[8]Thomas M. Doerflinger, *A Vigorous Spirit of Enterprise: Merchants and Economic Development in Revolutionary Virginia* (Chapel Hill and London: University of North Carolina Press, 1986), 205–06, 287–88; Virginia Delegates to Benjamin Harrison, 27 Aug. 1782, Edmund Randolph to James Madison, 30 Aug. 1782, *Papers of James Madison*, eds., Hutchinson and Rachal, 5:85, 91–92.

which were significant for reducing the demand for imported goods after the return of peace.[9]

Even in the midst of war, the shadow of Great Britain's former commercial domination of Virginia cast over every effort to establish an independent economy. As planters groped for new outlets for their crops and local merchants struggled to fashion new trading routes, many in Virginia realized how easily Great Britain might reassert its commercial authority even without the support of imperial administration. John Page went so far as to hope that the war would last long enough that the "deep-rooted prejudices" in favor of that "Artful People are Eradicated." If peace came in 1778, he feared the British would engross nearly the whole trade of America. While George Webb in the same year held out hopes that Virginia might forge a commercial as well as political alliance with France, he was saddened when he considered "with what eagerness our People would return to their Commerce with Britain, should a Peace shortly take place." As late as 1780, William Fitzhugh found widespread concern among "very sound Whigs & sensible Politicians" that their fellow Virginians retained too great a partiality "in favor of the Mother Country & Her Manufactures." From the perspective of the former colony, the threat of continued dependence on British merchants appeared to be the result of the Virginians' own failings rather than the superiority of Great Britain's financial structure. Webb despaired that Virginians did "not have Virtue, or even Gratitude, enough" to cultivate trade with France. Francis Lightfoot Lee in 1778 dismissed an entire generation as "too much infected with the vices of Britain" and placed his dwindling hopes on "proper regulations to inlarge the understanding & improve the morals of the rising generation."[10]

■   ■   ■

[9]*Virginia Gazette* (Dixon & Hunter), 24 Aug. 1776, 13 Dec. 1776, 7 Feb. 1777, 16 May 1777, 20 June 1777; *Virginia Gazette* (Purdie), 6 Sep 1776, 28 Mar. 1777; Selby, *The Revolution in Virginia*, 166–70.

[10]John Page to Richard Henry Lee, 15 Oct. 1778, in *Lee Family Papers* (University of Virginia microfilm publication); William Fitzhugh to Arthur Lee, 5 Jan. 1780, in ibid.; George Webb to Thomas Adams, 26 June 1778, Adams Family Papers, Virginia Historical Society; Francis Lightfoot Lee to Richard Henry Lee, 12 Aug. 1778, *Lee Family Papers* (University of Virginia microfilm publication).

The disappointments of wartime trade never completely dampened the enthusiasm for the commercial opportunities that might arise in an independent United States once peace was restored. As they had through-out the decade preceding the Revolution, Virginians who wrote about commercial opportunities anticipated that the state's economy would remain predominantly agricultural. The wealth of crops from the Chesa-peake naturally would attract the manufactures of various European nations. The commercial hopes for a newly-independent Virginia rested heavily on the conviction that other European nations, particularly France and the Netherlands, would establish direct trade with the Chesa-peake and thereby eliminate the need for the British to act as middle-men and financiers of transatlantic commerce. Before the Revolution, the greatest bulk of Chesapeake tobacco went to these nations through the reexport trade from Great Britain. Direct trade would presumably lower the cost for purchasers in Europe and preserve a higher percent-age of the return for growers in Virginia. As the war came to a close, traders on both sides of the Atlantic assumed that Holland and France would become the largest importers of Virginia tobacco. Merchant James Hunter of Fredericksburg received assurances from European corre-spondents that not only would the Netherlands purchase large cargoes of tobacco, but that the country's centrality would make it the most advantageous entrepôt for the collection of manufactures to be imported by Virginia. While his son served as a clerk to William Lee in France, Richard Henry Lee instructed him to learn the native language since "our future commerce with France will be so extensive as to render this indispensible." Robert Beverley similarly sent his son to train as a mer-chant in Holland in 1783 "as trade is perfectly understood there . . . and at least one third of our Tobo will enter there." Throughout the 1780s, even as the British reasserted their primacy in the Virginia export trade, planters like Washington maintained their faith that the natural flow of commerce would eventually carry most of the state's trade to Continen-tal markets.[11]

[11]Ingraham & Bromfield to James Hunter, Jr., 11 June 1782, Hunter Family Papers, University of Virginia; Richard Henry Lee to Arthur Lee, 20 Apr. 1777, Richard Henry Lee to Thomas and Ludwell Lee, 10 May 1777, *Lee Family Papers* (University of Virginia microfilm publication); Robert Beverley to William Beverley, [1783], Robert Beverley Letterbook, Library of Congress; George Washington to Chastellux, 5 Sep. 1785, Washington Papers, Library of Congress.

After years of trading under the mercantilist restrictions of the British Empire, free trade throughout the Atlantic world promised to be one of the most important commercial benefits of independence. By breaking the bonds of Empire, the American Revolution offered a vision of trade unencumbered by Navigation Acts and commercial reprisals. On the eve of the peace treaty with Great Britain, James Madison maintained that "The wider . . . our ports be opened and the more extensive the privileges of all our competitors in our Commerce, the more likely we shall be to buy at cheap & sell at profitable rates." Shortly thereafter constituents from Fairfax County, in instructions to their assembly delegates, identified the "true and permanent interest of America to admit the trade of all nations, upon equal terms, without preference to any, further than the goodness and cheapness of their commodities may entitle them to."[12]

The sentiment favoring free trade was sorely tested with the resumption of peacetime trade and the necessity of deciding whether or not British traders would be permitted to return to the Chesapeake. Governor Benjamin Harrison might lament the crowds of British merchants he likened to "locusts" luring the Virginians down "old and destructive paths" of trade with Great Britain, but as Robert Beverley noted with some bewilderment, many Virginians expressed a tremendous eagerness for a trading agreement with Great Britain. Harrison also reported a "violent inclination . . . for opening every avenue to them before a treaty of commerce was entered into." In fact, the state's delegates to the Continental Congress strongly urged the governor and assembly to reopen the trade with Great Britain that already was flourishing in other states. In May of 1783, an act of what Edmund Randolph described as an "eagle-winged" General Assembly immediately repealed all restrictions on British imports except for those duties and regulations that applied to the imports of all nations.[13]

---

[12]Merrill D. Peterson, "Thomas Jefferson and Commercial Policy, 1783–1793," *William and Mary Quarterly* 3rd ser., 22 (October 1965): 584–610; James Madison to Edmund Randolph, [20] May 1783, in *Papers of James Madison*, eds., Hutchinson and Rachal, 7:59–62; Address & Instructions of their Constituents to Alexander Henderson and Charles Broadwater, 30 May 1783, in *Virginia Gazette or American Advertiser*, 7 June 1783.

[13]Virginia Delegates to Benjamin Harrison, 6 May 1783, Edmund Randolph to James Madison, 15 May 1783, Benjamin Harrison to Virginia Delegates, 26 Sep. 1783, *Papers of James Madison*, eds., Hutchinson and Rachal, 7:17, 44–46,

While the debate on the merits of British trade continued into the mid-1780s, the market forces established before the Revolution drove Virginia and Great Britain into an almost inexorable resumption of old trade patterns. The Virginians' deferred demand for the kind and quality of manufactures available only in Great Britain, the British merchants' desire to collect the massive debts still owed them in Virginia, and the sustained market for Chesapeake tobacco on the Continent persuaded planters and merchants alike to renew familiar connections. Like waking from an eight-year long dream, prominent London merchant Samuel Athawes in April 1783 sent his former correspondent Robert Prentis of Williamsburg an account of sales from 1775, along with his hope that "we can renew our friendly & amicable intercourse . . . which may be for our Mutual Benefit & advantage." Even before he heard of the final terms of the treaty, Robert Beverley sent an old merchant correspondent ten hogsheads and announced that he intended to resume such annual shipments "as will furnish my family with goods & maintain my son."[14]

In many ways the British succeeded in restoring familiar patterns of trade with Virginia following the restoration of peace. By the summer of 1784 an agent of William Cunninghame & Company could report to Glasgow that the "ferment" arising in opposition to the return of British merchants had "nearly subsided." Now as businesses prospered around him in Petersburg, the agent found "the minds of the people perfectly tranquilized." Tranquilized or not, the tobacco growers of Virginia embraced the opportunity to sell their crops to British merchants and their representatives. Within a few years the volume of tobacco exports approximated pre-war levels and constituted 85 percent of the state's total exports by 1787. Great Britain received more than 60 percent of the crop even though at least two-thirds of that tobacco continued to be reexported to the Continent. Despite the growth of Virginia's own merchant fleet, British-owned ships and a few large carriers from Philadelphia dominated transatlantic trade. Once again Great Britain supplied the bulk of the goods imported into Virginia. Even ships carrying Virginia tobacco directly to France generally loaded their return

---

358–59; Robert Beverley to William Beverley, [1783], Robert Beverley Letterbook, Library of Congress; *Hening's Statutes*, 11:195.

[14]Samuel Athawes to Robert Prentis, 23 April 1783, Webb–Prentis Collection, University of Virginia; Robert Beverley to Samuel Gist, 2 Oct. 1784, Robert Beverley Letterbook, Library of Congress.

cargoes in Great Britain, and the planters' profits from the French trade were more often than not applied to their accounts with British merchants. The initial rush of British buyers and high prices, followed by a glutted tobacco market and depressed prices in 1785 marked a disheartening return to the boom and bust cycles of the colonial era.[15]

The reopening of trade between Virginia and Great Britain threatened to expose Virginia debtors once more to the demands of their British creditors. At Independence Virginians owed their British creditors close to £2,000,000, over half the total amount owed by residents of all the former colonies. During the Revolutionary War when courts were closed to recovery suits from the exiled British merchants and factors, the General Assembly in 1778 passed a Sequestration Act which, in addition to appropriating for the state all Virginia property owned by British subjects, permitted debtors to pay into the state loan office money owed British creditors. Despite the provision for payment in depreciated paper currency and the issuance of certificates absolving the debtor from any future obligations to British merchants, less than one percent of the estimated debtors in Virginia took advantage of the offer. In 1782, a year after closing the courts to executions on any debt cases, the assembly voted to reopen the courts in 1783 but continued to exclude British subjects.

Although the Treaty of Paris in 1783 forbade all impediments to the collection of debts, the assembly still refused to allow British citizens to sue for recovery in the state courts. Opponents of debt repayment, led in the assembly by Patrick Henry and the delegates from Southside where the debt was most pervasive, cited the British failure to accede to the treaty terms, notably that requiring the return of slaves, as justification for their exclusion of British creditors from the courts. Delegates from other areas of the state, particularly the Northern Neck with its long-standing interest in economic diversification, hoped that steady repayment would restore the flow of mercantile credit as well as maintain the credibility of borrowers. In the mid-1780s, Madison made several efforts to win assembly approval for a plan for the recovery of pre-Independence debts, often with provisions for payments in install-

[15]Alexander Horsburgh to William Cunninghame & Company, 21 Aug. 1784, American Loyalist Claims, Public Record Office, T.79/1, ff.162–64 (Virginia Colonial Records Project microfilm); Myra L. Rich, "The Experimental Years" (Ph.D. diss., Yale University, 1966), 213; Price, *France and the Chesapeake*, 728–38.

ments, but opposition hardened as prices for tobacco fell and the ensuing depression contributed to a severe shortage of currency, a growing burden of taxation, and the pressure of domestic debts that threatened planters with insolvency.[16]

■   ■   ■

For the architects of commercial resistance and others intent on achieving economic independence, the renewed influence of British merchants was as dispiriting as it was ironic. Within two years of the ratification of the Treaty of Paris, James Madison decried Virginia's dependence on Great Britain in words nearly identical to those of planters before the Revolution. "Our trade was never more compleatly monopolised by G[reat] B[ritain] when it was under the direction of the British Parliament than it is at this moment." Madison found ample evidence that the monopoly of trade enticed British merchants to exploit their dependent clients in Virginia. "Not only the private planters who have resumed the practice of shipping their own Tobo but many of our Merchants, particularly the natives of the country who have no connections in Great Britain, have received accounts of sales which carry the most visible & shameful frauds in every article." In the same year Washington conceded that the promise of commercial growth in port towns like Alexandria was chimerical. The traders of that town were merchants only in name, as dependent on British creditors as any planter before the Revolution. As they had when Virginia was a British colony, the local merchants in need of retail stock turned "chiefly to England, for every article they purchase; by which means such manufactures as Holland, Germany, France &ca. could supply upon much better terms, (being of their own production) come with accumulated charges."[17]

The persistence of this kind of colonial dependency raised questions about the very nature of Virginia's autonomy in the years following the Revolutionary War. A "Sentinel" from Caroline County warned

[16]Emory G. Evans, "Private Indebtedness and the Revolution in Virginia, 1776 to 1796," *William and Mary Quarterly* 3rd ser., 28 (July 1971): 49–74.

[17]James Madison to James Monroe, 21 June 1785, James Madison to Richard Henry Lee, 7 July 1785, *Papers of James Madison*, 8:306–08, 314–16; George Washington to Robert Morris, 1 Feb. 1785, Washington Papers, Library of Congress.

that a "Subjection to the Ledger" would make a mockery of political independence. "Amicus" asked "For what then did we wish to be independent, if not to secure these profits to ourselves, and turn the balance of trade in our favour?" To the organizers of a Richmond association for the promotion of economic diversification, Virginia in the mid-1780s presented "the wretched spectacle of a people, free in their government, but colonists in their commerce . . . emancipated by their spirit, but subdued by their manners."[18]

Yet, obviously, even within the context of a continued sort of colonial dependence on Great Britain, the commercial life of post-war Virginia was very different from the years before the Revolution. Few could disagree with William Lee, who, after fifteen years as a merchant in London and Europe, returned to his native Virginia in 1783 and found that "this country is nothing like it was, nor can it ever be the same." The changes extended well beyond a reorganization of the tobacco trade that diminished the role of Scottish factors and shifted production within Virginia to the west and the south. The devastations of war, ranging from the destruction of property and the loss of slaves to the prolonged absences of estate managers, prevented many Virginia planters from restoring full productivity until the mid to late 1780s. Independence reduced Virginia and the other states to an even less favorable trading position than when they were colonies. Not only were they outside the protection of Britain's powerful navy, Americans, as a result of a British Order in Council of July 1783 which sealed the British West Indies from all American shipping, now were excluded from what had promised to be the most favorable market for both the export of agricultural produce and the carrying trade of the incipient native merchant community in Virginia. Great Britain, free of the obligations of Empire and enjoying unchallenged economic sway in Atlantic trade, threatened to reduce the residents of Virginia and the other states to, in the words of Thomas Jefferson, "unimportant consumers of her manufactures and productions, and useful labourers to furnish her with raw materials."[19]

---

[18]*Virginia Gazette or American Advertiser*, 8 Nov. 1783; *Virginia Independent Chronicle*, 13 June 1787; *Virginia Journal and Alexandria Advertiser*, 21 June 1787.

[19]William Lee to Edward Browne, 31 Dec. 1783, William Lee Letterbook, 1783–1787, Virginia Historical Society; Walsh, "Plantation Management in the Chesapeake," 401; Price, *France and the Chesapeake*, 728–38; Charles Ritcheson, *Aftermath of Revolution: British Policy toward the United States, 1783–1795* (New York: W. W. Norton, 1971), 6–9.

Virginians faced the reassertion of British influence over the state's economy at the same time that they watched the merchants of Philadelphia extend their reach into the trade of the Chesapeake. From the very first word of an impending peace treaty and the prospect of trade to Great Britain, Madison feared that the merchants of Philadelphia would come to exploit the tobacco trade of Virginia. By the mid-1780s as much as a third of the Chesapeake tobacco was shipped through Philadelphia. In a commercial arrangement strikingly similar to that of the Scottish factors before the Revolution, merchants from Philadelphia also opened stores in Virginia where they sold imported dry goods and purchased tobacco for direct export to Europe. The commercial development of Philadelphia stood in disturbing contrast to, and even compromised, the growth of small trading centers in Virginia which once again became outposts for large commercial enterprises outside the state. Madison was mystified that Virginians could surrender the commercial initiative to Philadelphia traders when the adverse effects were so obvious. One needed only to look at the market value of goods in Philadelphia to discover that "The price of Merchandize here [Virginia] is at least as much above as Tobo is below the Northern Standard."[20]

Virginians offered little more than hostility and suspicion in response to the growth of Philadelphia. When Virginia Governor Benjamin Harrison in 1783 learned of proposals to fix the seat of Congress in Philadelphia, he feared that the political prominence to be gained would secure Philadelphia's economic control over the rest of the union of states. His instructions to the Virginia delegates in Congress matched the most exaggerated attacks on the rapacity of British merchants. "Philadelphia has been a continual drain to us and will continue to be so if the residence of Congress is either in it or its neighborhood. It is a vortex that swallows up our wealth and leaves us no prospect of recovering a single shilling." Four years later, when Congress again considered a relocation to Philadelphia, Arthur Lee predicted to George Washington that placement of the capital in that city would permanently reduce Virginia to a commercial subservience similar to its long dependence on Great Britain.

> The Commercial Cities of our State are struggling against the vast superiority which Philadelphia acquired during the war. So great an

[20]James Madison to Edmund Randolph, 13 Feb. 1783, *Papers of James Madison*, eds., Hutchinson and Rachal, 6:232–33; Doerflinger, *A Vigorous Spirit of Enterprise*, 288–91; James Madison to Richard Henry Lee, 7 July 1785, *Papers of James Madison*, eds., Hutchinson and Rachal, 8:314–16.

addition of money & influence, as the residence of Congress would give, to the Merchants of that place; would I apprehend give them a decided controul over our own commerce, if not an entire monopoly. Our native Merchants woud not be able to stand against their factors & all the profits of our trade woud center in Philadelphia.[21]

■   ■   ■

The failure to realize visions of economic independence in postwar Virginia, the commercial rise of Philadelphia, and the repeated efforts of the Continental Congress to formulate a uniform commercial policy for the United States contributed to a heightened awareness of the unique character of Virginia's economy. As the Congress commissioned negotiators for commercial treaties and debated the merits of an impost on foreign trade, Virginia's delegates to Congress recognized the need to protect what they began to refer to as "Southern interests." Governor Harrison greeted the nomination in 1784 of Jefferson as minister to Europe with delight that one "so well acquainted" with the trade of the southern states would be joining the other American ambassadors "whose interests so materially clash with ours." For some like Richard Henry Lee, who viewed national politics through the prism of regional jealousies and distrust, the interests of Virginia and the northern commercial centers were sharply opposed and perhaps irreconcilable. At the heart of Robert Morris's proposal to institute a continental impost on imports, Lee alleged, was nothing less than an effort to "strangle our infant commerce at its birth, make us pay more than our proportion, and sacrifice this country to its northern brethren."[22]

When Lee compared Virginia with the northern commercial states he focused on the cost of free labor and the scarcity of individuals with capital in his own state and frequently decried the lack of a mercantile structure in an economy so thoroughly dominated by Great Britain before the war. But what appeared to some as the structural legacy of a colonial dependence on Great Britain appeared to others as the cultural

---

[21]Benjamin Harrison to Virginia Delegates, 14 Nov. 1783, *Papers of Thomas Jefferson*, ed., Boyd, 6:354; Arthur Lee to George Washington, 13 May 1787, Washington Papers, Library of Congress.

[22]Benjamin Harrison to Virginia Delegates in Congress, 28 May 1774, *Papers of Thomas Jefferson*, ed., Boyd, 7:293–94; Richard Henry Lee to Robert Wormeley Carter, 3 June 1783, *Letters of Richard Henry Lee*, ed., Ballagh, 2:281–82.

manifestation of a planter society. James Madison found a basic lack of entrepreneurial instincts among the planters and even the merchants of his native state. "They seem to have less sensibility to their commercial interests; which they very little understand, and which the mercantile class here have not the same motive if they had the same capacity to lay open to the public, as that class have in the States north of us." Madison further despaired that the planters of Virginia "enter little into the science of commerce, and rarely of themselves combine in defence of their interests." These commercial shortcomings of Virginians were readily apparent to an anxious Philadelphia trader who warned his Virginia agent to beware of "the extraordinary inattention & want of punctuality in business which seems to prevail in the Southern States."[23]

The tastes and habits endemic to Virginia's planter society also appeared to impede the development of an independent economy. The imported goods that filled the houses of both the wealthiest gentry and the yeoman planters became the most potent symbol of economic dependence before the Revolution and the focus of the associations aimed at greater self-sufficiency. As the British trade resumed and imported goods once more flowed into the houses of the planters, the Virginians' standard of living seemed to perpetuate the dependence on British merchants. Within months of the reopening of trade with Great Britain, Edmund Pendleton watched in dismay as "crowds of people" hurried to the newly-opened stores, marking a "return to the Indolence & Extravagance that was our character formerly." Edmund Randolph in the spring of 1783 also noted "a general ardor after those commodities which public arts have so lately proscribed" and feared that "a hunger and thirst after cheese and porter" would erase the virtue and self-denial cultivated during the Revolution. Others decried the "trumpery" and English fashion to which Virginians "so servilely subscribe." After three years of nominally independent trade, Madison traced the state's manifold "political evils ... to our economic ones," and predicted that Virginia's commercial dependence would persist "unless the luxurious propensity of our own people can be otherwise checked."[24]

[23]Richard Henry Lee, "State of the Constitution of Virga," Lee Family Papers, Virginia Historical Society; James Madison to Thomas Jefferson, 20 Aug. 1785, James Madison to James Monroe, 21 June 1785, *Papers of James Madison*, eds., Hutchinson and Rachal, 8:344–46, 306–08; J. Burnet to James Hunter, Jr., 24 Jan. 1783, Hunter Family Papers, University of Virginia.

[24]Edmund Pendleton to James Madison, 26 May 1783, Edmund Pendleton to James Madison, 16 June 1783, Edmund Randolph to James Madison, 24

The frustrations and disappointments of post-war trade contributed to an anti-commercial sentiment more virulent than anything expressed before the Revolution. Richard Henry Lee identified what he called the essentially "avaricious spirit of commerce." Meriwether Smith charged that merchants entered the country either to make or to mend a fortune and then were gone with no consideration for the welfare of Virginia. Better, he said, to encourage the settlement of farmers and manufacturers than to allow foreign merchants in the state. A writer to the *Virginia Independent Chronicle* in 1787 went so far as to suggest that Virginians might be better off without any foreign trade.[25]

■   ■   ■

As tempting as the withdrawal from the vicissitudes of trade might seem, more practical minds recognized the inevitability of commercial development and the need for Virginians to assert greater control over their own trade. In commenting to Washington that "All the world is becoming commercial," Jefferson admitted that "Was it practicable to keep our new empire separated from them we might indulge ourselves in speculating whether commerce contributes to the happiness of mankind." But even the habitually speculative Jefferson understood that "our citizens have had too full a taste of the comforts furnished by the arts and manufactures to be debarred the use of them."[26]

Jefferson was preaching to the converted in writing to Washington who understood as well as any Virginian "that the spirit of Trade which pervades these states is not to be restrained." Washington admitted that foreign trade carried the risks of "luxury, effeminacy, & corruption," but Virginians could scarcely afford to indulge in the age-old debate over the merits of commerce while other states eagerly embraced trading opportunities in the post-war era. Washington was particularly anx-

May 1783, *Papers of James Madison*, eds., Hutchinson and Rachal, 7:81–83, 150–51, 72–75; *Virginia Gazette and Weekly Advertiser*, 13 September 1787; James Madison to Thomas Jefferson, 18 Mar. 1786, *Papers of James Madison*, eds., Hutchinson and Rachal, 8:500–04.

[25]Richard Henry Lee to Lafayette, 11 June 1785, *Letters of Richard Henry Lee*, ed., Ballagh, 2:369–71; "Mentor" in *Virginia Gazette or American Advertiser*, 17 Apr. 1784; *Virginia Independent Chronicle*, 13 June 1787.

[26]Thomas Jefferson to George Washington, 15 Mar. 1784, *Papers of Thomas Jefferson*, ed., Boyd, 7:25–27.

ious to see his native state match the trading ventures of Pennsylvania and New York, of whose commercial ambitions "no person who knows the temper, genius, & policy of those people as well as I do, can harbour the smallest doubt." Virginia could either take steps to direct its own commercial development or "submit to the evils arising therefrom without receiving its benefits." Should Virginians initiate commercial improvements of their own, the possibilities were endless. Washington assured a skeptical Benjamin Harrison that "A people . . . who are possessed of the spirit of Commerce, who see & who will pursue their advantages may achieve almost anything."[27]

Neither Washington nor Jefferson nor other proponents of commercial development in the 1780s intended to challenge the agricultural foundation of Virginia's economy. As planters themselves they shared an apprehension regarding the risks of an overemphasis on trade. Madison needed only to consider the case of the Netherlands to recognize that "wherever Commerce prevails there will be an inequality of wealth" and a decline in the "simplicity of manners." Washington also was determined to separate commerce "From those vices which luxury, the consequences of wealth and power, naturally introduce." But so too did they recognize the folly of turning away from the commerce that gave value to their investment in land and slaves. These individuals understood that the challenge for Virginia planters in the years after Independence, much as it was during the final days of Empire, was to gain some control over what Jefferson called "this modern source of wealth and power" and make it supportive of an agricultural society.[28]

Washington, Jefferson, and Madison each led one aspect of the movement to foster independent commercial development in Virginia during the 1780s. Washington, of course, had been a leader in the organization of commercial resistance before Independence, and his Conti-

---

[27]George Washington to Joseph Warren, 7 Oct. 1785, Massachusetts Historical Society; George Washington to Thomas Jefferson, 29 Mar. 1784, *Papers of George Washington, Confederation Series*, ed., Abbot, 1:237–40; George Washington to Benjamin Harrison, 10 Oct. 1784, Washington Papers, Library of Congress.

[28]James Madison to Edmund Randolph, 30 Sep. 1783, *Papers of James Madison*, eds., Hutchinson and Rachal, 7:363–64; George Washington to Thomas Jefferson, 29 Mar. 1784, *Papers of George Washington, Confederation Series*, ed., Abbot, 1:237–40; Thomas Jefferson to George Washington, 15 Mar. 1784, *Papers of Thomas Jefferson*, ed., Boyd, 7:25–27.

nental military experience heightened his awareness of the need for Virginians to emulate the kind of economic development that allowed northern states to prosper. Jefferson and Madison, through their service in the Continental Congress and their connections throughout the states, also sought for their native state the advantages of independent commerce that they understood were a foundation for the growth of northern port cities. In the mid-1780s, Washington concentrated on the diversification of production and private schemes for internal improvements that would support the growth of local ports. Jefferson, in Congress and as a minister to Europe, attempted to establish favorable trade agreements and retained his faith in the value of economic coercion. Madison led the efforts to effect economic independence and commercial development through statutory reform.

With his return to the Virginia assembly in 1784, Madison devised a legislative program that he expected to foster a native commercial class and lessen Virginia's dependence on the merchants of both Great Britain and Philadelphia. The centerpiece of his plan was a Port Bill submitted to the House of Delegates in 1784. In a stunning display of faith in the power of law to transform economic structures, Madison proposed to restrict Virginia's foreign trade to one or two ports. By forcing the considerable trade of the state through these channels, Madison hoped the bill would stimulate the growth of true commercial centers like those in northern states. The bill, as its unusual coalition of supporters testified, would serve several purposes including the more efficient collection of revenues. Madison's primary motivation was to preclude the reestablishment of the diffused trading system of the colonial period and to retain for Virginia the profits now absorbed by merchants in Philadelphia.[29]

Madison considered the trade to individual plantation wharves and small towns along Virginia's rivers to be both costly and a principal means by which British merchants had controlled the purchase of local commodities, the retail sale of imports, and the shipping of Virginia's external commerce before the Revolution. With foreign trade limited to a single or even a handful of coastal cities, British factors would be unable

---

[29]Drew R. McCoy, "The Virginia Port Bill of 1784," *Virginia Magazine of History and Biography* 83 (July 1975): 288–303; Robert B. Bittner, "Economic Independence and the Virginia Port Bill of 1784," in *Virginia in the American Revolution, A Collection of Essays*, eds., Richard A. Rutyna and Peter C. Stewart, (Norfolk: Old Dominion University, 1977): 73–92.

to reopen the myriad of small stores along Virginia's river system and throughout the Piedmont. Local merchants might then build their fortunes on the retail trade of imported manufactures and the purchase of local crops. The concentration of trade in a few ports also would attract merchants from European nations who did not have the resources to establish the expensive if lucrative store system favored by the British before the Revolutionary War. The resultant demand for services in these designated port cities would foster the growth of artisan crafts and a free class of seamen. Madison anticipated the growth of port cities. with a native merchant community and a full range of financial and retail services. The urban concentration of business, he hoped, would reduce the charges of intermediaries, retain for Virginia a higher portion of the profit on exports, and eliminate the price differential with Philadelphia.[30]

From his position as chairman of the committee on commerce in the House of Delegates, Madison drafted a bill that would have confined Virginia's foreign trade to the ports of Norfolk and Alexandria. Although Madison initially preferred to designate Norfolk alone, during debate in the full House he found it necessary to expand the number of ports to five. The addition of Tappahannock, York, and Bermuda Hundred provided for a designated port on each of the state's four principal rivers as well as at Norfolk just inside the Virginia Capes. Despite the opposition of Madison, the House also revised the bill to exempt resident Virginians from the restrictions on foreign trade. In the Port Act as passed in June 1784, all river and bay craft operating below the fall line were required to employ crews consisting of no more than one-third slaves, since "navigating small country craft by slaves, property of the owners of such craft, tends to discourage free white seamen, and to encrease the number of such free white seamen would produce public good." In order to build sufficient loading craft and prepare for what promised to be a significant reorganization of trade in Virginia, the assembly delayed implementation of the act until June 1786.[31]

During the intervening two years the Port Act faced an assault of opposition from traders and planters fearful that the arbitrary designation of a few ports would enrich the inhabitants thereof at the expense of the rest of the state. Emboldened by the onset of a commercial depression in 1785, opponents of the bill submitted numerous petitions

[30]Ibid.
[31]Ibid. *Hening's Statutes*, 11:402–04.

demanding repeal or at least the designation of additional ports. Madison ascribed the resistance to those who wished to see a reestablishment of the British trading system, but in truth the petitions came largely from individuals who sought to protect their tenuous trading positions throughout the state. Opposition was strongest in western counties and trading towns upriver from the designated ports. Yet the Port Act survived attempts at repeal largely because of its perceived value in the collection of revenue at a time when the state was in desperate need of funds. When revision came late in 1786 it was in the form of the addition of 17 designated ports and an increase in fines for violations. The amended act effectively reduced Madison's sweeping attempt to impose a new kind of commercial development on the state to little more than an administrative structure for the more effective collection of revenue.[32]

At the same time that Madison promoted the Port Bill, he submitted legislation to create a system of assize courts that might facilitate commercial transactions in the state. The idea dated back to the early 1770s and attempts to process court cases more swiftly than was possible in the largely autonomous county courts. Madison's bill, in part based on one proposed by Edmund Pendleton and Thomas Jefferson in 1776, was also part of the larger movement to reform the courts and Virginia's legal code in the early years of independence. The resumption of trade and peacetime business made clear the need for a more regular and predictable administration of debt cases if Virginia were going to attract commercial investments and sustain the growth of its own merchant community. As "Aristide" warned readers of the *Virginia Independent Chronicle*, every imported article bought in Virginia carried an extra charge to cover the delay in recovery of debts. The irregular judicial process of the county courts raised the cost of borrowed capital as well.[33]

Drawing on support from the Northern Neck and centers of incipient commercial growth in the eastern portion of the state, Madison's assize court bill passed in late 1784 with the proviso that its implementation be delayed until after the meeting of the next session of the assembly. As with the Port Bill, the intervening months allowed time for

[32]Ibid.

[33]A. G. Roeber, *Faithful Magistrates and Republican Lawyers: Creators of Virginia Legal Culture, 1680–1810* (Chapel Hill: University of North Carolina Press, 1981): 153–54, 192–202; Risjord, *Chesapeake Politics*, 181–84; *Virginia Independent Chronicle*, 4 Apr. 1787.

the opposition to mobilize support and demand substantive revision when the assembly convened again in December 1784. The opponents were largely delegates from the west and the Southside, the same allies of Patrick Henry who fought every measure to facilitate the recovery of British debts. They succeeded in revising the Assize Bill in ways that destroyed Madison's original intent, and the assembly eventually suspended the act before it ever went into effect. The passage of an act creating district courts in late 1787 embodied many of the long-standing proposals for judicial reform but came after Madison and others had transferred their interest in commercial development to the federal level.[34]

What Madison hoped to achieve through the statutory regulation of foreign trade and institutional reform, Washington sought to initiate through internal improvements that would tap western markets and transform Virginia's Tidewater towns into major ports. Since before Independence, Washington envisioned the growth of Virginia as much through the development of territory to the west as through the expansion of commerce in the Atlantic economy. The west beckoned not only as an object of land speculation but as an opportunity for the extension of agriculture that would stimulate the growth of cities in the east. Already grain produced in the Shenandoah and trans-Allegheny west moved along wagon roads to Baltimore and Philadelphia. Washington was determined to open river traffic on the Potomac and bring that valuable produce of the west to Alexandria. Others expected the opening of the James River to insure similar commercial growth in Richmond. Washington, who long appreciated the connection between commercial prosperity and political security, was equally determined to attach the west through ties of trade rather than risk links between the growing western settlements and the British or Spanish on adjacent frontiers.[35]

For all of Washington's concern with national security, he viewed the development of waterways to the west largely from the perspective

---

[34]Roeber, *Faithful Magistrates and Republican Lawyers*, 192–202; Risjord, *Chesapeake Politics*, 181–84.

[35]George Washington to Benjamin Harrison, 10 Oct, 1784, and George Washington to Henry Knox, 5 Dec. 1784, Washington Papers, Library of Congress; Douglas R. Littlefield, "Eighteenth–Century Plans to Clear the Potomac River: Technology, Expertise, and Labor in a Developing Nation," *Virginia Magazine of History and Biography* 93 (July 1985): 291–322.

of the promotion of Virginia's economic prosperity and maintenance of its primacy among the other states. In his determined search for political and financial support of plans for canals along the Potomac and James, Washington repeatedly emphasized the importance of exploiting Virginia's "superior advantages" and the urgency of matching the similar efforts of Pennsylvania and New York to draw commerce from the west. Virginia's assembly and that of Maryland responded with charters for the Potomac Company and Virginia's alone with a charter for a canal on the James River, but, as Washington conceded, the pressure of debts on both states rendered them "incompetent to a work of this sort." The canals thus would be funded by subscribers and a schedule of tolls that Washington feared was too high to encourage new trade. Washington's grand dream of active canals and port cities confronted a host of further impediments including what he considered a failure of entrepreneurial spirit among his fellow Virginians, regional jealousies ("as if the benefits of trade were not diffusive & beneficial to all"), and the chronic shortage of capital, particularly for a large-scale investment whose return seemed so distant. Work on the canals progressed in the 1780s, but repeated financial problems and technical challenges made clear that they would not yet provide the commercial growth Washington imagined.

As he had been before the Revolution, Washington in the 1780s was at the forefront of private efforts to diversify plantation agriculture and provide a foundation for new trading ventures from Virginia. In 1785 he vowed to enter "upon a compleat course of husbandry as practiced in the best Farming Counties of England" and hired an English farmer to serve as overseer of his estates. But while Washington continued to reject the cultivation of tobacco and Indian corn, he found that all too few of his countrymen were prepared to abandon the traditional agriculture that was "as unproductive to the practitioners as it is ruinous to the land-holders."[36]

Washington boasted that his plantation was able to manufacture sufficient woolens "to clothe my out-door Negroes," but as in the colonial period few planters in the 1780s had the labor or resources to provision their own families and slaves. Early calls for manufactures in an independent Virginia went largely unheeded as the flood of imports and high tobacco prices satisfied the demand for goods and once more

---

[36]George Washington to George William Fairfax, 30 June 1785, Washington Papers, Library of Congress.

made foreign goods more cost-effective in the short term. In the depression of the mid-1780s, a self-styled Patriotic Society in Richmond rallied Virginians to an association similar to those employed before the Revolution. The society's public resolution declared that the "only method in the power of the people, honestly and effectually to relieve themselves from the oppression of public and private debt, is by spirited exertions of industry, to encrease the productions of the country, and by a strict frugality, and avoiding all dissipation, to lessen their expences." The subscribers to the society pledged themselves "by our *examples*, to encourage and promote industry, frugality, œconomy." They identified the dependence of Virginia on foreigners "for almost every necessary and conveniency of life" as the most dangerous threat to independence and agreed "to promote every well founded scheme of trade and manufactures, the profits of which shall arise and center with our own citizens." Washington, although wary of private societies that assumed responsibilities best left with an elected assembly, congratulated his nephew as one of the organizers of the Patriotic Society and suggested the awarding of bounties for agricultural improvements which might soon "make us a rich & happy people."[37]

■   ■   ■

As long as Virginians were committed to trading throughout an Atlantic world circumscribed by mercantilist restrictions, the state government faced demands for the protection of Virginia's own commerce from the coercion of far wealthier and mightier nations, most notably Great Britain. The various efforts to achieve in Virginia an economic independence commensurate to the United States' political independence coincided with a prolonged debate on the proper diplomatic posture for promoting the commercial prosperity of Virginia and the Confederation as a whole. The free trade sentiment rooted in the ideology of the earliest days of the Revolution vanished in 1783 when the British, followed by other European powers, imposed restrictions on American trade in the valuable West Indies market. No action of the British, who already stood poised to reassert their control of the transatlantic trade in tobacco and European manufactures, could have con-

[37]George Washington to Bushrod Washington, 15 Nov. 1786, in *The Writings of George Washington*, ed., Fitzpatrick, 29:66–69.

"View of Norfolk from Town Point" is a watercolor sketch by Benjamin H. Latrobe, 1796. Its location near the Virginia Capes and its participation in the West Indies trade contributed to Norfolk's growth as the state's largest port. In drafting his Port Bill of 1784, Madison considered designating Norfolk as the sole port of entry for Virginia's foreign trade. (Maryland Historical Society).

veyed more forcefully the arrogance of imperial power than this exclusion of American shipping from a market where smaller merchants with limited capital formerly had an opportunity to compete with larger shippers.

The Order in Council of July 1783 provoked immediate demands for diplomatic and economic retaliation throughout the United States. A "Sentinel" in the *Virginia Gazette* advised that the British intended on nothing less than a monopoly of the trade of the states. The governor insisted that navigation act must be countered with navigation act and proposed to prohibit the importation of all British goods and commodities from the British West Indies excepting those carried in American ships. In December 1783, a resolution submitted to the Virginia House of Delegates called for the grant of congressional authority to prohibit British ships from carrying any trade between the United States and the British West Indies. The assembly approved the act contingent upon the concurrence of the other states. In an affirmation of at least the concept of free trade, the assembly condemned the British Order in Council as "repugnant to the principles of reciprocal interest and convenience which are found by experience to form the only permanent

foundation of friendly intercourse between states." The assembly offered Congress another, albeit temporary, grant of commercial authority in 1784 when it favorably responded to Congress's request for the
power to prohibit trade from nations with which the United States had
no commercial treaties. Although other states did not follow the lead of
Virginia, the clamor for retaliation against Great Britain continued
through the mid-1780s as British merchants regained ground in Virginia and the initial prosperity of peacetime trade gave way to lower
tobacco prices and higher costs for imported commodities.[38]

Consensus on the merits of diplomatic response offered no easy
solution to the far more divisive question of which government, that of
the state or the Congress of the United States, had proper jurisdiction
over the regulation of trade. The act approving congressional restrictions on the trade of the British West Indies came at the close of a two-
year debate on the similar grant of authority for Congress to lay duties
on the foreign trade of the United States. The impost originally proposed to the states in 1781 was part of Robert Morris's plan to establish
a more secure revenue for the Confederation and simultaneously extend the authority of the central government. Virginia's assembly in 1781
approved the provision for a five percent duty on imported goods out of
the conviction that "it will conduce to the general interest, that the commercial regulations throughout the said states be uniform and consistent." But the grant of congressional power over trade initiated a political
debate over commerce and the national government that would esca-
late through the contest over ratification of the Federal Constitution in
1788. In part the opposition to the impost was rooted in the Lee family's
visceral animus toward Robert Morris, but even that personal rivalry
was the result of a larger fear that the expansion of federal authority,
whether in the person of the superintendent of finance or in the form of
an amendment to the Articles of Confederation, would favor the development of commercial centers in the north at the expense of the staple-
producing states to the south. A year after their initial approval, the
assembly delegates rescinded their grant of authority for the impost,

---

[38]*Virginia Gazette, or American Advertiser*, 8 Nov. 1783; Benjamin Harrison
to Virginia Delegates[?], 3 Oct. 1783, *Papers of James Madison*, eds., Hutchinson
and Rachal, 7:366–67; *Virginia Gazette, or American Advertiser*, 6 Dec. 1783;
Hening's Statutes, 11:313–14.

[39]*Hening's Statutes*, 10:409–410; James Ferguson, *The Power of the Purse: A
History of American Public Finance, 1776–1790* (Chapel Hill: University of North

largely out of fear of the "great superiority, to be obtained by other states over ours."[39]

Virginia's assembly in late 1783 restored its approval of the impost, although this time the text of the act omitted all references to the benefits of uniform trade regulations and offered instead the delegates' expectation that creation of a national duty on trade "may contribute to lighten the burthen of taxes on real and personal property." The revised approval specified the acceptable rates for duties and stipulated that the governor of Virginia would reserve the authority to appoint all collectors within the state, thus withholding at least as much from the national government as it offered. New York's refusal to cooperate with the other states prevented this or any other form of the impost from going into effect.[40]

The state legislature's reversals and the continued impotence of Congress only exacerbated the debate in Virginia over the most effective diplomatic stance and the wisdom of expanding national authority. Although Madison despaired of the possibility of forcing repeal of British restrictions ("What could she get from us by yielding to our demands which she does not now enjoy?"), he remained the most forceful public advocate of enlarging the Congress's commercial powers. Washington concurred that a concerted response from the national government was the best protection of Virginia's commerce, and he remained considerably more confident that economic coercion on the part of the United States would force Great Britain to yield. As he had during the organization of commercial resistance before the Revolution, Washington contended that the trade of the United States, and of Virginia in particular, "in all points of view is as essential to Great Britain, as hers is to us—and she will exchange it upon reciprocal & liberal terms, if an advantage is not to be obtained." The folly of British policy, Washington predicted, would strengthen the national government more in a few years than it would otherwise have achieved in fifty.[41]

Carolina Press, 1961); Edmund Randolph to James Madison, 7 Feb. 1783, *Papers of James Madison*, eds., Hutchinson and Rachal, 6:207–08.

[40]*Hening's Statutes*, 11:350–52

[41]James Madison to Richard Henry Lee, 7 July 1785, James Madison to James Monroe, 7 Aug. 1785, *Papers of James Madison*, eds., Hutchinson and Rachal, 8:314–16, 333–36; George Washington to James McHenry, 22 Aug. 1785, Huntington Library; George Washington to Joseph Warren, 7 October 1785, Massachusetts Historical Society; George Washington to William

From his post in Europe, Thomas Jefferson implored Madison and others to obtain approval in Virginia for commercial regulations from the Continental Congress. If ever Virginians were going to enjoy the advantages of free trade, they must first demonstrate the ability to forego commerce with Great Britain. At the least, Virginia and the other American states needed to enact reciprocal prohibitions on British shipping from the West Indies. Jefferson and the other American ministers initially hoped to negotiate reciprocal trading agreements with European nations as part of the Congress's effort to establish a transatlantic trade that was not dependent on Great Britain. But however much Jefferson the Virginian might have wished to see the staples of his native state shipped without restrictions to markets throughout Europe, he soon confronted the realities of a world still marked by mercantilist restrictions. He quickly became convinced that the Congress must be able to enforce its own navigation acts if the wealth of American trade were to be used to open new markets in Europe and the colonies of the West Indies. After his first year in Europe, he wrote Madison that "the politics of Europe render it indispensably necessary that with respect to every thing external we be one nation only, firmly hooped together." In the meantime, Jefferson informed James Monroe, "On this side of the Atlantic we are viewed as objects of commerce only, and as little to be relied on even for this purpose while its regulation is so disjointed."[42]

Perhaps the most persuasive Virginia opponent of vesting commercial authority in Congress was Richard Henry Lee, who in 1785 served as president of the Continental Congress. Lee had opposed the impost out of a conviction that it would offer northern cities an insuperable advantage over southern states, and his resistance to a grant of commercial power to the national government intensified through the 1780s. His support of commercial resistance and leadership of the pre-Revolutionary movement for economic diversification had always rested on a far darker view of the prospects for Virginia and the planter gentry than the optimistic vision offered by Washington, his close ally in the forma-

Carmichael, 10 June 1785, Library of Congress; George Washington to George William Fairfax, 30 June 1785, Library of Congress.

[42]Peterson, "Thomas Jefferson and Commercial Policy, 1783–1793," 584–610; Thomas Jefferson to James Madison, 18 Mar. 1785, 8 Feb. 1786, Thomas Jefferson to James Monroe, 11 Dec. 1785, *Papers of Thomas Jefferson*, ed., Boyd, 8:38–41, 9:94–95, 264–67.

tion of the nonimportation associations. By 1785, Lee took a particularly dim view of all merchants whether they be from Great Britain or the northern states. The commercial interests of the eight northern states already enjoyed such great advantages that they could not resist the inevitable tendency of all mercantile establishments to impose a monopoly on societies that, like the southern states, were dependent on them for marketing and shipping. Lee was content to have Virginia's government respond to the restrictions of Great Britain with "a very careful, and considerate restraining of their Trade." In response to similar regional concerns from James McHenry of Maryland, Washington assured him that under congressional strictures on British trade from the West Indies, the southern states would soon develop their own commerce with native merchants and seamen to carry the produce that Lee and McHenry feared would fall permanently into the hands of northern traders. Madison also dismissed Lee's fears, attributing the opposition to Congress to a combination of provincial jealousies and the influence of merchants with ties and loyalties in Great Britain.[43]

By 1785, the collapse of tobacco prices, economic depression, and the failure to resolve the debate on congressional authority incited demands that the Virginia assembly take some action to protect planters and native merchants. "Mentor" in Essex County renewed calls for the exclusion of former loyalists who had returned to Virginia as merchants. Virginia, he insisted, should follow the model of New York and give legal preference in trade to native merchants. A committee of constituents appointed from Nansemond County publicly instructed their delegates in the assembly to forbid all trade with the British West Indies for as long as Americans were excluded from those islands. They also recommended the prohibition of all foreign merchants in Virginia and a requirement that all foreign goods be imported in vessels owned by residents of the United States. The *Virginia Gazette* printed "Thoughts on the Commercial Interests of Virginia" which proposed similar legislation creating a schedule of discriminatory duties designed to encourage native merchants and local shipbuilding, fully confident that "Merchants in Europe can lay in their goods so much cheaper than citizens that they will have the advantage, and continue to trade." In the

[43]Richard Henry Lee to James Madison, 11 Aug. 1785, James Madison to Thomas Jefferson, 20 Aug. 1785, *Papers of James Madison*, 8:339–40, 344–46; George Washington to James McHenry, 22 Aug. 1785, Huntington Library.

meantime, Virginia would develop its merchant fleet, its ranks of free laborers, and its commercial establishment.[44]

In response to these sorts of entreaties and numerous petitions calling for commercial protection and in an effort to avoid an irregular system of state commercial regulations, Madison proposed that the assembly which convened in October 1785 approve a new grant of congressional authority based on James Monroe's draft amendment to the Articles of Confederation. The amendment, which Congress had yet to approve or send to the states, would have given Congress the authority to levy commercial duties and regulate interstate and foreign trade. After initially expressing its support, the House of Delegates passed a resolution offering such a grant of authority, but only for the limited term of 13 years and with the crippling stipulation that all individual commercial regulations be approved by two-thirds of the state legislatures. Soon thereafter, an unlikely coalition of opponents to national power and strong nationalists like Madison who thought the act too restrictive joined forces to withdraw this limited grant of authority.[45]

With the intention of subverting additional calls for the expansion of congressional authority, Carter Braxton, supported by Speaker Benjamin Harrison, had introduced into the same session of the assembly a proposal to forbid the landing at Virginia ports of all British ships sailing from the West Indies. The measure also would have established a minimum residency requirement for all merchants operating in the state. This bill failed to win assembly approval, although the delegates agreed to apply a discriminatory duty of five shillings per ton to the entrance into Virginia waters of any ship owned wholly or in part by British subjects. Virginia, as Madison had feared, thus joined the ranks of states that were imposing disparate trade restrictions in the absence of any uniform commercial regulation from the Continental Congress. Finally, in the last days of the session and in a desperate effort to answer public demands for some action, the assembly agreed to send delegates to a proposed conference for the negotiation of an interstate commercial agreement with Maryland, Delaware, and Pennsylvania. In accepting the proposition from Maryland's legislature, the Virginia assembly ex-

[44]*Virginia Gazette, or the American Advertiser*, 30 July 1785, 12 Nov. 1785, 19 Nov. 1785.

[45]Risjord, *Chesapeake Politics*, 259–60; Brant, *James Madison, The Nationalist*, 379–81; Resolution Calling for the Regulation of Commerce by Congress, 14 Nov. 1785, *Papers of James Madison*, eds., Hutchinson and Rachal, 8:413–14.

tended the invitation to delegates from all the states. Although the localists who approved the resolution seemed not to have understood its implications, the decision to participate in what became the Annapolis Convention would change forever the debate over commercial regulation and congressional power.[46]

Despite broad support for some kind of commercial reprisal against Great Britain and a general recognition of the trade advantages to be gained from diplomatic agreements, internal political divisions in Virginia again and again paralyzed the assembly and prevented the formulation of any true navigation system for the state. Nor was the state legislature able to devise a consistent policy of support for the expansion of congressional authority over commerce. By the opening of the assembly session in late 1785, the political impasse had convinced nationalists like Madison and Washington that direct reform of the federal government was the only feasible means of securing the uniform commercial policy that they believed was a prerequisite for the economic prosperity of Virginia. The Annapolis Convention of 1786 provided the opportunity to shift the dialogue from the state legislatures to a gathering of delegates representing various states, and from there the nationalists won agreement on the need for a federal convention to consider broad-ranging revisions in the structure of the national government.

The decision of the Virginia nationalists to cast their lot with the Federal Convention and ultimately with the new Constitution arose in large part from their understanding of the requirements for trade with European nations still committed to a mercantilist protection of domestic production and foreign commerce. The framework of the new Federal Constitution had many sources, but with respect to the commercial issues that were the immediate impetus for the movement to reform the national government, the Framers endorsed a concentration of governmental authority in a determination to counter the trade restrictions of Great Britain and less powerful nations that had excluded United States' shipping from the most promising markets. Madison consistently maintained that for Virginians the most compelling argument in favor of congressional regulation of commerce was the potential damage it would inflict on the widely-resented British merchants. Madison, Washington, and other leading nationalists fully expected the new government to help Virginia at last achieve the economic indepen-

---

[46]*Hening's Statutes*, 12:32; Rich, "The Experimental Years," 60–63.

dence that had proved so elusive over the previous quarter century. So too did the nationalists' drive for greater federal authority over trade manifest an enduring confidence in the efficacy of economic coercion and governmental regulation. Rooted in both the mercantilism of their colonial experience and the organization of commercial resistance before the Revolution was the nationalists' belief that comprehensive restrictions imposed on the flow of America's invaluable trade would yield political and economic concessions from other nations.[47]

Ratification of the Constitution and inauguration of the federal government restored a measure of confidence in Virginia's economy and encouraged new investments, yet long before federal commercial policy had an impact in Virginia or elsewhere, European wars and shifts in distant markets brought an end to the staple trade as it had operated for much of the previous century. The demise of the French Farmer-General's monopoly in 1791, a decline in continental demand, and disruptions in shipping precipitated a 20 year stagnation of tobacco production in Virginia and its disappearance from many areas of the state where it had long been the principal crop. The transition to grain culture and mixed agriculture allowed planters with sufficient labor and land to maintain their income, but only at the expense of displacing many other families who left the state in a great exodus to settle on cheap, productive lands in Kentucky, the Northwest, and newly-settled regions from the Carolinas to the Mississippi. As many as 250,000 whites migrated from the region during the next three decades and carried with them 175,000 slaves. In their wake, the gentry families of Virginia managed to preserve their estates and retain their hold on the political establishment, but lost forever the expansive, self-confident prosperity that had marked the culture of the great planters for much of the eighteenth century.[48]

---

[47]James Madison to Thomas Jefferson, 20 Aug. 1785, *Papers of James Madison*, eds., Hutchinson and Rachal, 8:344–46.

[48]Price, *France and the Chesapeake*, 839–42; Walsh, "Plantation Management," 401–06; Kulikoff, *Tobacco and Slaves*, 428–32.

CONCLUSION

VIRGINIA INAUGURATED ITS BREAK FROM THE EMPIRE by striking at the bonds of trade that intimately linked the colony to Great Britain. Faced with an assault on political rights and the centralization of the tobacco trade in Great Britain, the gentry planters who presided over Virginia's society and government organized a resistance movement that withheld the agricultural produce of the colony and closed its markets to imported British goods. It was as producers and consumers that the Virginians assumed they held the greatest sway with imperial authorities and British merchants. The intended demonstration of Virginia's economic influence was the means by which Virginia's planters sought to guarantee political prerogatives against infringements by the Crown and to protect their estates against the demands of merchants and creditors in Great Britain. The support for a strategy of commercial resistance reflected the degree to which Virginians of all ranks were integrally tied to the fortunes of external trade and demonstrated a consensus on the importance of achieving economic independence as a foundation for political liberty.[1]

The search for economic independence in all its varied forms, from the commercial associations of the 1760s to the movement for reform of the federal government in the 1780s, rested on the assumption that Virginia's agricultural production was so valuable that it might be traded with advantage throughout the Atlantic world and support a free soci-

---

[1] For discussion of the importance of consumption in the organization of resistance in other colonies, see T. H. Breen, "Narrative of Commercial Life: Consumption, Ideology, and Community on the Eve of the American Revolution," *William and Mary Quarterly* 3rd ser., 50 (July 1993): 471–501.

ety, unencumbered by the ties of Empire. The organizers of commercial resistance before the Revolution and the later proponents of commercial development remained convinced that with modification and diversification the plantation system of agriculture would maintain its economic viability and continue to be as supportive of social and political order as it had been through the previous century. They accordingly set out to make Virginia's predominantly agricultural economy independent of British merchants and competitive with trading centers in the United States. They relied on a combination of voluntary associations and governmental policy in expectation that concerted action might utilize the state's great wealth to lay the foundation for political, diplomatic, and commercial strength.

As long-time participants in a complicated Atlantic trade, these wealthy Virginia planters sought to embrace the burgeoning opportunities of liberal commerce at the same time that they insisted on perpetuating the social and political structure that evolved under colonial rule. Few grasped the inherent contradiction. Only during rare moments like the debate over prohibition of the slave trade and in anxious comments about the planters' standard of living or the business acumen of northerners did proponents of economic independence reveal underlying doubts about the competitiveness of a plantation economy and bound labor, but none translated those misgivings into plans for the comprehensive reordering of the economic or commercial life of Virginia or into suggestions that planters abandon the land in favor of mercantile and manufacturing ventures. Most remained confident that adjustments in personal behavior and the organization of plantations would reinvigorate the state's system of agriculture and maintain Virginia's leading position in the United States' foreign trade. The architects of nonimportation and commercial development, for all their talk of diversification and the need for a native merchant community, were notable for their own lack of investment in ambitious mercantile or manufacturing schemes, save those that promised to make their individual plantations more independent and flexible.

No one in Virginia offered a compelling alternative vision of economic development outside the British Empire. Those intent on establishing a measure of economic independence for Virginia met with little internal opposition before the Revolution other than the massive indifference of yeoman planters who until 1772 continued to prosper through their trade with the factors of British merchants. After the Revolutionary War, the proponents of commercial development faced political resistance from many of the same small planters, particularly those of the

Southside and Piedmont, who had accepted earlier offers of British credit and instinctively recoiled from further involvement with the risks of a transatlantic trade that had left their lands encumbered with debt. The loose coalition centered around Patrick Henry resisted the repayment of pre-war debts as well as other proposals to facilitate commerce and encourage merchants in Virginia. Through the contest over ratification of the Constitution, the majority of property-holding Virginians accepted the more positive vision of economic growth articulated by Washington, Madison, and other nationalists, even if a sizable portion had grown suspicious of involvement in foreign commerce, the balance of which seemed always against Virginia.

More substantive if equally fruitless was the criticism of men like Richard Henry Lee who, though an early champion of commercial resistance and diversification, questioned the basic organization of Virginia's plantation economy and came to doubt the state's ability to compete with the entrepreneurial society born of a liberal capitalism emerging in Philadelphia, New York, and other commercial centers of the north. The "dearness of labour here & the want of Men of Fortune" would always restrict Virginia's commercial development according to Lee, who once contemplated moving to Massachusetts in order to escape the "hasty, unpersevering, aristocratic genius of the south." This scion of one Virginia's most notable families would not easily have left the state, particularly for a region he distrusted, but the remark to John Adams reflected a frustration with Virginia's seeming incapacity to develop the domestic economy that would protect its interests in trade. He thought it far preferable for Virginians to cultivate a merchant fleet and native seamen than to engage European nations in an endless game of countering restrictions on navigation. Until Virginia controlled its own shipping, he opposed any grant of commercial authority to a Congress dominated by what he called the "No Staple States." The response of Lee was all too often one of reaction and retreat, presaging the defensive voices of a declining Virginia in the nineteenth century. Yet if Lee was unwilling to challenge the structure of Virginia's economy, he nevertheless exposed fundamental flaws in the assumptions of commercial resistance and foretold the eventual failure of proposals for commercial development.[2]

---

[2]"State of the Constitution of Virga." Lee Family Papers, Virginia Historical Society; Richard Henry Lee to John Adams, 8 Oct. 1779, idem to James Monroe, 5 Jan. 1784, idem to [   ], 10 Oct. 1785, *Letters of Richard Henry Lee*, ed., Ballagh, 155–56, 286–90, 387–90.

Even in the wake of a successful political revolution and the dissolution of the formal ties of Empire, the Virginians' definition of economic independence all too often remained rooted in colonial dreams of great riches that would entice traders from Europe and enable the great planters to prosper on their largely autonomous estates. When the fortunes of the tobacco trade faded, the demands of British creditors became too pressing, and imperial regulations grew too restrictive, Virginia's wealthiest planters and political leaders sought to introduce greater flexibility and independence to the system of plantation agriculture and slave labor that had developed within the context of the staple trade with Great Britain. The unprecedented scope of their attempts never entirely obscured the degree to which these efforts mimicked similar schemes from throughout the colonial period. The interest in the diversification of agricultural exports, the experiments in domestic manufactures, and the attempts to establish port cities recalled earlier if more modest efforts that appeared during periodic depressions in the tobacco trade dating back as far as Governor Berkeley's administration and even Sandys' reorganization of the Virginia Company. Yet if the Revolutionary generation revived failed schemes from colonial Virginia, they also foreshadowed the agricultural reform movement of nineteenth-century Virginia with its focus on the development of a more skilled labor force and the alleviation of the wasteful effects of staple agriculture.

The prospect of political freedom and an end to the imperial connection obliged the great planters and political leaders to devise an economic foundation that would insure the continued prosperity of an independent Virginia and maintain the value of investments in land and labor. At the same time, Virginia's planters and local merchants reacted to the concentration of British mercantile firms and the more rigorous demands of the commercial capitalism of Atlantic trade in the second half of the eighteenth century. The proposals for independent economic development that emerged from revolutionary Virginia, like colonial plans for diversification and later proposals for southern agricultural reform, sought to make the state's economy more secure from the risks of trade at the same time that they accepted the basic outline of plantation agriculture and the employment of slave labor. Adherence to these colonial legacies preserved for Virginia's gentry a social and political order, while the failure to embrace the opportunities of a dynamic, liberal capitalism following Independence simultaneously hastened the state's declension in the nineteenth century.

Index

This book was set in Janson,
a seventeenth-century typeface
originally cut by Nicholas Kis.
The display type is Copperplate Gothic
designed by Frederic W. Goudy in 1904
in imitation of the lettering used by early metal engravers.
This book was designed by Gregory M. Britton
and William Kasdorf for Madison House.

Printed on acid-free paper